Contemporary Catholicism in the United States. Philip Gleason, ed.

The Major Works of Peter Chaadaev. Raymond T. McNally.

A Russian European: Paul Miliukov in Russian Politics. Thomas Riha.

A Search for Stability: U.S. Diplomacy Toward Nicaragua, 1925–1933. William Kamman.

Freedom and Authority in the West. George N. Shuster, ed.

Theory and Practice. Nicholas Lobkowicz.

Coexistence: Communism and Its Practice in Bologna, 1945–1965. Robert H. Evans.

Marx and the Western World. Nicholas Lobkowicz, ed.

Argentina's Foreign Policy 1930–1962. Alberto A. Conil Paz and Gustavo E. Ferrari.

Italy after Fascism, A Political History, 1943–1965. Giuseppe Mammarella.

The Volunteer Army and Allied Intervention in South Russia 1917–1921. George A. Brinkley.

Peru and the United States, 1900–1962. James C. Carey.

Empire by Treaty: Britain and the Middle East in the Twentieth Century. M. A. Fitzsimons.

The USSR and the UN's Economic and Social Activities. Harold Karan Jacobson.

Chile and the United States: 1880–1962. Fredrick B. Pike.

East Central Europe and the World: Developments in the Post-Stalin Era. Stephen D. Kertesz, ed.

Soviet Policy Toward International Control and Atomic Energy. Joseph L. Nogee.

INTERNATIONAL STUDIES OF THE

COMMITTEE ON INTERNATIONAL RELATIONS

UNIVERSITY OF NOTRE DAME

The
Catholic Church Today:
Western Europe

The

Catholic Church Today:

Western Europe

Edited by M. A. FITZSIMONS

CONTRIBUTORS:
Jean Becarud · Jean Delfosse · Desmond Fennell · M. A. Fitz-
simons · Thomas Hanlon · Ludwig Kaufmann · Erwin Kleine
Giuseppe De Rosa · Robert Rouquette · Harry J. van Santvoort
Antonio da Silva Rego · Erika Weinzierl

UNIVERSITY OF NOTRE DAME PRESS
NOTRE DAME—LONDON

Library of Congress Catalog Card Number: 68–58334
Manufactured in the United States of America

INTRODUCTION

The Catholic Church Today: Western Europe and the companion volume *Contemporary Catholicism in the United States,* edited by Philip Gleason, are the first volumes of a series devoted to the Church in the contemporary world. The objective of this series is to provide, in a time of change and controversy, the perspective and detachment that scholarship must initially command.

The Church is not alone in experiencing this ordeal of change and controversy. In our troubled and defective world community there may be seen aspects of a crisis to which many men contribute and almost every man experiences.

Western Europe and the United States have profoundly affected the rest of the world: their influence initiated in African and Asian societies, which in modern centuries appear to have passed their distinctively creative periods, a process of transformation and a will to change. But importing change from the West, that is, borrowing Western ways in the name of modernization, also means the importation of the West's unsolved problems, including the critical strains of Western society.

Whatever the relationship of Church and culture, it is unconceivable that the Church should be unaffected by the cultural disarray of the present world. Indeed, its impact on the Church has been partly responsible for a spectacular response to the world's anguish: reform through modernization. Drawing inspiration from the Christian simplicity of Pope John and from the Second Vatican Council, the Church has sought to become apostolically more effective by reorganizing responsively to modern needs and sensitivities and by speaking in a manner that would reach and affect the man of our culture.

Much of the change and controversy within the Church stems from this reform effort and will continue. For a long time there will be no secure vantage point or quiet period to facilitate writing about the contemporary Church. This series, undertaken with some awareness of its difficulty, will, it is hoped, be of interest to all concerned with contemporary man's wrestling with the spirit. The adjustments of the Church in various national societies to the reform efforts of this highly centralized universal institution may be of considerable scholarly interest. The story of these adjustments is also a contribution to the sharing of experiences. It may additionally minister the wan comfort of impressing on the reader that he is not alone in his anxiety and concern. The ordeal of change within the Church is underway in almost every country.

Philip Gleason, the editor of the American Church volume, suggests that some may regard our project, "The Catholic Church Today," as an attempt "to draw a map of a landslide." But to delay, he argues in his "Introduction," has the disadvantage of waiting for the dust to settle, that is to say, until the action is over. "But it is while a process is still in motion that people have the greatest need to discover its direction and significance." The processes are affected by human choice, which in turn is a response to what men think is happening. "The understanding men have of the movements in which they are involved, the attitudes they adopt, and the actions they take become factors in the outcome of these very movements."

To complete the project will require a number of editors and a host of authors, translators, and consultants. For the present volume I sought knowledgeable writers in each country of Western Europe. A chapter is devoted to the Catholicism of each country of Western Europe and I have not been legalistic about states and nations. Thus, there is a chapter for Scotland, but not for Wales, whose Catholics are less numerous and are more recent immigrants. In most cases authors are natives of the country which they describe. Practical considerations made for two exceptions, the authors of the chapters on Spain and England.

The decision was made to seek contributors solely on the basis of competence, without reference to their reformist or conservative views. In retrospect this impartiality appears somewhat naive or at any rate old-fashioned. In most countries only the proponents of reform were sufficiently interested to be able and willing to write on the present state of the Church. No matter how rooted in history conservatives may profess to be, as a rule only the proponents of *aggiornamento* were willing to write on the recent history of the Church.

This may be explained on the ground that the conservative position in the Church is antihistorical in spirit. The conservatives see in the historically formulated teachings and institutions of the Church time-lessness and changelessness. The consequent Platonic rigidity raises doubts whether evangelization and preaching can be anything other than a call to submission. Furthermore, this position within the Church is generally in opposition to modern civilization. This is sup-ported by its diagnosis that has proclaimed modern civilization as mortally ill. The latter would appear to call for nonconservative radi-calism—it is assumed that Western civilization would be judged and that the Church would survive. Variants of the conservative position were impressively framed by Evelyn Waugh: the Church's strength was its antimodernism, for contemporary art and literature testify to the horror of modern life; the young especially might be attracted to an institution that remained indomitably opposed to the ugly modern world.

The *aggiornamento* is almost a direct reversal of a papal position taken in the "Syllabus of Errors." There Pope Pius IX had condemned the proposition that the pope (and the Church) should come to terms with nineteenth-century civilization. In a major sense he stated quite accurately the position that should be taken by a prophetic Church which claims divine foundation. But in another and more immediately influential sense the condemnation was heard as a defi-antly hostile voice from a beleaguered ghetto. The "Syllabus of Er-rors" was, in effect, a cry of alarm and a call for security: in no way could it provide a major impetus for evangelization. In the nineteenth century Western Europe's missionaries overseas were more venture-some and enduring than the secular apostles of imperialism. Effort and zeal on a similar scale were less notable in evangelizing at home, where, apart from those countries depending on voluntary efforts,* the cities grew largely without benefit of new parishes and churches.

Young Albert de Mun and the Marquis de la Tour du Pin, after the suppression of the Paris Commune, observed how little charity was evident and how astonishingly ubiquitous hatred was. This ex-perience prompted them to espouse social Catholicism, but their sub-sequent activity had no impressive impact. They opposed liberal so-ciety and parliamentary government, which they sought to replace with what they believed to be an organic society organized on a cor-porative basis. This ideal has been singularly free of practical conse-

* England, Ireland, Scotland, and Holland.

quences apart from the Fascist, Austrian, and Portuguese use of cor-
porativism for antiparliamentary and antiliberal ends.

De Mun and La Tour du Pin are characteristic figures of Catholic
political and social action in the nineteenth and early twentieth centuries. For all of their compassion, they were conservative and even
reactionary figures. Indeed, Church leadership had been out of tune
with the leading cultural movements of Europe since the seventeenth
century. In England Cardinal Manning was at odds with Newman
and Acton, both of whom aspired to reach men of their time. He
would be a brave man who would define Manning's idea of a Catholic university. For his part, Manning, an ultramontane—was he an in-
novator or conservative?—responded to "the trade winds of the nineteenth century" with a vigorous concern for the social question. He,
however, had no English successors of comparable stature or influence. The social thought of English Catholics has inspired histories
but has exerted little social influence.

In general, the political, social, and intellectual movements of the
nineteenth century were suspect for their novelty. The changes en-
gendered were thought to menace the already reduced alliance of State
and Church, which Church leaders sought to maintain.

The First Vatican Council, the condemnations of Modernism and
Americanism (remarkably enough, a heresy without heretics), and
continuing liberal hostility strengthened the reactionary forces within
the Church. The ascendancy of conservatism and reaction within the
Church was no mere accident but expressed the intentions and will
of Church leadership.

The great change that *aggiornamento* may involve is suggested by
the title of the collected articles written by Father Rouquette, S.J.,
on Vatican II and its aftermath: *Le Fin d'un Christianisme* (2 vols.,
1968). The desire to move consciously and deliberately, to change
from a Church order and outlook that is culturally anachronistic and
evangelically ineffective to a flexible order and responsive outlook is
certain to have the most unsettling consequences. Reformers animated by the desire to bear Christian witness in a contemporary idiom
and to influence a world in rapid movement may expect to encounter
resistance in proportion to the magnitude of their aim and thus to repeat the experience of many reformers in our time: that espousal of a
reform program becomes a commitment to permanent reformism. Reforms, even when they are successful on first implementation, even-

tually turn out to be inadequate. The measures of reform programs usually prove to be superficial and inadequate.

The preceding is a formulation that seems almost inescapably forced on the observer, and it is primarily a conservative formulation. It is conservative in the implication that reform becomes a life's and a century's work which places a possibly intolerable burden on individual men. Perhaps it points to the characteristic and anxious ambivalence of our time. Many of us fear radical transformation as a likely source of totalitarian rule; yet we seem to be caught in its process and, in yielding to it as necessary, seek to promote radical change. Within the Church there are analogues to those who believe great change is impossible: some because they do not want change, and others because they wish to maintain the purity of their doctrine and program as enduring evidence of superiority to their unregenerate brothers and equals. It is this profession of changelessness, mistakenly identified with continuity, that for so long made the study of Church history of the modern age unprofitable.[1]

Since Vatican II the proponents of reform have gained a large measure of the initiative. Their ideas were first effectively propounded in the French- and German-speaking Catholic worlds. In France itself, for example, there was something of a cultural and social Catholic *ralliement*—a concern to be a force in French cultural life free of nostalgia for ancient privilege and of the hopes of a Maurrasian restoration. Among Catholics, modern religious sociology was pioneered under Gabriel Le Bras in France and has provided support and direction to reformist efforts. Among the episcopate of Western Europe it is likely that the most laggard in the study and appreciation of sociology are the Portuguese and English.

While French, German, Austrian, and Belgian spiritual leaders and thinkers were the avant-garde, Holland in the years after 1962 presents the spectacle of the Church of a nation in the course of reform. The greatest transformation has taken place among the most religiously observant people in Continental Western Europe. The Polish Church

---

[1] In *The Unreformed Church* (New York, 1965) Father Robert McNally, S.J., has noted the surprisingly and disturbingly insignificant role "that the history of the Church has played in Catholic intellectual life, especially in theological thought." There flourished in modern times "a static theology" with a method that tended "to concentrate on the propositional rather than the historical; possibly to dislodge, at least to overlook or disregard history in favor of speculation."

was beleaguered and not free. The Irish did not have the experience of the Dutch in reconciling Protestant-Catholic differences and in developing a new conception of authority. The magnitude of the Dutch enterprise is suggested by Harry van Santvoort. He noted that the Dutch bishops insisted their *aggiornamento* effort not be presented as a model to the Church, but that it was of interest to all Christians. It may be added that the Dutch bishops have been model pastors in their unwearying labors to guide a reform that included new conceptions of authority.

The *aggiornamento* initiated with Vatican II is an effort to organize the Church so that it can effectively discharge its contemporary responsibilities. The powerful antimodernist trend in the Church meant that this modernization effort would be a very sweeping one. Was this modernization effort a decisive break in the continuity of Church history or was it the fulfillment of movements already underway? Had the earlier movements culminated in a recognition that new directions and definitions were necessary? The earlier emphasis on the changelessness and the authoritarian structure of the Church discouraged the open discussion of change that might have documented the prehistory of the modernization movement. Episcopal pronouncements and the largest party of the Catholic press provide only the most meager hints of a possible prehistory. Indeed there was so little general preparation for this modernization effort that a distinguished Church historian once argued, in the fervor of a dinner conversation, that the only possible explanation of Vatican II is that most of the Catholic bishops of the world were secret revolutionaries.

There was, however, a prehistory in various movements such as those for liturgical reform, biblical study, biblical theology, the movement of the lay apostolate, and Catholic Action. Out of these and other sources came a new willingness to see the Church as the People of God. This involved a diminished concern with an objective order of authority as formally externalized.

How far was all this influenced by general events and movements of the twentieth century—by World War II, the experience with totalitarianism, and the threat of nuclear weapons? Such is an exceedingly difficult question, because the answer must be sought in the particularly intangible area of changing spirit, temper, and emotional expression.

Within the Catholic Church there developed, as an astonishing contrast with the recent past, an evangelical sense for action here and now. This sometimes reached the extreme of believing that spiritual fulfillment was to be achieved in the current moment rather than in some major way transcendentally. Ironically, you could find within the same movement men calling for ceaseless activism and defiant witness on behalf of the kingdom of God as well as for the greatest mistrust of all association with political power along with a condemnation of Church history as a kind of Constantinian heresy. One finds proponents of a reform to make the Church relevant to our culture side by side with individuals who believe that the Church is doomed to remain a sect, as though the world itself is impervious to reform.

The effort to make the Church a force in society and the world has its highly problematic aspects. Was this influence to be gained primarily by evangelical will and zeal? Obviously the Church could not have this influence in terms of simple competence under existing social systems. Furthermore, there was no strong tradition of Catholic scholarly accomplishment in the modern historical and social studies to provide the expert knowledge presumably requisite for any effort to achieve social influence and transformation. Almost all the authors of this volume recognize that Catholics have not been in the forefront of major artistic and literary achievements in this century. Indeed, their role has been a progressively declining one. Of the multitude of issues raised by the modernization effort within the Church and the attempt to make it responsive to society today, four observations may be made here:

1. There are enormous differences in the problems of various national societies, and there are great differences within the national cultures. In Switzerland, for example, it is almost as easy to speak of Catholicisms as to speak of Catholicism. The Catholicism of Belgium is very different from that of Ireland or that of Portugal. In Portugal a modernization effort may require a predetermination of what kind of society the Church should adapt to, for it is reasonably certain that Portugal is in a state of change. In other countries—Spain, for example—public life has perhaps been insufficiently secularized. In this sense secularization may be a necessary preliminary for effective human response. Elsewhere the persisting polarity of liberalism and the left on one side and the Church on the other serves to inhibit action. Other branches of the Church, England and Ireland being examples, are free of the burden of historical antagonisms to liberalism,

socialism, and even urbanism—but even in them it is objected that the Church has not been rooted in the respective national cultures, and so remains a stranger on any deep social level.

2. There is in all these modernization efforts a certain coming to terms with nationalism. This contrasts with the past in which the Church professed a universal character that was reflected in the use of Latin. Acceptance of the vernacular for the liturgy removed for many a feature that had distinguished Catholicism from the Protestant churches. The use of the vernacular certainly is a coming to terms with nationalism. Equally, the concern with the adaptation of the Church to local national conditions has its nationalist aspects, as is evident in the intensified Walloon-Flemish fight in Belgium. These efforts are bound to heighten tensions with the Roman Curia, whose universal claims might then be seen as excessively influenced by its own parochialism as well as by national and regional outlooks. Under the new arrangements the universal Catholic Church would have to become a less centralized monarchy and, for a time, partake a little of the character of the United Nations.

3. Some of the proponents of reform appear to be animated by a temper and a style very akin to that of the New Left. They believe in their own causes and insist upon them with a righteousness that is both destructive and intolerant. They urge the cause of the people and popular participation, but they seem to believe that for the time being the people are not to be trusted, for they have been corrupted by the old order. In short, they are most astonishingly elitist in the name of the people. They appear to be antiestablishment if the establishment has a history. There is an endless reform movement, a recklessness that seems to substitute will for rationality and persuasion, and there is equally a remarkable lack of objectivity with regard to life and society.

4. The Church in its new transformed period is presented as a prophetic and pilgrim church. The question is who converts whom— does the Church convert the world or does the modern world convert the Church? In view of the depressing lack of influence that the Church has had in recent times and in view of the meagerness of preparatory work—that is, thinking through the problems of theology and morality within the context of modern culture and society— some real hesitations may be suggested. Many Protestant churches had for substantial periods of time made the same modernization effort and generally had not been notably successful.

The reforms initiated in this modernization effort affect the training of seminarians, celebration of the Mass, the structure of the Roman Curia, and finally reach the geologic deposits of canon law. There is an impressive appearance of lively intellectual life. It is confusing, for theologians are addressing a wide audience of people. If theology is to be influential, obviously it will have to cease to be the arcane knowledge of a body of experts restricted to a highly technical and almost private language. Theology then will suffer some of the vulgarization of the market place. The Dutch Catechism and its unquiet history offer an illustration that may serve as a paradigm of the reform effort.

The modernization effort is presumably to be accompanied by a revival to stir the people. There remains the problem of attempting to keep people constantly alert and aflame with zeal. The congregations do not suddenly become alive and responsive. Indeed, the sheep seem irresistibly to drag their feet. In them it is not always easy to see the People of God. Nevertheless the concept of the Church as the People of God is bound to inspire a reexamination of authority on all levels within the Church. This reexamination and redefinition probably provide the clearest evidence of the liveliness of the Church.

The papal encyclical on contraception, *Humanae Vitae*, appeared after this volume had been submitted to the press. It was impossible to consult the contributors. The chapters, nevertheless, provide background and guide to the responses of the various countries. Perhaps only the middle-aged and elderly continue to note the novel emphasis on conscience.

In preparing this volume I have received substantial assistance. For typing assistance I am indebted to Mrs. Jane Fowler, Mrs. Anne Dietrich, and Robert Moss. For translations I am indebted to Mrs. Elisabeth Reinecke (German chapter), Mr. Adolph Schalk (Swiss chapter), Professor James A. Corbett (Belgian, Spanish, and French chapters), Miss Emily Schossberger (Austrian and Italian chapters), and to an unknown Dutch translator. For editorial assistance I owe a debt to John Madigan, Miss Suzette Ellsworth, and Mrs. Theresa L. Silio. For various reasons many helpers must remain unacknowledged here. Finally, I owe to my family thanks for their patience and occasional mutinies when preoccupation with this volume made me additionally insufferable. Indeed, all my collaborators will testify that I edited a tight book.

M. A. FITZSIMONS

CONTENTS

Introduction ix

1 HOLLAND 1
    Harry J. van Santvoort

2 GERMANY 29
    Erwin Kleine

3 AUSTRIA 61
    Erika Weinzierl

4 SWITZERLAND 87
    Ludwig Kaufmann, S.J.

5 ITALY 121
    Giuseppe De Rosa, S.J.

6 PORTUGAL 157
    Antonio da Silva Rego

7 SPAIN 183
    Jean Becarud

8 FRANCE 215
    Robert Rouquette, S.J.

9 BELGIUM 243
    Jean Delfosse

10 IRELAND 271
    Desmond Fennell

11 SCOTLAND 297
    Thomas Hanlon

12 ENGLAND   309
        M. A. Fitzsimons

    Index   345

1 : HOLLAND

Harry J. van Santvoort

Holland is rigidly divided into religious denominations. Catholics make up 40.4 per cent of the Dutch population, Protestants 39.1 per cent, and 18.4 per cent belong to no religious group. Although some foreign news media characterize the present condition of Dutch Catholicism as stormy and disturbing, the Dutch Catholic views the changes and tensions as a necessary evolution. After a long emancipation struggle, now at an end, the Catholic Church in Holland is searching both for a period of frankness and dialogue between the Church and the world and for an authentic Christianity that will promulgate and make understandable to men today the message of Christ.

Historically the movement has been from a period in which Dutch Catholicism became conscious of itself and obtained privileges equal to others to the most recent period, that of the Pastoral Council of the Dutch Church. In this latest period an attempt has been made to account for the process of growth, to make it intelligible and supple: necessary new structures of the Church have been energetically sought.

I. DUTCH CATHOLICISM ACQUIRES
SELF-CONSCIOUSNESS

By the papal letter, *Ex qua die arcano* of March 4, 1853, Pope Pius IX implemented his decision to establish the hierarchy in Holland. Somewhat earlier he had said of Holland: "Utrecht, the seat of St. Willibrord—I will let Europe see that the Dutch Catholics are not backward." The "reestablishment of the hierarchy" was based on the fact that until the year 1592 Holland and Belgium together made up one hierarchy. The Reformation made substantial and rapid progress, especially in North Holland, because of its adaptation to the Dutch way of life and because of dissatisfaction with the rule of the Catholic Spaniard Philip II.

The Calvinists and members of the Reformed Churches acquired power not only in North Holland but also in South Holland which had a large Catholic majority. When the Reformed Church was made the State Church and the practice of the Catholic religion was forbidden, a very close bond developed between the priest and his followers. Necessity and a desire for unity with Rome strengthened the bond. From Rome the ex-nuncio ruled the Dutch Church; he was forbidden to enter Holland.

For Holland, the French Revolution meant an end to the one State Church and the beginning of formal freedom of worship with equality of all religious denominations. Nevertheless, for a long time the Catholics remained an underprivileged and backward group. Of little importance in political, financial, and industrial affairs, they were chiefly to be found among the lower middle class and the country people. The so-called "*diaspora*-mentality," that two centuries of concealed Catholicism had fostered, lingered for a long time among the Dutch Catholics.

The Restoration of the hierarchy in 1853 followed political changes as well as a change in the consciousness of Dutch Catholicism. The Restoration itself provoked a flood of protest and extreme antipapist expressions, culminating in the stormy Reformers' protest, the April Movement. The government tried somewhat to restrict the freedom of the Catholic Church with the "law of religious denominations." This, however, was a fiasco. The fear of renewed papal domination increased Protestant suspicion which lasted for a long time. This fear does not appear so strange when one reflects that the pope and, with him, many Dutch Catholics, entertained the idea that Protestantism, which was going through a period of dissension, would eventually combine with the flourishing Catholic Church.

The period between the Restoration of the hierarchy and the celebration of the Centenary of this Restoration (1953) is dominated by the struggle for Catholic emancipation. It is the period which in Holland is ironically known as "the rich Roman life." Preaching the Gospel had the character of a defense of the faith and involved a strongly apologetical strain. Partly as a result of increasing emancipation in the political, social, and cultural fields, the practice of religion took on a certain triumphal aspect and again, as a result of this, a demonstrative character. Politically Catholics were concentrated in the so-called "Catholic State Party," which initiated the school conflict and fought for absolute educational equality for Catholics. Catholic leaders, such as Msgr. Schaepman, played an important part in social legislation. In the same period Catholic trade unions began, and Catholic Church art reflected the neo-gothic style.

At the end of the emancipation struggle, Dutch Catholicism emerges as a strong, closed group to whom unity with the pope and the episcopate as its symbols is precious above everything else. In all spheres the Catholics have gained a certain position of power and have formally organized themselves into seven dioceses.

In comparison with other countries, the number of practicing Catholics is very high. Of the 5,147,200 Catholics in a total population of 12,377,000 (January 1, 1966), 87 per cent go to church with some regularity and 77 per cent go every Sunday. The number of priests and conventuals is high. On January 1, 1965, the number of secular priests totalled 4,191, and of this number 31 worked abroad. On January 1, 1967, there were 9,999 order priests, of whom 5,244 worked abroad, and 6,732 monks, of whom 1,621 were abroad; the number of nuns was 31,767 and 3,269 of them were abroad. Until a short time ago, 2,000 student priests were to be found in 32 institutes for philosophy and 30 institutes for theology.

More than 10,000 Dutch missionaries, among whom there were at least 70 missionary bishops, worked in 76 countries (European nations, the United States, and Canada are not included). This means that Holland, with 2 per cent of world Catholics, provides 12 per cent of the number of missionaries. Although the number of vocations decreased during the period 1955-1963, the number of missionaries reveals the following increase:

1. 1955—3,750 priests, 1,160 monks, and 2,671 nuns;
2. 1960—4,215 priests, 1,204 monks, and 2,811 nuns;
3. 1963—4,397 priests, 1,251 monks, and 2,888 nuns.

While the Dutch Cardinal, van Rossum, has made a great contribution to the organization of mission activity in Rome, the Dutch Catholics have contributed generously to the financial support of the missions. For example, in 1967, they gave approximately 75,000,000 florins (about $21,000,000) exclusively for the missions.

The average size of a Roman Catholic family is always higher than that of other denominations. Children born to every 100 marriages consummated during the period 1924 to 1928 totalled 502 to Roman Catholics, 432 to orthodox Reformed Protestants, 318 to the Strictly Reformed, and 270 to couples who did not belong to any religious denomination.

The Dutch dioceses control Catholic schools from elementary through university: all Dutch schools enjoy complete equality. Ninety-six per cent of Catholic children attend Catholic elementary schools, and 86 per cent of them attend Catholic high schools. In 1960 Catholics provided 24 per cent of university students; this represents a 9 per cent increase since 1930, and the ratio is still increasing.

Politically all Catholics have been united in one strong Catholic People's Party and have built an extensive network of trade and professional organizations. Practically everything is organized on a Catholic basis. Holland possesses—and this is unique for the whole world —an independent Catholic radio and television broadcasting system (the KRO). There are numerous rural and regional Catholic daily and weekly newspapers. De Tijd and De Volkskrant, both of Catholic origin, are two of the largest daily newspapers in Holland.

With the Centenary of the Restoration of the hierarchy, the Dutch Catholics realized that they were emancipated and in celebrating this event Cardinal de Jong, who was then Archbishop of Utrecht, said: "We must stay united: what we achieved in the past especially in the field of public life we owe to our united front in the face of the outside world . . . . The more our emancipation increases, the more will our unity be confronted with greater dangers."

II. FROM EMANCIPATION TO BREAKTHROUGH TO DIALOGUE

At the time of the Centenary World War II was becoming a thing of the past. The German occupation, however, had seriously transformed the outlook of the Dutch people. Until then the various social groups grew in isolated development. Politically, Holland was extremely divided. The confessional parties formed strong individual groups, and opposing them were firm liberal and socialist parties. The oppression and misery of World War II fostered a national consciousness which, in turn, promised an opportunity for conversation and cooperation.

Many non-Catholics recognized that in the general resistance to the Germans Catholics had been true patriots, and notable among them was Cardinal de Jong, Archbishop of Utrecht, who openly criticized the measures taken by the army of occupation. With all the parties working together, the myths about each other vanished. The Protestant had proved to be very serious and convinced of his religion. The time was ripe for dialogue and working together. Until this time in religious circles the Church's, that is, the divine, command was something that men should obey without hesitation. But the absolute authoritarianism that characterized the army of occupation and that manifested itself in the trials of the war criminals after the war (with repeated appeals "Befehl ist Befehl," that is, "orders are orders") provided a stimulus to a new approach to authority and authorities.

In the history of the Dutch Church it will always be remarkable that in 1954, in the midst of these changes of thought and of a growing openness, the Dutch bishops issued a mandate concerning "the place of the Catholic in public life at this time." The bishops showed some understanding of the Catholic initiative for collaboration with other Christians and non-Christians but they plainly stated that it was the duty of Dutch Catholics to keep their ranks as closed as possible. This was a last spasmodic attempt to preserve the unity of Catholics.

The Dutch bishops expressed themselves in favor of a denominational political party and denominational trade unions. With strong negative arguments they dissuaded Catholics from joining the Socialist Party and declared that a Catholic was not allowed to join a Socialist trade union or to listen to the Socialist broadcasting agencies. Measured in terms of the intention of the composers of this instruction, namely the bishops of the southern dioceses, where socioeconomic change had already broken the closed ranks, this injunction had a reverse effect. The seclusive unity of the Catholic group appeared to have become artificial. The crisis became imminent. The political and social breakthrough of the Catholics became more and more a reality. Only two years later, in 1956, the bishops were forced to scrap the passages prohibiting Catholic participation in the Socialist Party and trade unions.

In the following years the view of the Catholic population was greatly influenced by a group of young Catholic intellectuals. At first the growth of this influence was a gradual matter stimulated by the weekly newspaper *De Bazuin* (The Trumpet) and the magazines *Te*

Elfder Ure (The Eleventh Hour) and *G* 3, a monthly for the military forces. Later, public opinion began to develop much more rapidly. This rapidity was a consequence of the numerous mass media of Dutch Catholicism. Among some people this extensive publicity created the impression that developments were moving too fast and that if old principles were discarded so easily, the upshot would be too much freedom of thought. Undoubtedly, this anxiety was so strong because there had been so little effective resistance from conservative thinkers. The latter had been content with negative criticism of all positive ideas and so had failed to provide a basis strong enough for repelling and destroying progressive ideas.

The unity of the Catholic population, once so highly praised, was gradually lost. In other words Catholic organization was preserved for the time being, but it had already begun to work in federal relationship with groups from other denominations, and Catholics, much more than formerly, were playing a part in the national life. Thus a beginning was made in the deconfessionalization and ecumenical work that was so conspicuous a feature of Catholic history in the 1960's. Throughout the 1950's questions were raised about the necessity of a Catholic university. Catholic parents did not consider themselves compelled, in all circumstances, to send their children to Catholic schools. Discussions arose over the questions as to whether the Dutch nation must necessarily be divided into Catholic, Protestant, and humanist groups. This was the beginning of a development which continues to foster more and more integration of all parties in the service of common causes within the community. At that point, however, the Dutch Catholics still had to learn how to relate their strong group ethos to that of others and to participate in truly ecumenical dialogue.

The development and change in the Dutch Catholic way of thinking may be well illustrated in changing opinions concerning marriage. The Dutch Catholic bishops inspired an investigation of marriage and the family conditions of Catholics. This investigation resulted in an open and critical discussion of marital problems. It became clear that the social responsibility for procreation was increasingly recognized and that "family planning" was more generally familiar and taken into account. One of those who exerted considerable influence in changing Catholic public opinion on these matters was Msgr. W. Bekkers, Bishop of 's-Hertogenbosch from 1960 to 1966. His television talks and addresses on numerous occasions about the primary importance of personal conscience created a climate in which it was recognized that, along with other values, sex is also a determining factor in the individual. This new atmosphere is undoubtedly one of the reasons that in recent years priests and laymen have joined in widespread criticism of Paul VI's encyclical on the celibacy of priests and, indeed, have emphatically urged that the office of priest and the state of celibacy be separated. The question of priestly celibacy is being debated as part of the extensive survey of the priests initiated by the Dutch bishops. It is believed that many priests will vote for the abolition of compulsory celibacy.

Thus far it has been suggested that the breakthrough to a personal conscience and a sense of personal responsibility was at first a gradual one. Later the pace quickened and the growth was more extensive, and a like pattern appears in nearly all spheres, for example, in dialogue within the Church and in dialogue with the world. On the eve of the Vatican Council the Dutch bishops in a letter dealt with the relationship between the collective belief and the authenticity of the Church, and, at the same time, they clearly pointed to the collegiality of the world episcopate with the pope in Rome. The dialogue of the Dutch Catholics has involved lively exchanges *with other Christians* (a subject to be developed later) as well as with others.

Finally the last has led to some talk of an actual dialogue with the world, notably with *humanism* and *Marxism*. Indeed, the interest of the younger generation in the fundamental inspiration of Marx is evidence that Dutch Catholics have acquired a feeling for reality. Of this generation, Dr. D. de Lange has noted that their interest in Marx's inspiration impels them to demand that the Church itself be dynamic. He further explains that the Church, constantly in interaction with historical circumstances, must testify to its truth and Gospel mission:

> For this generation the fact that one is a Catholic has ceased to be a social standard to which one inevitably conforms. For this generation being a Christian has become a life's concern. For them the Church has the most meaning when it forsakes the protection of its own traditional environment and, serving and defenseless, confronts the large and small realities of the present and the future. The great reality: the world problems which must be answered today and tomorrow; the small reality: the daily life of the common man who in the rapids of historical events is threatened by self-alienation and who may expect that the Gospel will restore him to himself. Here

is a point beyond the dialogue between the Church and the world, where an attempt must be made to understand the Gospel message from the contemporary world itself.

III. SCOPE FOR EXPERIMENTS

An inestimable service of the Dutch bishops has been their broad willingness to allow for experiments in the midst of the growth of recent years; a minority, however, have made this willingness a ground for reproaching the bishops. Experimentation is an essential part of the renewal of the Dutch Catholic Church. Many Catholics are convinced that the new forms are not so much a renewal of the old forms but are the result of continued experiments.

A. LITURGICAL EXPERIMENTS

In a pastoral letter of January 25, 1964, the Dutch bishops indicated the importance they attach to renewing the liturgy and expressed the conclusion that modernization can be successful only through the combined efforts of all the faithful and the hierarchy.

> This is not a matter of a fleeting adaptation and a superficial modernizing of ceremony: above all, it requires insight into and a pure experience of the reality which faces us, the reality of the world, of mankind, and of God who became man. This reality is not alien to the liturgy. . . . We all are very much in agreement with those who state that it is a task for all of us; and the creation of a vitalized liturgy depends on the bishops with their official assistants, laymen, and all religious orders.

In accordance with the instructions of the post-Conciliar commission for the execution of the *Constitution on the Liturgy*, the bishops introduced the Dutch language in various parts of the Mass, as the instruction provided, in all texts for baptism, confirmation, confession, and extreme unction, and in a few rituals of the Church year. Since 1967 the Dutch language may be used for the whole of the Mass, and, since there are no official translations, celebrants are free to use various texts that have been approved by the Church.

In the meantime experiments took place in many parts of Holland. These involved not only the Dutch language in the entire Eucharistic service, but also matters concerning the form of the ceremony. Well known for their experiments are the *Boskapel* of the Augustinian monks in Nijmegen, the *Pleingroep* in the Hague, and the youth Masses in Maastricht. In Holland one may also find churches where the Eucharistic service is celebrated with Gregorian music, and here and there churches where beat music is used. The experimental character of the translated texts for the communion celebration makes an impression of disorder on some people. Along with the translated Roman Canon, there are six new approved texts, four of which have been available from Rome. The first can be traced back to Hippolytus, the second and third are based on old models, and the fourth is based on the Greek Church-father Basil.

The Dutch experiments with the liturgy include the so-called house liturgy: on certain occasions the liturgy is celebrated in the family circle. The priest sits with all present around the table and everyone takes part in the Gospel reading and prayers. The communion service includes bread and wine for all, and the bread is placed in the hand of the communicant.

Since the renewal of the liturgy, the devotion of the congregations in Holland has become notably intense and the numbers attending communion have greatly increased. Liturgical experimentation is not confined to the communion celebration. Many parishes have gone over to a collective confessional service and for many this has taken the place of auricular confession. The Dutch bishops, however, have not made any statement as to the sacramental character of the collective confession. In addition many conventual communities are seeking new forms of saying the Divine Office.

In the Dutch Church the liturgy, in the full sense of the word, has a strongly pluralistic character, and many of the faithful have the impression that much has been gained in relevance and authenticity.

B. PASTORAL EXPERIMENTS

To promote communication among the higher Church authorities, the priests, and the faithful, the Dutch bishops, on November 1, 1963, established the Pastoral Institute for the Dutch Church Province. The Institute provides preparatory material for the pastoral decisions of the bishops and offers advice. The establishment of this Institute in itself is evidence of how much the bishops are convinced that they must work with their priests and the faithful in the formulation of policy and of how valuable is the flow of ideas issuing from every rank, from low to high. In this respect a new structure is growing within the Church in Holland, for on the diocesan level as well as the parish level, Diocesan Pastoral Centers, Deanery Advice Councils, and Parish Councils are chosen as democratically as possible. A consequence of the participation of parishioners in the pastoral sphere has been the growth of numerous discussion groups which meet in private homes to discuss various subjects concerning religion, the Church, and the Church and the world. Reports on these discussions are sent to a central address. As a result of the establishment of these discussion groups, the layman has experienced a closer and more influential association with the life of the Church. Moreover, in its life of five years, the Pastoral Institute has organized many study commissions on pastoral matters and consequently has provided important preparation for the Pastoral Council of the Dutch Church.

C. ECUMENICAL EXPERIMENTS

The ecumenical movement has developed very vigorously. Here, doubtless, the denominational richness and divisions of Holland have been a great influence. The Dutch Catholic grows up in a religiously divided environment. After World War II, a strong *rapprochement* among the different religious persuasions took place. Recently the Dutch Reformed and the Strictly Reformed Churches officially agreed to recognize their respective baptisms; this will shortly lead to an important step toward unity, namely the foundation of the Council of Churches, whereby the churches will combine in organizing pastoral activities and in issuing pastoral documents.

In Holland the St. Willibrord Association directs the national and international ecumenical movement. In 1966, a joint liturgical service including Cardinal B. Alfrink, Archbishop of Utrecht, and Msgr. A. Rinkel, Old-Catholic Archbishop of Utrecht, opened an official discussion that, hopefully, at no very distant date, will lead to the restoration of unity between the Church of Rome and the Old-Catholic Church.

Another important step toward unity of the churches is the issue of "intercommunion" which is developing among the churches in Holland. It involves meetings of the churches which recognize each other's celebration of the sacrament as authentic conformity to Christ's commandment: "Do this in memory of me." This is an issue which has inspired considerable publicity and unfavorable comment about the life of the Catholic Church in Holland. It has been particularly directed toward the ecumenical evening meal, or the ecumenical Eucharistic celebration of the *Sjaloomgroep*, which consists of Protestants and Catholics. This occasioned an illustrated account in the Christmas (1966) number of the weekly *Paris Match* that drew foreign attention to the initiative of the Sjaloomgroep, which had for some time organized so-called *agape* celebrations, that is, brotherly Christian meals. On March 15, 1965, and on January 14, 1967, the Dutch episcopate declared that these *agape* celebrations were not celebrations of the sacrament and were not to be thought of in the same sense that the Church gave to the celebration of the sacrament. For its part, the Sjaloomgroep declared that these Sjaloom evening meals were understood by the participants to be actual communion celebrations of the sacrament. The terms "evening meal celebration" and "communion celebration" have the same meaning for the Sjaloomgroep. This meaning may be determined by its constitutional forms such as "the purpose of the Lord," "faith in the Church," and the "function of office in the Church." Even without repeatedly calling attention to the initiative of the Sjaloomgroep, this question aroused considerable reaction in Rome and in other Church circles abroad. But additionally *Paris Match* and other foreign journals and papers committed the error of insinuating that the practice of the Sjaloomgroep was widespread in the Dutch Catholic Church.

Closely connected with this and considerably criticized and misunderstood abroad is the discussion about the Eucharist which originally took place between Dutch philosophers and theologians and which was later expanded into a discussion among the faithful. The point is not whether Christ is really present in the sacrament. Rather it is a more precise definition of the true presence—a new approach to the mystery of faith. The theologians Schoonenberg and Smits replace the scholastic definition *transubstantiation* with such terms as *transfinalization* and *transignification*. In effect, this is a theological question and does not affect the underlying belief.

Another experiment that attracted the attention of many people is the joint celebration of the sacrament by a priest and Protestant minister in Veenhuizen, a parish in the Diocese of Haarlem. This provoked discussion of the Catholic belief concerning office and sacrament in the celebration of communion. It must be explicitly stated that, on this occasion, intercommunion did not take place between two churches, but between two local officials. The difference of opinion about this experiment emerged clearly in the discussion among the theologians. According to some, Eucharistic unity between Protestant and Catholic must be the ultimate crown of the growing ecumenism: others thought it should be the starting point.

Some experimentation has also dealt with the problem of mixed marriages. Mixed marriages celebrated in church are increasing in Holland. In 1965, 15 per cent of the marriages in which a Catholic took part were mixed. In towns with more than 150,000 inhabitants the percentage of mixed marriages is 30 per cent. During the Bishops' Synod in Rome, the Dutch bishops pleaded for a more positive formulation concerning the *cautiones* that before ecclesiastical approval is given to a "mixed marriage" there should be moral certainty that the Catholic partner will preserve his faith and keep it as the guiding line in his life. They would also gladly have a common ceremony created in consultation with other churches. The church marriage ceremony between a Catholic and a non-Catholic Christian takes place in a Catholic as well as in a non-Catholic church, whereby the priest, as well as the *dominee*, leads the service. If a marriage ceremony takes place during a communion service, the non-Catholic partner can partake of the communion, at any rate, if certain conditions are satisfied. It is a case of so-called "open communion."

The growth of ecumenism in practice is certainly evidenced in naming non-Catholics as delegates of their churches to the Pastoral Council of the Dutch Church. As a matter of fact, they are not merely delegates, but full members of different study commissions in the cadre of this council and one of them even has a place in the official council.

D. The New Catechism

One of the most discussed experiments in the Catholic sphere, an experiment that brought reaction not only from the foreign press but especially from Vatican circles, is the publication of "the new catechism." On May 8, 1966, the Dutch bishops described the new catechism:

This new catechism will be a book that proclaims the creed for adults. In contrast to former ones, this catechism is not written in question and answer form. Rather it will be written on a broad basis and not in technical terms. It will give a description of our belief in the spirit of renewal as begun by Pope John, and, under his successor, further elaborated by the Council. It will not, of course, be a collection of ready-made answers. Nevertheless, we count on the fact that this catechism can be a support for everyone looking for a book which renders our belief in a form adapted to our time.

The so-called Higher Catechetical Institution in Nijmegen to which the development of the catechism was entrusted recorded the announcements of the Dutch bishops.

In our lives faith means something quite different from a study subject. The new catechism, therefore, must not be a collection of definitions. . . . It tries to describe human existence even as it lives in the faith. . . . Belief is not here proclaimed as a system of truths as in the old catechism. . . . The new catechism begins with mankind's searching for God. It ends with God's looking for mankind. It begins with human life and illustrates from it how the quest for God arises. There centrally is the basic theme of this entire book: that we only meet God, purely and veritably, if we recognize Him as the Son of Man. Only through Christ can we talk about God, and above all live in Him. This book expresses the belief that in Christ all great religions and world philosophies find each other and themselves. Thus, this catechism will show how through Christ, the Church develops in history, and how Christians are continually confronted with new problems.

The new catechism commanded unusual attention in Holland where more than 400,000 copies have been distributed. Difficulties began when a small group of conservative Catholics, secretly and without the knowledge of the Dutch bishops, sent a report with objections to the pope. In April, 1967, on the initiative of the pope, Dutch and Roman theologians met at Gazzada in northern Italy for a confidential discussion of the catechism. The Roman theologians had encountered twelve important and thirty-two less important difficulties concerning, among other matters, the virgin birth of Christ, the Eucharist, the sacrificial character of the communion celebration, original sin, and the direct creation of the soul—all questions which have come up in theological discussions during recent years.

The new catechism attracted much attention abroad: translations appeared in England, the United States, and Germany, and arrangements are under way for editions in French, Italian, Portuguese, and Spanish. The pope, acting partly in response to this interest, nominated a special commission of cardinals, which brought out a confidential report. In connection with the alterations suggested by the commission of cardinals, two theologians came from Rome to Holland in the hope that a discussion of the proposed changes would make possible a new joint edition. One of the Dutch theologians soon withdrew because he could not agree with a demand that alterations must be made. Eighteen of the thirty-two minor points concerned important questions such as the virgin birth of Christ, original sin, life after death, the supremacy of the pope, and birth control. He urged that proposed changes would impair the coherence of the work. In an interview one of the theologians from Rome later declared that there was no question of heresy but of error. The discussion of the three theologians continues. The Dutch episcopate has been informed of the progress of this discussion. The developments associated with the new catechism have irritated many Dutch Catholics, the more so because the intervention of Rome was accompanied by a campaign against the Dutch Catholics in some Italian newspapers, for example, *Il Tempo*.

E. Experiments in the Education of Priests

In the last few years the Dutch bishops have encouraged the study commissions of the Pastoral Institute to devote special attention to the subject of priests. The results of the work of these commissions have been published in the "Pastoral Directives for the Fulfillment of the Office of the Priest in Holland." The Directives begin with a description of the way of life and the work milieu of the priest and conclude with the education of the priest. In discussing the priestly way of life, the bishops treat the problem of celibacy:

> Convinced of the positive worth of celibacy, for our time as well as for the sake of the Kingdom of Heaven, we are on the other hand convinced that making celibacy optional should be the subject of further discussions and research. [In the meantime a special com-

mission has been set up for this purpose.] Primarily this is not—though we do not here provide conclusions—to meet the actual need of individual priests or to deal with the possible shortage of priests, but eventually to provide through this facultative position clearer shape for the new forms of the Church, and to elucidate the specific meaning not only of the priesthood but of virginity as well.

The question of separating office and celibacy is much discussed in Holland. Not so long ago in an open letter to the bishops, a group of theology students urged this separation, for celibacy is the principal reason given by many priests who lay down their office; in 1967, 115 out of 8,900, that is, 1.28 per cent, left the priesthood. It is estimated that between 1965 and 1980 the total will be approximately 500. The same influence is operative in the decline of vocations. An estimate made for the years 1965 to 1980 indicates that in fifteen years the number of active priests will decrease by 2,500, that is, a decline of 20 per cent. A consequence of the decline in the number of ordinations is that eventually most of the clergy will be in an older age group.

On April 28, 1968, Bishop Nierman of Groningen wrote to his flock that of the 181 priests in his diocese 40 are in the age group 60 years and older, 70 are between 50 and 60 years old, and only 9 are younger than 30 years. Even now he cannot provide a priest as pastor for every parish. For Holland, which has always produced so many priests and in the last one hundred years has sent thousands of missionaries to lands and churches that could not help themselves, this is a very surprising situation.

The decline in the number of student priests has prompted the consolidation of a large number of seminaries, for regular and secular priests, and the formation of five Catholic Theological Universities. An advantage of this concentration is that it makes possible cooperation and uniform standards. Additionally, the education of future priests will be in the hands of the best possible professors and teachers. Moreover because their main function is pastoral care, they receive more guidance than was previously the case and their pastoral education has been increased. They also have the advantage of taking refresher courses.

In Holland the study of theology today is not reserved for the clergy alone. Various educational programs are available to provide theological training for the layman so that he can become a teacher of religion on the high school level. In the future experienced laymen will be appointed to help with parish pastoral work.

F. The Renewal of Religious Orders

The modernizing of the life of religious orders in Holland has been greatly stimulated by the Commission for Dutch Religious Orders. The starting point of the Commission is that religious experiments are necessary. It has described experimentation as involving an existing order's or congregation's reflection on the original ideals of its founder. This reflection should be the basis for working out an authentic and modern form of life and work for the individual cloister.

In these experiments similar features appear.

1. There is the search for renewal through *small communities*, that is, small congregations. These smaller groups are less apt to become power structures and are more likely to be followers of the Gospel than large communities. In smaller groups common love and charity are more quickly realized. The personality of all members develops better, and the modality of the group is guaranteed.

2. There is need for *personal contact*, above all, there is a desire to join in the life of the common people. Accordingly, men wear civilian clothes, live among the people in small private houses, help with social work, and take part in ordinary recreations.

3. The experiments are marked by their *social character*. This reveals itself not so much through direct apostolate, but through normal contact with men in the outside world.

4. There is a *clarified conception of authority*. This goes together with complete democracy and brotherly fellowship. From the very beginning, the authorities recognized that experiments must be undertaken.

5. The experiments spring from the exigencies of a *radical consciousness* of monastic dedication: many forms and possibilities are allowed. The right of experimentation involves no impairment of the right of "old-fashioned" monasteries and cloisters with large congregations to maintain other ways of life and traditional customs.

In effect, there are three fundamental tendencies among these religious experiments and in the renewal of the life of religious orders: one is toward secular activity; another is a firm concern with personalism; and the last is an even stronger emphasis on democracy.

IV. CRISIS IN THE DUTCH CHURCH?

On August 16, 1966, the Dutch bishops issued a statement in which they declared that during their last episcopal conference they had concerned themselves with the "restiveness, the uncertainty, and the anxiety that appear to exist among many Catholics in the Dutch Church, as they become aware that matters which they had been accustomed, from their childhood, to consider as belonging to the Church, are now being changed, differently interpreted, or abolished altogether. Often the anxiety is increased by the manner in which these new visions are brought to public attention."

The bishops correctly stated that, among the clergy as well as among the laity, there is a great deal of uncertainty about what is going on in the Church. People are not yet able to view the many efforts to renew the thinking and life of the Church in such a way as to place them in the right context. As a result a small number of people have formed the so-called Confrontation-group and a still smaller number have joined the Michael-legion. These feel themselves obliged to offer open resistance against the tendencies favorable to innovation. A malicious foreign press has even accused the Dutch Church of aiming toward schism. The Italian press particularly so criticized the Dutch Catholics that during his stay in Rome in the days of the Council, Cardinal Alfrink was compelled to make a public and passionate defense of his people.

Are there really so many elements of crisis in the Dutch ecclesiastical province? In 1966, in a series of German radio talks, Father Schillebeeckx elaborately analyzed this question. Here only the main points of his analysis will be presented.

As a preliminary it should be recognized that Dutch Catholics, and this is part of their national character, are intensely interested in religious matters. Talking about matters of their faith comes naturally to them. Additionally, it should be said, Dutch Catholicism is notable for the staunchness of its people. In contrast to the noiseless apostasy in other countries, the kernel of the Dutch Catholic population as a community has remained fundamentally what it was, before a crisis in the Church of Holland was made the subject of discussion. All the same there is a crisis and the kernel of the Catholic population has encountered many difficulties in seeking a solution. Schillebeeckx in speaking about the crisis proceeds step by step.

A Dutchman, and a Catholic Dutchman as well, is accustomed to writing and speaking in all openness, boldness, and freedom. When he feels he must criticize authorities, including the ecclesiastical authorities, he will not remain silent. The very numerous Catholic publicity media, mostly in the hands of people who are in favor of renewal and forwardness, have strongly supported the new ideas and, as a matter of fact, they have exerted in behalf of these ideas a very great sociological pressure. Schillebeeckx even distinguishes between a Catholicism on the level of the publicity media and a "silent Catholicism" on the level of real daily life; that is, of the bulk of the Catholic population. To what extent this distinction is accurate cannot easily be discerned, because it never has been studied scientifically.

Schillebeeckx also cites the phenomenon of Catholic authors and writers who are staunchly religious and Church-minded, who, in short, are Catholics, but who disagree with the empirical form of the Church, the ecclesiastical provinces, the dioceses, and the parishes. They are strongly interested in religious matters, but they are not trained theologians. As a consequence, they express their intuitions and opinions, which, for the most part, are perfectly acceptable, in words which do not distinguish between the external "sociological structure" of the Church and its external but fundamental and basic structures. Therefore some people get the impression that they want a kind of exclusively spiritual, charismatic Church. Moreover they wish to express their belief in a modern way and to use their own contemporary accent in the expression of it. Thus there appear in the Netherlands some changes of accents which have nothing to do with a "crisis of the faith." Because the people in the Netherlands are unrelenting and adamant about the consequences of putting their newly acquired insights into practice, they often voice their ideas with a complete unconcern for traditional practices and customs and consequently contribute to the atmosphere of crisis.

The most striking point is that most of the elements of crisis are to be found in clerical circles, even in the preaching of the faith. Here, too, traditional or obsolete views are only too readily attacked and sometimes even denounced without style and cultivation. Some of the clergy are experiencing a crisis with respect to their priestly office. The departure of many from the priesthood is impelled by their uncertainty about its purpose. Many priests are tired of proclaiming truths against which doubts have risen in their souls. They are troubled by the contrast between what they are expected to say and what they know to be their own real existential needs, their concerns, and their authentic experience. The ensuing restlessness among the faithful provides fertile soil for a small, integralist group of conservatives, whose activities are confined to negative reactions against various phenomena. These reactions, in turn, elicit prompt and fierce response from the other side. The true and fundamental problem at the base of this crisis and restlessness —and this is true for more than the Netherlands—is the problem of religion and reality or humanness.

This is connected with the process of secularization. Schillebeeckx's analysis continues:

> It is noteworthy that this is not a process of doing away with the Church, nor is it even an "away from Rome" movement. Those matters, and even related problems, involving some historical blemishes of the Church are not the big problem, although it cannot be denied that, in many Dutch minds, *authority* and *dictatorship* arouse nearly the same feelings. Although this may often be historically understandable, it is essentially a bewildering experience. Even where the crisis takes on extreme forms (though no precise percentage can be given here), there is not even a thought about "schism" in the classical, theological sense of the word. The issue is quite different. *Within the Church,* that is, within the limits of Catholic-ecclesiastical practice, there is growing a new *interpretation* of the Church and of Christianity. Among some people—and here the percentage declines still more, although even an approximate estimate cannot be provided—there is growing something I can only characterize as a "liberal catholicism" on the model, so to speak, of the "liberal protestant" communities of faith. For the present I do not consider the question to what extent the term "liberal catholicism" is an intrinsic contradiction. I adopt this term only in order to delineate the extreme of a marginal situation: they wish to remain in a believing Catholicism but as liberals. In the Netherlands this movement is to be found mainly in private circles and is barely perceptible in the literary forum. Because they have not come into the open, all these tendencies provide grounds for anxiety and insecurity.

In its extreme form all this tends to a belief which is seen exclusively as a self-illumination, a self-interpretation or *Selbstverständnis* of man, in which Holy Scripture as well as the "holy books" of other great religions has a suggestive and stimulating function: this again is a case of uncertain and vague formulas with reservations added here and there. As to the Church, it is almost completely identified with the world. It is a man-made community or constitutes a provisional authority which, having fulfilled its functions, is to be thanked and dismissed. Of this whole process God is the bearing ground, as is manifested to us in Jesus.

I suppose that this tendency, as it has been sketched here, is consciously shared only by very few, but *as a tendency* it affects many people. With many (among this unknown percentage) it is more a question of searching and sympathetically reconnoitering this complex of problems.

Father Schillebeeckx concluded his analysis of the elements of crisis in the Dutch Catholic Church by stating that it is a crisis of growth. It is a seeking for the very core of believing existence. This is promising for the present and for the future. Moreover there are some indications that in a large measure people are aware of the fact that this indeed is a crisis of growth. This not only means that the crisis is acknowledged as such but also that this evolution is being considered as a historical process. Acknowledging this is a necessary condition for keeping the process under control. The Dutch Catholics who consciously participate in this evolution do not erect a separating wall between the Church and the Evangelical. However much they consider the local church as an essential value, they equally take for granted a central authority in the Church, the pope, who governs the Church in collegiality with the bishops of the whole world. The tensions that sometimes develop between the Dutch Church and Rome mainly involve the organs and machinery of government in Rome. This machinery, so the Dutch think, lags behind practical developments and may provide inadequate information to the central authorities. In the opinion of those Dutch Catholics who have closely followed the reformation of the Roman Curia, including its internationalization, the reformation has too few positive possibilities, because the papal directives as to age are neither strictly applied nor strictly followed.

The Dutch bishops have initiated a truly substantial attempt to make the growth process of the Dutch Catholic Church surveyable and to trace some structural lines in it. They have done this by establishing the Pastoral Council of the Dutch Ecclesiastical Province which provides a dialogue of the whole community of the faithful. Thus, this account of the present situation of the Dutch Church will conclude with a survey of the aims, procedures, and themes of the Pastoral Council.

V. PASTORAL COUNCIL OF THE DUTCH CHURCH

A. Some Historical Data

On November 16, 1965, the late Msgr. G. de Vet, Bishop of Breda, speaking to the Dutch missionary bishops in Rome, launched the idea of a Provincial Council (in the canon law sense of the word) in order to apply the Vatican Council's views to the Dutch situation. The Dutch bishops adopted this proposal which they communicated to the Catholics of the Netherlands in a pastoral letter dated December 26, 1965.

In line with the suggestion of the Pastoral Institute of the Dutch Ecclesiastical Province and its advisors, the idea of a Provincial Council was dismissed and replaced by a "Pastoral Council." On March 16, 1966, during the first press conference about this council, Msgr. G. de Vet made the following comment:

> Such a form of holding a council, with intensive deliberation taking place on the largest possible scale, will in the future be the normal way to secure clear advice, which may grow into the necessary decisions about the renewal that may be required. It may even be said that in the Dutch situation the Pastoral Council has already been proceeding for some time. So much is this the case that now the issue mainly is how may all the questions and all the views of our situation lead to acceptable decisions, that is, decisions which have arisen from the Church and are to be lived by the Church. As to what is already going on, we may, for example, point out that the Pastoral Institute of the Dutch Ecclesiastical Province has many working groups and advisory committees, which from the beginning have been concerned with a plan of pastoral renewal of the Church by studying closely the many problems which the Church faces in our Dutch situation. We may also point to the hundreds of discussion groups of priests, religious, and lay people in the various dioceses

who, under the supervision of the bishop and with the aid of the diocesan pastoral centers, have busied themselves and are still concerning themselves with the same problems which must constitute the agenda for our Pastoral Council. We also note the intensive opinion-building which our modern means of publicity have been effecting for a long time, sometimes, even, in a very engaged way.

B. Nature and Aims of the Pastoral Council

The Pastoral Council of the Dutch Ecclesiastical Province desires to hold a "faith-inspired deliberation of the Roman Catholic Church in the Netherlands under the guidance of the Dutch episcopate."

The *underlying idea* is that the Church as the whole People of God is responsible for the present and future renewal and for the self-realization of the Church as presented in the *Constitution on the Church* and the *Pastoral Constitution on the Church in the Modern World*. Therefore the whole People of God has to participate actively in this work.

This "faith-inspired deliberation" is presided over by the bishops, because as bishops they have their "own and irreducible authority and responsibility." The council therefore is characterized by its *mutual dialogue*, not in the sense of the People of God with the bishops, but of the People of God *and* the bishops, for *together* they constitute the whole People of God. This is more closely borne out in the structure of the council. The aims of this Pastoral Council are:

1. To make the Church in the Netherlands consider, in a way adapted to the needs and desires of modern man, the entire Christian life: the contents of the Gospel; the observance and the preaching of the Gospel; the structures of the community of the faithful; the existence and activity of the faithful in a changing world. In other words it aims at a *deliberation inspired by faith*, which must lead to a renewal of the Church in such a way that the Church of the Netherlands, on the one hand, answers the purpose for which Jesus Christ has founded it and, on the other hand, that it comes up to the expectations of men, believers and nonbelievers.

2. The further aim is to enliven the consciousness of the Roman Catholic Church in the Netherlands as to its own task and responsibility within the whole Church of Jesus Christ, its service to all mankind. It wants to enliven in this *local* Church of the

Netherlands the consciousness of its *own* task and mission within the frame of the one and whole Church of Jesus Christ. This therefore presupposes *communio* with the world Church as well as with the other Christian Churches. Hence the council has before it an *ecumenical* perspective. And this consciousness looks to "service unto the world."

3. Moreover, it wants to find ways and means to fulfill this task in a more faithful way. "In order to realize this aim the Catholic Church in this deliberation hopes for the closest possible contact with other Christian Churches, communities of believers, and the Ancient Chosen People, and for collaboration with groups of other religious and philosophical convictions." Thus if the Church of the Netherlands wishes to fulfill its task and mission faithfully, it will also have to listen to the voices of others and to allow others a voice in this deliberation. This has been provided for: there are officially appointed representatives of the Churches, the deputies delegated by communities of believers and by the Ancient Chosen People; there are observers from humanist groups; and there is the presence of Protestant and humanist participants in the discussion groups and the study committees.

The Structure of the Pastoral Council

The supreme organ of the Pastoral Council is the Plenary Assembly, which consists of: *all the bishops,* including auxiliary bishops, who *ex officio* constitute the presidium; *members of the Central Commission,* that is, the daily presidium of the council, in charge of the whole organization; *three priests* chosen by the clergy from each diocese; *seven lay people* from each diocese, chosen *by,* but not necessarily *from,* the members of the diocesan Pastoral Councils; *ten religious* from the religious orders for men and for women and from members of the secular institutes; *fifteen persons,* assigned, if necessary, by the episcopate; and the previously mentioned *representatives, delegates* and *observers,* who do not have a vote. Its tasks are:

1. To decide about the question whether the documents treated represent the religious thinking of the ecclesiastical community. Its primary task is to issue a faith-inspired statement about certain subjects, arrived at by means of dialogue.
2. To pronounce on the desirability of certain practical consequences to be drawn from the statements which it issued. In other words, the Plenary Assembly has no legislative power. It may advise the

bishops about practical consequences, but the bishops must act on such matters. Since the bishops are members of the Plenary Assembly (as well as of the presidium), they *individually and as a college* contribute positively to the whole course of formation of opinion and decision. When a vote is taken they, as the leaders in the faith, are the first to vote.

The agenda of a session and of a Plenary Assembly is prepared by the Presidium, that is, the episcopate. But additions may be made by the members of the Plenary Assembly.

The items placed on the agenda are to be studied by the Conciliar Board, which is composed of a group of eight experts in the field of ecclesiastical life and sciences, one representative from the working-teams of the "Conciliar discussion groups" and "Postboxes of the Council," and one representative of the other Churches and believing communities. This Conciliar Board forms study committees for investigating and elaborating these points; on these committees Protestants and non-Christians may be members.

Study committees have been established to consider the following sixteen subjects: 1. changes in the life and thinking of the Church—causes, facts, and consequences; 2. the meaning of the Christian life in a secularized world; 3. contents and realizations of the Christian life of modern man—his spirituality; 4. the lay Christian's moral attitude —inspiration and norms, liberty, conscience, and responsibility; 5. liturgy, or religious cult in the community, its forms, norms, and possibilities; 6. the preaching of the faith to young and adult people—the content, form, and responsibilities in modern catechesis; 7. authority in practice; 8. matrimony and the family; 9. the life of the religious; 10. ecumenical questions; 11. questions about the practice of faith; 12. youth, human development, education, and project of life; 13. the responsibility of the Christian for peace in the world; 14. Church and mission; 15. development-activities; 16. the priesthood.

The Conciliar Board formulates the questions for the diocesan discussion groups. These groups usually have ten to fifteen members and number about 15,000. The Board invites people to communicate their opinions through the diocesan postboxes. From the working-team of the "Conciliar discussion groups," the Board receives the results of the discussion groups and from the working-team "Council postboxes" the views presented to the postboxes.

The Conciliar Board may place these materials before the study committees. The reports of the committees and working-teams are placed before the Board. It examines them and eventually discusses them with the study committees. It may ask for additions and emendations and it may compile and collate several reports.

The *Central Commission*, in consultation with the presidium, decides when and how the reports are to be treated and presents them to the Plenary Assembly.

The sessions of the Plenary Assembly are *open to the public*. Documents, if possible, are published a month beforehand, so that all the people may study them. Additionally, they are sent to the Diocesan Pastoral Committees both for discussion and to assure diocesan co-operation.

The Plenary Assembly *proceeds* as follows: the report is first subjected to vote as to whether it shall be admitted for debate or not; after admission, it is debated, and it may be approved, amended, or rejected; also motions opposed to it may be made. At the end of the session the approved reports are accepted as official documents of the Council. The Pastoral Institute of the Dutch Ecclesiastical Province acts as the Council's secretariat.

D. THE PARTICIPATION OF ALL THE PEOPLE OF GOD

This participation is fostered by the possibility of making known one's personal opinions, desires, wishes, suggestions, and so forth on subjects to be treated in the Plenary Assembly and other subjects. The media are the diocesan postboxes and those of the KRO. A national working-team deals with such data. Until now some 3,000 letters have been received. Participation is promoted by the discussion groups, which are organized in the parishes under the guidance of a diocesan working-group. Each group has ten to fifteen members. The diocesan working-group fixes the agenda of the dialogues in consultation with the national working-group and the Conciliar Board. Each group sends a report of the discussions to the diocesan working-group, where a common diocesan report is compiled.

The national working-group for "Conciliar Discussion Groups" coordinates and stimulates the activities of the diocesan working-groups and serves as intermediary between them and the Conciliar Board.

The aim of the discussion groups is not to provide *information* to the

Conciliar Board, but to express the Church's mind in a dialogue and to reflect the consensus of the faithful and of the many non-Catholics who participate in these dialogues.

Organizations and associations which are allowed to form their own study committees for their own concerns and to submit appropriate subject matter to the dialogue of their members are another means by which participation is furthered. Then activity is coordinated by a working-team for "organizations and associations."

Thus the Dutch Pastoral Council wishes to establish a fruitful dialogue that will involve a mutual dialogue of the whole People of God, a dialogue with the other Churches and religious communities, with the Ancient Chosen People, with humanist groups, and a dialogue with the world. This fruitful dialogue will give to the Church of the Netherlands a form that enables it to accomplish its task and mission according to the will of the Lord as faithfully and as fruitfully as possible, in a *diakonia* unto the one Church of Jesus Christ and unto the world.

The Pastoral Council was inaugurated officially on November 27, 1967. The first Plenary Assembly was held from January 3 to January 5, 1968. Its subject matter was "Opinions about Authority and Authority in Practice." During the second Plenary Assembly (April 7–10, 1968) the subjects dealt with were Missions and Development-Aid. About four Plenary Assemblies are expected to take place annually.

Cardinal B. Alfrink noted that in the deliberations of the Pastoral Council "the faithful and the bishops found each other and understood each other." They learned with astonishment and joy that ". . . they did not stand as far apart from each other as was often suggested. They could think together, speak together about things which are important for the Church and humanity; this is quite a novel experience." The Cardinal also cited the important contributions made by younger representatives and by the delegates of non-Catholic Churches and groups. But perhaps most significant are the Cardinal's remarks made in an interview for KRO:

> The atmosphere behind this pastoral deliberation reflects the words which Pope Paul VI addressed to the KRO team during the general audience of February 8, 1968: "Now we want to welcome most cordially the reporters of the Dutch KRO who are present in this audience. Through them we address all our dear sons in the Netherlands. We know, dear sons, how intensely the faith is being lived

among you. You are not satisfied with a formalistic religion of exterior conduct; with you religious practice is the expression of a real interior conviction. Dear sons, always carefully preserve full fidelity unto the Church and its Head. . . ."

The attitude toward Rome became clearly evident in the first Plenary Assembly, that is there is no wish to attack the authentic mandate of the Pope, but there is a great deal of resentment about defective and indirect information and communication with Rome, about the methods and the place of the official machinery in Vatican City, and about the task of the papal legates. Openness is wanted and secrecy is rejected. Confidence in our own clergy is wanted as is true collegiality. And confidence in the laity is wanted. Decentralization and the collaboration of all, wherever necessary and possible, both on a secular and on the international level, is necessary. Pluralism of forms is wanted in all members and branches within the unity of the Church and without damage to its catholicity.

In commenting on the *progressiveness* of Dutch Catholicism in a press conference on November 14, 1966, Cardinal Alfrink stated:

In the Church today the course of our Pastoral Council can only be a progressive one, provided . . . that you are prepared to understand this word correctly and without the immediately emerging alternative. We are a Church on the move, and in this move we want to follow the Lord. He moves on in this world and in time. To follow Him means to go forward.

For some the progress is too rapid; for others it is too slow. On both sides there is anxiety. But real anxiety is called for only when people become entrenched in their own opinions and positions, for such entrenchment leads to decrying each other as heretics. This has always been the blow of death to love in the Church.

Our Pastoral Council is a free and open communication in faith and love, and it would make us happy if the entrenchments could be demolished and if there could be a growth toward unity and unanimity. It is meant as a common pastoral deliberation, where every voice may be heard and every opinion may contribute. Therefore, we hope that everyone will also be prepared to acquiesce in whatever conclusions will emerge from the common deliberation.

To those who must lead within the Dutch Catholic community it is of extreme importance that they learn as fully as possible to note what is alive in this community and to search in common deliberation for the best ways that may lead to a happy and flourishing Christian life in faith and love.

VI. CONCLUSION

This survey of the Catholic Church in the Netherlands cannot be concluded better than by quoting some passages from a speech delivered by Cardinal Alfrink on March 25, 1968, in Ghent (Belgium).

We feel no need to export our experiment [the Pastoral Council] to other countries, even if it should appear to be a good example. . . . Every diocese and every ecclesiastical province will have to seek, in terms of its own special situation, the means best adapted to building a post-Conciliar Church.

Our method gives to the faithful an opportunity to become interested in their own Church and to be engaged in it. It is a gratifying event when a community shows special interest in the Church and when the bishops have to think more about how to satisfy the demands for collaboration than about how to arouse the people's interest. Vatican II has opened many perspectives for the individual development of the local Church, for decentralization and pluralism of forms. This possibility we want to use, and we have such an opportunity because of our country's interest in the renewal of the Church. Our council is a novelty in the Church and this implies some risks. But the project, including its theological ramifications, has been thoroughly planned. There is no reason for distrusting this experiment only because it is new. In the Church it seems easier to accept the fact that a member of the body no longer exercises its function than [to understand and accept] our endeavors to make each member live its life to the full.

2 : GERMANY

Erwin Kleine

History is what happens to men and through men. Thus there can be no value-neutral history. Since every historical account is also the work of man, history should never be expected to be objective and free of accent. Objectivity can consist merely in the attempt to record events according to the facts. Yet the judgments of these facts are diverse since only those who are dead can experience and represent history without being engaged by it. The living see things in this way or that, reverberating with the echo history arouses in their existence.

These remarks may serve as my apology in presenting the following account of German Catholicism.

THE WAR AGAINST THE REFORMATION

The great confusion of Luther's time which affected the political sphere no less than the spiritual was somewhat lessened by the Peace of Augsburg: the subject of a Catholic sovereign had to be Catholic; that of a Protestant ruler had to be a Protestant. This settlement was as questionable as it was fateful. Ultimately it falsified the religious substance of encounter between the confessions, for thereafter political coercion choked the possibility of a true inter-Christian dialogue. Dictatorially established confessional regions made a spiritual confrontation of Christ's separated disciples impossible.

At the beginning of the nineteenth century Napoleon and the Congress of Vienna caused a rather sudden collapse of the malign confessional geography. The Constitution of the German Bund of 1848 contributed its share; it guaranteed in all Federal States equal civic rights to every German, regardless of his confession. Thereby was German Catholicism deprived of the decisive means of power which it had so long employed to increase and solidify its "possessions." Against this change, however, was the fact that the Peace of Augsburg had prevented the confessions from participating in dialogue; two centuries of living under it had led to complete alienation among Christians.

Although the Church in Germany still suffers from this fact—we need think only of the pain caused by the unsolved problem of mixed marriages—the problem is more deep-rooted: it is a subconscious and unadmitted suffering resulting from an unfulfilled mission. The German Church, more than any other, was asked by God and history to solve the problem of the Reformation in a brotherly spirit. It was helpless in the face of this command; it allowed the much-discussed "historical coercions" to predominate.

German Catholicism cannot detach itself from the Reformation, for ultimately the Reformation is its own child. That, in view of these historical forces, it espoused a war against the Reformation rather than Evangelical dialogue necessarily had fateful consequences that shape its present profile.

MILITANCY AND INFERIORITY

The radical rejection of the Reformation involved as a consequence a fundamentally disturbed relationship with the world and with the times. What else could one expect of a highly intellectual country in such a religious division? If we allow that this rejection was inspired by unrevised dogmatic and traditional pastoral concerns, we must also recognize that it was not free of power aspects. The clash with Protestant political conceptions was unavoidable. Equally unavoidable was the conflict with the intellectual and social emancipation movements which, legitimately or illegitimately, used the freedom of the Reformation for their own purposes. In the political area the Cologne Church controversy of 1830 and Bismarck's *Kulturkampf* (1872–1879) were prominent high-points of this battle. If this struggle is seen in the proper perspective, Catholicism was here victorious.

To compensate for the loss of political power, German Catholics at the beginning of the nineteenth century attempted to exert direct influence by forming Catholic associations and by publicist activity.

These efforts were nourished by the anti-Catholic foolishness of non-Catholic groups which inspired bitterness and anger among the Catholics—at times more was at stake than the mere defense of questionable Catholic rights. Some Catholic groups with worthy and generally relevant goals undertook a double role and in doing so forfeited their true worth, since they coupled their essential purpose with a militant Catholicism concerned with power. Outstanding figures like Ketteler, the great socially alert bishop, and Kolping, the patron of the journeymen, as well as the members of the then progressive Catholic *Volksverein*, undoubtedly would have been more important to the nation and the world if their work had been free from the pressures of an ecclesiastical-political alliance and if they could have separated evangelical mission and ecclesiastical power.

On the one hand, partial victories could be registered. On the other, the Church has never recovered from its historic loss of power. The experiences of the ghetto situation, a result of the *Kulturkampf*, left deep feelings of inferiority that today greatly determine the mentality on which Catholic action and reaction in Germany are based.

THE REACTIONARY POSITION

The tie-up of basically healthy Catholic initiatives with political concerns of the Church was all the more deplorable, since in principle the Church stubbornly remained politically reactionary. Consequently the history of German liberalism as well as of German socialism acquired antiecclesiastical accents. In spite of the Cologne Church controversy and the *Kulturkampf*, the Church's pact with yesterday reached back to the emperors of the house of Hohenzollern. Obsolete but similar regimes joined together in order to resist the push toward a new social order. This morganatic marriage held on to life tenaciously and, beneath the threshold at least, crept into the Weimar Republic. True, historians maintain that German Catholicism needed little time to adapt to historical facts, yet it is notable that even in 1925 a great many German Catholics preferred the Protestant Monarchist Hindenburg as president of the Reich rather than Marx, the Catholic Republican.

The spiritual-ideological situation corresponded to the social-political one. The Church was not willing to respond in dialogue to a world in process of secularization and the increasingly imposed papalism was incapable of such conversation. Hence its adaptation to a changing history of ideas did not occur. Bishops and theologians like Sailer, Hefele, Wessenberg, Döllinger, and Schell tried by their liberal and ecumenical ideas to force the traditional element to respond to new trends. But rather than the Church's assimilating liberal ideas and goals, it forced the liberals to be silent or to break away from a traditional Church. It is small wonder that an intellectualism that encountered so much misunderstanding progressively broke away from traditional forms.

The question arises whether the fundamental difficulties of German Catholicism derive from a seriously defective relationship with Rome. Counter-Reformation Catholicism was known as the most faithful son of the Church and of the Jesuits. Did it perhaps feel that it had to make a special effort to destroy Rome's distrust of transalpine people? This would follow quite naturally, since its intellectual leadership has a strong contingent of pupils from the *Collegium Germanicum*, founded by the Jesuits in 1552. Because of this situation German Catholicism never gave what it more than any other regional Catholicism owed to the Church, namely, a decisive contribution toward a fruitful confrontation with the Reformation.

Until today the products of the *Germanicum* have set the pace for the German episcopate. According to rumor the bishops of Germany on one occasion promised the papal nuncio to "reestablish order" in the country after Vatican II. Rumor though it be, one may still be constrained to ask, among other questions: what was it that had to be put in order in Germany? That such a rumor could exist characterizes the atmosphere of the situation.

THE CHURCH AND THE NAZIS

With the formation of the Center Party in 1870 German Catholicism created a means of public political power, whose range and strength are uncontestable. It stood decisively for Catholic concerns. Apart from that, it proved to be a generally authentic democratic factor, as is evidenced by the large number of non-Catholic members. To the Weimar Republic it provided four chancellors and a number of ministers, all persons of merit, who contributed considerably to the democratization and social transformation of Germany. The importance of the Center Party as a Catholic stronghold against National Socialism ended in 1933, when, deceived by false promises, it consented to

Hitler's Enabling Act—ultimately the grave of democracy. A reestablishment of the Party after World War II produced only abortive results.

Not only the voluntary abandonment of the Center Party but the attitude of the German bishops, and they were not alone, placed the relationship between German Catholicism and the Brown dictatorship in a fatal twilight where only the most experienced and perceptive observers could see halfway clear contours. In fact, close-ranked episcopal resistance was as weak as was the fidelity of many Catholics. The number of those who left the Catholic Church during the Third Reich is estimated to be 480,000. Nevertheless, it would be unfair to conclude that German Catholicism in general was friendly to National Socialism. The situation was far more complicated.

During the period of free, democratic elections, studies of electoral geography reveal a massive rejection of National Socialism in predominantly Catholic areas; these were strongholds of the Center Party which best suited the Catholics. It is, however, difficult to estimate the extent to which reflective political thinking here played a role.

We can ask whether more intelligent deliberation would not have saved the party from a too hasty suicide, but in asking we should also recognize that few had read Hitler's revealing *Mein Kampf*. And where a man had done so, would he in a nationalistically heated period have adequately appreciated its disclosures? For the program of the Nazi Party propagated with demagogical skill a "positive Christianity," and Hitler's coming to power stopped the dangerous movement away from the Church. Numerous Church weddings of SA members were part of the false front of the "revolution."

However, once the anti-Christian dictator shed his mask, German Catholics lost no time in making significant contributions to resistance. It was in those years that bishops like Galen, Preysing, and Sproll became symbols of a better Germany, and not only Catholics clung to them. The number of priests and laymen persecuted, arrested, and killed did not cease to mount.

THE BISHOPS OF THE NATION

No right-thinking person would want to defend mistakes and omissions. But this is not the issue when one attempts to reconsider more objectively those bishops who were more or less failures with respect to Hitler. It is only fair to speak of a tragic rather than of a subjective guilt—a guilt which was the result of definite a priori views and circumstances.

First of all, we should not forget that the Vatican, undoubtedly because of honorable motives, conveyed an impression of the situation which did not inspire the episcopacy, in its utter fidelity to Rome, to set up a timely resistance. Eugenio Pacelli had secured what never had been won before: the *Reichskonkordat*. For the dictator this was a piece of paper, a kind of international alibi; for Rome it was the feeble hope of being able to preserve through the Concordat what, without it, would have been endangered from the very start. Additionally it was a hard-won diplomatic success.

The world's judgment of the German episcopate would probably be more lenient if astonishingly foolish Catholic attempts had not been made to whitewash the bishops and to throttle well-deserved objective historical criticism, if there had not been an enslavement to the way of thinking that refuses to mention the inadequacy of a person —and to do so solely because that person is a bishop of the Roman Catholic Church. An unhesitant demythologizing of the image of the bishop on the Catholic side would have noticeably facilitated discussions about the dark years.

But the Church's historic liaison with reactionary political and social systems had so shaped the psyches of the hierarchy that the occasional anarchism that accompanied the birth of German democracy was alien to the mentality of the bishops. They secretly cherished a longing for a ruling authority that would be in general accord with their own ideas about pastoral undertakings. Is it surprising, then, to find a susceptibility to Hitler's phrase about national order? Certainly not everything about this man was reassuring. But they found it noteworthy and more important that he cleaned up an uncontrolled republicanism and constantly referred to the "providence of the Almighty." Was one not justified in sharing the calculation of conservatives and German nationalistic groups that the "lance corporal of World War I" should be allowed to "clean up" the place and that at the opportune moment he would easily be brought under control? Although this was as unrealistic as it was unpolitical, it cannot be imputed to everyone as sin.

Moreover, to remain indifferent to the misery of one's flock is to be a bad bishop and the Germans had suffered bitterly following World

War I. A British writer has said that there was no Allied reparation demand that struck so hard as did the abolition of the German monarchy. Germany was simply not ripe for democracy. The end of the monarchy brought about a dangerous psychic void in feelings about the State. This vacuum gave room not only to antidemocratic, revolutionary developments but also to every kind of national symbol or pseudosymbol that might serve as an ersatz for the lost crown.

This opened up countless possibilities for Hitler. Many accepted him—consciously or unconsciously—as a crown-surrogate. Doubtless his prospects in this subliminal process would have been much poorer had not the Allies at Versailles and afterwards compounded the national tribulation and the moral political discrimination by making economic demands that made for conditions leading only to chaos. In these circumstances there developed a macabre German solidarity of hope in the strong man. Indeed it would have been unnatural if the State's entire episcopate had remained an outsider to this solidarity.

Moreover, one should not succumb to the illusion that a correctly timed anti-Nazi Catholicism could have prevented the catastrophe. Until 1938 the Catholics represented no more than one-third of the German population and in this third were only a very limited number of leaders and intellectuals.

THE FRUITS OF TRIBULATION

When we investigate the effects on Church history stemming from the tribulations of the Third Reich, we enter into the new climate that made possible the Council of John XXIII. Ecclesiastical tradition and hierarchical stability had proved to be foundations of secondary value —at least for many. Of primary importance was one's personal attitude of faith. For many, the historical events had pointed up and clarified the essential. Leading thinkers such as the Jesuit Alfred Delp, who was killed by the brown-shirted executioners, began to sense the radical and bitter consequences of the Church's failure, by reason of indifference or hostility, to aid in the formation of modern society. Therefore, these men insisted on the need of an authentic Christian encounter with their era and its thought, and this, although a timid beginning, marked the first breakthrough in the complacent ghetto of German Catholicism. Reflection, self-examination and criticism, and repentance helped to impel this change.

The resistance against Hitler, which did not draw its support from obedience to an infantile examination of conscience and which could drive a conscience directly in contact with God even to face the possibility of murdering a tyrant, included both Catholics and Protestants. Here is seen the promise of a rebirth of Catholic responsibility for the world. Man's salvation was no longer viewed as depending on the jealous and exclusive guarantee of Catholic positions but on a presence of Christ which formed every day's reality—a presence that can be summoned into being only by replacing rulership with service and law with charity. Fundamental values of the Reformation broke through the dilapidated wall separating the Churches.

The community of suffering gave birth to the recognition of the community of the crucial foundations of faith. Historically conditioned confessional characteristics lost their relevance. Many learned to pray and work together—without official Church approval, of course. Ordinarily this growth was limited to the lives and circles of awakening laymen and clerics. That it scarcely, or not at all, succeeded in involving the official Church indicates the tenacity and rigidity of the traditional system. For this traditional system curtailed the beginnings of renewal and as soon as the external pressure was lifted, Rome was again free to give vent to its distrust of any form of "interdenominationalism."

The momentum was evidenced most conspicuously in the interdenominational *Una Sancta* groups. Outstanding in many respects was the important Munich group, which during the persecutions nurtured German ecumenism. The life of these groups is characterized by names such as Max Josef Metzger (a victim of the so-called People's Court under Roland Freisler), Emanuel Maria Heufelder, and Matthias Laros, all of whom exemplified active brotherly love, courage, and a spirit of sacrifice.

Yet this vitality was not exclusively the fruit of suffering. Courageous theological pioneers had long ago laid its foundation; for example, Josef Lortz, the internationally influential Catholic expert who reinterpreted the Reformation, and Robert Grosche who daringly and sensitively built bridges of the mind. Strong currents flowed from the liturgical and bibilical movements connected with the names of Romano Guardini, Abbot Herwegen, and others. They came closer to the heart of the true Reformation Christian than any impersonal sacral objectivism could do. Whatever was temporary in these movements was wiped out in the times of trial while the lastingly valid took on clearer contours.

SERVICE AMID CHAOS

The end of World War II was a time of inconceivable catastrophe for Germany, when it seemed no longer possible even to dare to hope for a worthwhile national future. In this situation the Churches persecuted by Hitler took a leading role in the work of salvage and service. Because German Catholicism above all had at its disposal a relatively large reserve of "politically unblemished" (that is, verifiable non-Nazis), it was able to bridge many serious gaps. The reconstruction of Germany offered the Catholic Church enormous possibilities of influence. In order to provide collective effort for the suffering nation, Catholics and Protestants joined together in the "Christian Democratic Union" and in the "Christian Social Union" (Bavaria).

The ecclesiastical rescue service was not confined to the realm of domestic politics. What to the Protestants was ecumenical foreign relations was to the Catholics their universal Church: the field of first, significant, international contacts. Here they struggled not only to acquire new moral credit but also to elicit considerable help from foreign countries for suffering Germany.

It was here that German Catholicism realized, perhaps for the first time, what it means to be a universal Church. This awareness could not remain content with itself but called for expression. The experiences gained in helping their own country evoked a realization of brotherhood in the chaos of the world. So an unforeseen renewal occurred: the sense of responsibility for their own nation expanded into responsibility for others, too. German Catholicism was not unresponsive when it was able to give, where before it had to receive.

By the mid-fifties the Archdiocese of Cologne gave a visible example by entering into a kind of sponsor-relationship with the Archdiocese of Tokyo. Substantial contributions were sent to the Japanese. In August of 1958 Cardinal Frings of Cologne made an appeal to the German Conference of Bishops for German-Catholic development aid. *Misereor*, a yearly Lenten collection, begun in 1959, was established and with it an unexpected reputation for German Catholicism in the world. *Misereor* is an exemplary undertaking, if only for the reason that it is founded on the sound insight that the proclamation of the good news is unauthentic, as long as one preaches about heaven while allowing the "missionary objects" on earth to perish from hunger and sickness.

And more than that: this development aid was based exclusively on Christ's command to love *all* men, to help everybody without discrimination. This deserves special emphasis, because here Christian responsibility for the world presents itself with a realism hitherto all but unknown. The German-Catholic development aid became a reality long before many other people were able even to comprehend the idea. Its precocious beginning and its accomplishments created a sensation.

This is not a matter of idealizing the event. Much is praised as sacrifice that does not even approach its true meaning. Yet, in fact, many real sacrifices can be reported, especially among the economically poorer population. Only when one realizes to what extent poverty puts the little it possesses to the service of the still poorer of the world do the statistics of the contributions take on life. This deserves respect.

From approximately 35 million marks in 1959, the Lenten collection increased to 58 million in 1967. If we include the intervening years the total reached approximately 440 million marks. Approximately 5,000 development projects have been carried out or supported by these collections. Thirty-five Catholic associations and institutions united to form the *Arbeitsgemeinschaft für Entwicklungshilfe* (Working Community for Developmental Aid). From 1959 to 1967 it trained 874 qualified development helpers and sent them into projects supported mainly by *Misereor*.

While *Misereor* contributions are in general destined for underdeveloped countries, in 1961 the bishops began to call for special consideration of the plight of the Church in Latin America. And not without success. By 1966 more than 221 million marks was collected to which can be added the sponsorship-contributions which for the years 1963 to 1966 amounted to almost 262,000 marks.

These figures demonstrate a considerable broadening of viewpoint and a realistic vision of German Catholicism which no longer sees the Church and its problems of existence in the shadow of its own steeple.

However, these figures did not remain static. *Deutsche Caritas-Ver-*

band (German Charity Association), sometimes in connection with *Misereor*, participated considerably in development aid. From 1960 to 1966 its multifaceted "overseas" aid (including approximately 1.3 million marks for training purposes) added up to more than 28 million marks. *Katastrophenhilfe* (Disaster Aid), which is integrated in *Caritas*, spent about 7 million marks—a sign that German Catholics not only can be called upon for routine contributions but are also willing to help with extraordinary cases of human need.

Finally there are numerous individual sponsorships as well as diocesan sponsorships of extra-European dioceses. And for the sake of completeness, we cannot disregard the assistance given especially by the Diocese of Osnabrück to the Catholic *diaspora* in Scandinavia; in addition this diocese regularly made a considerable contribution to the extensive *diaspora* in North and Middle Germany.

AT THE EXPENSE OF TRADITIONAL COMMITMENTS?

At this point the reader may be tempted to ask whether the "unmissionary" efforts toward development did not push the missions themselves into the background. Although the war was a painful blow to the missions, the personnel bottlenecks caused by it were quickly resolved. From 1955 to 1966 the number of German apostolic workers in the missions increased from 10,066 to 17,000. In 1962 German missionary associations maintained 5,393 institutions for training personnel and providing humanitarian help.

The keen missionary interest of German Catholicism may be suggested by some statistics of the German division of the Society for the Propagation of the Faith. In 1950 it counted about 445,000 members; in 1966 the membership came to 1,150,000. In the same period the contributions increased from 1,270,000 marks to 24,100,000 marks. Other associations and institutions with missionary interests report similar results.

So far we have failed to mention the unascertainable but by no means small sum donated by individual contributors to missionary orders and individual missionaries. This effort, however, is evidence that the problem of the "forgotten missions" is nonexistent. The 4,140 sponsorships of catechists from 1961 to 1967 are no mean witness to missionary zeal. Through the Society for the Propagation of the

Faith, "sponsors" help to maintain no fewer than 107 schools which are dedicated to providing pastoral care by native laity in the missions.

In short, German Catholicism gives considerable help to foreign countries. Does this affect German Catholic response to the help needed in Germany itself? Without the subsidies of the government, which in turn benefits from its social action, the German *Caritas* would not always be in the best of shape. But the reason for this is not that the Catholics treat *Caritas* as a stepchild but rather that it must meet tremendous demands. The German *Caritas* has a vast scope: 4,800 hospitals, recreation centers, and similar institutions totalling 390,000 beds. It provides for 7,700 kindergartens and maintains social work training centers with 21,000 places. All these institutes employ a full-time paid personnel of 153,000.

No financial accounting is needed to demonstrate how many painful sacrifices make this service apparatus possible. It is also apparent that the large development effort maintained overseas does not involve a shifting of contributions from the internal realm of misery to the external. The contributions for development are not instead of the active help "at home" but in addition to it.

More than anything else, this active co-responsibility for the world and the universal Church has aided Germany in stamping its image on the community of nations. German Catholicism, therefore, enjoys a high reputation and has developed in self-confidence. This sense of co-responsibility gave German Catholicism an importance in the universal Church that it had not enjoyed previously. Vatican II revealed the new situation. There, when the German bishops presented well-worked out reform ideas, they had an authority and impact that is partly to be explained by the confidence and affection of those who had received German help. These bishops had practiced the principle of collegiality long before the Council fathers had formulated it. The collegiality of the Council was an echo of the active brotherliness of the German bishops.

GERMAN PROBLEMS

The active concern of German Catholicism with world problems and the reform calls of some of its bishops in the Council may suggest that here we are dealing with an extremely progressive area of the Church.

But realistic piety, no matter how farsighted, and pioneering proclamation in an unusual situation do not necessarily indicate an entirely
progressive attitude. One of the most conspicuous characteristics of
German Catholicism is that while in one area it may be quite responsively modern, in other areas it lingers sleepily in the shadows of its
past.

The accurate description of the situation is hampered by the
unavailability of statistics. On the one hand, there is the division of
Germany by the Iron Curtain. Additionally there is the ecclesiastical
reluctance to furnish information. The latest edition of the *Kirchliches
Handbuch* (Ecclesiastical Handbook) of the Catholic Church of Germany covers the years 1957–1961 and is six years old. The author's
request for more recent information was refused. The vicariates-general
as well as other Church authorities generally answered questionnaires
by saying that no information was available because of a lack of data
or lack of personnel.[1]

Out of almost 76,800,000 Germans a bare one-third belong to the
Catholic Church. The establishment of the German Democratic Republic in 1949 and the German split institutionalized by it created a
situation in which thereafter one had to deal with two German partial
states of quite different confessional structure. In predominantly
Protestant East Germany the number of Catholics (who live mostly in
the *diaspora*) is estimated as hardly more than 10 to 11 per cent of the
17,000,000 citizens while in the Federal Republic of Germany with
almost 59,800,000 inhabitants (in 1967), the proportion of Catholics,
according to the 1961 census, was about 55 per cent.

The Catholic population of the whole of Germany is divided into
twenty-four dioceses or archdioceses. Because some extend partially
into the Eastern zone, for pastoral purposes they are stricken areas
where the West-German bishops must arrange to be represented by
fully authorized deputy prelates. Included in this number is a small
portion of the Diocese of Breslau, the greatest part of which is within
the Polish area. The Eastern regions that are under Polish administration are not mentioned here. These are in the care of Polish bishop-

---

[1] The author acknowledges his gratitude to the excellent work of N. Greinacher
and H. T. Risse, *Bilanz des deutschen Katholizismus* (Mainz, 1966). Without
its material and the questionnaire replies received from various institutes, as well
as some pertinent press reports, the author would have been at a loss. But even
with their help, much that is stated here can only have the status of probability.

administrators who since 1967 have had juridical independence, yet the Vatican has not declared them to be Polish dioceses.

In contrast to the harsh restrictions imposed on the life of the Churches by the German Democratic Republic (DDR), Catholicism in the Federal Republic enjoys great freedom. It can express itself in the energetic activity of many associations and organizations, but it is difficult to acquire the actual statistics. The membership of some organizations reaches into hundreds of thousands while other groups are quite limited in size. In all there may be considerably more than 300 organizations. This is a respectable potential which provides a sizable Catholic representation in ecclesiastical and public life.

The Central Committee of German Catholics, which is also responsible for the famous German *Katholikentage* (Catholic days), is erroneously considered to be a kind of holding company of all these organizations. Although it occupies a key position in the work of Catholic laymen, it by no means officially represents all these groups. The Central Committee does not grant membership to organizations and clubs but merely to individuals as such and these are not considered delegates of their organizations. The number of groups represented in this way in the Central Committee could not be established. Yet since the individual members of groups work side by side with representatives of the broad and extensive branches of directly diocesan lay activity, the Central Committee can, in a certain way, claim to represent German Catholicism. But this representation should not be viewed in terms of democratic-parliamentarianism.

The representative basis is rather narrow. In past years the committee has frequently been criticized for being too narrow, on the ground that it pays almost no attention to unorganized Catholics. But this situation is expected to change with a restructuring that is now in the planning stages. In accordance with Conciliar intentions, this restructuring also intends to end dependency on the hierarchy. The goal is to establish with the bishops an official relationship that approximates a partnership.

THE PRESS AS MIRROR

The Catholic press in Germany also reflects the widespread activity of the Church. In the Federal Republic there are more than 420 Catholic magazines constituting a colorful bouquet of titles and aims. At the moment there is some concern regarding how their influence can be intensified through greater concentration. These magazines publish copies totalling in excess of 15 million. An association of the ecclesiastical press arranges exchanges of experiences among its members (over 70 publishing houses with about 140 magazines turning out over 12 million copies) and strives for a coordinated representation of its members to the public. KNA, the Catholic News Agency, based on diocesan newspapers and Christian-oriented dailies and financially supported by the dioceses, furnishes ecclesiastical and secular publications with information about Catholicism.

There is no purely Catholic daily. The Catholic weekly press has not yet been able to share the success of the Protestant press. A weekly newspaper, planned by the bishops and announced for 1968, is intended to compensate for this lack and to provide a proper representation of German Catholicism. This project has been the subject of heated debate.

In the DDR the circulation of the ecclesiastical press is severely restricted. The communist State blocks all Christian influence on public life; recently it even attempted to deny the Church the status of a corporation in public law. *St. Hedwigsblatt*, the East Berlin diocesan paper, is forbidden to publish more than 25,000 copies weekly. The Leipzig *Tag des Herrn*, which covers the rest of the DDR, is limited to 100,000 copies biweekly.

SOCIOLOGICAL ASPECTS

The Catholic press reflects the situation in Germany not only in respect to Catholic activity and political constellation, but it also offers striking religio-sociological information. For example, 1) Catholic publications are read less in cities of more than 500,000 population; 2) they are read more in towns of 2,000 and under; and, 3) Catholics of lower and middle educational levels tend to be more interested in Catholic papers than are the highly educated. Such evidence, indicative of an essential characteristic of German Catholicism, perhaps explains some of its plebeian tendencies and some of its other aspects. German Catholicism is closer to the country districts and to little towns than it is to the concentrations of big cities which energize and determine modern life. Catholicism, too, is more pervasive in the lower social levels than in the upper strata.

One expert has maintained that the modern work-world and technological civilization, along with its prerequisites, have come to the fore and as a result have, figuratively speaking, left the Catholic in the lurch. One sees evidence of this in dealing with the much discussed Catholic educational gap in Germany. Catholics are poorly represented in intellectual and administrative leadership (estimates of the professorships held by Catholics in German colleges and universities vary from 15 to 30 per cent), but even the number of Catholic students in universities and high schools is disproportionately low relative to the total Catholic population; further, Catholics are seldom found in schools with progressive tendencies.

Though much substantial and admirable work has been done in various fields devoted to the education of both youth and adults, the unachieving record of Catholics is deeply rooted in general history and in the history of ideas and cannot be quickly or easily changed, for its deepest cause lies in the traditionally negative attitude toward science and reason which still prevails. The Protestants, on the other hand, learned quite early to deal with this attitude in a more natural and fruitful way.

Does this suggest that there is a numerous and extensive Catholicism which in the twentieth century stalwartly persists in its naive piety? Experts estimate that churchgoers who center their life around their faith may total 20 per cent; 30 per cent are Sunday-Catholics; 40 per cent are occasional churchgoers; and total abstainers number 10 per cent. These figures may be curtly explained: industrialization and technology have initiated critical changes which the German Church has not escaped.

Other postwar statistics point the same way. Even though the exodus of many during Hitler's ascendency was followed by return and conversions after the catastrophe—until 1950 the curve was upward—it has since been on the decline. This decline is not steep but steady. For quite some time conversions to the Catholic Church have not kept pace with the defections. If we can rely on a recent survey made by a sociological institute, the intensity of religious life is also declining. In 1962, 68 per cent of the population of the Federal Republic professed themselves to be practicing Catholics. In 1966 only 64 per cent went to Sunday Mass with fair regularity. The middle-aged and elderly are far in the lead and the rural communities proved to be twice as church-concerned as the big cities.

Of course, this is no proof of faith or nonfaith, but it does raise the serious question as to whether the Church's behavior and work are oriented to the times. We cannot disregard another survey which revealed that 84 per cent of West Germans maintained that one can be a believer without going to church. The fact that the younger and more educated were the most vehement advocates of this opinion is one more indication of the Church's impending obsolescence.

SHORTAGE OF CLERGY

Is it any surprise that the clergy, too, is also affected by this process of obsolescence? The secular clergy, at least, plays an unmistakable role in it. The older generation predominates while the younger suffers from a noticeable shortage. The most densely populated areas have the most obvious shortage of priests.

In 1954 a parish priest had to administer to 1,568 Catholics. This placed Germany third from the last in European "priest-density" and since then the proportion has hardly changed. The 20,125 secular priests (together with 6,428 priests of religious orders) listed in 1964 cannot keep up with existing and increasing demands. Foreign priests who come to assist cannot fill the gaps. Even if we include the 28 per cent of secular clergy in West Germany who serve in administrative and in various other nonpastoral offices, we would still be far away from the ideal number of 1,000 Catholics per priest. Taking this theoretical proportion of 1:1,000 as a basis, Germany has a shortage of about 12,000 priests. The result of this situation is that 70 per cent of the existing parishes are "one-man parishes" with, at times, seriously limited possibilities for pastoral care.

What is the reason for this alarming shortage? It is estimated that the war cost approximately 1,150 priests. The number of theology students and aspirants for the priesthood who fell or are missing is unknown. But even today's prospects are affected by the war's blood-letting and by the reduced birth rate immediately following the war.

But the war can only be partially blamed for the shortage of priests, for the decline in priestly numbers appears in traditionally Catholic areas and in the seminaries. The secularization of the times and the

failure of Catholic parents are excessively simplistic explanations of
this problem. Undoubtedly affluence and materialistic attitudes play
some role. This is supported by noting that there are three well-at-
tended seminaries in the DDR where affluence and its attendant super-
ficiality are unknown. In communist Germany tribulation cannot be
mastered by inane religious formalism. Is, then, the Church responsible for its unattractiveness? It has been observed—and lends support
to my argument—that the Council and the reform efforts in the
Church awakened in many a new interest in the priestly vocation.
Nevertheless, there is a high wall between German Catholicism and
the priestly office. Traditional systems and structures and a revolution-
ized and ever more revolutionary society work at cross purposes. In
this society the attractiveness of the image of the priestly office is increasingly overshadowed.

The exact number who fall as victims of this dilemma is restricted
information. It is estimated that only about 50 per cent of those who
begin studying for the priesthood after finishing high school persevere
until ordination. The connection of priesthood and celibacy, moreover, plays a not insignificant role in this dilemma.

Finally the cleavage between ecclesiastical and secular reality is
clearly manifested by the social background of theology students. In
the Federal Republic, at any rate, they reflect very inadequately the
social composition of the German population. While the middle-class
element has a disproportionately high representation in the Federal
Republic, the working class represented almost 90 per cent of the population, but only one-fourth of the students of theology are from this
class (1950 statistics).

DANGEROUS TRIUMPHALISM

In turning from sociology and statistics and toward the more internal
course of ecclesiastical history since the end of the war, we may see
that in many respects the catastrophe of 1945 was a turning point. It
forcefully shattered the ghetto of fatal introversion and led the Germans into a not unproblematic, but much more natural, dialogue with
the world, and this is the yardstick of inner development. The significant participation of German Catholics in this dialogue has already
been mentioned.

It is more difficult to record the deep-reaching *inner* Catholic changes. The spiritual yield of the times of suffering indicated that little ground had been previously tilled. It appeared as though the institution of the Church and a great part of the people had merely experienced an episode which was not powerful enough to initiate a truly new chapter in German Church history. It almost seemed as though there was a naive belief that the Germans could take up where they had left off in 1933. There was not enough openness to permit a deeper penetration of the experience endured. So the experience was looked on more as a bitter current event and was not examined as the symptom of a fundamentally shattering revolution of mankind. And it was for this reason alone that it was possible to fall into the utopian dream of a restored old world in which an uncorrected traditionalist Catholicism could function without friction *in saecula saeculorum*. Multitudes of apostates streamed back to the Church. The occasional suspicion that the brilliant statistics of baptisms and Church collections might present a superficial and misleading picture aroused little concern.

Protestantism, led by men who had proved themselves in the struggle against Hitler, could not pass so lightly over the precipitous and essential situation. Its *Stuttgarter Schuldbekenntnis* (Stuttgart Confession of Guilt) documented a promising new reflection, which, however, bore only meager fruit. But in broad Catholic circles an alarming triumphalism began to spread. Slogans like "and the Church was victorious after all" were a frightening commentary. The fall of the tyrannical State and the possibility of a Catholic restoration were rashly interpreted as proof of the dependability of Christ's promise that the gates of hell could not destroy the community of the Lord. A "springtime of Christianity" was childishly enjoyed.

It is true that the circumstances almost begged for a triumphant attitude. It required religious maturity not to succumb to the temptation. According to the figures, Catholicism went through the Third Reich much more impressively than Protestantism. It registered conversions of persons of rank and name, of persons whose experience of the tribulations had prompted doubts regarding the validity of the Protestant system and, more exactly, doubts which had subtle theological implications. The moral authority of the Church took on a halo and its political capabilities acquired an importance and influence on the commonwealth that had not been witnessed previously. The Church was no longer merely tolerated but was respected and strong, with a strength disproportionate to its ultimately valid presumptions. This appeared all the more conspicuous, since Protestantism had to cope with a far more problematic past and, because of its great numbers in East Germany, was much more affected by the partition of Germany.

In retrospect it can be concluded that the basic attitude of triumphalism blocked the Catholic repentance and prevented German Catholicism from undertaking the great and long overdue task of building the bridge between Wittenberg and Rome. This triumphalist attitude was quite foreign to Protestant thinking and feeling. It aroused fears of a Catholic urge for hegemony and in certain cases even expressed such an urge.

Of course, the shared experience of trials had its aftereffects. Whenever the need arose one would offer the other his church for services. Many other encouraging actions can also be reported. But as sincere and honest as these individual actions may have been, officially they did not exceed minute formal concessions. These were not enough for the breakthrough from Catholic insulation. These could not make possible brotherly dialogue. Although in time expert theologians established committees for discussion, they were essentially limited to spadework in the history of dogma and to "working up" unsettled centuries of Church history.

The burning question they inevitably avoided. And this had to be— only illusionaries could have approached it courageously. For one had to take Rome into account. Decisive questions remained unchanged and inflexible, especially those concerning the mixed marriage problem. Because of the great immigration of expellees and the growing mobility, the problem became more and more acute so that today almost every third marriage in the Federal Republic is interconfessional. The traditional rules prevented a realistic pastoral insight into the new circumstances. The contemporary task with its challenges and opportunities was lost in the fear of a dilution of dogma and of a weakening of the position of the Church—and a similar situation with similar results prevailed in Protestantism.

IN THE OLD GHETTO

The restraints were applied not only to interconfessional but also to intersocial developments. The more and more sharply prominent con-

tours of an ideological and political pluralism were watched with un-
easy feelings. The antiquated ideal of a Catholic, or, at least, of a
Christian state stood in the way. There was only a limited openness to
the appeal for a revision of major sociopolitical viewpoints. Individual
groups were willing, but the predominance of the political Catholic
outlook dissipated their *élan*. An ideological aversion against anything
smacking of socialism was another contributing factor.

Certainly the unified trade union established after the war with
Christian approval was not blameless in the origin of a *Christliche
Gewerkschaftsbewegung* (Christian Trade Union Movement). But in
the last analysis this special, Catholic-Protestant project, which enjoyed
only slight success, was evidence of a basic incapacity to break open the
old ghetto. Distinguished men of vision fell victim to suspicion and
discrimination; the most important of them were the great Catholic
social scientists, von Nell-Breuning and Wallraf.

It could hardly be otherwise; inferiority feelings, a heritage of the
Kulturkampf, still persisted. There was a basic defensive tendency
against everything that appeared dangerous to the Catholic position.
Yet, even here, there was no impressive unity; many nuances were
represented and divergent Catholic in-group interests were also
noticeable.

Did the previously mentioned "Christian" union parties offer help
or even attempt a solution? Founded, as they were, by farsighted men
who had recognized the need of the hour, they could have, if they had
adhered to their original principle. But in these political formations,
too, payment was obstinately demanded on the historical mortgage of
German Christianity: on the one hand there was a Catholic *Kulturkampf* bloc-mentality, and on the other there was the ingrained Protestant fear of "Roman hegemony." These were bound to complicate
matters. The Catholic episcopate's indiscriminate support of the
"Christian" party intensified widespread Protestant uneasiness.

Within this context Konrad Adenauer with his political greatness
and undoctrinaire Catholicism made it possible for the tension-filled
positions to be brought together. Among the Protestants such exemplary
figures as Hermann Ehlers and Eugen Gerstenmeier should not be
forgotten; their particular religious formation and common sense were
too strong for them to permit sectarian problems to block efforts to
achieve Christian community in a sense of responsibility for the nation.

It is understandable that the designation of "Christian" for the

Union was passionately defended. That its constituent members succumbed to the temptation to claim exclusive use of it illustrates how little they had grasped of modern social and ecclesiastical structures.

While the party was endangered by the pull of a powerful traditional Catholicism, the Catholic position was endangered by the main lines of the leadership of the party. Being a member of the party was a part of being a good Catholic, which obviously led into political fields of different orientation at the expense of Catholic-apostolic work. It followed that the autonomous repute and character of Catholic social groupings especially had to suffer from it. A fruitful conversation with political socialism was out of the question; the progressive social forces were doomed to splinter.

This led to serious consequences, especially when the Christian Democratic Union relaxed its ideological ties and fell more and more under the influence of pragmatic economists of the old school. Thus, it happened that finally some Catholics even became the lackeys of a liberalism and neocapitalism which signed itself Christian.

Nevertheless, no one would dare denigrate the great merits of the Union, not the least of which was to have proven that separated Christians can work together—in spite of dogmatic discrepancies—when they respect one another and realize that what unites them is more important than what separates them.

POWERLESS NONCONFORMISTS

These remarks suggest that postwar German Catholicism presents a rather conformist panorama. The totalitarian character of conformism suppressed every divergent opinion wherever possible. It rejected everything that did not fit into its ideological landscape. Daringly critical publications, for instance, *Hochland* and *Frankfurter Hefte,* circulated only in limited and predominantly intellectual circles. Progressive theological publications could not count on being defended against Roman verdicts. We will never learn how much human tragedy and loss of ecclesiastical substance was connected with this. Only a single bishop showed truly nonconformist courage and dared to stand up bravely to the last consequence even against Rome in defense of convictions under attack. This was Wilhelm Weskamm, Bishop of Berlin, who died in 1956. That at his grave the Evangelicals spoke about their "brother Weskamm" casts a characteristic light on this great figure.

Repeatedly the question arises as to why until now it has not been possible to bring the many individuals and small groups devoted to constructive opposition within the Church into a socially effective organization. Is it because of the typically German dichotomy of intention and principles? Is it because the Germans have so much trouble with the practice of democracy in general? Is it because of resignation to the power of the hierarchy? No one can really say. It is a fact that the intensive counterstruggle of the conformists has nullified many positive nonconformist initiatives in their formative period. This happened, for instance, to the progressive circle supporting the *Werkhefte für katholische Laienarbeit* (Publication for Practical Catholic Laywork). It was charged with heresy and the extremism here displayed can no longer be called an intra-Catholic function. Even a figure like the poet Heinrich Böll (now outside the Church) is without doubt only partially to be blamed for the acid he pours on the Church. Whenever a nonconformist attitude is so strong that it cannot be forced into resignation and insignificance, it is more and more in danger of an interior emigration. The case of Böll is all the more weighty since he is the only German Catholic writer that may worthily bear this name in world literature.

Those who founded their meditations on peace in the world on sources other than scholastic ideas concerning just and unjust wars and justifiable and unjustifiable methods of war also disturbed the conformists. Additionally the latter were upset by those who, like Boeckenfoerde, dared to demythologize the German Catholic picture of recent history and to call the Catholic failure in the Third Reich by its true name.

Only a few have survived the period of thirst and suffering without resigning or emigrating and these may be represented by such men as Walter Dirks and Carl Amery. The intellectual quality and integrity of Dirks and the true humility in which he conducted his progressive attack have probably served as a shield to preserve him for a time that will clamor for nonconformist authorities. And Amery's victory over his persecutors may be grounded in the fact that with his devastating book *Die Kapitulation* he stirred up German Catholicism at a time that called him to be the spokesman and interpreter of inner changes for which the Council had opened the way.

In spite of all political and ecclesiastical reaction and restoration, the theological and ecumenical seed of the past decades germinated and grew. The work of men like Karl Adam, Steinbuechel, Schmaus, Rademacher, Pascher, among others, was not in vain. They proposed to lead the Catholic Christian back from a nonexperiential formalism into the existentially demanding proximity of the Gospel, which would then lead him into the world of today where he lives with his fellow man and fellow Christian. It is a movement which at present is characterized by names like Karl Rahner, Rudolf Schnackenburg, Voegte, Joseph Ratzinger, and Hans Küng. It provided inspiration and basis for the Council of John XXIII.

Their work became the guidelines of a postwar ecumenical movement, not broad, but inwardly effective. Whatever was sentimental in this movement was swept away in the times of crisis that the official Church abundantly provided. Events like the definition of the Assumption, the Vatican *Monitum*, and the "instruction" from Rome concerning ecumenical activity (all in 1950), Germany's consecration to Mary at the *Katholikentag* in Fulda in 1955, unbearable attitudes in Saxony regarding mixed marriages and conditional baptism, and many other incidents, put German ecumenism to hard trials. But it could not be smothered. Continually it returned with new vigor. When, in 1962, after a catastrophic flood in Hamburg, Bishop Wittler of Osnabrück, as chief pastor of the stricken area, sent his Lutheran colleague 50,000 marks for the flood victims, the promising growth of ecumenism was vividly illustrated.

The Eucharistic World Congress that met in Munich in 1960 was a glorious moment for Catholic-ecumenical progress. Against much official resistance laymen and priests on the periphery of the event made possible an unforgettable hour of Christian community. As the number of participants exceeded all estimates the prepared facilities proved inadequate. Bishops and abbots presented themselves in numbers far beyond anything experienced by the universal Church at an interdenominational event.

Whoever speaks about the development of ecumenism in Germany, which is quite clearly documented by a series of ecclesiastical-scientific institutes as well as by abundant literature available almost from its inception, will have to note that there were many things which perhaps could not have come to pass without the support and help of the delegate for ecumenical questions of the German Bishops' Conference,

Archbishop, and now Cardinal, Lorenz Jaeger of Paderborn. Though not at all a progressive figure, he often displayed a clear decisiveness that finally kept things moving and a patient capacity to see things through to the end.

These were the tendencies of German Catholicism at the convocation of the Council of John XXIII: there were both reactionary conformity in questions of faith and life, and world-openness and brotherly helpfulness; there was a widespread, rigid traditionalism and, in the same Church and people, progressive theological dynamism and ecumenical purposiveness. The assembly of bishops in the hall of St. Peter's saw the German bishops as messengers and interpreters of new insights which were the fruit of a rather unofficial reform effort in Germany. Yet it certainly was also a consequence of the fact that they were secretly agitated by the sense, hitherto concealed, of ecclesiastical impotence rampantly growing in the abyss between the reality of the world and of the Church. The voices of the fathers echoing from the dome of St. Peter's promised the German Catholics a future more closely concerned with realities and so a time of greater effectiveness.

What has come out of it? Two years after the Council, a foreign journalist voiced this well-grounded observation:

> The rejection of a narrow past and the breadth of inspiration were a challenge for Catholicism in the whole world, but the German Catholics, priests and laymen, are not yet ready for it. German Catholicism is still too much attached to the pre-Conciliar Church with its tightly organized, hierarchically controlled block and still has not enough room to cope with a fullness of opinions and tendencies. The renewal of German Catholicism is starting very slowly. . . . And the unrest that characterizes German Catholicism is not evidence of a desire for renewal but rather a sign of insecurity.

This explains why those who expected from the Council a decisive break in the Catholic life of their country were disappointed. This break did not take place. Hopes and promises were not fulfilled. Shaken out of its inherited routine by an unquestionably violent shock, official German Catholicism consistently subscribed to a policy of "small steps." The main achievement of the Council is considered to be the reform of the liturgy and similar issues and in some areas even this is a very slow and painful process. Conciliar "piety" is in high gear, but Conciliar spirit is at work only in insignificant measure.

Except for a few isolated, timidly groping attempts, nothing essential has happened such as, for example, subjecting the training of priests to the law inherent in a Church renewing itself. Modern theology, whose chief exponent is Thomas Sartory, must, just as before, theologize basically independent of the Church. Its efforts to build a bridge between current spirituality and the Gospel are, except in the colleges, practically tabooed. To the exception should be added those safety valves, certain institutions of adult education, especially the Catholic Academies. The pastoral task of relaxing the tension between the faith of the people and scientific theological insight still awaits even a plausible beginning. As the people still receive much of their information from the "revelations" of the mass media, they are in danger of finding themselves in serious confusion.

The old system is trying to assert itself both spiritually and structurally. The question as to how pastoral contact can still be maintained or made anew with the progressive, the intellectual, and especially the youth, is only inadequately grasped especially when we recognize its fateful significance. It is no surprise that the "layman" is still one of the great unsolved problems. Whether the establishment of priest senates prescribed by Rome, in which the layman is supposed to have a voice, and whether the planned restructuring of the Central Committee of German Catholics will effect satisfactory changes remains to be seen. There are, certainly, a few bishops and priests who are seeking extra-institutional ways to establish a true dialogue with the laity, but they remain only a few. For instance, the dioceses of Osnabrück and Rottenburg have made some quite remarkable beginnings in sounding the people's opinion through surveys, the results are then made a factor in episcopal consideration and decision.

In the political realm we can notice, in spite of the enduring sympathies of the episcopate and the Catholic majority, a slight loosening of the Church's tie with the "Christian" parties. This creates some possibilities for a conversation with Christian groups of different orientation. At the same time it places the Church and the *Unionsparteien* in a state of tension never before experienced. Yet, according to the results of the latest election it is unlikely that the general Catholic political situation has greatly changed. One should not, however, undervalue the scattered Social Democratic breakthroughs into traditional Catholic bastions. Here appear symptoms which would have been inconceivable a few years ago. The aftereffects of the Council are being felt: its impulses for independent judgment and personal free-dom in the areas of choice and discretion.

Unfortunately, exciting changes are not coming to the fore in the field of ecumenical relationships. There is no doubt that the inter-denominational climate has improved: a helpful committee of promi-nent delegates of Catholicism and reformed Christianity has been established with a view to engage in dialogue. Efforts are being made for official manifestations of friendly neighborliness which, however, at times give the unfortunate impression that ecumenism might make its greatest progress where the fear of an overthrow of the *status quo* is shared. On occasion a few bishops, for instance, Josef Stimple of Augs-burg, Helmut Hermann Wittler of Osnabrück, and Franz Hengsbach of Essen, even try something out of the ordinary in order to promote the coming together of the separated. The big picture, however, is that of a *status quo* that is not seriously responsive to the ecumenical desire of increasing Catholic groups.

In regard to the problem of mixed marriages, which German Prot-estantism has proclaimed to be the test case for the credibility of Catholic ecumenism, no progress has been made. On this matter it appears that the German hierarchy is more narrow-minded than Rome itself. Even the possibility of making application for dispensa-tion to Rome, presented in the *Motu Proprio* of March, 1966, is hardly ever used in Germany. The interpretation of the Catholic rules has been so narrow that in Westphalia a Catholic married by a Protestant minister was denied a Catholic burial even in 1967.

Since every third marriage in the Federal Republic is mixed, this backwardness means, among other consequences, that a considerable number of Catholics are lost to the Church and pastoral care. Here again appears the rigidity of the Catholic approach to the Reformation: it may be argued that to present the Counter-Reformation as the main concern of German Catholicism unquestionably overstates the matter. But it is incontestable that the basic relationship to the Reformation is still very tense. In pastoral care this manifests itself in an often ques-tionable tendency to "preserve the *status quo*" and to neglect the pas-toral aspects of our own times. Perhaps, then, a still lingering Counter-Reformation inflexibility is partially responsible for Catholic Ger-many's painful and inadequate treatment of the problems posed by history and the present day. Is this inadequacy a penalty for German Catholicism's failure to do its special and proper task: to begin and carry through the reconciliation of the Reformation with the Roman Church?

Diminutive Holland has courageously deputed itself to fulfill this task. Its ecclesiastical renewal is important as a Catholic integration of the Reformation. Fascinated and full of hope, the progressives among German Catholics look across the northwestern border. True, the majority is still suspicious, but interest in the events of the Netherlands is constantly growing. The conservative wing and most of the official representatives of the Church remain uncomprehending and negative. The first European symposium of bishops, which took place in Noordwijkerhout in the Netherlands, was attended by only one resident and two suffragan bishops of Germany. Alien Church movements can expect agreement only to the degree to which they can still somehow be fitted into the conceptual world of the traditional system.

It is difficult for superficial observers to square the courageous forward-thrust of the German bishops at the Council with their subsequent slowing down. But when we see the assembly of the bishops in Rome not only in its pneumatic but also in its psychological aspects, many attitudes became more understandable. The German bishop has always found himself isolated in his position of power. Thus the "community of St. Peter" was probably his first experience of an existential community of bishops allowing a certain relaxation of inhibitions. The return to the homeland found him once again in a constricting solitude; for, while the ecclesiastical guideline in Rome had changed, the milieu of the local residences of the bishops had not. Even those bishops who had made a clear decision to move forward were soon worn down by the widespread conservatism of the Cathedral chapter (practically all-powerful in Germany) and by the slow and familiar routines. In order to effect revolutionizing reforms and courageously to develop their own initiative, the bishops would have needed a true community of enthusiasm and boldness.

They succumbed to many different fears: to the fear of not doing justice to the older generation and to the conservatives, to the fear of the tenacious resistance of their administration, to the fear of a shattered ecclesiastical unity, if they should break down the oppressive conformity of the conference of the bishops. There was, of course, also fear of alarming and disturbing the immature faithful. Finally, some even feared the fall of traditional positions of power.

This complex of fears explains the actions of the bishops after the

Council. Concern about the past that is ebbing away supplants the more legitimate fear of a future that could shape itself completely without the Church. There has been, as a result, a series of inglorious and unsuccessful engagements inspired or, better, dispirited by the conviction that the struggle was in defense of a lost cause.

The constant outbreaks of the "battles over the schools" faithfully reveal the situation. Against the growing opposition of Catholic parents and teachers, the bishops at every opportunity defend the Catholic schools which are attended by 1,720,000 German children. It is nonetheless certain that new arrangements must be provided if the religious and educational needs of the children are to be met. Moreover, until recently, initiatives to improve the pastoral care of children would have had favorable prospects. Today, there are so many urgencies that compromises are to be the order of the day.

The difficulties which stand in the way of the German episcopate (and which certainly include much that is subjectively excusable) would be described only fragmentarily, if we did not take into account the German tendency toward perfectionism in everything and everybody. This perfectionism plays an important role in the antipathy to the Dutch who are skilled in experimentation—the contrary of perfectionism. The quest for the perfect postpones even what is most necessary. This is illustrated by the prospects of diocesan synods. These (not to speak of a national synod) are still far in the future. The hierarchy wants to have the situation set up perfectly before a move is made and fails to see that today's fast pace will have already invalidated the situation by the time action is taken. Here is another characteristic example. In the spring of 1967 Rome granted permission for the vernacular in the Canon of the Mass. The German episcopate did not want to make use of this permission before suitable texts were available in the mother tongue. For decades, however, the German Catholics were encouraged to use the *Schott*, that is, the German translation of the Roman Missal: hence an "imperfect" transition would have been easily possible.

Most of the German bishops are recruited from professors, instructors, and superiors of seminaries, and in that background is perhaps one source of this crippling perfectionism. They are, therefore, from the ranks of those who are especially familiar with that which is principled and perfect. Adherence to principle and perfectionism, however, has given the post-Conciliar episcopate the reputation of being more

Roman than Rome itself. As many of the bishops received their decisive formation on the Tiber, they acquire as a kind of subconscious heritage an urge to compensate for the "German sin" of the Reformation with a model Catholicism.

The unavailability of data makes it impossible to include the East German bishops in this account. But for the most part, they cope with far more fundamental worries than confront their episcopal colleagues in West Germany.

The Government of Pankow does not allow its bishops to attend the Bishops' Conferences in the Federal Republic. The Bishop of Berlin, who resides in East Berlin, is merely allowed to visit the western part of his diocese a few times monthly. In such difficult circumstances every effort must be made to keep pastoral care alive and to cope with the danger of defections which communist pressure makes unavoidable.

Finally, besides other burdens, the East-zone bishops must also bear serious financial problems, which, within the framework of its possibilities, West German Catholicism attempts to share. There is no governmental apparatus to collect taxes for the Church. Everything depends on voluntary contributions. And these are all the more to be appreciated since in the DDR a man no longer becomes a social outcast when he turns away from the Church.

In the Federal Republic the Church's advance would probably be more impressively convincing if the Church were not supported by social convention and laws that place obstacles to leaving the Church and guarantee the Church a considerable financial cushion in state-collected taxes. Experience teaches that those bishops who depend on the free will of their people have less difficulty in establishing a living and sincere dialogue. Because numerous Catholics are no longer attracted by the forced marriage of Church and State revenue, diocesan administrations face the financial future with growing concern.

The hierarchy, which is certainly well intentioned, is not so difficult to describe as are the priests. The latter reacted to the Council's impulses in quite different ways. Many, even among the older generation, display a delightful openness and welcome moderate reforms, although most of them shun revolutionary changes. Quite a few of the clergy seem to be overwhelmed by the post-Conciliar tasks requiring a change of thinking for which foundations are lacking. The habits of the pulpit-perched "Reverend" are too ingrained, and to be a brother among

God's people is an inconceivable idea for many. The noticeable fermentation among the assistants is disturbing to the old guard.

In what proportions nuances and variations are distributed is not easy to discover. Not everyone speaks his mind openly. The mentality that solicits orders for obedience is still too pronounced: facing censure is not readily risked. In 1967 a number of pastors in North-Rhine-Westphalia created a sensation when, in open letters to their bishops, they expressed their dissatisfaction with the episcopal tactics in the school battle. The response was an equally public reprimand from the bishops and no wide demonstration of sympathy from the laity, who themselves are not in favor of denominational schools.

The post-Conciliar profile of the German Catholic laity, with the exception of the progressive wing of the avant-garde, is also troubled by the same historical mortgage that falls on the hierarchy and clergy. Yet the hierarchy is obviously afraid to grant this wing a truly legitimate function, for if it were integrated into the Church, it would encourage bishops, priests, and the people of the Church to take longer strides. It could also be a "stumbling block," a challenge that would stir German Catholicism to delineate itself more clearly than it has done so far and make it easier for the bishops to realize the spirit of the Council in their own homeland.

No one knows, at this point, what the German laity really is. In many ways it seems to be quite promising. In 1966 the conservative *Una Voce* made a representative survey. Its results revealed that only 17 per cent of German Catholics still cling to pre-Conciliar liturgical practice, and only 20 per cent of practicing Catholics are opposed to interfaith association. Sixty-seven per cent were in favor of more vernacular in the Mass and 70 per cent advocated active ecumenism.

In sum, 42 per cent were quite satisfied with the reforms introduced by the Council and no less than 26 per cent expressed their regret that in the last analysis nothing had changed at all. Thus the desire to move ahead and the possibility of persuading large contingents to go along should not be underrated. On the other hand, however, a random sample made by a large sociopolitical association revealed that the presence of a desire for innovations, beyond what has so far been allowed, cannot be established and, hence, a forward-thrust can hardly be expected from this sector of the laity.

This sector probably reflects the attitude of a significant portion of

German Catholics while "progressive" answers to the *Una Voce* survey generally come from groups of the well educated and of the intellectuals. As it stands, there seems to be contentment with the situation as it is and with due obedience that involves no strain on one's personal conscience. In short, there is a disregard of anything that may be upsetting or disturbing. For many it is inconceivable that the life of the Church can proceed democratically. Their life has settled into an easy chair, undisturbed by the intellectual and spiritual distress of our times.

The *Una Voce* survey shows how dangerous this situation is. It uncovered an alarming lack of interest among the youth regarding the affairs of the Church of the post-Conciliar epoch. That is to say, regarding the future—the future of the message of Christ, of the Church, of Christianity.

The task of German Catholicism in regard to the Reformation was left undone. It will probably suffer from this for a long time to come. Will it also fail to confront with the Gospel those who are to come and so leave them with no call to decision? It has come to the crossroads. It must take the road of Conciliar dynamism without delay or it will eventually come to a dead end that can only look back to the lost generations.

3 : AUSTRIA

Erika Weinzierl

I. RELIGIOUS LIFE OF THE CHURCH

A. CHURCH ORGANIZATION

The largest administrative and organizational entities of the Church in Austria are the church provinces of Vienna and Salzburg. These consist of eight dioceses, which, because of Austria's eventful history, have foundation dates extending over more than one thousand years. The church province of Vienna has the archbishopric of Vienna (bishopric in 1469, archbishopric in 1722) with the suffragan bishoprics of Linz (1785) and St. Pölten (1785) as well as the bishopric of Eisenstadt (1960). The church province of Salzburg consists of the archbishopric of Salzburg (798) with the suffragan sees of Gurk-Klagenfurt (1072) and Seckau-Graz (1219), the bishopric of Innsbruck (1964), and the general vicariate of Feldkirch (1820). In 1961 these dioceses had 242 deaneries with 2,980 parishes and pastoral agencies.[1] Nearly two-thirds of these were established by the Emperor Joseph II (1780–1790). Including all the parish-affiliated and convent churches, there are more than 6,000 places of worship in Austria, 1,400 of them in the archdiocese of Vienna which with more than two million Catholics is the country's largest diocese. Since 1918, that is, in the Austrian Republic, only the bishop of Vienna has become a cardinal. Since 1956 it has been under the leadership of the former bishop of St. Pölten, Dr. Franz König, in 1958. Coadjutor Archbishop

[1] Erich Bodzenta, *Die Katholiken in Österreich* (Vienna, 1962), p. 23.

61

Dr. Franz Jáchym and two vicars-general, Suffragan Bishops Dr. Weinbacher and Dr. Moser, assist him.

The Archbishop of Salzburg, Dr. Andreas Rohracher, like his predecessors, has the honorary title of *primas Germaniae*. In the government of the archdiocese, he is assisted by Suffragan Bishop Dr. Macheiner and Vicar-general Dr. Simmerstätter. The remaining Austrian bishoprics are administered by their diocesan bishops, mostly in collaboration with a vicar-general. The Vicar-general of Feldkirch is Suffragan Bishop Dr. Wechner. The boundaries of the dioceses coincide with those of the Austrian Federal provinces (Länder), except for the part of the Tyrol in the bishopric of Salzburg. The general vicariate of Feldkirch coincides with the Federal province of Vorarlberg. All Austrian bishops have one or more academic degrees. All Austrian bishops belong to the Bishops' Conference which regularly holds spring and fall sessions. The chairman of the Conference is the highest-ranking bishop, usually the cardinal of Vienna.

B. The Clergy

1. *Numbers and Recruitment*

An investigation made in 1956 showed that there were then 6,467 Catholic priests in Austria—4,239 secular priests and 2,228 order priests. From both groups there were 4,220 priests active in pastoral care. Since, for the most part, conditions have not changed, the conclusion then established is still valid: a parish priest takes care of an average of 1,500 Catholics; in 1956 the number was 1,578 and in 1963, 1,544. Thus, in ranking European countries according to the proportion of priests to Catholics, Austria is in the next to the last place. In addition, about 30 per cent of the clergy is above 60 years of age and only 12 per cent is between 25 and 35.[2] Several dioceses have already been compelled to import priests from abroad (principally from Holland and the West German Federal Republic). In all of Austria 162 priests were ordained in 1961 and 54 in 1963. These facts are disturbing enough. But when Archbishop Jáchym conducted an inquiry into priestly ordination in Austria during the last century, it was revealed that for the years 1919 to 1964, the Archdiocese of Vienna was the only diocese which in drawing from its own area was able to augment

[2] Bodzenta, p. 26.

the number of its priests.[3] Archbishop Rauscher as early as 1854 was lamenting Vienna's lack of priests.[4] The present lack of priests in Austria is not a new phenomenon, but extends far back into the past. From the establishment of the republic, excluding the years of Nazi rule, the number of yearly ordinations has remained stable:[5]

SECULAR PRIESTS ORDAINED

Diocese	1924	1934	1944	1954	1964
Vienna	24	27	1	24	22
St. Pölten	7	1	1	14	5
Linz	19	0	1	12	16
Eisenstadt	0	6	0	2	9
Salzburg	12	9	1	5	12
Klagenfurt	18	11	0	1	6
Graz	24	17	1	15	11

In spite of this relatively constant level, special efforts to increase the number of priestly vocations will soon be necessary. In both the major and the minor seminaries as well as in existing diocesan institutions, a great percentage of the students do not seek ordination upon concluding their studies. Today only about one-half of the students in the clerical preparatory schools go on to a seminary and of them, only one-fourth or one-third are ordained.[6] Some expressions of public opinion appear to indicate that the rule of celibacy may be the reason for this.

2. Formation of Priests

The formation of priests and theologians takes place in the Catholic faculties of theology in the state universities of Vienna, Graz, Salzburg, and Innsbruck and in the diocesan philosophical-theological institutes in St. Pölten, Linz, and Klagenfurt. In addition there are two extra-diocesan seminaries: the Collegium Pazmánianum in Vienna; and the

[3] Franz Jáchym, "Zur Priesterfrage in Österreich," in Klostermann, Kriegl, Mauer, and Weinzierl, eds., Kirche in Österreich, 1918–1965, Vol. I (Vienna-Munich, 1966), 410.

[4] Jáchym, 421.

[5] These tables are from the figures published by Jáchym, 429–443. His figures do not cover the diocese of Innsbruck.

[6] Gottfried Griesl, "Die Priesterbildung," Kirche in Österreich, 80.

Canisianum in Innsbruck; the latter with 200 theology students is the largest Austrian seminary. The order priests have eight teaching institutions in their own houses: the Cistercians in Heiligenkreuz, the Augustinian prelates in Klosterneuburg and St. Florian, the Society of the Divine Word in St. Gabriel, the Camillians in Vöklamarkt-Pfaffing, the Redemptorists in Mautern, the Franciscans in Schwaz, and the Capuchins in Innsbruck.[7] Some of these houses of study are very small and often have difficulty in procuring qualified teachers. The other congregations and orders send their members to the state institutions of higher learning and to diocesan institutions. In terms of the religious order represented by the professors, it appears that two theology faculties have been largely the domain of two orders. Until recently the Benedictines were strongly represented in Salzburg while the theological faculty in Innsbruck is almost entirely composed of Jesuits.

The professional formation is governed by the rules of the Roman constitutions. The baccalaureate, secured after twelve years that include compulsory elementary schooling and high school years, is a prerequisite. Since 1927 this has been followed by a five-year course of studies. A reform of the curriculum now being discussed will add another, that is, a sixth year to allow for greater attention to sociology, psychology, pastoral medicine, and similar subjects. In carrying out the Conciliar decree *De institutione sacerdotali*, two new courses were introduced during the winter semester of 1965–1966. These are biblical theology, and, for the beginning of the program of study, a basic course in theology.[8]

Nearly 40 per cent of Austrian theology students come from peasant backgrounds, 25 per cent are from the working class, that is, from skilled and unskilled labor, 20 per cent are from civil servant and government employee families, and the remaining 15 per cent are from mercantile professional classes. Only one-fourth of the theology students are urban; three-fourths come from the country. In proportion to its percentage of the total population, the peasant class provides twice the number of priests.[9] This disproportion creates additional problems in the training of priests since those from one class are unfamiliar with the outlook of another class and have difficulty in adapting to it or identifying with it. A few dioceses have initiated special vacation programs so that the seminarians can gain practical experience. Innsbruck,

[7] Griesl, 78.
[8] Griesl, 83.
[9] Griesl, 80.

for example, has engaged help from industry for the special training of priests for pastoral duties among workers.

The gratifying increase of late vocations, that is, vocations among mature adults, nearly 15 per cent of all theology students,[10] requires a shift of stress in the preparation of priests. Formerly the traditional humanist educational ideal was emphasized while now the need of a new orientation of the theoretical and practical training of priests is stressed.[11] At Innsbruck the reform process has begun, for there the Regent of its seminary, Gottfried Griesl, has introduced some innovations and is hopeful that the educational program for secular priests will also require the introduction of a pastoral year between completion of theological studies and ordination. This provision, it is argued, should accompany a strengthening of the diaconate.[12] Those in charge of the impending diocesan synods of Vienna, Salzburg, Graz, and Eisenstadt have asked study commissions to consider these problems.

3. The State of the Theological Sciences

State control of the Vienna theological faculty since the time of Joseph II, Pope Pius IX's condemnation of one of the preeminent Austrian theologians of the nineteenth century, Anton Günther, and the Modernist dispute at the beginning of the twentieth century—each of these has left a distinctive mark on the development of Austrian theology. Although in Vienna there was no real flowering of speculative theology,[13] since the 1900's Heinrich Swoboda—author of a pioneer book on urban pastoral work—Karl Handloss, Karl Rudolf, Michael Pfliegler, and Ferdinand Klostermann have fostered the study of pastoral theology and with their work gained eminence. Klostermann, of the University of Vienna, is well known for both his substantial work (1962) on the Christian apostolate which is largely devoted to the layman and for having been a *peritus* at Vatican II. Two of his latest works, mainly concerned with the new structures of the Church, *Prinzip Gemeinde* (Community in Principle) and *Priester für Morgen* (Priests for Tomorrow), are his best known. His very broad

---

[10] Griesl, 81.

[11] Ferdinand Klostermann, *Priester für Morgen* (Innsbruck, 1966) and "Geistliche Berufe in Westeuropa," in *Der Seelsorger* (March, 1967), esp. pp. 119–123.

[12] Griesl, 83.

[13] Johannes Nedbal, "Die theologischen Wissenschaften," *Kirche in Österreich*, 119. Nedbal's article provides a base for the following treatment.

interests and his extraordinary creativity have made him, after Josef Jungmann and Karl Rahner who has left Austria, the best-known Austrian theologian outside of the country. At Vienna, Josef Pritz, concerned with fundamental theology, has devoted his work to a theological account of the teachings of Anton Günther, who is one of the prominent theologians of the nineteenth century. Kurt Schubert, professor of religious science, teaches in the department of philosophy; his research interests involve the historical Jesus. Adolf Holl, assistant professor of religious science in the department of theology, specializes in the sociology of religion, and more recently has turned to research in communication. Christian social teaching is represented by Rudolf Weiler, a disciple of Johannes Messner, whose standard work on the social question and natural law has gone through many editions and was translated into several languages and who is unanimously recognized as the "grand old man" of the entire discipline.

In the theology faculty of Graz, Winfried Gruber has attempted to initiate a dialogue with modern theology, including that of other Christian denominations. From a historical point of view Karl Amon, church historian, shares the same concern and in addition is greatly interested in liturgical questions. History of dogma is taught by Johannes Bauer, the first layman to be appointed full professor in a faculty of theology. The moral theologian from Luxembourg, Marcel Reding, formerly at Graz and now professor of ideology at the Free University of Berlin, has been working for more than ten years on a comparison between the Christian and the Marxist view of the world.

In keeping with their historical tradition, the Benedictines have filled most of the positions in theology at Salzburg. There Thomas Michels not only concentrates on liturgical studies but also edits the religious-scientific periodical, *Kairos*. Today secular priests and members of other orders are in the majority. Until a short time ago, Josef Dillersberger, a New Testament scholar and a pioneer in the theological understanding of the New Testament, taught in Salzburg. The canonist and Rota lawyer Carl Holböck is also active in Salzburg theological studies, although he has taught in the law faculty since its foundation. The professor of philosophical sociology and political theory in the department of theology, Franz-Martin Schmölz, O.P., is a disciple of Eric Voegelin, and is distinguished for his studies on the political ethics and teachings of Thomas Aquinas. Recently he assumed the direction of a department for research in atheism.

Until 1964 two *periti* of the Council taught at the University of Innsbruck: Josef Jungmann, S.J., the world-famous liturgist, and Karl Rahner, who during his many years of teaching on the faculty at Innsbruck made it an internationally known theological center. It was here that Roman and German theology intersected and from here many of the theological points of Vatican II originated. Karl Rahner's brother, the patrologist Hugo Rahner, also contributed to the eminence of Innsbruck.

The Innsbruck faculty in 1964 not only lost Karl Rahner and his work in the field of fundamental theology, but also the dynamic and open-minded scholar Johannes Schasching, S.J. Father Schasching is both rector of the Germanicum in Rome and editor of a review, *Zeitschrift für Katholische Theologie*, that publishes the results of theological research and that, since it reaches the whole German language area, exercises internationally a great influence upon theology.

With no affiliation with any faculty but still of great importance for Austrian theology is Otto Mauer, the Vienna cathedral preacher and pastor of the university community. He has advanced individual and fruitful ideas that have appeared especially in *Wort und Wahrheit*, which he has co-edited since 1946. Before the beginning of the Vatican Council, the journal published a survey whose demands and recommendations won the attention, if not the full implementation, of the Council.

C. DENOMINATIONAL STRUCTURE AND PROFESSION OF FAITH

In the last quarter of the sixteenth century four-fifths of the Austrian population were adherents of Protestantism. Since the Counter-Reformation was successfully imposed by the Hapsburgs in the seventeenth century, Catholic tradition has continued uninterrupted, at least nominally.

The last population census, available in published form, was taken in 1961.[14] There were then 7,073,807 people in Austria.[15] At least 89 per cent of that number were baptized Catholics. The proportion of Catholics varies with the region, declining to a minimum of 81 per cent in the city of Vienna and reaching a maximum of 96 per cent in the

[14] The results of the Census of 1967 were not available at the time of writing.
[15] *Statistisches Handbuch*, 1962 (Vienna, 1962), p. 5.

diocese of St. Pölten.[16] Furthermore, there are variations according to age. Thus we note an increase in the over-sixty group in Krems and Salzburg, while the number constantly decreases in Vienna-Heiligenstadt. There is hardly any variation according to professional groups. In the present analysis the difference between the group of liberal professions, civil servants, and employees on the one side and workmen on the other is 6 to 8 per cent.

Since 1954, an annual net loss of about 5,000 Catholics has been noted. There are 5,000 returns and conversions as opposed to 10,000 withdrawals. The big cities of over 100,000 inhabitants account for two-thirds of such losses: Vienna accounts for one-third and in 1965 for 41 per cent. The greater part of these withdrawals or fallings away occur between 30 and 50 years of age. Of live births in Austria in 1963, 94 per cent were baptized. In Vienna 85 per cent of live births in 1963 were baptized Catholics.

In 1963, 79 per cent of all marriages were performed in church; this represented 93 per cent of those marriages that could qualify for a church ceremony. For Vienna the corresponding figures are 53 and 70 per cent respectively. In 1962, 92 per cent of all deceased Catholics had a church funeral while in Vienna 90 per cent did. Although nationally 96 to 98 per cent of Catholics pay their church dues without being sued, in Vienna only 66 per cent do so.

Apart from the duty to contribute to the Church, which was only introduced in 1939 by the National-Socialists, the figures quoted indicate the continuing high totals in the traditional evidence of belonging to the Church: baptisms, marriages, and funerals. Quite a different picture appears in answer to the question about how many Austrians are practicing Catholics: in 1964, 31.5 per cent of Catholics fulfilled their Easter duty and in 1962 some 39.5 per cent. But regular Sunday church attendance has changed very little in the last seven years. It reached a maximum of 54 per cent in the Diocese of Innsbruck-Feldkirch, and a minimum of 22 per cent in the Archdiocese of Vienna (within the city proper only 19.5 per cent). With the exception of

[16] All figures presented in these paragraphs are taken from the following mimeographed studies: Institut für kirchliche Sozialforschung, "Zur Situation der Kirche in Österreich," text edited by Father M. Zulehner, contained in a study packet published by the Working Section of the Post-Conciliar Study Commission I and the Austrian Pastoral Institute; Institut für kirchliche Sozialforschung, "Zur Situation in der Erzdiözese Wien," Working Section of Commission VI, "Diagnoses of the Situation of the Dioceses," Document I, prepared for the Diocesan Synod of Vienna, 1968.

Innsbruck, however, fewer than 30 per cent attend Sunday Mass in the big cities. In 97 per cent of 67 parishes analyzed, women were more regular in practice than men.

In 40 of 42 parishes, the 18 to 50 age groups took the smallest part in worship, and in 32 out of 38 the participation in religious services was highest in the 6 to 18 age group; the next highest group are those over 65. The group which has the majority of withdrawals, that from 30 to 50, is also least represented in church attendance. Such attendance varies according to the profession. In 72 out of 84 parishes analyzed, working men showed the least participation and in 48 out of 84 parishes the employees showed the greatest. In 88 per cent of all the parishes analyzed, those without an occupation show the highest participation in religious services. If this is compared to the results of the elections to the National Assembly, a variation according to political structure can be noted. In general, increased attendance at church corresponds to a bigger share of the votes cast for the Austrian People's Party.

In 1966 a survey of religious faith was carried out in Salzburg. An inquiry along the same lines circulated a questionnaire among the workmen of the Vereinigte Österreichische Stahlwerke (VOEST— Federated Austrian Steelworks) in Linz. Both inquiries show that the existence of a supreme being is almost generally accepted. The lowest degree of confessional adherence was discovered in Salzburg among the self-employed, the highest degree among the employees of public services, and the greatest contrast in accepting specific items of belief is found in the ranks of labor. The span extends from a minimum of 19 per cent concerning belief in an afterlife to a maximum of 56 per cent concerning the conviction that Christ is the Son of God.

Although these results cannot be extended to all of Austria without significant modifications, they still are an important indication of the piety of people in a traditionally Catholic country. As such, it is not among the most depressing documents. The results are at any rate clearer than those derived from the rare attempts to estimate the profession of religious truth, made in Austria in the nineteenth century in connection with the suppression of sects[17] and the expulsion of Protestants in 1837.[18] Those resulted in even more confusion and diffuse statements. The intensive use of today's better research methods

[17] Erika Weinzierl-Fischer, "Visitationsberichte Österreichischer Bischöfe an Kaiser Franz I," *Mitteilungen des Österreichischen Staatsarchiv* (1953), pp. 296 ff.
[18] Ekkart Sauser, "Die Zillertaler Inklinanten und ihre Ausweisung im Jahre 1837," *Schlern-Schriften*, 198 (Innsbruck, 1959), 51 ff.

accounts for the clearer data. This advance has been facilitated by the foundation in 1952 of the Institute for Ecclesiastical Sociology in Vienna, established by Archbishop Jáchym.

It can be assumed that the kind of church connection explored by the Institute in 1960 is still valid: one-third of the baptized Catholics in Austria are practicing. The activists and the members of Catholic organizations, constituting 9.5 per cent, belong to this one-third. Another third, the so-called "seasonal Catholics" practice only on great feast days; the last one-third has for the most part fallen away.[19] But we must not overlook that even among Catholics with a minimum of formal profession of religious truth, there still exists a strong, informal religiosity. An opinion reported in the VOEST inquiry—"Religion is necessary for the family"—closely parallels one advanced by the workers in 1848.[20] Undoubtedly then as now the answer was determined by the prevailing spirit of Josephinism, the legacy of the Enlightened Despot Joseph II, who respected and promoted religion chiefly because of its ethical influence. Ultimately, these polls reflect deep-rooted conservatism among all social groups. This conservatism must be taken into consideration in every attempt to "Christianize" popular piety in the spirit of Vatican II. Additionally, it should be recognized that the trend for loosening ties with the Church is not to be equated with a decrease of informal religiosity.

D. AUSTRIAN CATHOLICS AND VATICAN II

1. Liturgy

There were a number of Austrian precursors of the Second Vatican Council in the liturgical movement, the Bible movement, and early ecumenical contacts—some of them as early as the nineteenth century. Father Anselm Schott belonged to the first monks of Beuron who reopened the old Benedictine Abbey of Seckau in Styria. When he came here, he had already signed a contract with his German publisher for a popular Latin-German missal. The wish expressed by a Seckau peasant, that he might understand what the monks were singing, strongly confirmed Father Schott in his purpose.[21]

[19] Bodzenta, p. 81.

[20] (Dr. Witlaci), "Verhältnisse der Bevölkerung in Wien," *Zeitschrift des Vereins für deutsche Statistik* (No. 2, 1848), 177 ff.

[21] Karl Amon, "Volksliturgische Messreform," in *Die Kirche in Österreich* 1918–1965, Vol. I, 137. Much of this section is based on Amon's article.

After World War I the liturgical movement in Austria received new impact from students and the Abbey of Klosterneuburg. The *missa recitata*, where the congregation recited most of the prayers with the priest, was adopted by students in Vienna and Salzburg around 1920, particularly by those who gathered around Wilhelm Schmidt, S.V.D., Virgil Redlich, O.S.B., and Karl Rudolf—later publisher of a journal, *Der Seelsorger* (The Pastor), and the first Director of the Vienna Pastoral Institute. After 1918, the center for the liturgical and biblical movements was the Abbey of Klosterneuburg, where in the Abbey institute Pius Parsch taught pastoral theology. Under Parsch's direction the first popular liturgical celebration of the Mass in German-speaking countries took place on Ascension Day in 1922 in the small church of St. Gertrud in Klosterneuburg. From the *Klosterneuburger Mass Texts*, which have appeared since 1923, has developed the extensive publishing activity of the Liturgical Apostolate for the People. And finally, the sung participation Mass that became customary in all German language countries originated in Klosterneuburg. It was sanctioned by Rome in 1943, together with the High Mass in German and the Evening Mass in German, celebrated for the first time in Vienna on December 8, 1940. In 1914, the then Archbishop of Vienna experienced considerable difficulty in keeping off the Index a book about evening Masses by the Caldense Father Zimmermann.

In 1940 the Austrian Bishops' Conference arranged for regular reports on the liturgy and entrusted the work to the later Bishop of Linz, Fliesser. The Austrian episcopate, then, in contrast to the German bishops, displayed considerable understanding and sympathy for the liturgical movement. During the war the meetings with Protestants in Vienna initiated by Cardinal Innitzer provided the inspiration for a report on questions involving the reunion of the confessions made at the All-German Bishops' Conference at Fulda (1943).

After 1945 the Abbot of Seckau, later Archabbot of Beuron, Dr. Benedikt Reetz, made it a major concern to provide a suitable place for the evening Easter Vigil in the Holy Saturday Liturgy. Although in 1948 the petition of the Abbey of Seckau to be allowed the privilege of celebrating the Holy Saturday Feast in the evening received a negative reply from Rome, in 1951 the celebration was established for the whole Church. In April, 1945, Linz and Graz became new centers for the development of the liturgy of the Mass. In Graz, the church historian Karl Amon was especially prominent in the reform of the liturgy. At the International Congress for Church Music (Vienna,

1945), there was a sharp exchange between the reformers and the representatives of Rome who decidedly rejected both the form of the *missa recitata* celebrated in St. Gertrud's at the tomb of Pius Parsch and the report of Josef A. Jungmann, S.J., the author of a standard, two-volume work, translated into many languages, *Missarum Solemnia*. The Bishop of Linz, Zauner, in his capacity as reporter on the liturgy to the Austrian Bishops' Conference quite firmly sided with the liturgists. The Vatican Council's vote for the Liturgical Schema as a whole and the election of Bishop Zauner to the Liturgical Commission with the highest possible number of votes may be rightly interpreted as recognition accorded by the ecumenical Church to the Austrian liturgical movement.

The Council's liturgical recommendations have already been effected in Austria. Under the chairmanship of the Suffragan Bishop Macheiner of Salzburg, the liturgical commission set up by the Bishops' Conference worked out guidelines for the concrete shape of the Divine Service. The Bishops' Conference approved them on February 8, 1965, and on March 7, 1965, they went into effect. One year earlier the reading of the Epistle and the Gospel in the vernacular had been allowed. Since Advent of 1965 the vernacular has been used in the Preface and since Advent of 1967 it has been used in the Canon of the Mass. Because of the many years of the Austrian liturgical tradition—Pius Parsch long ago celebrated Mass facing the congregation—the necessary changes have generally been made quickly and without friction.

Moreover, all earlier forms of the Mass including the Latin high Mass are preserved. They are, for example, celebrated every Sunday in Vienna's Cathedral of St. Stephen as are the vernacular Masses. Consequently, the *Una Voce* movement has gained only a few members in Austria.

2. *The Austrian Bishops and the Council*

From the beginning the Austrian bishops took a positive approach to the Council and its reform efforts. Mainly it was at the Council that Vienna's Cardinal König came to prominence. König himself selected as his Council *peritus* Karl Rahner who at that time was having difficulty with the Roman censorship. The Cardinal was one of twenty-four selected in 1964 for the American series "Men Who Make the Council." During the Conclave of 1963, König, who had been very close to Pope John XXIII, was said to be the only non-Italian, apart from Cardinal Suenens, who was believed to have any chance for the tiara. His interventions in the Council reveal the Cardinal not only as a linguist and scholar of religious studies, but as a moderate reformer and forward-looking theologian. His extensive United States' lecture tour in the spring of 1964 increased his reputation, and his role during the Eucharistic Congress in Bombay in December, 1964, made him well known outside the Christian denominations. Early in April, 1965, he was appointed President of the new Vatican Secretariat for Non-Believers.[22]

During Vatican II Bishop Zauner of Linz, whose election to the Liturgical Commission has already been mentioned, played a prominent role in discussing liturgical questions. Bishop Laszlo of Eisenstadt served as a member of the *Consilium de laicis*, and Bishop Rusch of Innsbruck was elected by the Austrian episcopate to be the Austrian representative in the Synod of Bishops. Not only did the Austrian bishops take an important part in the Council, they also urged its importance on the laity in the Synod of Bishops. All Austrian bishops wrote pastoral letters devoted to the Council and Bishop Rohracher of Salzburg wrote many. To implement the Council decrees, the bishops of Vienna, Salzburg, Eisenstadt, and Graz have announced diocesan synods with lay participation; such synods had earlier been allowed only in the Seckau diocesan synod of 1960 under the direction of Bishop Schoiswohl. The preparatory commissions, composed of priests and laymen, treat all problems raised by the Council and give special attention to basic statistical data. Letters from the Archbishops of Salzburg and Vienna have solicited every household for suggestions. Archbishop Rohracher personally took part in a massive rally of the Salzburg Catholic Educational Project, *Fragen an die Kirche* (Questions for the Church), for which more than a thousand written questions were sent in. In implementing the principle of collegiality, the bishops of Salzburg, Linz, St. Pölten, Graz, and Klagenfurt instituted councils of priests with members elected by majority vote.[23] Bishop Zak of St. Pölten called a Pastoral Council. In Vienna an ap-

---

[22] Material on this and the following topic may be found in Richard Barta, *Kardinal Franz König* (Vienna, Freiburg, Basel, 1965); in Erika Weinzierl, "Die Kirche," in *Zwei Jahrzehnte Zweite Republik* (Vienna, 1965); and in Weinzierl, "Der Episkopat," in *Die Kirche in Österreich, 1918–1965*, Vol. I, 21–77.

[23] Ferdinand Klostermann, "Neue diözesane Strukturen" in *Diakonia* (1967), p. 261 and Kathpress releases for 1967.

pointive lay council has its own statutes and meets regularly at the bishop's call.

The spirit of Vatican II characterized interdenominational relations. In January, 1965, an ecumenical commission appointed by the Bishops' Conference and the leaders of the Evangelical Church of both the Augsburg and the Swiss Confessions met for the first time and made arrangements for regular meetings in the future. On the occasion of the introduction of the first superintendent of the new Evangelical diocese in Salzburg-Tyrol, Archbishop Rohracher, in a welcoming address, publicly apologized for the expulsion of Protestants in 1732.

The ecumenical spirit extends to Orthodox Christians and Jews as well. Cardinal König is curator of *Pro oriente*, a foundation that cultivates contacts with Orthodox Christians. The Cardinal, in honoring the Patriarch of Constantinople Athenagoras on his eightieth birthday, wrote an appreciative essay on him for a Viennese newspaper. He also promised the director of the American Jewish Committee to examine textbooks for passages hostile to the Jews and to do it through a coordinating committee for Jewish-Christian cooperation. In addition to the collaborators of the Secretariat for Non-Believers to which Karl Rahner also belongs, the *Katholische Akademiker verband Österreichs* (The Catholic Association of University Graduates) is also concerned with dialogue with atheists, as evidenced by a symposium planned by the Viennese scholar of religion Kurt Schuberth and Professor Franz-Martin Schmölz.

In general it can be stated that Vatican Council II has strengthened the readiness of the Austrian bishops for a dialogue with other denominations and with nonbelievers as much as it has strengthened their readiness to cooperate with the world Church. Since the Council they have granted a greater voice to the laymen. Yet a number of bishops are worried about some progressive theologians and hence the 1967 Lenten pastoral letter of the Austrian episcopate was addressed to the clergy. But generally the progressive attitude of their bishops has spared Austrian Catholics the tensions and differences of opinions about the Council and its consequences that have appeared in some other countries.

3. Effects of the Council upon Austrian Catholics

For the present, an account of the Council's impact on Austrian Catholicism can be based only on an attempt to comprehend the outward sphere of Church life and the new initiatives developing in the spirit of the Council. The Catholic Youth Movement is especially concerned with the renewal of the liturgy and occasionally attempts experiments. In order to strengthen ecumenical efforts, interdenominational prayer services have been held at various times in Vienna, Innsbruck, and Linz. In January, 1966, a Protestant pastor preached for the first time in Innsbruck Cathedral. Among the many ecumenical meetings organized by young people, here mention may be made only of "Possibilities of Faith Today" which the Catholic and the Evangelical Student and Graduate Associations of the University of Vienna organized together with Karl Rahner and Wilhelm Dantine. The Diocese of Linz introduced for the first time a common telephone pastorate in the fall of 1966. In Vienna, in the fall of 1967, a branch of the Teilhard de Chardin Society was founded with ecumenical membership.

Doubtless, an outcome of the Council appears in the initiative taken to hold so-called Youth Councils as well as the fact that a nun is now a regular speaker on the radio and television program "Christ in der Zeit" (Christian in Our Time). Mention should also be made of the attempts to establish a *Forum katholischer Begegnung* (Forum for Catholic Encounter) to activate dialogue among Catholics; the dialogues of the Paulus Society and the new forms of sociopolitical instruction of the Catholic Academy of Sociology have been received with increasing interest in Austria. Informative dialogues, instituted in the Bohler Works in Styria in August, 1966, between industrial councils and theologians as well as the assignments of priests and theologians for one-month periods to Austrian centers of industry were praised by *Osservatore Romano* as a "unique initiative."

From the trend of the questions which were submitted for the Salzburg *Fragen an die Kirche* (1966), it is possible to indicate what concerned the Austrian Catholics a year after the closing of the Vatican Council. In Salzburg there were the following problems: liturgy, Church and money, Church contributions, pastoral and social action of the Church, celibacy, morality in marriage, birth control, Church and politics. In nearly all these fields the questions asked were from the conservative as well as the progressive point of view, if such simplified and general terms may be applied here. The "new" liturgy received much adverse criticism, though an 81-year-old woman declared that she was very satisfied with it.

A cautious summary would report that Austrian Catholicism, for the greater part traditional and unconditionally faithful, has been roused by the Council. Compared to such a country as Holland, the movement is not very strong but by working within the confines of Austrian conservatism, the Church can continue reform and the spirit of the Council can achieve fulfillment in Austria—if reform is proclaimed with patience and in freedom becomes effective.

II. CHURCH, STATE, AND PARTIES

The relationship of the Church to the State and to the political parties of the Second Republic cannot be treated separately, at least not for the era of the coalition of the ÖVP (Österreichische Volkspartei—Austrian People's Party) with the SPÖ (Sozialistiche Partei Österreichs—Socialist Party of Austria) which lasted from 1945 to 1966. Basic decisions taken by the Austrian bishops as early as the fall of 1945 determined this relationship.[24] At Salzburg, in their first postwar meeting, the bishops decided to retain the rule imposed in 1933 that the clergy should refrain from active politics and so to preserve the esteem won by the Church's rejection of political association in the course of the National-Socialist struggle with the Church. In the fall of 1946 the Bishops' Conference again proclaimed that it was not considering the situation of the Church before 1938, that is, before Anschluss, as a model. In that earlier period the Church had been closely allied first with the Christian Democratic Party of Msgr. Seipel and later with the corporate state of Dollfuss and von Schuschnigg. As a result of those experiences the Church did not desire any future connection with a political party. In 1946 the president of the Bishops' Conference, Cardinal Innitzer, who had had bitter experiences with a policy of appeasement, coined the slogan "A free Church in the new State." The Church also wanted to pay for personnel and materials from its own means and so retained the Church contributions which had been introduced by the National-Socialists.

At its Fall Conference (1950), the episcopate decided to annul its

[24] Richard Barta "Religion—Kirche—Staat," in *Bestandaufnahme Österreich 1945–1963* (Vienna, Hanover, Bern, 1963); Alfred Kostelecky, "Kirche und Staat," in *Kirche in Österreich, 1918–1965*, Vol. I, 201–217; Otto Schulmeister, "Kirche und Ideologien und Parteien," *Kirche in Österreich*, 218–240; Weinzierl, "Der Episkopat," *Kirche in Österreich*, 21–77.

own ordinance of July 18, 1938, concerning the introduction of obligatory civil marriage ordained by the Nazi regime. Under that arrangement religious marriage ceremonies were allowed to take place only after it had been established that the civil ceremony had been performed. The episcopal act of annulment formed part of their dispute with the State concerning the validity of the 1933 Concordat. In the dispute the Socialist Party under the leadership of Vice-Chancellor Adolf Schärf lined up against the Austrian People's Party which substantially was the heir of the Christian-social tradition. The Socialists rejected the Concordat because the Dollfuss regime in 1934 had vanquished the Social Democrats in civil war. The rejection was made and defended on the basis of the so-called theory of annexation, for Austria was not occupied in 1938 but had been annexed, that is, crushed in its existence as a State. This condition, it was argued, lasted until 1955 when the State Treaty was signed. At that time the Church tried to clarify future legal questions by positive preparatory work and continued to keep aloof from party politics. On the Concordat issue its demands were clearly formulated in the bishops' guidelines for the May, 1952, Students' Conference that met at Mariazell to prepare the first postwar *Katholikentag* for which the motto was "Würde und Freiheit des Menschen" (Human Dignity and Liberty). As the result of its deliberations, the Students' Conference, with the participation of priests and laymen from all over Austria, published what has since become a classical definition of a free Church in a free society: "No return to the state-controlled Church of past centuries. . . . No return to the protectorate of one party over the Church . . . !" Since this view still determines the relationship between the Church and the State and parties, it approximates a kind of Austrian "Catholic Manifesto."

Immediately after the liberation of Austria and until the signing of the State Treaty, the episcopate pressed for a final clarification of the Concordat, as far as could be arranged in the difficult political situation then prevailing. Charged by the Bishops' Conference, Archbishop Jáchym published a "White Paper" on July 1, 1955, in which he presented quite unequivocally the Church's point of view. In the same year the Church successfully won the abolition of Paragraph 67 of the personal estates law. The result was achieved by legal means, for the constitutional court declared Paragraph 67 to be unconstitutional as it provided for legal prosecution of those priests who celebrated a church wedding without previous civil marriage.

Since 1956 a new attitude of the Socialist Party toward *Kulturpolitik* has been apparent. This change may have taken place for reasons of electoral tactics; the efforts of the small but very active Union of Socialist Catholics may have played a role; certainly, the change of guard in the Socialist Party is part of the explanation; just as certainly the social pastoral letter (1956) of the episcopate and the contacts of the episcopate and the contacts of some Church people with party and union functionaries, who might have some understanding of their claims, from another part. At any rate, in his inaugural address the new Federal President, Adolf Schärf, expressed his pleasure that a new climate concerning culture prevailed in the land: "I shall do my utmost to see that the relations between Church and State are stabilized in this new climate and that they are not swayed by ancient sentimentalities."

Six days later, the Council of Ministers of Chancellor Julius Raab's coalition (ÖVP-SPÖ) government decided to tackle the Concordat question. For this purpose a committee of ministers was formed to draw up an Austrian note to the Holy See informing it of the unanimous decision of the Federal government to recognize the validity of the Concordat in principle. The government assumed that the sequence of changes following the conclusion of the Concordat in 1933 would predispose the Holy See to negotiate a new Concordat. However, more than a year of silence intervened before Vatican pressure received a response. The government's note was delivered to the Papal Secretary of State on December 21, 1957. The detailed and rather cool rejoinder received on January 30, 1958, stated that the Vatican would not be satisfied with a mere recognition of the validity of the Concordat but had to insist that the content and the obligations contracted should be recognized. The Holy See, however, would be ready for negotiations involving "retouches, that is, changes which might be considered necessary."

Thus it was not until March, 1959, in the pontificate of John XXIII, that new negotiations were begun on the open questions involving property, school, and marriage. The starting point for these negotiations was the Federal government's petition to raise the Apostolic Administration of Burgenland to a diocesan level—the government's case was based upon the provisions of the Concordat. The first results were the treaties signed on June 23, 1960, by the Holy See and the Republic of Austria. The treaties provided for the Apostolic Administration of Burgenland to be a diocese and for rules to settle the disputed property matters. On July 12, 1960, the Austrian National Assembly approved the treaties: the supporting votes of the ÖPV and the SPÖ were opposed by those of the Freiheitliche Partei (Freedom Party) which continued the anticlerical tradition of the national liberals.

The school problem, insofar as it involved the Holy See and the Concordat, was settled on July 9, 1962, by a treaty dealing with issues affecting education. Thereafter the coalition parties in the National Assembly on July 18 accepted a constitutional amendment dealing with schools. The amendment filled a gap in the Austrian Constitution that had existed since 1920. On July 25, 1962, eight new school laws were passed by the National Assembly. And so for the first time denominational schools in Austria were assured of state financial support. The successful passage of these laws resulted principally from the efforts of Heinrich Drimmel, the Catholic Minister of Education. The laws, moreover, may be considered an outstanding success of the new democratic Kulturpolitik of Austria, for treaties with a generally respected Church are no longer, as in 1855, the result of absolutist politics of the monarch, or, as in 1933, of the determined efforts of an individual "Catholic" party.

After the establishment of the Innsbruck-Feldkirch Diocese, for which a treaty with the Holy See (July 7, 1964) provided, the only remaining issue from the discussion of the Concordat, begun in 1945, is the marriage question. In view of the conciliatory attitude shown by both parties, an agreed solution should be possible. For example, facultative (that is, optional) civil marriage should be introduced. In addition, the Catholics of Vorarlberg have indicated to both Church and State their desire for the establishment of their own bishopric. This indicates that the relation of the Church to the State as well as to the two great parties can be termed quite satisfactory. The politicians' understanding and moderation and the Church's strict observance of the disengagement from party politics and acceptance of both the constitutional state and democracy as a free development of political forces in a pluralistic society have brought this about. But the achievement was not made without resistance—within the Catholic sphere as well.

Independence from party politics, repeatedly stressed and demonstrated by Cardinal König, and openness to dialogue with all who are ready for it, still do not pass unchallenged, especially from the generality of those Catholics who, following the prevailing tradition, are politically active in the Austrian People's Party. This is evident from the controversy provoked by a meeting organized by the Socialist Party at the beginning of November, 1967, which was devoted to the theme, "Socialists and the Catholic Church." It convened at St. Pölten and was attended by prominent Socialists, headed by Party Chairman Bruno Kreisky, and by Catholic sociologists, historians, and reporters, who participated as speakers or served as observers.[25]

The line which since 1945 the Austrian bishops have deliberately pursued for pastoral reasons has already convincingly proved itself. And it will have to be preserved in the future. For Federal Chancellor Klaus's single party (ÖVP) government which, after the elections of March 6, 1966, took over from the twenty-year-old black and red coalition and which consists of the majority of practicing Catholics, can no longer lay claim to the historically conditioned equation of the interwar years: Christian social party=only representative of the Church interests or vice-versa. The close bond with a political party, even a meritorious one, and, above all, with the corporate State from 1934 to 1938, has had such negative effects on the Church both with respect to its authority and to its role as society's conscience, that a return to that tradition cannot even be considered. Nor does the Church desire a revival of political Catholicism in traditional or new forms.

All the more necessary, therefore, is the political involvement of the individual Catholic in that kind of democratic party which, in theory and practice, holds up under his conscientious examination. This principle, represented by the bishops and by Catholic Action, one of the biggest Catholic organizations in Austria, will ultimately be maintained only if the Socialist Party of Austria does not again take up the radical hostility to the Church that characterized Austrian Marxism during the interwar years. That hostility has by no means disappeared. The movement for an opening which was to be observed at the end of the fifties and the beginning of the sixties, and can be noted in the Socialist program of 1958, came to a standstill in the mid-sixties. Recently the movement has been deliberately and intensively resumed by the new Party Chairman Kreisky who wants to reform the party on the Scandinavian example. This effort has provoked considerable discussion in the Socialist Party. Whatever the future development of Austrian parties, the years since 1945 form a new period, not only of Austrian

[25] *Die Furche* (November 22, 1967) published all the reports.

Church history but one that should influence future relations between the Church and a democratic state.

III. CHURCH AND SOCIETY

A. CATHOLIC SCHOOLS AND EDUCATION

Austria does not have a Catholic university. The plan to establish one in Salzburg has been considered since 1848 and entertained by all Catholic university societies in the twentieth century; however since a state university was established there, the Church, in order to establish a significant distribution of emphasis between research and teaching, founded a Research Center in 1961 with funds provided by *Katholisches Hochschulwerk*. The Research Center, consisting of seven institutes, headed by professors from state universities, maintains a research program and provides opportunities for the professional growth of Catholic scholars.

With fourteen Catholic teachers' colleges among the existing twenty-eight teachers' colleges,[26] the Church is strongly represented in the training of teachers. Until the new school laws of 1962, their graduates had fewer chances for appointment in the public service of some of the federal provinces. And the level of education offered by some of them was very uneven. As a result of the new laws, all are now being transformed into fine arts, pedagogical *Realgymnasia*, and future teachers have to take two more years of study in a teachers' college after graduation from these schools. The Catholic pedagogical academies now being established by the dioceses are intended to be the spatial framework for spiritually important centers of Catholic teacher formation. Their effectiveness, however, will depend mainly on the quality of professors they can engage and on their employment of modern methods.

The new school laws also silenced Catholic demands for the introduction of Catholic public schools and for "free parental choice" schools. The demands had reached a climax in 1952. These new laws gave existing Catholic schools the character of public schools and the State assumed the obligation of filling 60 per cent, or 1,300 of the posi-

[26] On this and the following consult Hans Kriegl, "Kirche und Schule," in *Die Kirche in Österreich, 1918–1965*, Vol. I, 302–315.

tions necessary to carry out the curriculum in the academic year 1961–1962; this is in the same proportion that the State staffs the public schools. In 1966, the breakdown of Austrian Catholic schools was: 33 high schools, 15 teachers' colleges, 65 secondary schools, 93 primary schools, 50 home economics schools, 5 special schools, and 14 institutes for the preparation of kindergarten and manual-work teachers. To a great extent these are schools for girls; technical schools and vocational schools for men are lacking. Though Austrian Catholic schools have a long and proud ancestry, they will have to be restructured and redistributed geographically if they are to meet the exigencies of modern times.

Such adaptation has already been accomplished in Catholic adult education, which has been increasing since 1945, especially in the country. In adult education the Catholic educational enterprises of the dioceses of Linz, St. Pölten, Seckau, Innsbruck, Salzburg, and Vienna have done pioneer work. Because they are fully conscious of their importance for the sensible use of leisure time in the interest of social education, their activities are often devoted to important problems of state and society in Austria, their historical development, and the possibilities for a realistic solution. The Vienna Catholic Academy, founded in 1945, and especially the Catholic Social Academy, founded in Vienna in 1958, as well as the educational enterprises of the Catholic organizations which are numerous among young people, have been oriented toward these goals. An increasing attempt to take account of social realities and to evaluate facts accurately has been generally noted in all Catholic social work since 1945. It must be judged to be one of the most important changes of Austrian Catholicism in the twentieth century.

B. Representation of Catholics in the Mass Media

In the sphere of mass media, such as radio and TV, Catholics often have a voice, that is, there are special time slots given over to church broadcasts. Their actual influence upon programming is much smaller in proportion to their numbers, since formerly only very few Catholics had the necessary special training and practical experience; hence, many occasions were missed at a time when long-range and forward-looking professional planning in the Catholic sphere was necessary. Catholic attempts to make their own productions, for instance, in films, never went beyond mere beginnings.

The situation is different in the press.[27] There is no overall Austrian Catholic daily. Otto Kaspar's attempt, in the Catholic weekly *Offenes Wort* (Open Word), to provide independent criticism of events inside and outside the Church failed in 1956 because of economical and political difficulties. But a wide range of Catholic publishing does exist. Graz's *Kleine Zeitung* (Little Newspaper) has a large circulation in Styria and Carinthia. Many dioceses publish church bulletins, the most modern of which is that issued by the Diocese of St. Pölten. There are, as well, Catholic weeklies and the numerous publications of Catholic movements and organizations. In addition, the news agency Kathpress, established in 1945 and since 1955 directed by Richard Barta, daily furnishes the whole Austrian press with domestic and foreign Catholic news.

The oldest Catholic weekly of the Second Republic, *Die Furche* (Furrow), was founded in 1945 by Funder, the former Editor-in-Chief of the Social-Christian newspaper, *Reichspost*. It was intended to be an open forum of Austrian opinion with stress on the Catholic. The famous intellectual historian Friedrich Heer, who in the fifties defended conversation, that is, dialogue, with the enemy, has been one of its chief contributors. Although the paper could have maintained and served its original purpose, after the death of Funder in 1959 and especially under the editorship of Kurt Skalnik, financial as well as practical and personal difficulties dissuaded the Herold publishing house from providing the means essential for the timely development of the paper. The circulation declined so sharply that at the end of 1967 Skalnik and nearly all his staff had to be dismissed. The future of this distinctive periodical which fulfilled an important function in Austrian journalism is quite uncertain. Quite secure, however, now as formerly, is the weekly *Volksbote*, since 1946 published in Innsbruck by the Tyrolia publishing house and distributed throughout Austria.

Established in 1945 was the monthly review of religion and culture, *Wort und Wahrheit* (Word and Truth) published by Herder in Vienna and edited by Otto Mauer, Otto Schulmeister, Anton Böhm, and Karlheinz Schmidthüs. This review of opinion for Catholic intellectuals has acquired an honored place alongside of the older religious-

[27] Kurt Skalnik, "Die Katholische Presse," *Kirche in Österreich*, 363–315.

cultural reviews, such as *Stimmen der Zeit* and *Hochland* in the German Federal Republic. But periodicals of this kind require great sacrifices by a publisher in view of the increased production costs and a limited number of subscriptions. Thus changes have also occurred in *Wort und Wahrheit* which until 1967 was edited by the former Editor-in-Chief of the independent newspaper *Die Presse*, Otto Schulmeister. Since January, 1968, it has appeared as a bimonthly under the editorship of Otto Mauer. In Austrian journalism, too, there is a crisis which involves a tendency toward concentration in a few papers and journals and the crisis has not spared the Catholic press. As a consequence, the activity of Catholic journalists and of reporters for newspapers and periodicals which are ideologically or religiously neutral assumes an ever-increasing importance.

C. Catholics in the Scientific and Cultural Life of Austria

Catholics are more widely represented in professorial and academic circles than was the case in 1918 or even before 1938. The efforts of *Katholische Hochschuljugend* (Catholic Academic Youth) alone, founded in 1946 under the leadership of the academic pastor Karl Strobl, have helped to develop and bring to the fore thirty professors and university teachers of lower rank almost equally divided between the humanities and sciences. The CV (*Cartell Verband*), the main support of the *Arbeitsgemeinschaft der katholischen Verbände* (Association of Catholic Organizations) recognized by the bishops in 1955, has already produced several of the younger professors. *Pro Sancta*, an enterprise initiated in 1967 by the Austrian bishops and Catholic Action for the advancement of studies, will increase the Catholic potential for professors. As a matter of course, practicing Catholics among scientists as everywhere else in Austrian society are in the minority, but it can be said with a measure of assurance that the majority do not reject the Church. This is a real change from the days when the Austrian universities were bulwarks of liberalism. This change is an indication of the increased respect for the Church that was gained during the times of Nazi persecution.

In literature[28] and in the plastic arts the balance sheet is less encouraging. Immediately after 1945 there was a great receptivity to religious

[28] Rudolf Henz, "Die Katholiken in der Literatur," *Kirche in Österreich*, 357–362.

literature. This may be explained, in part, by the necessity of catching up after seven years of Nazi rule. Many of the younger authors showed themselves open to religion. This gave rise to a hope for substantial Catholic poetry in Austria. The social and economic development since the fifties, however, has not fulfilled this hope. Many of the younger generation of writers emigrated to the German Federal Republic or now write only for German publishers. At the same time they turned away from religious problems or at least did not give them literary expression. Today Catholic literature in Austria is represented by men like Max Mell and Rudolf Henz, who had been writing poetry before 1938.

Another indication that in the Catholic literary sphere first-rate young talent is lacking is furnished by the attitude of Ludwig Ficker's periodical *Brenner*, in whose pages Georg Trakl and Theodor Haecker became known between the wars. The stagnation of Catholic literature coincides with that of the general literary situation in Austria which in 1966 lost the last poet of world distinction with the death of Heimito von Doderer. He had also been a practicing Catholic.

In the arts the primary influence has come from the old masters, such as Clemens von Holzmeister in architecture and Herbert Boeckl in painting. During the fifties there was considerable progress in modern church architecture which is also due, it is a pleasure to state, to young architects like those of the "Group 4" (Spalt, Kurrent, and Holzmeister) and Ottokar Uhl.[29] The painter Josef Mikl has made church windows and Ernest Fuchs altar pictures. Toni Schneider-Manzell has acquired fame beyond the confines of Austria for his sculptured church doors. The meeting place for the Catholic artists of the avant-garde has been the Wiener Galerie next to St. Stephen's Cathedral, founded and directed in the fifties by Msgr. Mauer. Recently a small new gallery was established in the Catholic Academic Community House in Salzburg and is managed by the press agent of the Archdiocese of Salzburg, Hans Widrich. The *Christliche Kunstblätter* (Pages of Christian Art) in Linz, and the *Biennale christliche Kunst* (Biennial of Christian Art) in Graz are concerned with the furthering of modern art, with the accent on sacred art.

In general, we may say that the Church has developed a series of initiatives principally in the plastic arts, not always to the pleasure of Church people who in the majority are as conservative in their taste for

[29] Günter Rombold, "Sakrale Kunst," *Kirche in Österreich*, 153–161.

art and as progressive in that for music as the rest of the Austrian population. Yet the liturgical reform should provide the occasion for the Church to commission modern poets, musicians, architects, painters, and sculptors to a far greater extent than formerly and the consideration should be the quality of the artist rather than his Catholicity.

All doors are open for the Church in the social and cultural life of today's Austria. They are open for the Church to enter without hesitation or pusillanimity and to be the servant Church in the spirit of the Council.[30]

[30] In addition to the preceding footnotes, the following books and articles are useful: Richard Barta, "Freie Kirche in Freier Gesellschaft" in *Zwanzig Jahre Zweite Republik* (Vienna, 1965); *Custos quid de nocte? Österreichisches Geistesleben seit der Jahrhundertwende*, edited by Karl Rudolf and Leopold Lentner (Vienna, 1961), a Festschrift for Michael Pfliegler; *Diener Jesu Christi*, a Festschrift for the Archbishop of Salzburg, Dr. Andreas Rohracher, on the Fiftieth Anniversary of his Priesthood (Salzburg, 1965); *Institut für kirchliche Sozialforschung* (Vienna, 1962); *Katholisches Soziallexikon* (Innsbruck, Vienna, Munich, 1964); *Löscht den Geist nicht aus, Probleme und Imperative des Österr. Katholikentages 1962* (Innsbruck, Vienna, Munich, 1963); *Österreichischer Katholikentag 1952, Festführer* (Vienna, 1952); Erika Weinzierl, "Österreichs Katholiken und der Nationalsozialismus," I, II, III, in *Wort und Wahrheit* (1963 and 1965); Weinzierl, *Die österreichischen Konkordate von 1855 und 1933* (Vienna, 1960); Josef Wodka, *Kirche in Österreich* (Vienna, 1959); Ignaz Zangerle, *Zur Situation der Kirche* (Salzburg, 1963).

4 : SWITZERLAND

Ludwig Kaufmann, S.J.

"Switzerland exports not only cheese, chocolate, and watches, but in recent times theology as well." This remark has been making the rounds among students at Catholic theological faculties in Germany where Swiss theologians hold several chairs. The observation, of course, is not a guide to the statistics of Swiss exports among which pharmaceutical products of the powerful chemical industry hold first rank. But it is significant in expressing the astonishment that this small, fortunate country that escaped both world wars and experiences material prosperity should also be looked to for its spiritual potential.

The same phenomenon appears with more illustrious examples in other areas. These indeed suggest that there is something akin to a historical law—that in a small fatherland the prophet is without honor. If he wishes recognition, he must emigrate. This was the case with the composer Arthur Honegger and with the architect Le Corbusier; even the dramatists Max Frisch and Friedrich Dürrenmatt first acquired fame abroad.

Catholic theology in Switzerland, in contrast with Protestant theology, has had few favoring circumstances. On the university level the material and structural groundwork is still unfavorable. This partially explains why a substantial part of the Swiss contribution to international theological discussion has been made on foreign platforms: even more does it explain why the Swiss theological contribution to Vatican II was conspicuous by its absence.

Until the Council, the Swiss presence at the Vatican was exclusively of a militaristic and musical comedy nature. Instead of an ambassador or even a cardinal, the *Confederatio Helvetica* was represented by a guard detail. With their halberds and motley uniforms allegedly designed by Michelangelo, the Swiss Guards recall an epoch long past, during which both the Swiss Confederation and the papacy sought military glory.

But at the Council there were spiritual battles to be fought. The attack on the closed "system" thinking of the Roman textbook theology and the routine of the curial apparatus required not only strong personalities with civil courage, as Cardinals Achilles Liénart and Joseph Frings demonstrated on the Council's first day; it also required the tools which only expert theologians could furnish. Thus the Germans, the Austrians, and the Dutch not only had Frings, Döpfner, König, and Alfrink but behind them stood Ratzinger, Rahner, Schillebeeckx, and more.

Among the Swiss, neither was visible. The ecclesiastical structure of Switzerland did not make for any preeminent archbishops and there was no inspiring personality who might have united the Swiss bishops. The latter, not well-endowed materially, came to Rome without large entourages, and were scattered throughout Rome. They were too modest and too oblivious to appreciate that the appointment of theologians might have made a difference so that the "Voice of Switzerland" would carry weight and validity at the Council. Even then there were Swiss theologians available who had something to say, although they were mainly "comers."

One of them, Hans Küng, has become especially well known in the United States. Küng's works directly contributed to the formation of ecclesiological consciousness before, during, and after the Council.[1] Significantly he did not come to the Council with a Swiss bishop but with the Bishop of Rottenburg, West Germany.[2] In his diocese is the

---

[1] At the beginning of the Council (1962) appeared Küng's *Strukturen der Kirche.* In English it appeared as *The Structures of the Church* (London, 1966). Küng's lectures in the United States (1962) made a decisive impact as did his best-selling book, *The Council, Reform and Reunion* (New York, 1961). After the second session of the Council he cooperated in editing a selection of Council Talks (*Konzilsreden*). Two years after the closing of the Council (1967) appeared *Die Kirche* (Volume I: Ecumenical Research), which was published as *The Church* (London, 1968).

[2] Bishop Josef Leiprecht. Later he chose another collaborator, who assisted him in his work in the Commission for Religious. Küng, who was interested in the Theological Commission, but only expected a fruitful cooperation if there had been a completely new lineup of commission members, declined direct, active par-

University of Tübingen, where Küng held a chair for dogma and where another Swiss, the Old Testament expert Herbert Haag (editor of *Bibellexikon*), had taught before him.

The Swiss bishops did not bring a single theologian of rank to the Council. Thus were missing the moralist Franz Böckle, who has since been appointed to the University of Bonn, and Leonhard Weber, who has meanwhile moved to Munich as pastoral theologian. This in spite of the fact that at the time both men were working near their bishops, the first in Chur, the second in Solothurn.

Even the most prominent of them all, Hans Urs von Balthasar, was absent. Nor has he yet acquired a university chair: he merely holds a preeminent place for his theological writings as well as his works of literary criticism and spiritual writings in German and French publications. Von Balthasar had serious contributions to make on such timely questions as lay spirituality and secular institutes.

Only Otto Karrer, a pioneer in ecumenism, widely known for his translation of the New Testament and religious-historical-spiritual writings, was summoned to the Council. The Bishop of Basel had him come to Rome for the last three weeks of the fourth session—a gesture made so late that nothing could be accomplished.

The theologians mentioned so far come from German-speaking Switzerland. In this largest of the three language districts are located the three universities of Basel, Bern, and Zürich, each with an Evangelical-Reformed theological faculty, as well as a very small Old-Catholic faculty in Bern. There is no Roman Catholic theological faculty at any of these universities. The new generation receives its theological training in isolated cantonal theological faculties in Lucerne and at several seminaries. In the years preceding the Council the one in Chur made a name for itself far beyond Switzerland's borders. On the occasion of its one hundred fiftieth anniversary a jubilee publication entitled *Fragen der Theologie Heute* (Questions of Theology Today)[3] reached the incomparable circulation, for a theological subject, of 50,000 copies, thanks to its translation into French, English, Dutch, and Spanish. During the last Council session one of the editors, Johannes Feiner, together with a Swiss Benedictine in Rome, Magnus

---

ticipation in the Council. He remained a papal *peritus* and made appearances from time to time.

[3] Edited by Johannes Feiner, Josef Trütsch, and Franz Böckle (Einsiedeln, 1957). American Edition: *Theology Today* (Milwaukee, 1965).

Lohrer, was able to present the pope with the first of a planned five-volume work on the dogmatic of salvation history, *Mysterium Salutis*.[4]

Although no one bothered to give Feiner the title of a Council theologian, he surely achieved far more than many others who officially ranked among the *"periti."* His notable contribution was in the field of the theology of salvation, so dear to the heart of Paul VI, as the guide-line for ecumenical and Conciliar theology. Feiner appeared regu-larly on the observers' tribune; commissioned by the Secretariat of Unity, he was available as a modest advisor and interpreter to non-Catholic delegates. Thus he was often seen in discussion with the Protestant expert on history-of-salvation-theology, Oscar Cullmann of the University of Basel, and with Lukas Vischer, the Basel-born Secre-tary of the Conference on Faith and Order of the Geneva-based World Council of Churches. Among the men surrounding Cardinal Augustin Bea, Switzerland was not badly represented: a Swiss archivist and a secretary as well were employed by the Secretariat for Unity from the beginning, and since the Council, a young Swiss Luther expert, Augustin Hasler.

GERMAN-FRENCH BRIDGE?

Anyone who considers the geographical location of Switzerland in the heart of Europe will examine Swiss participation in the life of the Church for contributions that may be compared to those of its neigh-bors or that may be especially distinctive of Swiss life. The mission field, for example, might be regarded as particularly suited to the Swiss, who have been politically neutral and have never been tainted by colonial possessions. In view of its special location at the convergence of three languages and cultures, it is natural to ask whether the Church might expect assistance and initiative from Switzerland in regard to such matters as cultural exchanges, the bridging of disparities, and the mu-tual enrichment of various language areas. Or, on the other hand, whether the Church or churches contribute noticeably to the fulfill-ment of this special mission of Switzerland.

---

[4] Thus far two volumes of 1,000 pages each have appeared. The first is dedicated to Hans Urs von Balthasar on his sixtieth birthday; in the second von Balthasar himself wrote the first chapter, "Der Zugang zur Wirklichkeit Gottes" (Admittance to the Reality of God).

This question may be raised with respect to the German-French exchanges in theology. One would think that precisely here the Swiss might have performed a bridging function. There has always been a strong group of Swiss students at Innsbruck, where Karl and Hugo Rahner used to teach. The contingent of Swiss students who again and again went to the Institut Catholique in Paris or as Jesuits to Lyon-Fourvière and thus came in contact with Congar and Chenu or de Lubac, Bouillard, and Danielou was equally strong. However, their education was principally limited to one place or the other: only rarely did something like a deep encounter of the two cultures or a synthesis take place in one and the same person.

As is well known, essential, dynamic impulses of the Council came from French as well as German-Austrian theology, but ultimately it must be stated that intensive German-French dialogue simply did not take place during Vatican II any more than before the Council. The language barrier was just too great; too few Germans could speak French and too few French spoke German. Was this not due to a lack of mediation?

A prominent French Conciliar theologian told me that in the last analysis neither the French nor the Germans but the Belgians from Louvain took the lead in most of the theological negotiations and treatises. On the other hand, the Dutch attributed their theological "convulsions" to the fact that everything dynamic and exciting simply seemed to flow into their country. Why did not Switzerland similarly become a melting pot of theological ideas?

The question is all the more justified inasmuch as large areas of Switzerland, more precisely everything lying west of the Gotthard-Schaffhausen line, once belonged to the Kingdom of Burgundy, which had assumed the function of the European center. Its first name is associated with Charlemagne's son Lothar. This *Lotharingia* that once extended to parts of Belgium and Holland is still present in today's Lorraine which bore the same name. Under Charles the Bold this middle land had the name of Burgundy and extended all the way up to Flanders and Brabant, Gelderland, and Holland. The militant Swiss played a decisive role in Burgundy's dismemberment. At the beginning of the last quarter of the fifteenth century, they shattered the European middle kingdom from the eastern flank.

The city which was joined to the Confederacy from the battle zone is called Freiburg (or Fribourg). As Fribourg, in contrast to Bern, preserved the faith during the Reformation period that soon followed

(Peter Canisius is buried there), it especially merits consideration for its role as an intermediary center.

Here, directly at the language borders, stands the only Swiss Catholic university. It is a state-sponsored, bilingual institution of higher learning which is partly supported by this hitherto poor, purely agrarian canton, and partly by the donations of Swiss Catholics from the rest of the country.

Fribourg once played a very important role—in the preparatory work for Leo XIII's social teaching in *Rerum Novarum*. Since the founding in 1927 of the Foyer St. Justin by the present Bishop François Charrière, it has also accomplished a great deal of pioneer work in the education of students from mission countries overseas, especially Asia. Moreover, Fribourg is the city in which very many colleges, schools, and institutions of various orders, as well as missionary centers and the international student groups of the *Pax Romana* have been established. For this reason it has been, not inaptly, called "little Rome." At the Council, however, Fribourg did not at all play the role that some might have expected of it. This judgment refers primarily to the theological faculty. Like the philosophical faculty this has been in Dominican hands since its foundation. Why was it not put to use for the Council? Could not, for example, an exegete, such as the New Testament expert, Jean-Dominique Barthélémy—who today collaborates, together with other, especially Protestant, Swiss in the great French *Bible Oecumenique*—have given good service to his bishop and through him to the Secretariat for Unity? But exegetes and biblical theologians were on the whole thinly spread over this Council, which so decisively tried to convert to the Bible. One can hardly blame the Swiss that they proved to have less imagination and foresight in this respect than their colleagues from all over the world.

Toward the end of the Council, Fribourg Dominicans did appear in the company of Bishop Charrière, who earlier had been engaged in a papal mission to Moscow. One of them, Heinrich Stirnimann, has since become a key figure for ecumenical contacts in Switzerland and heads the Ecumenical Institute at Fribourg University. One of his confreres, Henri de Riedmatten, who was for a time the prior at the Fribourg Community, played a significant role as secretary of the special papal commission for marriage and population (the so-called "Pill Commission"). He also participated in the work of the mixed commission for "Schema 13" (*Pastoral Constitution on the Church in the Modern*

World). According to a letter of November 27, 1965, signed by Cardinal Ottaviani and sent to the pope, it is thanks "primarily to the criticism of P. de Riedmatten" that the expression *"artes anticonceptionales"* was not included in the text concerning the famous *Modi* of the section on birth control introduced by the secretary of state. This was the case, although the Cardinal (as was the experience of other commissions) presented the views of the minority to the pope as the "better" view. Today Riedmatten is the official observer of the Holy See at the International Organizations in Geneva.

If one speaks of Fribourg, one does not think merely of Dominicans. Chairs for pastoral theology and liturgy have for some time been given to professors from the secular clergy. One of the most industrious workers and quiet helpers of Msgr. Bugnini, the architect of liturgical reform, was Professor Anton Hänggi, who was called to Rome by the Swiss bishops collectively. He comes from Solothurn in German Switzerland and was consecrated Bishop of Basel on February 11, 1968.

In addition to the theological faculty of the university in Fribourg, there is also a diocesan seminary, where for more than forty years Charles Journet has taught. In his earlier years the present pope learned to esteem Journet in connection with Jacques Maritain's Neo-Thomism. Hardly known in German Switzerland, Journet was the more bound to *Suisse Romande*. For many years he edited the theological-cultural magazine *Nova et Vetera* and devoted himself to being a distinguished and enthusiastic chaplain to students in Geneva. His elevation to the cardinalate can be included among the special "gestures" by which Paul VI departed from the prevailing tradition. If there ever was a man who was not a "career" man, it was Journet, who upon his elevation asked to be allowed to continue his quiet, simple mode of life in the Fribourg seminary.

During the fourth session of the Council he took the floor at a last important moment in order to speak, it is generally believed at the request of the pope, in favor of the schema on religious freedom. He knew, as few others at the time did, how to dispel the objections of the opposition that in spite of many revisions, still remained and how to clear up misunderstandings. He can also be mentioned as an early partisan of *rapprochement* with the Jews and as an opponent of Nazi anti-Semitism. He took part in the so-called *"Thesen von Seelisburg"* of 1947,[5] which treats this subject. (His book *Destinées d' Israel* did not

[5] Cf. *Orientierung*, No. 6 (1967).

receive an imprimatur until after the American invasion in Normandy and the capture of Paris.)

If he was ahead of his time more than many others in this matter, on the other hand his defense of indulgences proved that he did not wish to be included among the "progressive" theologians. His concern today is above all an inner deepening—*theologia cordis*—even though during the Nazi threat he did not restrain his courageous pen from the subjects of politics and public life.

Of course one could mention many other worthy names from Fribourg. At the Council there were two lay auditors, Soranyes de Franc, who had made a name in *Pax Romana*, and de Habicht, presently a member of the Curia's lay council. But they have little to do with Switzerland. For the fulfillment of a possibly specific Swiss mission originating in Fribourg, we should be especially interested in *a meeting and mutual enrichment of the various cultures within the spiritual sphere of the Church*. But at the Council one could hardly perceive the least help or initiative in this direction from Fribourg, and the same, unfortunately, must be said of Switzerland. If the Germans and French came together at the beginning of the Council without Swiss help, so too, at the end, when Germans and French disagreed in connection with Schema 13, Swiss mediation was absent. To the extent that all-European meetings took place at all at the Council—twice there were such meetings dealing with pastoral problems of transient populations and foreign guest workers—the initiative came from the Bishops of Metz and Strasbourg, that is, from the same Alsace-Lorraine area that produced Robert Schumann, the spokesman of European unity.

THE CHURCH AND LANGUAGE AND CULTURAL PROBLEMS

The preceding account will not greatly astonish anyone familiar with Church life in Switzerland. The language and culture boundaries are by no means less effective within the Church than they are elsewhere. German-Swiss and French-Swiss concepts of ecclesiastical lay organizations, for example, have long been radically different. The latter followed the example of the "milieu theory" of the specialized movements of French and Belgian *Action Catholique* (Jocist, JEC, JAC), while the former clung to the German system of *Standesvereine* grouped according to age and sex. Common organizations to embrace all three language groups exist more on paper than in practice. One positive exception is the trilingual magazine *Civitas*, collectively published by the Catholic student association. The Boy Scouts have a general organization that is all-Swiss and extra-confessional. But within it, the Catholics are the very people who divide their national associations according to language.

The Council has not at all improved cooperation across language frontiers. This obstacle was already in evidence during the sessions in Rome. The Bishops of Basel, Chur, and St. Gallen, which are predominantly German dioceses, together with the Abbot of Einsiedeln, regularly attended the meetings of the German and Austrian bishops. With them, they established a common liturgical commission, which was joined by the Bishop of Luxembourg. Since the end of the Council this commission has accomplished a great deal of work that the Council's advocacy of the vernacular in the liturgy made necessary. Thus the German Swiss bishops made a very natural opening to the north and east and at the same time pledged a greater degree of cooperation among themselves.

For the bishops of Western Switzerland and Ticino the same opportunity did not arise. Apparently it was not particularly enticing for the Apostolic Administrator of Ticino to seek admittance as the only foreigner to the general assembly of several hundred bishops that make up the Italian episcopate, even though from his seat in Lugano he is in regular contact with his neighbors in Como and Milan. Neither did the Bishop of Lausanne-Geneva-Fribourg on his part feel impelled to join the French. He could only have had the Abbot Bishop of Saint Maurice as companion. The Bishop of Sion, who presides over the evenly bilingual canton of Wallis (Valais), is in a most difficult situation. He has chosen a certain degree of isolation rather than to show a preference for one or the other language group by joining a unilingual episcopal-collegial alliance.

Thus the minority problem has been emphasized rather than diminished by the Council and has had repercussions on the Church authorities. The centrifugal tendency of the language groups needs to be regulated by increased all-Swiss cooperation.

Soon after the bishops had returned from the Council, a certain disarray in this matter appeared. The occasion arose when Rome authorized new fasting regulations. The Diocese of Lugano immediately followed the Italians, while the rest of Switzerland held back to note the course that their neighbors would take. They had to consider the numerous border commuters of the eastern and northern regions who work in Switzerland but live "abroad." Finally the Swiss found their own general solution applicable for all of Switzerland. Swiss Catholics like their many Italian guest workers may eat meat on Friday; and this arrangement differs from, for example, German regulations.

This small incident made the bishops aware how necessary and timely for Switzerland is "collegial" cooperation of the bishops on the national level. Because the diocesan conditions in Switzerland are very singular and complicated, they require a short explanation.

DIOCESES AND BISHOPS' CONFERENCE

Unlike many other countries where dioceses are grouped around metro-politan sees, all Swiss dioceses are independent, that is, immediately under the jurisdiction of the Holy See. This has not always been the case. For more than two centuries after the independence of the Swiss Confederation in 1499, the ancient boundaries of Church provinces overlapped the new Swiss frontiers. Disengagement from foreign ecclesiastical dependence was achieved, but not without the political pressure of the Federal Government which was established in 1848 and since then has reserved the constitutional right of approving every diocesan change. On the other hand, the present circumstances are codetermined by the historical requirements and intervention of in-dividual "diocesan cantons" (for example, Grisons). The relationship of Church and State differs among the cantons and there are many variations, from close ties (*Landeskirche*) to complete separation.

The possibility of uniting all Swiss dioceses into one Church prov-ince has never been seriously considered. Beginning in 1863, however, an annual Swiss Bishops' Conference began to take place. Today it consists of the Bishops of Basel-Lugano (seat in Solothurn), Chur (which includes the General Vicariate of Zürich), St. Gallen, Sion, Lausanne-Geneva-Fribourg (seat in Fribourg), as well as the Apostolic Administrator of Ticino (Lugano), the Abbot Bishop of Saint Maurice, and the Abbot of Einsiedeln. Except for the latter well-known mon-asteries in Valais and the heart of central Switzerland respectively, there are in effect five dioceses of very unequal size, whose seats, except for Fribourg, are all in border regions. Moreover, their boundaries as well as territorial conditions are to a great extent still canonically "provisional," even if this *provisorium* has already been in existence for more than a century. A serious revaluation as required by the Conciliar decree *Christus Dominus* has so far hardly begun. The formal elevation of the Ticino canton to a diocese is in praparation, since the now-retired Bishop of Basel, Franziskus von Streng, offered to relinquish the annexation title of Lugano (first added in 1888).

The number of priests in the various dioceses gives some indication of their size: Basel, 706; Chur, 425; Lausanne-Geneva-Fribourg, 365; St. Gallen, 225; Sion, 138. Two dioceses, Basel and Chur, are especially criticized for their boundaries and size relationship, and because their bishops' sees are located on the periphery of the respective dioceses. That Catholic inner Switzerland does not have its own diocese with its seat in Lucerne can be explained historically. There, the papal *nuntius* resided for nearly 300 years, until 1873, the time of the so-called *Kulturkampf*. Since World War I, the *nunciatura apostolica* has had its seat in the Confederation capital, Bern.

In 1961, shortly before the Council, Rome provisionally approved the statutes of the Swiss Bishops' Conference. Meanwhile it has become clear that progress must be made in solving urgent common tasks on a national level. The Bishops' Conference has now established a secretariat in Sion, meets more frequently, and elects its chairman on a rotating basis. The present chairman for a three-year term is Johannes Vonderach, Bishop of Chur. Together with Professor Sustar, the seminary Rector, he has evidenced a new style. The Rector is his contact man with the press, which previously learned about the holding of a Bishops' Conference only from a noncommittal communiqué issued afterwards. Now, by contrast, the press is invited beforehand and immediately following the sessions the bishops hold a news conference which includes a question period.

PASTORAL PLANNING FOR ALL OF SWITZERLAND

More drastic, however, is the decision to use the methods of social research in investigating pastoral relations for all of Switzerland and to draw up a plan for the future shape of the pastorate. This plan is to be binding on all dioceses. The task has been entrusted to a commission composed of priests and laymen. A prime consideration in making this decision is the ever-growing dearth of priests. True, the number of diocesan priests has remained constant since 1950. But in this same period the Swiss population has increased from 4.7 million to 6 million; the increase affects Catholics to a far greater extent than it does Protestants, not only among the Swiss themselves, but especially among the foreigners in their midst. This is principally due to the large number of Catholic workers from Italy.

Between 1950 and 1960, when the last census was made, the Catholic population had increased from 1,900,000 to 2,400,000; of this one-half-million increase 242,000 are Swiss and 262,000 are foreigners. By 1960 Catholics made up 45.4 per cent of the population. Today the proportion may be 48 per cent, that is, above 2,900,000 Catholics. To put it another way: hardly a single new diocesan priest is available for the one million Catholics added since 1950.

Even though there are already a considerable number of vacant posts, circumstances continually call for the establishment of new pastoral posts. If these are estimated at only four per year—as a matter of fact there are many more—the prediction for 1970 is 204 unoccupied ministerial posts, and by 1980 the figure will be 477. The forecast is based on the premise that in the coming years the priestly death rate and the number of newly-ordained will remain constant. Unfortunately this is hardly possible, since the average age is fifty-five. In recent years, the deaths of priests in Switzerland have exceeded the number of ordinations.

Not only has the population increased; it has also shifted with the urban and industrial migration. The clergy seldom accompany the migrants and generally stay behind in the villages and towns among the dwindling population. The result is that there are now city parishes with 15,000 or more Catholics, in which an average priest must care for 3,000 or more faithful, while in the country, especially in the mountain regions, one priest often has only 300 persons or less to look after.

More effective distribution of the clergy is an urgent problem for the new planning program, but this is extremely difficult to achieve. Often there are complicated legal conditions. There are very few parishes in the Catholic rural areas that are willing to relinquish a centuries-old right to their own pastors. Nor can a bishop remove a properly installed pastor against his will or that of the parishioners. Moreover, not every country priest is suited for the urban or specialized ministry. The same applies to priests who for many years have taught in secondary schools. In principle they should be replaced by laity, but in concrete cases this cannot always be done.

Inevitably, however, deacons and laymen (and women) will increasingly assume tasks that have been discharged by priests. To this end the pastoral planning commission has submitted to the Bishops' Conference a plan for the implementation of a permanent diaconate. Under its terms deacons will be empowered to assume responsibility for entire Christian communities in regions where no priests are available.

Another difficult problem is the revision of the financial structure. Hitherto the bishops have not only lacked the wherewithal for matters of common interest—until the Council they had a mere 10,000 francs (less than $3,000) available, but the individual diocese likewise has few sources of income. In many cantons a voluntary system or a compulsory, state-administered church tax system provides a guaranteed, fixed income, but this revenue is almost exclusively for the use of the local ecclesiastical treasury: that is, it is directly earmarked for the use of individual parishes, an amalgamation of parishes, or, at best, for perhaps certain cantonal institutions. The tax money is never available for the benefit of the entire diocese or the Swiss Church as a whole. In Germany, by contrast, the situation is the exact opposite: compulsory church tax revenue from the parishes and additional sums from other sources flow into the diocesan treasury.

Such diocesan concentration of fiscal and administrative power would hardly find approbation in Switzerland. But it is important to focus attention on the disadvantages of the decentralized Swiss system and to study possibilities for reducing them to a minimum.

First, a way must be found for a just distribution of funds between well-to-do and needy parishes and institutions. Secondly, supraparochial projects and movements require financial assistance to relieve clerical and lay leaders from enervating and time-consuming fund-raising chores. For the present a central, voluntary tax system would not only remedy this problem but would also simultaneously eliminate the proliferation of countless individual collections. Meanwhile, an emergency source of national income has been found through *Fastenopfer*, the annual all-Swiss Lenten collection.

CONQUEST OF PARTICULARISM THROUGH MISSION RENEWAL

The idea of the *Fastenopfer* goes back to the Mission Year 1960–1961 and so precedes the Council. Until then the various religious congregations had been primarily concerned about their own missions and so were in competition with one another. This same attitude was characteristic of youth organizations in their parish work. But after the initiation of *Fastenopfer,* a communal sense of cooperation began to appear. Activities were no longer restricted to fund raising and consequently a great deal was accomplished by renewing and modernizing the traditional concepts of the mission world. For example, the highlight of the Mission Year was a huge departure ceremony for missionaries in the Cathedral of St. Gallen and in the presence of Cardinal Gregorio Pietro Agagianian. In the ceremony lay assistants participated side by side with priests and religious. Thus for the first time, the vocation of lay assistant was given recognition along with the traditional missionary vocations.

The financial returns of *Fastenopfer* exceeded all expectations. Whereas, for example, the annual Advent collection in all dioceses for Fribourg University usually amounted to one million francs ($250,000), the Lenten collection for the missions totalled 17 million francs (nearly $4,000,000).

Since then, the Lenten collection has been equally distributed between the missions and pastoral work at home. A commission of clergy and laity decides on the allocation of these funds and publicly accounts for them. Development projects in the mission areas are reviewed by a commission of experts. These projects have proven to be so effective that they can also qualify for grants from the Swiss Confederation's office for technical aid to developing countries.

The other half of the Lenten collection, designated for domestic needs, is also intended for "development projects," that is, for new undertakings such as prefabricated churches for needy areas of the *diaspora.* As long as the above-mentioned central revenue system is lacking, however, this sum is unavoidably absorbed by maintenance costs of numerous subsidized operations, and so a quarter of the total is placed at the disposal of the bishops. The total collection ranged from 4.2 million francs (nearly $1,000,000) in 1962 to 9.1 million francs (nearly $2,000,000) in 1966 (India's famine year). This year (1968) the higher amount is again expected.

An analysis of these collections on a per capita basis and according to cantons provides a surprising insight into the regionally differentiated attitudes of Swiss Catholics to such an undertaking. The pendulum swings wide: from 6.67 francs (about $1.60) per Catholic (including children) in Canton St. Gallen in eastern Switzerland to 0.82 francs (about $0.20) in the West Swiss canton of Vaud (Lausanne).

THE "INDIVIDUALISTIC" MINORITIES

St. Gallen is the capital of a canton that was first established in the nineteenth century and is today 62 per cent Catholic. It is famous in history for its Benedictine abbey (dissolved in 1805) founded by the Irish monk and missionary Gallus, after whom it was named. The postwar economic boom made an impact here later than in the western cantons. This delayed impact is to be explained by the severe blow dealt by the depression in the thirties to its delicate textile industry. This canton has continually produced the most missionaries, and this small, enclosed diocese,[6] which includes in addition only the tiny canton of Appenzell, has taken the lead in the Lenten collection.

Canton Vaud, by contrast, with its capital, Lausanne, constitutes by far the largest and the economically leading canton of French Switzerland. The Vaud, which is only 27.1 per cent Catholic, is after Bern (19.1 per cent) the "most Protestant" canton of Switzerland. This *diaspora* situation as well as the low social status of the Catholics here do not provide the decisive reason for their poor showing in the Lenten collection. It is, of course, true that the Lausanne Catholics for the most part have migrated from the large-family mountain and country regions of Fribourg and Valais (Wallis), and their first concern is the establishment of their livelihood in Lausanne. But, even Geneva, where migration has gradually put Catholics in a slight majority, and Fribourg, where they have always predominated (1960, 86 per cent), have remained in the lowest group of contributors to the Lenten collection. The same is true of the nearly all-Protestant canton Neuchâtel

[6] The present diocese is the heritage of the former Abbey-principality of St. Gallen and the Diocese of Konstanz (Germany), which until 1814 included the largest part of Switzerland up to the Gotthard line. Appenzell at first belonged to the Chur diocese, but since 1866 has been provisionally annexed to St. Gallen. St. Gallen is not only territorially but also administratively a "cantonal diocese" with influence in the choice of councillors in the cantonal Parliament and in a Catholic "administration council." These institutions play a far greater role than in most other cantons in keeping confessional consciousness alive and, as a consequence, confessional opposition.

and of the almost exclusively Catholic, Italian canton, Ticino, which forms a world in itself.

The language minorities, then, do not account for the poor support they give to Church drives that concern Switzerland as a whole.[7] This impression must be modified somewhat by the relatively good returns of the trilingual mountain canton of Grisons, where the Catholics principally speak Romansch and Italian and consistently reach a per capita quota above the Swiss average. Perhaps the two cantonal minorities here feel more closely integrated with the Swiss Church because of their direct ties with the Bishop of Chur.

ECUMENICAL CENTERS AND CONTACTS

The Catholicism of French Switzerland is almost at the opposite pole from the "organized" Catholicism of German Switzerland. The French Swiss is more attracted to personalities than to institutions. He is more apt to follow the ups and downs of French movements and to prefer the spontaneous and improvised to the perfectionism of German Switzerland. He does this in relation to the ideal of a "Church of the poor" as expressed in the new type of religious order established by Charles de Foucauld, and in the style expressed by the *Taize* formula, "Dynamisme du Provisoire" (the dynamism of the provisional).

Taize was founded by two French Swiss, Roger Schutz and Max Thurian. Their monastery consists of monks from various Protestant denominations, but its ecumenical work and well-developed vernacular liturgy have attracted many Catholics. Today its influence has spread

---

[7] The picture of the recent Lenten collection is modified somewhat by the findings of the long-established collection for the *diaspora*, the so-called "Inland Mission." Neuchâtel and Fribourg here reached an average almost equal to that of the country, while Vaud, Geneva, Wallis, and Ticino, as well as Basel and Bern again were to be found on the bottom rungs. At the head are the ancient Catholic regions of inner Switzerland, from which this "mission" is launched and which thereby extended aid to their own migrants who had wandered to the predominantly Protestant industrial zones, notably Zürich. How much the situation has changed is shown by the fact that Zürich today is no longer a recipient but a donor city. According to the absolute figures of donations, Zürich is barely exceeded by Lucerne. According to per capita count, it is in ninth place. The best per capita returns came from the tiny canton of Obwalden, the canton with the lowest income tax quota!

in all directions so that in the territory, which is also the historical area of Cluny, it fulfills the ancient role of Burgundy in consciously working for universal reconciliation.

A community of women similar to Taize has been established on Swiss soil in Grandchamps near Neuchâtel, with a branch house in Gelterkinden near Basel.

Western Switzerland, then, may be regarded,[8] and not merely because of the World Council of Churches in Geneva, as especially significant for the ecumenical movement. Oscar Cullmann, the Protestant New Testament scholar and church historian at Basel, popularized "Unity Prayer Week" among Protestants before the Council. He made it even more popular with his intriguing suggestion of an ecumenical collection (Protestants collecting for Catholics works and vice versa). And that great renewer of Protestant theology, Karl Barth, has in his later years repeatedly sought discussion with Catholics (which formerly he held only in private with Hans Urs von Balthasar). The Council deeply influenced him and he decided, on the occasion of the post-Conciliar theological congress, to make a "Protestant journey" to Rome. His account of that journey appears in a small work entitled *Ad Limina Apostolorum.*[9]

Since the beginning of the Council there has appeared a Protestant ecumenical series *Begegnung* (Encounter) edited by one of Barth's successors, Heinrich Ott, and also published in Basel and Lucerne. In

[8] We mean here the zone along the Jura mountains, in which the language boundary runs through Biel (Bienne), and which ends in northwestern Switzerland at Basel. Basel too belonged to Burgundy for nearly 100 years (912–1006) before it was annexed to the German Reich. Accordingly, the possessions of the Bishop of Basel penetrated far into French-speaking Jura: indeed, this latter remained episcopal state territory until 1815. Basel's intellectual influence extends as far as Strasbourg, which is represented not only by the Protestant commuter theologian (Basel-Paris) Oscar Cullmann, but also by the bilingual Catholic theologian, Professor Hans Urs von Balthasar.

For ecumenism Basel offers a long humanistic tradition of tolerance. It is here that the separation of Church and State at the beginning of the century found a fruitful soil, which gives rise to the hope that theologians may open the way for institutional ecumenical initiative on the university level (and perhaps, eventually, a chair of Catholic theology at the secular university?).

[9] Karl Barth, *Ad Limina Apostolorum* (Zürich, 1967). In a letter to the Jesuit biweekly *Orientierung* (Zürich) Barth said that, in spite of the fact that he is "a stubborn Evangelical theologian," in his retirement he is occupying himself "almost full time with Catholic matters, old and new."

this series French-Swiss theologians from the Evangelical faculties of Geneva (Franz J. Leenhardt) and Neuchâtel (Jean-Jacques von Allmen) are represented.

These faculties, together with that of Lausanne, have taken the initiative in cooperation with the universities of Basel and Fribourg and established a Swiss Theological Society (*Schweizerische Theologische Gesellschaft*) which includes Protestants, Old-Catholics, and Roman Catholics. One of its first conferences was devoted to the critical subject "Kanon im Kanon," that is, to internal biblical criteria. The Catholic viewpoint was presented by the New Testament expert of the Swiss Mission Society of Bethlehem-Immensee, Georg Schelbert, while Pierre Bonnard from Lausanne represented the various Protestant viewpoints. Both men, incidentally, are connected with the worldwide ecumenical Bible movement. Schelbert represented the Roman Catholics at the first confidential meetings with the Protestant Bible associations. In 1967 Bonnard presented the Sorbonne with the translation of the Epistle to the Romans, the first product of the *Bible Oecumenique*, which is jointly edited by Catholics, Protestants, and Orthodox. Although its Swiss collaborators are mainly Protestants, Fribourg exegetes also participated under the patronage of Federal Councillor Roger Bonvin, a Catholic from Canton Valais. An important seminar of the same theological society, which is presided over by the Neuchâtel Protestant ecumenical theologian, Jean-Louis Leuba, was devoted to the theology of marriage. The society thus did serious preparatory work on possible solutions of the mixed marriage problem.

MIXED MARRIAGE AS CRUX AND TEST

Perhaps in no other country does mixed marriage represent the "crux" and "test" of ecumenical *rapprochement* than in Switzerland. Immediately after the announcement of the Council, a Basel group took the initiative and prepared a petition which was then presented by the former Bishop of Basel, Franziskus von Streng. Their chief consultant was Dr. Theodore Bovet, a Protestant physician and well-known marriage counsellor who, for his part, recognized the sacramental character of marriage.

The *votum* submitted to the pope at the end of the third Council-session aroused certain hopes in Switzerland. In 1965 these, however, were almost totally destroyed by the Spring Instruction of the Holy Office. The first commentary of the Swiss Bishops' Conference on this Instruction did not improve the effect. Indeed, it increased public apprehension. Then an ecumenical weekend conference of academicians held at the University of Zürich was devoted to the marriage question. Soon after the Council, officially permanent groups, established to maintain contacts between the Swiss Bishops' Conference and the Swiss Evangelical Church Federation and between the Roman Catholic and Old-Catholic Churches, held intensive talks on this subject. Finally, the three national Church bodies issued a joint statement on the mixed marriage problem and in it emphasized pastoral care for existing confessionally-mixed marriages and expressed a decisive wish for the modification of Roman Catholic regulations. Although the statement did not contain many concrete suggestions or offer solutions, it did improve the climate between the Churches.

MIXED MARRIAGE VOTE AT THE BISHOPS' SYNOD

Switzerland was represented by Bishop Johannes Vonderach of Chur, whose viewpoint on the mixed marriage problem had attracted considerable attention. The Swiss example of dialogue in this matter was immediately seized upon by Cardinal Bea for the purpose of improving the ecumenical climate. Although Vonderach's far-reaching suggestion regarding the reform of Canon Law on mixed marriage was not carried out, the Swiss were pleased that, at the Synod, the German bishops dissociated themselves from the canonists of the old school. The latter had successfully spurred opposition to decentralization concerning mixed marriage rights. Their influence also was manifest in Ottaviani's Instruction, which represented a relapse from the Conciliar *votum*.

Official talks on the mixed marriage question between the Secretariat for Unity and the World Council of Churches provoked reactions that varied from puzzlement to anger. Although the talks resulted in a joint recommendation, the substance of the talks reached the Bishops' Synod only after they had been filtered through the former Holy Office and then only indirectly. As a result Cardinal Bea was unable officially and in the name of his Secretariat to report on the talks. It was just as regrettable that the synod did not react to the recommendations on mixed marriage submitted to it by the Lay Congress that convened in Rome at the same time. Indeed, according to the information provided at a news conference, the synod did not even permit Cardinal Maurice Roy of Quebec to read the document, because the synod could only deal with questions submitted by the pope and was not concerned with other matters.

Yet it was noted in Switzerland that the non-Catholic observers at the Lay Congress expressed a generally favorable opinion. This was true of their spokesman, the Swiss Hans-Ruedi Weber of the Ecumenical Institute of the World Council of Churches at Bossey near Geneva. His idea, that ecumenism must consist primarily of common work in the world, however, has not yet penetrated all quarters. There are still voices, even if they are justly regarded as not objective, that wish to make every concession to Catholics dependent on the reform of the canonical regulations on mixed marriages.

CONFESSIONAL EXCEPTION LAW

Primary among such concessions is the proposed repeal of the anti-Catholic *Ausnahmeartikel* (Exception Article) of the Swiss Federal Constitution. The Constitution originated in 1848 and established the existing Federal State, which the Catholic cantons, then seeking independence, had opposed. Their *Sonderbund* (Separate League), in part a response to the illegal dissolution of monasteries in the so-called "radical" camp, was destroyed in a brief military action. The victors expelled the Jesuits, who were also formally denied "activity in Church and school" by the Constitution. An amendment in 1874 strengthened the ban. The erection of new monasteries or the restoration of demolished ones was likewise prohibited; in addition the establishment and alteration of dioceses were made subject to government approval.

Today leading politicians regard these constitutional provisions as anachronistic. In the fifties the Federal government issued a relatively broad-minded interpretation of the Jesuit ban: Jesuits may not preach officially, especially on radio or television, but are allowed to give talks and disseminate information. In two predominantly Catholic cantons the Benedictines and the Cistercians, respectively, reoccupied a partly abandoned monastery. There is no general conviction, however, that the referendum on this question, required for a constitutional amendment, would at this time be successful, and there appears to be evidence of widespread latent resistance from the older generation. The fear of an "invasion" of Jesuits is irrational. In Switzerland as well as in the surrounding countries, the upcoming generation of Jesuits cannot even meet the personnel requirements of existing institutions.

The same applies to all religious vocations. The establishment of the Spanish *Opus Dei* in Switzerland was observed with some surprise. Of course, this community, which Rome no longer recognizes as a secular institute, falls under the constitutional ban even less than all the congregations and religious societies that have been established in Switzerland in the 120 years since the Constitution.

Concern for the problem of vocations was one reason for the pre-Council formation of an alliance of the superiors of religious orders in Switzerland. Although the religious boarding and day schools, especially the much sought-after intermediary schools for boys and for girls, continue to prosper (the boys are taught mostly by Benedictines and the girls by the Sisters of Menzingen and Ingenbohl), they no longer supply the number of vocations by which it was hoped they would compensate for the vocations that the country regions once supplied.

In the public intermediate schools of the large cities, which are predominantly Protestant, religious instruction is provided by both confessions, but officially only in the lower classes. The improvement of these conditions, especially the presence of the Church in the trade schools and in all activities affecting problems of daily life, is a common ecumenical goal of the churches, for which the use of lay teams is being considered and, in some places, is actually being tried.

One of the most gratifying developments of post-Conciliar Catholicism in Switzerland is the large enrollment in the four-year lay-theology courses and two-year "faith course." Some 4,500 participants have already taken these courses. The executive secretary, Joseph Duss-von Werdt in Zürich, is a layman with a doctorate in theology.

The practice, so widespread in Germany, of studying theology at the university in conjunction with other subjects (mathematics, languages, and so forth) has not yet become a vogue in Switzerland. At present it is unrealistic to attempt the same here. Catholics might very well aim for the modest goal of affiliating existing seminaries and theological institutions with the secular universities in the large cities or at least of establishing closer contacts between them. Such a plan has been drawn up for Zürich. It is, however, in competition with another plan for the expansion of the existing theological faculty in Lucerne, where a new university is being planned.

THE FIELD OF THE LAITY—CATHOLIC POLITICS?

The Council's elevation of the status of the laity has made an impact in Switzerland, where, as in a number of countries, the reform had to some extent been anticipated. Among university students and graduates, whose spiritual care in German Switzerland is primarily in the hands of the Jesuits, a lay spirituality has developed. Special credit for this and for the establishment of student communities must go to Hans Urs von Balthasar.[10] Among the adult middle class something similar is being done by the Pallotines, who publish a lively magazine called *Ferment*, and by the Franciscan Third Order, which recently established two modern centers, conducted by the Capuchins.

In general the trend is toward adult education institutions, which have taken over many of the functions formerly fulfilled by retreat houses and the like. One new form is called the "Social Seminar." Another group, "Aktion 365," is inspired by the provocative and controversial techniques of the German Jesuit street preacher, Father Leppich.

One of the most important new institutions is the lay training center *Paulus Akademie* in Zürich, under the direction of the well-known theology professor, Dr. Johannes Feiner. It is modelled after the famous German academies (Protestant and Catholic) and the highly successful Protestant *Heimstätte* (homesteads) in Switzerland. Their basic principle is to be open to all men, especially to those who otherwise avoid close ties with specific organizations. Their weekend conferences treat controversial theological questions, such as the Resurrection, the modern concept of God, and faith; timely subjects such as Vietnam; or inflammatory subjects such as "Catholic schools."

Views on this last subject vary considerably. While in St. Gallen there are regular election clashes for and against the retention of confessional schools, in Chur a large and long-established Catholic school was speedily relinquished to the State after larger subsidies for the school were turned down in a referendum. A local priest observed:

[10] Von Balthasar, who once belonged to the Jesuit Order, left it before taking his final vows. He conducts a lay institute and from his base in Basel is also active as a free-lance author and lecturer.

"Anyway we will soon have a majority of school children in Chur."

A similar difference exists between Basel and Zürich. In Basel Catholic teachers work in public schools and excepting one Catholic school, all pupils attend public school to implement the "presence" of the Church. In Zürich, by contrast, Catholics have continued to build secondary Catholic schools and to expand existing ones.

Although the Swiss generally hold that politics is the special field of the laity and that the priest has no business interfering in it, this is not adhered to everywhere. The coupling of religion and politics, especially among Catholics, has deep historical roots. There has been the defensive position of Catholics since 1848, and especially since the *Kulturkampf* of the seventies. Catholic associations (even for gymnastics and sports), Catholic trade unions, and Catholic political parties have been prized or accepted both in so-called "traditional" regions where the "liberals" who did not belong to this bloc were regarded as second-class Catholics and in the *diaspora* of the expanding cities where the stream of country migrants was noticeably attracted by the Socialist Party and trade unions.

The influence of the Council has worked against any of the divisive groups of Catholics speaking in the name of the Church and for the realistic acceptance of pluralism as the consequence of secularization. For that reason it is understandable that politically liberal Catholics welcome the reforms of the Council more readily than the die-hard representatives of traditional Catholic "solidarity."

INTERNAL REFORM

The renewal trends of the Council have here and there encountered resistance from conservative Catholic politicians, who in turn are supported by well-known clergy favorable to authoritarian leadership. On the other hand, discerning pastors were conscious of the opportunity that the universal openness of the Council provided. Notably, the Church could offer a new image of itself to those who, for whatever reason, had emigrated—an image that more clearly than heretofore distinguished the essential from the nonessential and the eternal from the ephemeral. All this, of course, comes more easily to a Capuchin who makes house visits or a Jesuit who gives speeches and attends conferences throughout the country than to many parish priests who have been trained under the old "system" and have been primarily con-

cerned with keeping the sheep in the fold. Inevitably certain pastors
and deans have reacted against open discussions, especially those which
appear in the ten Catholic daily newspapers in the *diaspora* areas (for
example, *Neue Zürcher Nachrichten*), for these papers opened their
columns to Council discussion and one even initiated critical reviews
of sermons.

The Catholic press, however, saw in the new outburst of inner-
Catholic dialogue a new, or even last, justification for its existence. For
some time it appeared as though internal Catholic criticism was only
possible in independent secular newspapers. Indeed, since the Council
that sector of the press has become much more receptive to theological
and Church matters. For example, the Conciliar and post-Conciliar
commentaries of the world-famous and lengthy *Neue Zürcher Zeitung*
received a wide response. But they were understandably written from
the lofty elegance of Switzerland's "grand old lady" of the press and
lacked the candid housecleaning approach that is so urgently needed
today, especially in the relations between the younger and older
generations.

Such post-Conciliar housecleaning talks should assist the parish and
diocesan pastoral councils. These have been established in Switzerland
but pastors have not always been willing to cooperate. In some places
the establishment of new, and parallel, committees has merely increased the unproductiveness of existing committees, while in many
places there are parishes that since ancient times have had an active
and effective system of assemblies which even today have the right of
electing their own pastors. No one in Switzerland seriously wishes to
abolish this time-honored right, in spite of the Conciliar recommendation and regulations that would make this practice dependent upon
the bishop's choice.

The State, on a cantonal level, still formally exercises its right of
jurisdiction in the selection of a bishop, at least in the largest diocese
(Basel), as was the case in the election of Basel's new bishop.[11] Other
bishops in Switzerland are traditionally elected by the cathedral chap-

[11] Seven out of nine cantons are permitted to have a hand in the Basel episcopal
elections, whose governments send representatives who are permitted to examine
a list of six candidates drawn up by the cathedral chapter and may eliminate three
of them. Mostly it is a mere formality. The cathedral chapter makes a free choice
of candidates and then Vatican acceptance and confirmation of the elected bishop
are necessary. The present voting procedure can be traced back to a regulation of
1828.

ter. A growing number of persons think that it would be much more meaningful to drop those procedures that have become anachronistic and to let priests and laity vote directly for their bishops. But as long as no concrete new forms for such representation are found (which would also require Vatican approval), the old methods will prevail.

SWITZERLAND IN "MUTATION"

In order to understand the role of Swiss Catholics in society, one must first of all understand the Swiss mentality in politics. It is a mixture of stickiness and common sense. In church matters the Swiss will generally show the same conservatism that he shows in politics. Whereas in economic life he is entirely capable of thinking expansively and finds regrouping or constant adjustment quite normal in huge industrial concerns, he prefers a rigid frame of stability in his politics and does not lightly permit the *status quo* to be questioned. Although he exercises, it is true, his democratic right to criticize the government, as well as his own superiors, he would find the hasty abdication or removal of his cantonal and Federal governments unthinkable. He complains about the excruciating slowness of road construction, the frustrating inequities of the cantonal school systems, and the educational budget for cantonal universities; yet he is aware of the necessity of regional and national planning and would never surrender the autonomy of the individual communities or the sovereignty of the cantons. In short, political stability is everything. Here there is no unrest to fear. This is the basis of Switzerland's reputation as a paradise for international and intercontinental economic enterprises.

But within Switzerland itself the Swiss can no longer accept this contentment. More and more leaders, especially the younger ones, are concerned that the rapid development of the rest of the world may leave Switzerland behind. There is more talk of "Helvetian Malaise" and "Swiss survival." There is concern about the declining voting percentage and the political paralysis afflicting the much needed revision of cantonal and Federal constitutions. Until today constitutional change has been a patchwork matter—66 partial-revisions of the Federal Constitution alone. Little wonder that the economic and population changes have outgrown and strained the whole structure. For the past two years there has been talk of a "general revision." The traditional structures of Switzerland are being officially questioned.

THE CHURCH'S CONTRIBUTION?

What are the Catholics doing about all this? What can or should the Church contribute? If recent literature on the fate and future of Switzerland is used as a source, the conclusion is discouraging, for the works do not mention even an indirect contribution expected of the Church. Nevertheless, a sober sociological evaluation of the Churches, all the more in that many cantons officially recognize them as *Landes-kirchen*, that is, as cantonal corporate institutions, must also be considered in studying the Swiss transformation. A Church can be a restraining factor, if it is itself stagnating, or it can be a driving force, if it is capable of changing and developing itself. As a matter of fact, the Churches have played their role in the formation of an era and the outlook of the era was conducive to stability. They have favored supporting concepts of family, private property, authority, and obedience. This close interlacing of values, however, has produced a static ideology which is regarded as the answer and is identified with Christianity. But precisely here is the danger that the Church-oriented Swiss will withdraw from new solutions in the social and political sphere, even when they intrude upon him.

One can ask whether this danger is greater for Catholics or for Protestants. The Fribourg pastoral theologian Alois Müller[12] recently gave an interview on this subject for a special issue of the Geneva magazine *Choisir*, devoted to the characteristic theme, "Growth or Decline of Switzerland."[13] According to Müller, the danger for Catholics and Protestants appears wherever they enjoy recognition as public corpora-

[12] Alois Müller first attracted public attention for a statement favoring a socialist proposal that would have forbidden atomic weapons in Switzerland. The Bishop of Fribourg publicly opposed it. It is to the University of Fribourg's credit that in spite of this it appointed Müller a professor.

Müller is author of a theological investigation of the problem of obedience in the Church, *Das Problem von Befehl und Gehorsam im Leben der Kirche* (Einsiedeln-Zürich, 1964). Father Müller is also spiritual advisor of the Swiss Student Association. His theses are especially appealing to students—especially in Fribourg—among whom a trend toward socialism is perceptible. Contributing to this student orientation are the influence of the encyclical *Populorum Progressio*, and the proximity of the Communists in West, that is, French-speaking, Switzerland.

[13] The title recalls the famous pastoral letter of the former Archbishop of Paris, Cardinal Emmanuel Suhard, *Essor ou déclin de l'Eglise* (1947).

tions and are established as *Landeskirchen*.[14] But an additional handicap exists for the Catholics. Since the eighteenth century, and especially since the time of the *Kulturkampf* and the *Syllabus of Errors*, the Catholic Church has taken a negative attitude toward social changes. In Switzerland the odium of the *Sonderbund* had a notably strong effect, so that Catholics opposed progressive tendencies because they were, at the time, identified with anticlerical and sometimes even anti-Christian ideas. As the rebel "underdogs" they had to "confirm" themselves in the new state, that is, continually prove their loyalty.

Historically, this clearly appears toward the end of World War I. A general strike was called throughout the industrial cities. The liberal Federal State was threatened and was saved by the state-subsidized troops from inner, rural, Catholic Switzerland. The Catholics failed to take advantage of the opportunity to join the socialist movement; thereafter, they were immediately integrated into the bourgeois class, which "monopolized" the national mind. They were rewarded by the reinstatement of a papal nuncio (which annoyed the Protestants considerably more than it helped the Catholics), and after World War II they succeeded for a time in placing three conservative Catholics in the seven-man Federal Council (a nonmunificent concession).

The Catholic workers were pressed from two sides. On the one hand, the bishops had forbidden them to join the socialist trade unions; on the other hand, when they formed their own Christian trade unions, they were harassed by their socialist colleagues and restricted by con-

[14] Müller points out that the idea of the *Landeskirche* (cantonal Church as a corporate body) is more characteristic of German Switzerland than of western Switzerland, where since 1907 Geneva and since 1905 Basel have enjoyed separation of Church and State. The cantons of Bern and Zürich in German Switzerland have only recently restored Roman legal rights which they had lost to the Old Catholics during the *Kulturkampf*. In Zürich this restoration came one month after the death of Pope John XXIII, which had a favorable influence on the local climate. More recently, the former purely Protestant canton of Schaffhausen also restored legal rights to Catholics as a result of the "ecumenical climate." The occasion for this was the previous tax regulation by which Catholics had to contribute to the support of the Protestant Church in addition to their own. In the canton of Zürich all business until recently had to pay a church tax that went exclusively to the Protestant Church.

Some Catholics were opposed to these changes on the ground that they would inevitably lead to passivity on the part of Catholics. On the other hand, the Zürich Catholics no longer wished to be beholden to the donations of Catholics of inner Switzerland.

servative Catholic entrepreneurs. On the political level, the members of the Christian trade union had no other choice but to vote for the Christian Party along with their conservative fellow Catholics or to vote socialist, and so, in the eyes of the Church, to deny their faith. For a long time joining the Christian trade unions meant isolating oneself in a remote nook of society.

Now that socialists are finally represented in the Federal government, it is seldom that Catholics will form an alliance with them on the cantonal level. The old accusation, which even the most zealous workers' chaplain was at a loss to deny, namely that the Church is in cahoots with capital, is continually reaffirmed by its close association with bourgeois politics, even though in Switzerland today the charge has ceased to have the influence that it commanded when it was still possible to speak of a proletariat.

The Protestant Church, wherever it was long established, likewise presented itself as a "bourgeois institution." But its pastors could freely join the socialist or free-thinking or farmers' parties. For a long time an Evangelical party as such did not exist, and where it now exists, it is not regarded as representative of the Protestant Church.

Since Church consciousness was less developed in the Reformed Church, this commitment in restraint of change made an even less significant appearance in the Reformed Churches as a whole. Moreover, the Reformed Church had no historical mortgage to pay and reacted to social developments more impartially, uncritically, and less dogmatically. In the first quarter of our century Leonhard Ragaz was a teacher in the Zürich theological faculty and a leader of the religious socialists of Switzerland. His influence on Karl Barth may be described as profound. For his part Emil Brunner was impelled to deal with social problems in part because he had been influenced by the papal social encyclicals.

Moreover a number of Reformed clergymen had been active socialists and even today Protestant church announcements appear in the weekly edition of the socialist newspaper in Zürich, where one looks in vain for Catholic information. This absence is regrettable, inasmuch as a large percentage of workers have migrated, and still come, from Catholic regions; many could be reached through this newspaper.

But in Switzerland today, the "social problem" is no longer the "workers' question." Additionally, it may be said that, although nearly one million guest workers present an acute problem, the over-all social question is not concentrated in a specific area such as industry or agriculture, but affects nearly all fields of activity. In the public con-sciousness it acquires an ever greater world dimension. Thus the key question for the Church is: is the Church on the side of development, openness, and world solidarity, or is it supporting with obstinacy that narrowness which with some appropriateness has been called "church tower politics"?

EFFECTIVENESS OF THE COUNCIL

In this respect the Council and its aftermath have had a significance that is not to be underestimated. What amazed both Catholics and non-Catholics at the Council was this: discussion. And the generally observed effect was again the same: a discussing Church, a Church that questions many things hitherto regarded as unchangeable. Because the Church itself did this, because it is on the move and prepared to make changes as a matter of principle—for this reason it has again awakened interest. It is not only possible to quarrel with Catholics but it is also possible seriously and meaningfully to discuss with them. Because the Catholic is no longer under a dictatorship and subordinated to a uni-form program of action but has been emancipated by his Church in order to search for pluralistic contemporary realizations of the Christian message, he meets with less distrust. In particular, when humor, ob-jectivity, and self-criticism reveal that he is detached from his own con-cerns and no longer represents a "bloc," he encounters a greater will-ingness to cooperate. In this way, convinced and zealous Catholics with professional competence find an entrée to groups, for example in the mass media, that, in the main, had been closed to them.

If this is valid for the external impression that the post-Conciliar Church makes, it is not yet certain to what extent the changes in the Church have won internal acceptance and have been carried out. Large-scale surveys are not available, but there is a convergence of opinions based on a considerable number of local experiences.

One local survey is especially revealing because it was made in a town that is fairly representative of German Switzerland: Rapperswil. Its predominantly Catholic population was questioned extensively on their reactions to a lecture series on the Council.[15]

Rapperswil, founded in the thirteenth century, is a picturesque town of 8,500 persons situated on the upper end of the Lake of Zürich. Even before the Reformation it had been a source of contention in the dispute between Central Switzerland and Zürich. The town became an outpost against Reformed Zürich as a result of a Catholic victory in the Battle of Kappel in which Zwingli fell.

Today the Catholic community consists of 6,000 persons, including 1,000 foreigners. Here Catholic "mother country" and *diaspora* meet. On the one hand, centuries-old traditions are kept alive by the natives who are reluctant to abandon or modify them. An example is the *Musikgesellschaft Caecilia*, the Church Choir, a dignified fraternity whose bylaws go back to the eighteenth century.

On the other hand, new conditions have developed: these are typical of heavily industrialized, confessionally-mixed populations with a Protestant majority. The changes are mainly to be explained by urban migration from the adjacent rural regions. Moreover, the surrounding industrial areas do not belong, as Rapperswil does, to the Canton and Diocese of St. Gallen, but to Zürich and to the Diocese of Chur. These various factors make minimal the ties of the migrant workers with the Rapperswil Catholic community.

As for politics a Christian-Social Party was founded at the beginning of the century, although until then the long-established Rapperswil Catholics voted for the liberal party. Today the Catholics are spread throughout all the parties.

The lecture series was reported at length in the local press, and, according to the survey, ecumenism had awakened the greatest interest. The majority was pleased most by the ecumenical contacts and the "opening" of the Church in all respects to the world. This overall impression outweighed "disappointment" over the Church's failure to solve marriage problems, such as mixed marriage and birth control.

The second greatest interest of the respondents was the position of the laity, specifically their relationship with the clergy and their role in regard to Catholic schools, trade unions, and so on. There appeared a

[15] *Neues Denken in der Kirche* (New Thinking in the Church), with essays by R. Schmid, L. Kaufmann, J. Feiner, W. Dirks, E. Egloff, J. Duss-von Werdt, P. Vogelsanger; edited by Max Lehner and Augustin Hasler (Lucerne-Munich, 1968).

certain sense of helplessness about lay collaboration with the clergy: this was especially evident in the disappointment, voiced by the respondents, with clergy who apparently would not move with the times and were unwilling to have discussion or were unprepared for it. There was impatience in demanding the abolition of many details such as titles and the elaborate dress of the higher clergy and the Curia; moreover considerable annoyance was expressed at delays on these matters. The initial survey revealed little interest in the theological subjects which formed the background of the individual reforms and provided the coherence and guidelines of the Council's work. Later, these very topics occasioned tensions and aroused heated discussions.

According to the poll, the three main age groups reacted as follows:

1. The eighteen-to-thirty-year-olds were the most positive. The respondents unanimously professed to have a new, happier outlook on personal and religious problems. This, however, was the smallest group. A large majority in this age bracket did not attend the lectures. They were preoccupied with their professional training and with the care of their children, or, as was the case with the majority, they expected nothing significant or applicable from the Church or theology.

2. The majority of the thirty-to-fifty-five age group also reacted positively to the survey. It included many who do not attend church regularly. Most of them found that here at last the gulf had been bridged between what they themselves regarded as right and what the priests had told them. Though they recognized that priests are overworked, this group accused them of lacking a sense of professional involvement and of not keeping up with theological developments as laymen have to keep abreast of new developments in their professions.

   In the middle age group are also found the strongest critics of the "new thinking." They are mostly zealous churchgoers who think of the generally valid declarations of the Council only in terms of the small and narrow world of their little town and raise their objections from this perspective. Thus, the Council talks were judged by a teacher, described as "just-thinking and prudent," as "the greatest scandal in our Catholic community in thirty years."

   It is tragic that priests and chaplains meet more frequently with this group which continually blocks renewal in the Church and that they overestimate the significance of its views. This was the judgment of the specialist, a local resident, who evaluated the interviews.

3. In the age group of over fifty-five a strong minority surprised the survey-takers. Perhaps because their experience had made them wise and given them a broader perspective of thinking which is inner-directed and which compels them to a splendid, broad view of our faith, they are pleased with the new thinking. The majority of this age group does not oppose renewal, but regrets that they suffer under it and cannot come to terms with it. "Are we with our old-fashioned views no longer useful to the Church?" complained one old lady. Even some young people were touched by this consideration. Themselves open to change, they ask, "but how will my grandmother take this?"

The conclusions to draw from these findings are obvious: 1) There must be an intensified "postgraduate" training of the clergy. No longer may they seek refuge in the modern churches, vestments, and vessels expressing the new aesthetic direction of liturgical reform that especially in Switzerland existed before the Council, while bypassing the deeper reforms. 2) Real, patient, and reciprocal discussion must be fostered among small groups and between the generations. From the clergy is expected an increasing willingness to hold such discussions in informal groups, especially since the traditional Catholic associations, run by the clergy, no longer have much appeal.

ECCLESIA SEMPER REFORMANDA

Mario von Galli, S.J.,[16] the best-known Council reporter and commentator in the German-language area and the editor of the biweekly

---

[16] Mario von Galli continually speaks in Germany, Switzerland, and Austria on the theme, "Ecclesia semper reformanda," especially to those who are truly concerned about today's questions and tormented by them. In Orientierung, which he edits, he tries to reach precisely this public, not just those who are superficially confused or annoyed by this or that change. With a very simple format and layout the magazine has, without advertising or publicity, tripled its circulation since the Council.

Von Galli is also the author of the text in the monumental volume The Council and the Future (New York, 1967). His collaborator is the photographer Bernard Moosbrugger, whose photographs richly complement the commentary. Von Galli magazine *Orientierung* (Orientation) in Zürich, has a somewhat different classification that cuts across all age groups: 1) his first group, mostly university graduates, had many concrete hopes of the Council and are disappointed because not all their hopes have been realized; 2) his second group consists of a mixture of educated and simple people, including young persons, who find that the Council has caused everything to move and change; and 3) the third group is formed of those who would really like *to do* something, to go into action but do not know how. No one has really invited them or appealed to them to take up specific tasks. They miss guidance.

Von Galli sees the common basis of these apparently diverse disappointments in the past view that the Church consists primarily of external manifestations and regulations. In that perspective regulations were to be strictly observed and such conformity was accounted as right action. This position encouraged belief in pat answers. In this view, therefore, the removal of regulations does not mean that anything is "accomplished"; there has only been the negative act of abolition.

This group can only be satisfied if the emphasis is placed on the *spiritual* and *continuing* alignment of the Council in such a way that the point of departure should not be the individual documents themselves but the general direction that transcends all of them. As a matter of fact this approach surprisingly reveals the continuing novelty and timeliness of the Council. And *the* most penetrating, single dominant line is surely the conception of the Church on the move, the *Ecclesia semper reformanda*.

Among the Protestants too the expression "Reformata reformare" (to reform what has been reformed) is again valid. What is involved, as Paul VI said after the Council, is the continual *conversio*, the rethinking and turnabout of *metanoia*.

According to Alois Müller, among Swiss Catholics this should involve, in the political and social sphere, a readiness and courage to adopt courses that may be diametrically opposite to decisions taken in

---

has held great success with a series of thirteen commentaries on the Council televised for West German television under the direction of the well-known TV publicist, Werner Höfer. These have come out in book form in the German language, in collaboration with Karl Rahner and Otto Baumhauer, who also contributed to the TV series: *Reformation aus Rom: Die Katholische Kirche nach dem Konzil* (Tübingen, 1967).

the past. The future will show whether they have the courage to do this. Advance will also eventually depend on the openness of the Church in certain progressive countries. The Dutch example, which at first was rejected and maligned because of sensational press reports, is now followed with growing interest and good will. Developments in the Church of the United States are also beginning to receive wide attention.

Only the continual exercise of renewed civil courage can counteract the feeling of belonging to a Church that is frightened by its own courage. There is also needed what Pope John XXIII acquired from his consciousness of history and his trust in God: confidence.

5 : ITALY

Giuseppe De Rosa, S.J.

An inquiry into the state of the Catholic Church in Italy today may proceed in two ways: the presentation of a picture of the organization and the structure of the Catholic Church in Italy as complete as possible and furnished with all sorts of statistics; or penetration beyond the study of external structure and figures in an examination and measuring of the degree of vitality in Italian Catholicism.[1] Here both approaches will be attempted. The first three parts of this study will be devoted to the structural and organizational picture of the Catholic Church in Italy as well as to an account of its presence in Italian society; the fourth part, "The Vitality of Italian Catholicism," will undertake a

[1] The following works were consulted in the preparation of this study: *Annuario Pontificio 1967* (Vatican City, 1967); *Annuario Cattolico d'Italia 1961–1962* and *1966–1967* (Rome, 1962 and 1967); *Compendio Statistico Italiano 1960* (Rome, Istituto Centrale di Statistica, 1960); *Annuario Unione Cattolica Stampa Italiana 1964* (Rome, 1964); *Seminaria Ecclesiae Catholicae* (Rome, Typis Polyglottis Vaticanis, 1963); C. d'Agata, *Statistica Religiosa* (Milan, 1943); C. Falconi, *La Chiesa e le organizzazioni cattoliche in Italia, 1945–1955* (Turin, 1956); I. Weiss, *Politica dell'informazione* (Milan, 1961), Chapter VII, "La Stampa periodica cattolica in Italia," pp. 219–250; S. Burgalassi, "La sociologia del cattolicesimo in Italia," in *Orientamenti pastorali*, XIII (1965), Nos. 5–6, 120–246; "La dinamica post-conciliare in Italia," in *Il Regno* (November 1, 1966), 552–560, and *Italiani in Chiesa: Analisi sociologica del comportamento religioso* (Brescia, 1967); S. Burgalassi, *Il comportomento religioso degli Italiani* (Florence, 1968); A. Prandi, "Come studiare la religiosità italiana?" in *Il Mulino*, No. 131 (September, 1963), 868–876; R. La Valle, "La christianità italiana oggi: carenze, fermenti, responsabilità," in *Humanitas* (1965), No. 5, 515–531; L. Pedrazzi, "Il rinnovamento dei cattolici italiani," in *Il Mulino*, No. 161 (March, 1966), 232–247, and P. De Sandre, "Religiosità e cultura di massa in Italia," in *Il Mulino*, No. 158 (December, 1965), 1181–1198.

critical examination of Catholicism in Italy by studying its advantages, its deficiencies, and its dynamics and then present a few hypotheses about its future.

I. THE CATHOLIC CHURCH IN ITALY

If consideration is limited solely to official statistics, Italy is a completely Catholic country: over 99 per cent of the population are baptized Catholics. There are very few non-Catholics—Jews, Protestants, Waldenses, or adherents to other religions. It is impossible to say precisely how many there are, for in the last population census of Italy (1961), the question concerning religious adherence was omitted. In recent years there appears to be a growing number of parents who do not have their children baptized. This is especially the case in the so-called "Red Zones" (the provinces of Emilia, Romagna, Tuscany, and Umbria).

A. DIOCESES

From the religious viewpoint, Italy is divided into eighteen large areas, the so-called "conciliar regions." There are 322 dioceses, but since some of these have been combined, the *Pontifical Yearbook* (*Annuario Pontificio*) shows only 261 dioceses for about 52 million Catholics. This number is large compared to other countries: in France, there are 88 dioceses for 43 million Catholics; 136 dioceses in the United States for 40 million Catholics, and 23 dioceses in Germany for 24 million Catholics. There are, however, fewer bishops than dioceses because some minor ones are administered by the neighboring bishops.

For quite some time there have been expectations that the number of dioceses would be reduced and that in certain cases efforts would be made to provide a better distribution of territory among the dioceses, for the smallness of some dioceses involves a waste of personnel and makes it impossible to have specialized and competent priests in every diocese. Thus the Diocese of Gallipoli in the province of Lecce (Puglia) has 13 parishes, 26 diocesan priests, and 28,000 inhabitants, and it is not the smallest.[2] Finally, reform has begun under the impulse of Pope Paul VI: on the one hand, he nominates bishops only for the

[2] The diocese of Ostia (Rome) has 3,827 inhabitants.

dioceses which will remain after the prospective reform; on the other hand, the Italian Bishops' Conference has already prepared a new reordering of the Italian dioceses which will, as much as possible, correspond to the regional provinces of which there are ninety-one. It was stipulated in the Concordat (1929) between the Holy See and Italy that "the diocesan boundaries should be revised to make them correspond, where possible, to the provinces of the State" (Art. 16). It will not be easy to effect the disposition called for by the Concordat, because for many small Italian centers the diocese is the only thing that gives them prestige. Losing the status of diocese would mean that they would count even less than they do today. Thus there will probably be a great deal of opposition to the implementation of this reform, once the pope has approved it.

In addition to the reform of the dioceses, which, it is hoped, can be completed quickly, there has been the reconstruction of the Italian Bishops' Conference. The latter existed before Vatican II, but it was then a vertical organization comprised of only the heads of the conciliar regions. Its functions were limited: the fact that the pope is the primate of Italy has meant that the Italian Church has always been more closely tied to the Holy See than other Churches. The Conference acquired a new aspect when Paul VI approved (December 16, 1965) its new statutes. Now all resident bishops have a seat in it; its major deliberative organ is the general assembly which has annual sessions; decisions are taken by a two-thirds majority of votes and have the power of law only if this is provided for by civic law or if there is a special disposition by the Holy See. The president is appointed directly by the pope, while the assembly elects the vice-president and the members of the commissions for the study and solution of problems in the various spheres of pastoral action. The Cabinet Council, consisting of the president, the vice-president, the presidents of the regional conferences, the vice-regent for Rome, the military ordinary, and the bishop who presides over the National Council of the laity, meets three times a year. The first General Assembly took place from June 21 to June 23, 1966; the next one was planned for February of 1967. The Italian Bishops' Conference proposed as its main objective the implementation of the Vatican Council in Italy. Its first acts augur well for the future of Italian Catholicism. It is, however, unfortunate that the Italian episcopate is rather old: the average age of the Italian bishops is 67. In 1966, 28.3 per cent of them were under 60 years; 30 per cent were between 60 and 70; and 41.6 per cent were above 70 years of age—including 18.3 per cent who were over 81 years old!

B. Parishes

Today there are hardly less than 27,000 parishes in Italy. In 1881 when the Italian population had reached 28 million, there were 20,465; in 1966, with the population figure beyond 52 million, the parishes had risen to 26,664. This means that the average parish had risen from 1,400 inhabitants in 1881 to 1,968 in 1966. In reality, however, there are very few average parishes with 1,500 to 2,000 inhabitants. According to 1951 statistics, there are 6,916 parishes with 500 souls or less. On the other hand, 4,712 parishes have between 2,000 and 5,000 people, while 2,150 of them had more than 5,000 souls. Today, as a consequence of the large migration of recent years, some big city parishes have reached 30,000 to 40,000 souls.

While parishes have increased and have become much bigger, the diocesan clergy has greatly diminished. There were 84,834 diocesan clergy in 1881; forty years later, in 1921, the number had dwindled to 55,633; there were 44,500 of them in 1961 and 42,157 in 1966. This means that in less than a century, while the population has doubled, the diocesan clergy has been cut in half. The result is that, while in 1881 there was one priest for every 270 souls, today there is one priest for every 1,245 souls. In less than a century statistically the pastoral work of a diocesan priest has quadrupled although in actuality, while the small country parishes became even smaller, the peripheral parishes of the big cities, in the course of accelerated urbanization, have grown so enormously that they surpass the population of many dioceses. Thus the pastoral work of the priests in those parishes becomes extremely heavy, so much so that sometimes, and even quite often, they cannot keep in touch with the very people who need them most—the immigrants who, feeling isolated and abandoned, give up their religious practices. A calculation shows that there are more than 19,500,000 people living in 2,150 parishes; this leaves an average of 9,500 souls for each parish. If we take into account that many parishes of the urban centers are small, we come to the easy conclusion that in the parishes on the periphery where the immigrants are more numerous, the number may range from 20,000 to 40,000 souls.

C. Seminaries and Seminarians

What are the prospects for the future of the Italian clergy? When we consider the average age of Italian priests, we see that in 1911 it was about 46 years, in 1931 51 years, and today presumably about 60 years. This means that the Italian clergy is relatively old and destined to diminish greatly in the coming years as the mortality of its members increases. In the last thirteen years (from 1955 to 1967) the number of priests declined by about 1,700; newly ordained priests numbered 10,476, while death accounted for 12,192. This situation becomes even more dramatic when we consider that the number of seminarians, instead of growing, has also been drastically reduced. In 1955 there were 25,738 seminarians; in 1962 the number increased to 30,595, but in 1967 the total decreased to 27,454, which is a decline of 3,141 in five years.

There are 119 major and 277 minor seminaries—a considerable number in comparison to the number of young people attending them. Fortunately there had been created in Italy several regional seminaries for the conciliar regions (especially in the South and the center of Italy)—in fact, 15 minor seminaries and one major seminary. The results have been good. In addition, there are interdiocesan seminaries for those dioceses which cannot maintain their own major seminary although a seminary and especially a major seminary represents prestige for a diocese: hence all the efforts to maintain them. Thus it happens that some dioceses have maintained a major seminary with very few pupils for five years. The major seminary of Carpi, in the province of Modena, had only 16 major seminarians in 1960–1961, and that of Guastalla in the Province of Reggio Emilia had only 11. This surely is a negative sign for the formation of future priests.

D. Religious and Sisters

Italy represents one of the most fertile cradles of religious life in Christianity, both female and male, and has done so not only in the distant and recent past but in times close to us. In 1931, there were 11,907 order priests, and by 1966 this number had risen to 18,288; the number of men who were professed religious (not including priests) was 25,823 in 1956 and 31,966 in 1959. There were 28,172 sisters in

1881, 40,251 in 1901, 71,679 in 1921, and 112,208 in 1931; in 1956 the number had increased to 146,201 and in 1959 to 150,366. In 1966 there were 156,000

It should also be remembered that many secular institutes flourish in Italy—indeed, many of them originated there. It is impossible to estimate their number, but their influence upon the religious life of the country is noteworthy.

The religious and the sisters—in addition to the valuable help they give the secular clergy, for many parishes are in the care of religious—have a particular stake in two fields of activity: schools and service and welfare.[3]

E. The Catholic School

In 1927 Catholic schools, dependent on ecclesiastical authority and run by religious orders and congregations or by dioceses, numbered 425 and had about 31,000 pupils; in 1934 there were 510 with about 43,000; in 1940, 1,004 with about 104,000; in 1961 there were 2,087 with 188,000 pupils; in 1966 2,100 with 208,000 pupils—that is, about 6.6 per cent of the number of pupils in the state-run schools (in 1966, 2,869,145). Some 4,000 priests and men in religious life and about 10,000 sisters were employed in teaching.

These figures apply to secondary schools, that is, to schools for ages 11 to 18. The Church also works on the kindergarten level, for children 3 to 6 years of age, and in the elementary schools, from 6 to 11 years of age. In 1961–1962 there were approximately 21,917 religious employed in kindergartens with 822,000 children—the overall total of children in kindergarten was 1,195,000; in other words, 69.4 per cent of the children who went to kindergarten were in the care of sisters who represented 66.9 per cent of the teaching body. In 1961–1962, there were 2,085 elementary schools with 243,000 pupils taught by religious or sisters.

---

[3] Today the nuns administer: 1,905 orphanages and foundling homes, 131 institutes for reeducation (reform), 154 for psychically damaged, 1,335 old peoples' homes, 515 summer and preventive colonies, 1,497 social assistance societies, 1,855 sanatoria, 226 ambulatories, 1,705 catechetical schools, 1,639 recreation and prayer halls, 3,296 parochial activities. In addition, 361 sister communities provide assistance at home for the sick.

In the university field, the Church is represented by the University of the Sacred Heart of Milan, founded in 1920 by Father Agostino Gemelli. It now has five faculties in Milan (Law, Political and Social Sciences, Economics and Commerce, Letters, and Teachers' Training), and one for medicine and surgery in Rome and one for agriculture in Piacenza. Sacred Heart with its large enrollment enjoys the reputation of being one of the best Italian universities. In Rome there is, in addition, the Free International University "Pro Deo" with faculties of Political Science, Administration, and Syndicalism, and the Institute for Higher Studies in the Social Sciences. In Rome there is also the University Teachers' College "Maria Assunta" founded in 1939 and frequented by religious from every part of Italy. Recently a new Institute for Social Science has been established in Trent.

The Italian State juridically recognizes the schools that are under ecclesiastical authority; as a consequence, the degrees and diplomas that they award have the same standing as those granted by the State schools. Nevertheless, the Italian State does not finance the Catholic schools; only the kindergarten schools receive state subsidies. That is one reason why the Catholic schools of Italy are in grave difficulty today; it is also the principal reason that the Catholic school is the school of the rich, for only they are able to pay the substantial school fees that the Catholic schools, in order to make their way, are compelled to demand of their students. The Catholic University of Milan receives some support from the State, but the subsidies are rather small compared to those given to the State universities.

In turning from secular culture to the consideration of religious culture on the university level, it should be noted that there are only three theological faculties outside of Rome. These are: Venegono (Varese) which soon will be transferred to Milan where the episcopate of Lombardy, Venice, and Piedmont intend to create a Faculty of Theology open to laymen as well as clergy, in Cuglieri (Noro) for students from Sardinia, and in Naples for students from Southern Italy and Sicily. This scarcity of theological faculties may be explained by the great attraction the pontifical universities in Rome have for the youth of Italy: in addition to the Gregorian University with the Biblical and Oriental Institutes (they are an integral part of the university), there are three pontifical universities in Rome, the Lateran, Urbanian, and St. Thomas Aquinas; three pontifical institutes, St. Anselm, the Antonianum, and the Salesianum; and three theological faculties. Italian students particularly frequent the Gregorian and the Lateran universities.

II. CATHOLIC ACTIVITIES

A. CATHOLIC ACTION IN ITALY

There are many apostolic activities and organizations in Italy; the most numerous and best organized is Italian Catholic Action. When M. Fanni and G. Acquaderni founded it in Bologna in 1868, it was called the Society of Catholic Youth. Its formative development was the work of Pius XI and Pius XII. It was close to the heart of Pius XI who lavished attention and favors upon it. In his first encyclical *Ubi arcano* (1922), he defined its nature, goal, means, and obligations; then, on October 2, 1923, he gave it new statutes and throughout his pontificate never tired of recommending it to the bishops. This meant giving it a powerful impetus, even where this worked to the disadvantage of other organizations. In 1931 the Fascist government dissolved all non-Fascist youth organizations: this of course included Catholic Action. Pius XI, reacting very strongly in his letter *Non abbiamo bisogno* (June 29, 1931), compelled the government to give up its claim. As a consequence, under Fascism, Catholic Action, even though it labored under many restrictions and difficulties, was the only free association where it was possible, through study and action, to prepare the forces that upon the fall of Fascism could represent the Catholic soul of Italy in political and social life. Indeed, the major cadres of Christian Democracy which rose in 1943 came from the ranks of Catholic Action.

In 1939, Pius XII placed the direction of Catholic Action under a commission composed of three cardinals residing in Rome and a secretary who fulfilled the function of director-general of Catholic Action and of general ecclesiastical assistant. Thus the dependence of Catholic Action on the hierarchy was made clear. In 1946 the statutes were again brought up to date: Catholic Action became the principal establishment ordained for militant Italian Catholics; its function involved coordinating other Catholic institutions in education, propaganda, and welfare so that they would be serviceable instruments of its apostolate; its fundamental unity was reaffirmed even where its diverse branches were enumerated; the commission of cardinals was replaced by a commission of bishops and the director-general became a simple general ecclesiastical assistant. When the Council of the Lay Apostolate in Italy was established in 1959, all other apostolic activities of the country were allowed to take part on the same basis as Catholic Action. Thus Catholic Action has lost the preeminence that it had formerly had over other apostolic associations because it was the "principal establishment ordained for militant Italian Catholics." In practice, it still preserves its preeminence because it is the best organized and most widespread of Catholic organizations, for it is (or should be) in every parish.

Actually Catholic Action, constituting a unified organization with a general presidency and a central council as its highest deliberative organ, consists of seven associations whose presidents form part of the general council. These are:

1. Catholic Action: Men's Union. The Union is for married men or those over 30 years old and is particularly concerned with the apostolate in public life and in the social milieu: the protection of the family, Christian education of youth, and the maintenance of public morals. In 1946 there were 6,140 societies with 150,866 members; in 1954 they had increased to 12,224 with 285,455 members; and in 1961, there were 14,500 societies with 320,000 members. For its members the Union published a weekly, *Noi Uomini* (We Men).

2. Catholic Action: Women's Union. This is for married women or those over 30 years old and its sphere of activity is within the family and women's world: the spread of Christian principles concerning the rights and duties of women in modern society, the protection of family, and public morality. They are also responsible for the Children's Society of Catholic Action which has the task of giving children their first religious and moral formation and to prepare them for later membership in the Italian Youth of Catholic Action. In 1946 there were 10,965 societies with 369,015 members; in 1961, there were 18,000 societies with 750,000 members. At that time there were 540,000 in the Children's Society. A monthly house organ is entitled *In Alto* (Up).

3. Italian Youth of Catholic Action. This society is for unmarried young men from 10 to 30 years of age and is devoted to the spiritual and cultural formation of its members and to the apostolate among the young. It is divided into three sections: candidates (from 10 to 14),

juniors (from 14 to 20), and seniors (from 20 to 30). This is the liveliest and also the most problem-ridden branch of Catholic Action. In 1946, there were 9,951 societies with 367,392 members; in 1954, 15,706 with 556,752 members; in 1961 the numbers had increased to 16,500 societies with 650,000 members. For them it publishes two monthly journals, *L'Aspirante* (The Candidate), and *Gioventù* (Youth).

4. Female Youth of Catholic Action. This association has the largest membership of any Catholic Action organization. It is for young, unmarried women up to 30 years of age and is concerned with the spiritual, cultural, and moral formation of young people, with the apostolate in the field of female youth and with the preparation of young girls for the duties of family and social life. Its four divisions are arranged according to age. In 1946 it counted 13,898 societies with 884,992 members; in 1961, 21,000 with 1,320,000 members. It publishes two weekly organs for its membership, *In Cammino* (Underway) and *Incontro* (Encounter).

5. The Italian Catholic University Federation. Membership in the Federation is open to young university students of both sexes who may remain members until two years after graduation. The Federation is concerned with the spiritual and cultural formation of its members, who in addition devote themselves to the apostolate within the universities and to affirming Catholic thought in every field of university life. In 1961 there were about 380 clubs with 8,000 members. The Federation publishes a biweekly house organ, *Ricerca* (Research).

6. The Graduate Movement of Catholic Action. Their sphere is the apostolate among the educated classes. The Movement's membership consists of men and women graduates who seek to carry on their religious, intellectual, and cultural formation. The Movement also seeks to aid its members in their efforts to live a Christian life in their professions. In 1961 there were 540 such groups with 18,000 members. The Movement publishes for its members the biweekly *Coscienza* (Conscience) and for the educated public a monthly, *Studium*.

7. The Teachers' Movement of Catholic Action. This is open to men and women who are teachers in elementary schools or kindergartens. Its objectives embrace the development of its members in the spiritual life, in Christian pedagogy, and in the work of the school apostolate. In 1961 it numbered 310 groups with 12,000 members. It publishes the monthly house organ *Maestri di A. C.* (Teachers of Catholic Action).

For the extension of its apostolic work to particular sectors and surroundings, Catholic Action has promoted the establishment of many activities or works dependent on it. These amount to some twenty-two quite disparate activities—sports, tourism for young people, pharmacists, nurses, obstetricians, artists, merchants, technicians, high school teachers, journalists, entrepreneurs, managers, physicians, mothers of families, craftsmen, students. Of these the most important are the Catholic Union of High School Teachers and the Italian Association of Catholic Teachers which have large memberships and have great influence in the schools. The former publishes for its members a monthly, *La Scuola e l'uomo* (School and Man), and a bimonthly for spiritual professionalism, *Fede e scuola* (Faith and School); the latter publishes the biweekly *Il Maestro* (The Teacher); the Catholic Medical Association publishes *Orizzonti medici* (Medical Horizons); and the Italian Catholic Legal Association publishes *Iustitia* (Justice), a juridical quarterly of a high scholarly level.

There are also a few activities which are not dependent on Catholic Action but as coordinate associations work together with it. The Italian Female Center is a federation of Catholic female groups. Its efforts are directed to describing issues of concern to women in the social and civic field and to treating them in the light of Catholic thought. In general, the federation seeks to contribute to the education of women, to urge the advancement as well as the presence of women in social life, and to carry on welfare activities. The Italian Catholic Scout Society promotes the Christian and social formation of boys and youth according to the scout method of Lord Baden-Powell, interpreted in a Catholic way and adapted to the nature of Italian youth. The Association of Italian Guides, its feminine counterpart, is adapted to the needs of young Italian girls.

Among the coordinate activities the Christian Associations of Italian Workers (ACLI) deserve special mention because of their importance on the national level. In Italy this is the social movement of the Christian workers. The Associations constitute neither a party nor a syndicate: their aim is the religious, cultural, and social formation of the workers so that they can make their contribution to the transformation of a society revitalized by Christianity. A secondary activity is to study problems affecting laboring men as well as, by influencing public opinion, Parliament, and the government, to seek the resolution of their problems in the interest of the workers and within the framework of the common good. The Associations also endeavor to offer certain services to the workers. One of the most important is the Patronato ACLI, which offers the workers 8,000 people's secretariats, more than 100 ambulatories, 18 X-ray laboratories, 140 physicians for insured, 564 medical consultants, and 432 legal consultants. The ACLI helps promote professional instruction for workers, and over 700,000 have taken the classes offered. In addition, they promote recreational activities for the workmen. Founded in 1945, the ACLI has 7,500 clubs all over Italy as well as some thousand plant nuclei and groups in factories: the membership exceeds one million. In addition to special-interest publications, addressed, for example, to workmen, peasants, young workers, and managers as well as to ecclesiastical assistants, the ACLI publishes the weekly *Azione Sociale* (Social Action) and a quarterly review, *Quaderni di Azione Sociale* (Notebooks for Social Action).

In addition to the dependent and coordinate activities there are other groups who are described as "adherents" of Catholic Action. The most important of these are: the Christian Union of Entrepreneurs and Managers, which is concerned with the spiritual formation of its members and aims at the knowledge, spread, and application of Christian social doctrine in the industrial field. The Union of Catholic Publishers brings together publishers who put out books and periodicals inspired by Christian principles or who in their publishing activities are inspired by such principles. The National Confederation of Direct Producers is a Christian-inspired syndicate for the peasants who work their own piece of earth. Its membership amounts to 1,891,730 families with a total of 3,683,823 working individuals. Finally there are the "collateral" activities of Catholic Action, such as the National Civic Committee which coordinates the activities of 300 zonal civic committees and of more than 20,000 local civic committees; its aim is the political education and orientation of the Italian people in a Christian sense.

To complete the picture of Catholic Action activities in Italy, there should be added various entities and secretariats which are directly dependent on the central presidency of Catholic Action. Examples include the Catholic Institute for Social Action which promotes studies and the orientation of Catholics in the social field as well as the Catholic Educational Institute and, above all, the Council for Performances, which is concerned with problems of the cinema, radio, television, and the theater; in particular, it takes care of religious broadcasts and classifies films from the moral viewpoint. It publishes a monthly review of cinematography. Finally, there is the Institution of the Social Weeks of the Catholics of Italy which organizes a yearly week of study of a socially important topic.

B. OTHER APOSTOLIC WORKS

Even though the extent of Italian Catholic Action and its organizational strength give it an unequalled place in the country, there are other works of a more limited character which carry on precious apostolic activities. Only the most important are mentioned here.

1. The Marian Congregations were founded in Rome in 1563 and, following the example of the Spiritual Exercises of St. Ignatius of Loyola, are concerned with the formation of Christians with a deep inner life; Christians who by the testimony of their lives, words, and actions, are capable of unfolding an apostolate for evangelization and of filling the workaday surroundings with Christian liveliness. There are more than 400 congregations with over 25,000 members. Their house organ is the monthly *Christiani nel mondo* (Christians in the World).

2. The Movement for Christian Rebirth is a movement of small groups (8 to 10 persons) devoted to spiritual formation and an apostolate which seeks to bring the influence of Christian principles to middle class and aristocratic circles. It publishes the biweekly *Rinascere* (To Be Born Again).

3. The Apostolate of Prayer has about twenty centers with four million members. It publishes *Il Messaggero del S. Cuore* (Messenger of the Sacred Heart).

4. The Third Order of St. Francis, Franciscan Youth, the Pious Co-operative Union of Salesians, and Salesian Youth—all do excellent work in religious formation and the apostolate in connection with their orders or congregations.

5. *Pro Civitate Christiana* (For the Christian City) is a pious association founded in Assisi by Giovanni Rossi and composed of volunteers, both men and women, who dedicate themselves to the apostolate of evangelization through the word, the press, art, and every modern cultural means. By their own preference they work in surroundings farthest removed from faith, or among the world of the young. Their

"Christological Courses" attract about 2,000 persons annually and have national importance. With the help of the institutions of *Domus Christianae* (Christian Homes), of missions, and the biweekly *La Rocca* (The Rock), the influence of *Pro Civitate Christiana* radiates from Assisi all over Italy.

6. The Legion of Mary is very widespread among Italians. It has a Senate, two Councils, and also various Curiae. In many parishes there is the FAC movement, *Fraterno Aiuto Christiano* (Fraternal Christian Assistance) which by the exercise of charity seeks to lead people to the love of Jesus and directs its apostolate especially to those who suffer. In recent years the *Movimento dei Focolari* (Movement of the Hearths), established in Trent by Mrs. Clara Lubich, has made an extraordinary advance; its members who can be found in every social class and in all categories, including priests, work to revive in Christians an awareness of the Mystical Body and the spirit of charity. Today it includes a core of 1,500 consecrated persons (priests and single and married men and women), has a few thousand volunteers devoted to the spread of the Movement's work, and more than a million members. It is also very active in the ecumenical camp and publishes the biweekly, *Citta Nuova* (The New City).

C. WELFARE AND CHARITABLE WORKS

Quite widespread throughout Italy are the Conferences of the St. Vincent de Paul Society, whose members visit poor families in their homes, bring them the help of Christian assistance and the comfort of the word of God; men and women, but especially young people, belong to these Conferences and they, like the founder of their society, the young Frederic Ozanam, find in exercising charity an impulse toward the Christian life and to social action in favor of the poor. Good work is also done by the Ladies of St. Vincent de Paul and by the Catholic Association for the Protection of Young Girls, who are concerned with the young, especially minors who are away from home for reasons of study or work. Additionally there is the Spiritual Assistance for the Nomads of Italy which is concerned with gypsies and circus people; the *Apostolatus Maris* (Apostolate of the Sea) which helps seafaring people spiritually and materially; *Pro Juventute* (For Youth) was founded by Father C. Gnocchi, a military chaplain with the Alpine regiments during the war in Russia, to care for children—particularly for boys wounded or mutilated during the war. Today the organization provides assistance for infants and children stricken by polio.

There are a great many other charitable and welfare institutions. Here I shall limit mention only to those concerned with helping the sick to accept their sufferings. Thereby the suffering becomes an instrument of the apostolate, because in it is seen a special vocation in the Mystical Body of Christ. Such are the Voluntary Center of Suffering, which counts 60,000 members in Italy and abroad, and the Apostolic Movement for the Blind, which attempts to create a sense of brotherhood among the blind in Italy and to teach them to make an apostolic use of their blindness.

In its postwar days—and even today—the Pontifical Assistance Work has been particularly important in the sphere of charity and of rendering assistance. This work was organized in 1944 at the desire of Pius XII who wanted to create a charity organization that would substantially alleviate the tragic human situation that prevailed in Italy as a consequence of the war. This work, originally called the Pontifical Assistance Commission, was under the direction of Msgr. Ferdinando Baldelli, a man of extraordinary organizational capacity and strength of mind and spirit in his undertakings. Animated as he was by great Christian charity, he and the commission achieved true miracles for the hungry, the refugees, and those returning from prison camps and the various war zones. After these first activities directed to Italy's immediate postwar situation, the Pontifical Assistance Work moved in two directions: to bring help to those parts of the country suffering from natural disasters, such as floods or earthquakes, and mishaps of all kinds, such as mining, train, and other accidents and to continue assistance to the underprivileged, especially the children, for whom were established hundreds of summer camps at the seashore and in the mountains. These camps at times have cared for more than one million children. In addition to continuing work in these two areas, it has also created four specialized institutions for young diabetics and polio victims and has organized technical preparatory schools. In every region of Italy it has created social centers on the parochial and interparochial level; it assists the emigrants abroad and their families left behind in Italy; it gives help to prisoners and assists them in the arrangements and adaptations required by their return to society.

The Pontifical Assistance Work is paralleled by the National Moral and Religious Assistance for Workers, founded in 1922, which aims to provide religious, moral, and social assistance for factory workers through the work of a priest, who serves as plant chaplain, and of auxiliary social workers. The Pontifical Assistance Work then has created the Pious Union of Hired Agricultural Workers, Shepherds, Fishermen, Peasants, and Farmers for the spiritual and material assistance of these social categories which comprise the poorest groups of the nation.

D. Missionary Activity

Among European countries Italy has always been one of the most fertile in missionary vocations. In 1940, Italian missionary personnel numbered 10,661: 2,637 were priests, 1,013 brothers, and 6,511 sisters. Even today the missionary institutes, both for men and women, have the greatest number of vocations and do not experience the present crisis in priestly vocations. Characteristic of recent years is the increasing number of lay vocations, involving men and women who wish to serve the missions either directly in the apostolate of evangelization or in welfare and assistance work as doctors, teachers, and technicians. A response has been the establishment of some thirty organizations in Italy which have assumed the task of preparing the lay missionaries, of sending them out to the missions, and of aiding them there. Some of them require a lifelong commitment as well as celibacy, such as the Women's International Auxiliary, the Franciscan Lay Auxiliary Missionaries of the Immaculate Virgin, and the Society of Lay Missionaries. Others only require a commitment for a limited time and do not impose celibacy. Examples are the Center for International Cooperation, the University College of Candidate Mission Doctors, which since 1956 has sent about 120 physicians to the missions; the recently established Lay Movement for Latin America (CEIAL), which has already sent 175 young men and women to assist local churches in South America.

   In addition to the three pontifical missionary organizations—the Propagation of the Faith, the Work of the Holy Infancy, and the Work of Peter the Apostle, which spread the missionary idea among the people—there is also the Students' Mission League, which brings information about missions and their problems to the students. Above all there is a high-level mission press which manages to reach many sectors of the population, for example, the reviews *Missioni* (Missions),

Le Missioni Cattoliche (The Catholic Missions), *Gentes* (People), *Fede e Civiltà* (Faith and Civilization), *Continenti* (Continents), and *Nigrizia* (Black People).

E. THE ITALIAN CATHOLIC PRESS

The *Yearbook* of the Italian Catholic Press is edited by the Italian Catholic Press Union. It lists an impressively large number of Catholic publications, more than 1,700, that appear in Italy. For the most part, of course, they are diocesan or parochial bulletins, reviews published by orders and religious congregations, and publications edited for the members of the great variety of organizations which flourish in Italy.

There is no national Catholic daily newspaper in Italy that can be regarded as the official voice of Italian Catholicism. For some time, talk and thought have been devoted to establishing such a press organ and all sorts of soundings and experiments have been carried out. But such a project seems likely to be unsuccessful for various reasons: a Catholic newspaper would not be able to pay its own way; the size and shape of the Italian peninsula would prohibit such a paper from reaching all regions simultaneously, and finally there is the attitude of Italian Catholics who do not "feel" the necessity for a newspaper of their own and prefer the best distributed and locally best known paper to a Catholic newspaper, even if, as is usual in Italy, these are of laicist inspiration.

Although there is no *national* Catholic newspaper, there are six Catholic papers which have a substantial circulation in one or more regions of Italy: *Il Nuovo Cittadino* (The New Citizen) in Genoa, *L'Italia* (Italy) in Milan, *L'Eco di Bergamo* (The Echo of Bergamo), *L'Adige* in Trent, *L'Ordine* (Order) in Como, and *L'Avvenire d'Italia* (Italy's Future) in Bologna. Obviously these newspapers are all concentrated in the north. Their printing runs are fairly modest—their total circulations probably do not reach 150,000 copies. In addition, there are twenty-one daily papers of Catholic inspiration and these enjoy a total circulation of about 500,000 copies. That is not much when it is noted that one single newspaper in Milan, *Il Corriere della Sera*, has a daily edition of 500,000 copies. In other words, the Catholic papers represent 22.5 per cent of the total number of dailies, but only 10.5 per cent of the total circulation (sporting papers excluded).

More than 120 Catholic weeklies, mostly diocesan, carry on valuable apostolic work: usually they have an edition of 3,000 to 5,000 copies per week, but the circulation of some of them, like *Luce* (Light) in Varese, *Verona Fedele* (Faithful Verona) in Verona, and *Vita Cattolica* (Catholic Life) in Udine, fluctuates between 40,000 and 50,000 copies. The qualitative level is usually good, though it does not reach an especially high grade. Sometimes it is excellent, as in the case of the weekly *Il Nostro Tempo* (Our Times) in Turin. A special mention is due the *Osservatore della Domenica* (Sunday Observer) which is published in Rome.

The press that may be called "pious" or devotional is quite numerous. Among them the *Messaggero di Sant'Antonio* (St. Anthony's Messenger) in Padua is outstanding because it has the highest circulation of all Italian publications: more than 1,600,000 copies per month.

In addition there are the news weeklies produced by rotogravure which try to compete with the lay rotogravures that are so numerous in the peninsula. The most widespread is *Famiglia Christiana* (Christian Family), a weekly with a circulation of over one million. The situation of the children's press is also good: thus *Il Giornalino* (The Little Journal) has a circulation of over 200,000 and *Vitt* has about 100,000.

Finally, there are the cultural journals, devoted either to general culture or to a specialized aspect of it. Among the first we must mention *La Civiltà Cattolica* (Catholic Civilization), founded in 1850 and edited by a group of Jesuit writers, which is the oldest Catholic review and even today one of the most outstanding in the Catholic field; *Vita e Pensiero* (Life and Thought) published by the Catholic University of Milan; *Humanitas*, in Brescia; *Citta di vita* (City of Life) in Florence; *Il Regno* (The Kingdom), edited in Bologna by the Fathers of the Sacred Heart; *Studi Cattolici* (Catholic Studies) published by *Opus Dei* in Rome; *Studium* published in Rome by the Graduate Movement of Catholic Action; and *Testimonianze* (Witnessing) in Florence, until a short while ago edited by Father Ernesto Balducci and now in the hands of a group of laymen—similar to *Il Gallo* in Genoa. Among specialized periodicals devoted to theology, and apart from those published by the international academies in Rome, the following may be mentioned: *La Scuola Cattolica* (The Catholic School) of the faculty of theology at Venegono (Milan); *Rassegna di Theologia* (Review of Theology) of the Jesuit theology faculty of Naples; and *Sacra Doctrina* (Sacred Doctrine) issued by the Dominican Fathers in Bologna. In the social field there are: *Aggiornamenti sociali* (Social Renewal) published by the Center for Social Studies in Milan under the direction of Jesuits; in the educational field there are *Orienta-*

menti pedagogici (Educational Orientations) published by the Salesian Fathers; and *Pedagogia e vita* (Pedagogy and Life). In the pastoral field there are: *Orientamenti Pastorali* (Pastoral Orientations) published by the Center for Pastoral Orientation in Rome; *Catechesi* (Catechesis) issued by the Centro Catechistico of the Salesians in Turin; *Rivista di Liturgia* (Review of Liturgy) published by the Benedictines of Finalpia in the Province of Savona; and *Rivista Liturgica* (Liturgical Review). In literature there is *Letture* (Readings), a publication of the Jesuit Fathers of Milan, and many others. There are also numerous Catholic publishers in Italy: the best known are the Paoline (Sisters of St. Paul) in Rome, Marietti in Turin, Morcelliana in Brescia, Borla in Turin, Ancora in Milan, and Salani in Florence.

III. THE CATHOLIC CHURCH IN ITALIAN SOCIETY

The Catholic Church is present in the most varied fields of Italian society—labor, culture, education, and politics—and it exerts vast influence in Italy in spite of the strong presence of laicism in the country.

A. THE JURIDICAL POSITION OF THE CHURCH IN ITALY

Above all, what is the juridical position of the Church in Italy? It is common knowledge that after the fall of Rome to the Piedmontese troops of Victor Emmanuel on September 20, 1870, the relations between the Holy See and the Italian State, already bad during the Risorgimento, became even worse. The pope regarded Victor Emmanuel's conquest of the Papal States as a usurpation and considered himself to be a prisoner of Italy in the Vatican Palace. He refused to accept the Law of Guarantees by which the Italian State unilaterally sought to regulate the juridical position of the Church and of the Holy See. For its part, the Italian State, dominated as it was by anticlericals and Freemasons, did everything to worsen the relations of Italy and the Vatican. As a matter of fact, 134 religious communities were abolished in Rome alone; the theological faculties in all the universities of the kingdom were abolished; religious instruction was hampered in the elementary schools and removed from the secondary schools; the religious value of the sacrament of matrimony was not recognized; the pious activities as well as the charitable congregations were laicized. On the evening of July 13, 1881, while the mortal remains of Pope

Pius IX, in accordance with the dead pope's wishes, were being moved
for burial from the Vatican to the Basilica of St. Lawrence, outside the
Walls, a band of excited anticlericals stoned the cortege without any
police interference; they hurled insults at the dead pope, and pushing
into the funeral procession threatened to throw in the Tiber "the car-
rion of Pius IX."[4] This and similar actions, like the erection of a monu-
ment to Giordano Bruno on the Campo di Fiori, heightened the tension between Church and Italian State and created a serious "crisis of
conscience" for the Catholics. They were torn between love and
loyalty to the pope and love and loyalty to the fatherland.

This painful situation, a soul-tearing experience for many Catholics, was rectified in 1929 with the signing of the Lateran Pacts which
consist of a Treaty with 27 articles and a Concordat of 45 articles. The
Treaty solved the "Roman Question" that had originated with the
Italian Government's occupation of Rome. The creation of the State
of Vatican City assured the complete independence of the Holy See in
the fulfillment of its mission; the sovereignty of the Holy See was reestablished in the international field. There was a reaffirmation of the
principle of the statute of Charles Albert (1848) which stated that
"the Catholic apostolic and Roman religion is the only State religion."

The Concordat regulated "the conditions of religion and of the
Church in Italy." To the Church was assured "the free exercise of its
spiritual power, the free and public exercise of worship, as well as its
jurisdiction in ecclesiastical matters." The Holy See "may freely correspond and communicate with the bishops, the clergy, and the whole
Catholic world without any interference from the Italian government." To ordained clerks and to professed religious was granted ex-
emption from military service. The parties agreed that the boundaries
of the dioceses should be revised to coincide as far as possible

---

[4] This expression is found in a publication of that time, *The League of Democracy*, which reads: "The corpse of Pius IX was being moved. His embalmed body
was deposited in the vault amidst shouts: without the bayonets of the soldiery
and the revolvers of the secret guard it would have been thrown off the funeral
carriage. . . . Our heart was with those who shouted and whistled. Pius IX was
an imbecile. He personified the Catholic Church which is now reduced to a
monstrous nonsense. . . . The clericals of Rome were taking advantage of this
movement of a pontifical parricide and clown. . . . They were hissed. We were
applauding those who hissed and would have applauded even more if the relics
of that clown had been thrown into the Tiber from the Sant'Angelo bridge."
Reprinted in *Civiltà Cattolica*, "The Night of July 13 in Rome," Series XI, Vol.
VII, 263–264.

with those of State provinces. While the choice of bishops remains with the Holy See, before a bishop is appointed, his name should be communicated to the government which could then make sure that there were no grounds of protest of a political character to raise against the nominee. Before taking over their new dioceses, the bishops must swear an oath of allegiance to the Head of State. The *exequatur* and the royal *placet* were abolished. The Italian State "recognizes the sacrament of matrimony as regulated by Canon law to be valid in civil law." Religious instruction was extended to secondary schools. The State recognized the organizations which issued from Catholic Action, but these organizations were bound to carry on their activities outside of every political party; and all ecclesiastics and religious in Italy were again forbidden "to join, or be active in, any political party."

Even today the relations between Church and Italian State are governed by the Lateran Pacts, as is stated in Article 7 of the Italian constitution. Recently, encouraged by a parliamentary vote, the Italian State has taken the initiative to begin negotiations with the Holy See for a bilateral revision of some Concordat provisions which no longer correspond to the present Italian situation and are in opposition to the democratic Constitution governing Italy today.

It is true that the Concordat contains some provisions which do not conform to the Italian constitution: for example, Article 5, which says that "fallen away priests or those who have incurred censure, cannot be retained, or employed in teaching, in an office or employment in which they are constantly in touch with the public," and Article 43, which prohibits all ecclesiastics and religious from becoming members or being active in a political party. In addition there are outdated provisions which make reference to the Fascist regime. Finally there are provisions which do not conform to the freedom of the Church as reaffirmed by Vatican II, such as Articles 19 and 20 referring to the nomination of bishops and the oath imposed: these provisions involve an undue interference of the State in the life of the Church. Clearly, there are good prospects for a revision of the Concordat through bilateral action of the Italian government and the Church. It should not be difficult to reach an agreement on the points indicated, since the interests of the State and those of the Church converge.

There are, however, two Articles, 34 and 36, of the Concordat with which the laicist parties wish to dispense. For her part the Church considers these articles as beyond the possibility of renunciation, so much so that, should they fall, the whole Concordat would fall with them.

Article 34 reads: "The Italian state in its desire to restore to the institution of matrimony, as the basis of the family, the dignity corresponding to the Catholic tradition of its people, recognizes the validity in civil law of the sacrament of matrimony regulated by Canon law." Article 36 reads: "Italy considers as the basis and crowning achievement of public instruction the teaching of Christian doctrine according to the form handed down by Catholic tradition. It therefore agrees that religious instruction which is now imparted in the elementary public schools should receive additional development on the secondary level in keeping with a program to be established between the Holy See and the State."

The laicists desire the abolition of Article 36 because it conflicts, as they say, with freedom of conscience; but this is only an apparent motive because nobody is obliged to attend the classes in religion and parents who do not want their children to be instructed in the Catholic religion may ask to have the children excused. The true reason is that with religion in the school the Church exercises a great influence upon Italian youth that displeases the laicists. They also ask for abolition of Article 34 so that divorce legislation can be more easily introduced. As a matter of fact, the battle now going on in favor of divorce (which does not exist in Italian legislation, although ten attempts have been made to introduce it) confronts a big obstacle in Article 34, at any rate, in respect to the dissolution of marriages made according to the Catholic rite. Recently a parliamentary commission has ruled that the introduction of divorce even in marriages contracted according to the Catholic rite is not unconstitutional, because it does not prejudice Article 34 of the Concordat. But the reasons advanced for that position are certainly not valid and a law allowing divorce even for Catholic Church marriages could be found unconstitutional and ruled invalid by the constitutional courts.

What will happen in proceeding to a revision of the Concordat, and how far such a revision will go, is impossible to tell. It is, however, quite sure that the Church will fight to retain the substance of Articles 34 and 36 of the Concordat.

B. The Church in Italian Life

The Church is present in the world of labor. There is no professedly Christian union: the Italian Confederation of Free Syndicates to which the Catholic workers belong is not a confessional organization. Nevertheless, the majority of its directors are Catholic. The Association of Christian Workers of Italy (ACLI) demonstrated a courage and lack of prejudice in the position they took in behalf of labor—and have thereby gained great influence. Additionally in some factories there are labor chaplains who carry on a fruitful apostolate. Italy, however, has never felt the need to create "worker priests," for they would not have been accepted even by the workers themselves.

In school matters the Church is represented not only by the schools that the ecclesiastical authorities maintain, but also through the teaching of religion by priests, and the apostolic activities of many Catholic teachers. It is also present through the societies of professors and teachers and the Catholic student associations, especially *Gioventù Studentesca* (Student Youth), a student organization which in recent years has expanded greatly in state schools.

The Church is represented on every level of culture. Catholic professors are numerous and influential in all university faculties. Are there also good Catholic writers? It cannot be said that high culture is of Catholic inspiration—that is far from being the case. Theological culture so far has been somewhat flaccid and depends much on that of other countries. But lately there has been a remarkable awakening.

C. The Church in Italian Political Life

In the last twenty years, and for the first time since Italy's unification in 1861, Catholics have had preeminent political responsibilities. From the days of *Non expedit* (1874) until 1919 when the Popular Party, founded by the Sicilian priest Don Sturzo, was established, Italian Catholics were complete strangers in the political life in Italy.[5] No Catholic could present himself as a candidate for Parliament and

[5] The *Non expedit* was the formula by which the Holy See prohibited Catholics from taking part in political life. This was a form of protest against the conquest of the Papal States and of Rome by Victor Emmanuel II. The *Non expedit* goes back to 1874: at first some interpreted it not as a prohibition but only in the sense that it was not opportune to participate in politics. It was only on June 30, 1888, that the Holy Office, on orders approved by Pope Leo XIII, established that the *Non expedit* meant a real and true prohibition. Amended in 1905, the *Non expedit* was practically revoked by Benedict XV in 1919, when all Catholics were permitted to take part in the new *Partito Popolare Italiano* founded by Don Luigi Sturzo.

Catholics could not vote: *Nè eletti, nè elettori* (Neither elected, nor voters) was the charge given to Catholics. But they could vote and seek office in elections to city and provincial administrative positions. After 1905, Pius X made *Non expedit* less rigid: Catholic candidates could present themselves for political elections, if the bishops held this to be in the interest of the Church and of souls. Nevertheless, the deputies then elected were not "Catholic" deputies because they were Catholic, but were Catholics who had been elected deputies. "Catholic Deputies" held 35 seats in Parliament in 1913.

It was only in 1919 that Italian Catholics entered the political arena with a party of their own: *Il Partito Popolare Italiano* (The Italian Popular Party). It had immediate success: on November 16, 1919, it attracted 20.4 per cent of the votes and elected 100 deputies. But its fortune lasted only a short time. It participated in governments with the Liberals and then with Mussolini, who abolished it on November 9, 1926, along with other democratic parties opposed to the Fascist regime, which only at the beginning of 1925, when all liberty in Italy had been suppressed, showed its true totalitarian nature.

With the fall of Fascism in 1943 and the termination of the war in 1945, Catholics again entered the political arena: the old Italian Popular Party was replaced by *Democrazia Cristiana* (Christian Democracy). On December 10, 1945, Alcide de Gasperi, the last secretary of the Popular Party and then head of Christian Democracy, formed his first cabinet: he was to be Prime Minister without interruption until 1953. Thus, after having been excluded from political responsibilities for 80 years, Italian Catholics assumed political leadership in the country. On April 18, 1948, Christian Democracy had an extraordinary victory at the polls when it gained 48.5 per cent of the votes. In succeeding elections the party's total moved from 40.1 per cent in 1953, to 42.4 per cent in 1958, and to 38.3 per cent in 1963. In spite of these variations, it has dominated the Italian political scene for more than twenty years: all the governments of the last twenty years were headed by Christian Democrats. Voting in the elections of May 19, 1968, confirmed Christian Democracy in its position as the Party of the relative majority of the country. At that time the Party secured 39.1 per cent of the votes, a.gain of 0.8 per cent over 1963.

In running the country, the Catholics have rendered distinguished service. It was largely because of them that Italy, which after the war had been reduced politically, economically, and morally to a heap of ruins, was able to recover and become a modern country, prosperous and democratic. This achievement was made, in spite of the serious problems, not yet solved, such as the industrial development of the South, for which, however, much has been done. Among those who deserve to be remembered for their services to Italy, the first is Alcide de Gasperi († 1954), a great Christian and a great statesman. Of the present group of Italian politicians greatly esteemed Catholics include Professor Aldo Moro, President of the Council since 1963, and Professor Amintore Fanfani, three times President of the Council and today Minister for Foreign Affairs, Dr. Emilio Colombo, present Minister of Finances, Professor Giovanni Leone, President of the Council, and many others.

The charge that Christian Democracy is nothing but the long arm of the Vatican and an instrument of the Holy See to recapture the "temporal power" lost in 1870 is false and unjust. Christian Democracy is a popular, democratic, political party and not a confessional one. It does not represent the Church and the Vatican and it is not in the service of their temporal interests. Rather, where the Holy See was rather diffident in its relations with the Popular Party of Don Sturzo, it has shown every sign of confidence in Christian Democracy and has always supported it. For their part, the Italian bishops have asked Catholics to vote unitedly for Christian Democracy.

To understand the actions of the Church, it is necessary to appreciate the situation in which Italy found itself after World War II. Immediately after the war, for reasons which cannot be explored here, Italy found itself with a heavy Communist Party that soon became the biggest and most belligerent Communist Party in Western Europe; it was headed by the former Comintern Secretary, Palmiro Togliatti, a man of great ability and political acumen. Allied with the Communist Party was the Socialist Party of Pietro Nenni. There was, then, a very real danger of Italy falling into the hands of a popular front formed by Communists and Socialists and of so becoming a satellite of the Soviet Union in the manner of Czechoslovakia and Hungary. Italy's religious and political liberty could be saved only by unity among all Catholics, by Catholics closing ranks in a party of Catholics, as Christian Democracy, and around such a man of stature as De Gasperi. To dam the advancing flood of communism effectively the Italian bishops exhorted all Catholics to vote unitedly for Christian Democracy. Thus the great victory of April 18, 1948, was achieved: the popular front of Togliatti-Nenni was decisively beaten, while De Gasperi's party gained 48.5 per cent of the votes. But the menace of the Communist-Socialist popular front did not disappear: this accounts for the fact that in succeeding elections the bishops have asked Catholics to vote unitedly for Christian Democracy.

The communist menace has declined somewhat with the birth and reinforcement of the left-center, that is, with the detachment of Nenni's Socialists from Togliatti's Communists and with Socialist participation with Christian Democrats in running a government. This explains why in a recent intervention (January 23, 1968) the bishops again asked for Catholic unity in politics to provide for the preservation and promotion of important religious values, such as the stability and indissolubility of matrimony. This request was not advanced as a matter of obligation: the bishops hoped that such decisions of the voters would not be the response to a command, but the issue of maturity and of a sense of political responsibility in Italian Catholics. Thus, the Italian hierarchy plans to remove itself more and more from concrete Italian politics in order to allow Catholics full autonomy and responsibility.

IV. THE VITALITY OF ITALIAN CATHOLICISM

In observing the religious aspect of Italian life one question immediately poses itself: is Italy today still a Catholic country? To what extent? What "religious" value has Italian Catholicism?

A. Is ITALY A CATHOLIC COUNRTY?

Population statistics, as noted earlier, indicate that Italy is almost wholly a Catholic country. If, however, religious practice is taken as the index of a country's religiosity, it cannot be said that Italy's general level is very high. But it is impossible to be precise about the level of religious practice of the Italian people because there are no scientific inquiries concerning the entire population of Italy. There have been inquiries into single cities, for example, Bologna,[6] into a diocese, for

6 A. Toldo, *Risultati dell'inchiesta sulla frequenza alla Messa festiva nel Comune di Bologna* (Bologna, 1960).

example, Mantua,[7] or into a region like Tuscany.[8] But Italy is a country of great diversity, in spite of its relatively small size, and its 52 million inhabitants differ profoundly in temperament, outlook, historical and cultural traditions, and religious sentiment and traditions. Consequently, it is impossible to apply norms valid for a city or a region to all of the country.

A study by Father Silvano Burgalassi[9] has provided some helpful and suggestive data concerning Italian religious practice. He has made an analysis of religious practices in 3,418 parishes situated in 1,072 communities with a population of about seven million, equivalent to 13 per cent of the Italian population. Now, when it is recognized that the number of the parishes and communities under scrutiny represents about 14 per cent of the parishes and the communities of Italy, it must be allowed that the sampling is sufficient; it is, however, not entirely conclusive, because it was not possible to select the parishes and communities at random. The results of Father Burgalassi's research, therefore, are not "representative" of the religious situation in Italy, but only "indicative." For instance, the North is fairly well represented, for 2,523 parishes in 899 northern communities were studied: in the South he had material only for 388 parishes in 82 communities. Moreover, the collected data are not statistically homogeneous because they were obtained by different methods: census-taking, statistics, questionnaires, and interviews.

Father Burgalassi's data indicated that in the cities the rule about Sunday Mass attendance is observed by 26 per cent in big communities with more than 300,000 inhabitants, 30 per cent in median communities of 100,000 to 300,000, and 40 per cent in smaller communities of under 50,000. A difference should be noted between the central parishes where Mass attendance is more frequent and the peripheral ones where it is less regular. In addition, the religious practice of men is 12 to 15 per cent lower than that of women. Finally, children and young people attend Mass on Sunday more regularly than adult men and women.

[7] A. Leoni, *Sociologica e geografia religiosa di una diocesi* (*Mantova*) (Rome, 1952).
[8] S. Burgalassi, "Elementi per un'analisi della religiosità toscana," in *Il Mulino* (1965).
[9] S. Burgalassi, "La sociologia del cattolicesimo in Italia" in *Orientamenti pastorali*, XIII (1965), Nos. 586, pp. 120–246.

Mass attendance is better in the rural parishes than in the urban parishes. In the latter attendance is 35 per cent while it is 37 per cent in the mixed and rural parishes. Adult men go to Mass less frequently in the rural areas than in the cities whereas adult women go in greater numbers. At any rate, by combining the data for city and country it may be seen that in Italy 27 per cent of the men and 43 per cent of the women attend Sunday Mass. According to Father Burgalassi, in Italy only 36 per cent of those obliged to attend Sunday Mass do so.

But this national average varies greatly from region to region. If a distinction is made between the provincial capital cities and the rest of the diocesan territory, Mass attendance in Lombardy is 44 per cent in the capital and 49 per cent in the surrounding territory; in the Venetian province it is approximately 54 per cent and 80 per cent; in Piedmont 30 per cent and 45 per cent; in Emilia 26 per cent and 39 per cent; in Tuscany 27 per cent and 30 per cent; in the Marches 43 per cent and 45 per cent; in Puglia 38 per cent and 39 per cent; and in Sicily 30 per cent and 38 per cent. From these figures it is clear that the situation in the North is good and that it is rather less good in the center; data from the South are too scarce to permit a general judgment.

But the index of Mass attendance, even though it is important in defining the level of religiosity of a country, is not absolutely the decisive one. There are many people in Italy who do not attend Mass regularly, or attend it only occasionally, for example, on the major feasts, and yet they retain their religiosity and above all retain their faith. If they do not go to church, it is not out of hatred or contempt but mostly from laziness or negligence, or because they were never accustomed as children to go to Mass. But the same people who do not go to Mass on Sunday want their children to be baptized, want to be married in church, and want a religious funeral, even though they may not have thought of calling a priest to the bedside of the dying person, perhaps out of fear that to do so would frighten the invalid. Of course, some people seek these religious services in response to social pressure. Not to have one's children baptized, not to marry in church, and to refuse a religious funeral are not regarded favorably in Italy and in some areas are severely condemned. Yet it may not be said that all those who carry out such acts are responding to social pressure and are not acting out of real religious feelings, contradictory and incoherent as they may be, and yet sincere and authentic: people want to keep in touch, in however desultory a way, with God and the Church.

The great majority of Italians are religious, even though their religiosity may often be rather feeble and poor. The areligiously indifferent and professed atheists do exist but they are a minority—I would estimate that they do not exceed even 10 per cent of Italians. Actually absolute indifference to religion and explicit negation of God are extremely rare phenomena. Anticlericalism, however, is quite widespread: indeed, many expressions of what appears to be irreligiosity are simply expressions of anticlericalism. The politico-religious struggles of the nineteenth century and the "Roman Question" have greatly influenced religiosity. Hatred of the Church and the clergy has today become hatred of religion and God. It is no coincidence that the least religious regions today are the former territories of the Papal State.

B. COMMUNISM IN ITALY

If Italians for the most part are religious, how does one explain the fact that of all European nations it has been precisely Italy in which communism has found the most favorable soil and has achieved the greatest successes?

The fact is undeniable: the Communist Party is very strong, even though its membership declined from year to year; in 1960 there were 1,792,974 party members and 1,571,245 members in 1966. Its membership has been decreasing annually so that between 1953 and today its total declined by 900,000 and the Young Communists have lost two-thirds of their membership. But its electoral strength has increased with each election. In the general election of 1963 the Party secured 7,763,854 votes, that is 1,059,000 more than in the preceding elections (1958). In 1968 the voting again registered a gain for the Party, which won a total of 8,555,477 votes, 787,876 more than in 1963. How is this fact to be explained and what relationship does it bear to the religious life of the country?

The communist success in Italy may be explained by economic conditions, especially those of the immediate postwar period. The hunger and unemployment of those years aroused the Italian people to a movement of violent protest which was immediately seized and channeled by the Communist Party. Not only was the Communist Party the only organized party that had been able to survive the Fascist persecution; it was also the party which, rightly or wrongly, had acquired the greatest credit in the Resistance movement against the Nazis. This explains why the communists drew so many votes in the very first elections. With ability and without scruple they played upon the discontent and protests which rose with ever greater force throughout Italy as the country finally succeeded in emerging from hunger and misery (and it is a sociological fact that social protests grow more violent not when people are badly off, but when people begin to be better off and to see additional possibilities for improvement). In its increasing electoral success, the Communist Party benefitted from the divisions and quarrels of the other parties, from their slowness and improvidence. Two other factors should be mentioned: the voters display a certain laziness, for in general they continue voting as they had voted earlier; and in certain regions where nearly everything is in Communist hands, it is virtually impossible not to vote Communist if a man wishes to live in peace and attend to his affairs. Such is the case in Emilia-Romagna.

How, then, should adherence to communism be interpreted? Most party members and voters for the party's candidates do so because they are dissatisfied with the political, social, and economic situation in which they live and think that only communism can improve their situation. They see in communism a great political force capable of radically transforming the Italian situation. As for communist doctrine, it is mostly ignored; in any case it is not accepted in its philosophical and religious principles. Most of those who profess communism are neither atheists nor irreligious; at the most they hold it against the Church and the priests that they side with the rich, the *padroni* (landlords). They do not intend to break completely with religion. Indeed, they want to have their children baptized, want to marry in church and from time to time, attend certain church functions. In fact, many Communists do not think that there is any radical opposition between being a Communist and being a Catholic. In 1963 DOXA (the Gallup Poll of Italy) made a survey in which 100 Communist voters were asked: "Is it possible to be a good Communist and at the same time a good Catholic?" The answers provided the following result: 71 per cent answered "Yes"; 9 per cent said they did not know, and only 20 per cent replied "No."[10]

Membership in the Communist Party or electoral support of it does

[10] Fegiz Luzzatto, *Il volto sconosciuto dell'Italia*, Second Series, 1956–1965 (Milan, 1966), pp. 1305.

not mean that a person is an atheist, even though among its followers there are a number of avowed and convinced atheists. But we should note that in general they are not atheists because they are Communists, but are Communists because they are atheists; in other words, they did not become atheists because they joined the Communist Party (though this occasionally happens) but because they were already atheists or about to become atheists. Italian communism, instead of being the diffuser of atheism, has been the beneficiary of both the atheism and irreligion of nineteenth-century liberalism and the socialist and anarchic movements inspired by positivism and materialism. As a matter of fact, the massive adherence of Italians to such an irreligious and atheist system as communism, which has been strongly condemned by the Church and has been made the subject of Church admonitions, does not so much denote an absence of religiosity on the part of Italians but rather reveals the crisis of their religiosity.

C. ITALIAN CATHOLICISM IN CRISIS

In other words, communism is a sign of crisis in Italian Catholicism. It shows that the Catholicism of many Italians is only superficial and consists more of sentimentalism and of attachment to religious traditions than of profound convictions based on knowledge of Catholicism. Religious ignorance is widespread in Italy, so much so that in our opinion it constitutes the true weakness of Italian Christianity. It is precisely this ignorance that has permitted communism to have such great influence upon the Italian Catholic masses.

Communism is not the only sign of the crisis of Italian Catholicism. Its other manifestations include: the infrequency and decrease of religious practice; the decline of religious and priestly vocations; the dissolution of the family by the ever increasing number of legal separations of marriage partners (in 1967 there were 12,800 petitions for separation and in 1966 there were 11,600); the propaganda in favor of divorce and its effect in some Catholic circles; the large circulation of the pornographic press; the annual increase in the number of offenses and crimes, some of them really inhuman, committed by unscrupulous gangsters.

The cause of this crisis, especially involving the young people and those who have migrated from small rural centers to the cities to become industrial workers, is certainly the domestic migration which has resulted in an excessive urbanization. In a few years an enormous population shift has taken place: from the country to the city, from the South to the North and to other European countries including Switzerland, France, Germany, and Belgium. It is estimated that the migratory movement has encompassed about one-third of the entire population: that is, about 15 million Italians have changed their residences either temporarily or permanently. While the countryside is being depopulated and the South is losing its better energies, the cities have enormously increased: Rome, Milan, Turin, and Genoa have witnessed a spectacular growth on their peripheries where the Southern migrants have settled. This great displacement of population has caused the gravest problems which are not only economic, political, and social: they are also religious. Indeed, emigration from a familiar countryside and from a long-familiar environment has meant for very many a spiritual and religious uprooting, a loss of contact with religion and with the Church. Accustomed to the forms of a traditional and popular religiosity they did not find upon coming to the great cities what they had known and taken for granted. On the other hand, in the great cities they did not find parishes and priests who could accommodate and understand them and could help them to adapt to the religious rhythm of the city. Thus they have given up all religious practice. This effect is intensified by the fact that in the factories, where they work, they find themselves in surroundings that are either directly hostile to religion or certainly indifferent and areligious.

But even though the immediate cause of this crisis, at least as it involves those who make the move from the countryside to the city and from the agricultural South to the industrialized North, is immigration, the less immediate cause is the weakness of the religious structure of the country. This weakness is due to religious ignorance and to the fact that nothing has been done in depth. There was contentment with a Christianity consisting of religious traditions and of religious practices, without a compelling effort to help the faithful to develop a personal Christianity born of conviction, an effort that would involve instruction and personal participation in the liturgy and the life of the Church.

D. The Structural Weaknesses of Italian Catholicism

The present summary account of the structural weaknesses of Italian Catholicism will treat of the distribution and formation of the clergy, the parishes, the phenomenon of religious ignorance, Catholic culture, and the Catholic organization.

The number of the clergy is sufficient. The proportion of Catholics to priests is quite good, certainly better than in other Catholic countries of Europe: there is one priest for every 1,245 Catholics and this ratio does not include the priests of religious orders. Nevertheless, apart from the fact that many are employed in administrative tasks and in teaching secular subjects in the schools, the clergy is rather badly distributed: thus, next to regions like Lombardy and Veneto which have an abundant supply of clergy, there are poor regions like Tuscany, Sardinia, and Lucania; while, for instance, in the Diocese of Bergamo in Lombardy there is a priest for every 580 Catholics, in Leghorn there is only one priest for every 3,000 Catholics; while there is one priest for every 843 Catholics in the Diocese of Aversa in Campania, there is only one for 2,507 in the Diocese of Crotone in Calabria. But the major weakness of the Italian clergy is that a majority of them in their seminary years went through a course of training that scarcely prepared them to exercise the priestly ministry in Italy today, where radical transformations in outlook, habits, level of education, and life are in progress. Fortunately the training which aspirants to the priesthood receive in today's seminaries is much better and is more directly related to the times. Yet there still are seminaries where the old methods are in force. We must add here that the greater part of the clergy is eager for *aggiornamento*, to learn the new pastoral methods, to try new courses, so that they can approach the "distant ones" or provide for practicing Catholics the possibility of a better Christian formation. In this respect the Council has shaken up the Italian clergy.

The migratory tide has made the crisis of the parish acute: the mountain parishes have become too small and anemic; the city parishes have become too big and therefore unable to welcome the newcomers and to integrate them into the parochial community. Yet the parish crisis antedates migration and is more deeply rooted: the parish, at least in some regions, has not been successful in fostering around itself an authentic parish life that can keep the interest of those who belong to it. Thus it is easy to run into Italian Catholics who do not even know to which parish they belong or who come to the parish only when they need documents to get married, or when they want to have their children baptized.

The phenomenon of religious ignorance, so widespread in Italy, even among the educated classes, is connected with the parochial crisis. Actually it is not possible to say that there is in Italy an effort to give Catholics a complete religious instruction. Catechetical formation is nearly everywhere restricted to preparation for First Communion. There is almost no catechesis for adults. In all schools, however, there is obligatory religious instruction at least one hour a week. But apart from the fact that many boys leave school and go to work, for various reasons which cannot be developed here, religious instruction in the schools does not yield the fruits that should be expected. Many boys also leave school as soon as they reach the legal age—14 years. There is, therefore, a great religious ignorance among Italian adults, even the educated ones. To remedy this situation, there have been recent attempts in a few cities to establish courses of religious instruction for adults and there are even theological institutes for laymen in Milan, Turin, Florence, Rome, Naples, Assisi, and many other cities. Their radius of activity is rather limited, although they have been remarkably effective. For their part all Catholic institutions insistently call for religious instruction of their members, but these organizations reach only a small part of Italian Catholics. At the moment, almost all Italian circles have a lively interest in religious problems especially in the documents of the Council. Conferences, round tables, cultural meetings, which study the great themes of Vatican II, have multiplied. But the lack of basic formation prevents people from progressing beyond a point of information that is rather fragmentary and, all things considered, superficial.

This state of religious formation explains another grave deficiency of Italian Catholicism: the absence of a valid and strong Catholic lay culture. As a matter of fact, without a profound theological basis there can be no contribution to Catholic culture. And in Italy there is no lack of Catholic writers, poets, dramatists, producers, historians, scientists, critics, and philosophers; yet their cultural work is often only superficially Catholic. There is an absence of Christian impregnation such as may be found, for example, in Dante, Manzoni, Vico, and Rosmini. Since the death of Papini a few years ago there no longer is a major Catholic writer in Italy.

Finally, there is the crisis of the Catholic organizations which are responding to the transformations that have taken place or are taking place in the country. They are, therefore, in search of new organizational methods. The recruitment of new elements has turned out to be particularly difficult. Modern Italian youth shows on the one hand a strong inclination toward disengagement and on the other hand a tendency toward new formulas of organization, more elastic and free and less straitened in fixed schemes. Thus, while the large organizations are experiencing a crisis affecting their numbers and capacity to attract interest, free groups of every kind multiply, generally around some activist review. The best known and most influential, on the national level as well, are *Testimonianze* (Florence), *Il Gallo* (Genoa), *Il Momento* (Milan), *Il Tetto* (Naples), *Il Dialogo* (Palermo), and *Questitalia* (Venice).

E. PROSPECTS FOR THE FUTURE OF ITALIAN CATHOLICISM

The crisis of the Church in Italy today and the structural weaknesses of Italian Catholicism should not lead to pessimism about the future of the Church in Italy. Even though, in some respects, Italian Catholicism is in crisis and shows serious weaknesses, there is still a noteworthy reserve of living forces that have been aroused by Vatican II, which has already made an impact for renewal. From the thrust exerted by the Council, something is moving in Italy and in the rest of the Christian world. There is a profound desire for the renewal of the life and the structure of Italian Catholicism; this has led to the study of the Conciliar documents which the efforts of Catholic editorial houses have made available to everybody. It has also inspired Catholics to read and study the Bible which had never been popular in Italy. The deepening of the Conciliar doctrine and personal contact with Holy Scriptures create a new problematic and new and boldly striking perspectives for Catholic life in Italy.

There is a certain tardiness in the Council's impact, for Italians were not prepared for the Council. Nevertheless, the Conciliar spirit is a ferment in Italian Catholicism: at the moment, renewal is slow and tedious, but renewal is certainly on hand and will improve the aspect of Catholicism in Italy, if not quantitatively then certainly qualitatively. A notable advance has already been made with the reform of the liturgy that nearly everywhere was greeted with enthusiasm. More will be achieved with the impending reform of the dioceses and the restructuring of seminaries, the renewal of Catholic organizations, and the ecclesiastical programming which the new Italian Bishops' Conference can plan and carry out. One can only hope that these structural reforms will be accompanied by an inner renewal, that within individual Christians and in all the Italian Church there will be the growth of faith, hope, and charity. Added to this is the wish that Italian Catholicity respond to the travail of its present crisis—with sanctity, as in the past it has many times responded to crises perhaps more serious than the present one. In the past Italy has been a fertile soil for saints. May it still be so today and tomorrow.

6 : PORTUGAL

Antonio da Silva Rego

I. INTRODUCTION

The expansion of Rome placed the Iberian Peninsula in intimate association with the world of classical civilization. The entire Peninsula was finally occupied and politically organized by Emperor Augustus. Shortly afterwards Christianity came to Roman Hispania. Writing to the Romans, Saint Paul clearly stated his intention of visiting "Hispania" (Romans 15:24, 28), but whether or not such a voyage ever took place is still a debated point. During Diocletian's reign (284–305), Hispania was divided into five provinces: Lusitania, Galicia, Carthaginensis, Betica, and Tarraconensis. What afterwards constituted Portuguese territory was taken from Galicia (North) whose capital was Braga (in the present province of Minho), from Lusitania (Douro in northern Portugal to the Guadiana River), and from Betica.

In 409 barbarians rushed through the Pyrenees and spread throughout the territory. There followed years of strife and confusion, during which the Visigoths and the local inhabitants finally merged into a heterodox community. Christian Visigothic Spain reached its highpoint at the National Council of Toledo (589), attended by over 70 bishops representing all Hispania's dioceses.

In 711 the Arab invasion of the Peninsula began. The Visigothic kingdom melted away under the continuous pressure of the Arabs who came in ever increasing numbers via Gibraltar. The remnant of the resisting Christians took refuge in the hilly northern regions of Spain where the Arabs dared not attack them. In 720 came the reaction, the beginning of the long Reconquista, which lasted until 1492 and culminated in the recapture and occupation of the last Arab stronghold, Granada.

As the Arabs were forced southward, the Christians organized themselves around five main nuclei: Asturias, Castile, Navarre-Aragon, Catalonia, and the Portucalensis county. This small county was to give its name to Portugal. The county was under the suzerainty of Castile, when in 1128 Alfonso Henriques succeeded to its government and soon gave firm indication that independence was his ultimate goal. In 1139 Henriques broke off the ties of allegiance which linked the county to Castile. The following year (1140) independence was openly declared. Castile's displeasure and disapproval lasted for several years, but in 1143 Henriques came to terms with his previous overlord. In the same year, to strengthen his political position in the Peninsula, he placed the newborn nation under the protection of the Holy See and bound himself and his successors to pay an annual tribute, which was duly paid for many years.

Alfonso I, the first Portuguese king, realized that expansion could and should be carried forward in a southern direction, toward the Algarves, toward the ocean. He did not intend to quarrel with his Christian neighbors to the east. After the successful negotiations of 1143, he immediately inaugurated his southern campaigns. Lisbon passed from Muslim into Christian hands in 1147, and it appeared that the Algarves would be reached within a few years, but that hope proved illusory. The Portuguese had to live another century bordering the Moors who were firmly established in modern Alentejo and Algarve. The latter province was occupied in 1249, the year Portugal attained her continental shape and boundaries. Portugal is, therefore, among the European nations with the most venerably well-defined national frontiers. Spain's boundaries, for example, were not established until nearly two and one-half centuries later, in 1492, when the Moors were finally expelled from Granada.

During these first years, the ecclesiastical history of Portugal parallels that of other European countries: there are frequent disputes between Church and State, mainly over ecclesiastical properties and privileges.

In 1361 there is a first mention of the royal *placet*, that is, royal permission for bringing into the kingdom papal documents, such as bulls, rescripts, and briefs. This royal intervention was meant to assure the authenticity of such documents. Actual conditions favored the accumulation of false evidence even at the cost of pontifical authority. From the very beginning the *placet* gave rise to so many abuses that the popes regularly and the clergy often protested against such intrusion into ecclesiastical matters. The kings maintained it as a weapon to be used against what they might consider to be intrusions into secular affairs. The royal *placet* was to be a recurring stumbling block in the relations between the two powers. It was abolished in 1487, but somehow was periodically revived.

Before independence, there were only three dioceses: Braga, Coimbra, and Porto. Afterwards others were restored: Lamego, Viseu, Lisbon, Guarda, and Silves, which had been suppressed after the Arab invasion.

The kings also claimed and secured their authority in the appointment of bishops, parish priests, and other ecclesiastical officers. This was done mainly in the name of the royal patronage. This all the more fostered secular opposition to the Church, because the Church possessed large tracts of land. The ecclesiastical immunities, on the other hand, constituted another cause of dissatisfaction.

Religious orders established monasteries and other houses all over the territory. From the beginning the Cistercian monks became famous for their work at Alcobaca. From Alfonso Henriques, the first king, they received in 1153 the land situated between the two castles of Leiria and Obidos. The monks soon converted vast forests into magnificent arable fields and flourishing villages. Today this monastery is one of the principal national monuments and is visited by thousands of tourists.

In the thirteenth century two famous Mendicant Orders, the Franciscans and the Dominicans, were founded and both came to Portugal within a few years. The Military Orders, especially the Templars, were also well represented in the country. When Pope Clement V, acting under French pressure, dissolved the Order in 1312, King Denis of Portugal, who wished to have at his disposal Templar property and wealth in Portugal, used the occasion to establish a purely Portuguese Military Order, the Order of Christ approved by Rome in 1319. This Order was to play an important role in overseas expansion.

In 1290 Denis also founded the Portuguese university of Lisbon which finally settled at Coimbra one of the great European universities of the century. This century gave Portugal two internationally known personalities: Pope John XXI who died in 1277, and St. Anthony, who was born in Lisbon but is known the world over as St. Anthony of Padua, where he died in 1231.

The occupation of Ceuta (1415) in North Africa initiates a second period in Portuguese history: that of Portuguese expansion with which the name of Prince Henry the "Navigator" is inseparably associated. The Order of Christ was placed wholly at the disposal of what was termed "service of God and service of the King." Together with overseas expansion went the spreading of Christianity. The Portuguese kings, deeply interested in the Order of Christ, soon obtained a "royal patronage" not only for the occupied territories, but also for all other lands discovered and to be discovered. Indeed, this right of patronage extended not only over Portuguese territories, such as Portuguese Africa, India, Brazil, but also reached out to Ethiopia, India, Ceylon, Japan, China, and Indonesia. Francis Xavier, the Apostle of the East, worked in India and Japan under this *padroado* structure.

It was the extraordinary development of all these Portuguese missions that led the Holy See to establish in 1622 the Holy Congregation for the Propagation of the Faith. Initially relations between the royal Portuguese patronage and the new congregation were quite friendly. After 1640 they deteriorated and gave rise to serious conflicts mainly in India, Tonkin, Cochin-China, and China. The explanation for this change is to be found in the national revolution of 1640, when Portugal broke off ties which from 1580 had linked her to Spain. Strong Spanish pressure resulted in delaying recognition of Portuguese independence by several powers, including the Holy See. The latter acted in recognition only in 1668. Meanwhile all Portuguese overseas missions went into marked decline, and the period (1640–1660) may be regarded as the most serious crisis ever undergone by the nation.

The Inquisition, a semireligious and semiofficial tribunal, was introduced into Portugal in 1536, after rather difficult and long negotiations between King John III and Pope Paul III. Being a "Tribunal of the Faith" it dealt mainly with Judaism, witchcraft, heresy, and such matters, including the censure of books. Its principal aim was to secure the confession and win the repentance of those accused: the penalties were mostly of a spiritual nature. Only the dissenter and the impenitent were corporally punished. The Inquisition had no jurisdiction to pass a death sentence. This was reserved for the "secular justices," to whom the Inquisitors sent such hard cases.

In the eighteenth century the most important of several fateful events was the genesis and outbreak of the French Revolution, for both the Church and Christianity were openly attacked. Gallicanism and regalism found unchallenged general approval, and the Church was expected to serve the State in every respect. When Louis XIV boasted "L'état, c'est moi," he was indeed offering a motto to all crowned European heads of the century. And so they understood it.

Eighteenth-century Portugal's history extends over three reigns: John V (1706–1750), Joseph I (1750–1777), and Mary I (1777–1816). Each reign was a manifestation of royal absolutism. For their part, the popes, in effect, yielded to all royal whims and wishes. The bishops became more dependent on the Crown than on Rome. In 1728 John V reestablished the royal *placet* which had been abolished in 1487. Diplomatic relations with the Holy See were interrupted several times. Following the example of France, where the clergy defended the "liberties of the Gallican Church," most of the Portuguese clergy maintained the "liberties of the Lusitanian Church."

The almighty Prime Minister of Joseph I, the Marquis of Pombal, took direct charge of the Inquisition and raised it to the rank of "royal tribunal," entirely dependent on the Crown. His discourtesy toward the Jesuits was rapidly transformed into hatred. In 1759 they were expelled from Portugal, Brazil, and all mission lands. Portuguese Jesuits working in Portuguese territories were placed on board ships and sent to Lisbon. Here many went to prison while others were sent to the pope. Those working in China and India stayed on at their posts but could not be replaced. As they died, these missions were handed over to other missionaries or were disbanded. Not satisfied with that, Pombal, together with other European courts, exerted such pressure on Rome that Pope Clement XIV capitulated and agreed to suppress the Society of Jesus (July 21, 1773). When in August, 1814, Pope Pius VII revived it, the Portuguese government, no longer in Pombal's hands, declared that the Jesuits would not be permitted in the country.

During this period the entire area of Angola constituted a single diocese. Mozambique was limited to a "nullius prelacy." Macao was the seat of a diocese of a large and extensive jurisdiction, an inheritance from past years. Goa, the main ecclesiastical division in the structure of the overseas Church, was an archdiocese, having several dioceses under its jurisdiction, some of them in Indian territory. The Goan clergy was known all over India and the East. Nearly every Goan

Catholic family had a son in God's service. In the eighteenth and the early nineteenth centuries, when vocations were becoming scarce in Portugal, the Goan clergy maintained Portuguese missions not only in India, but in East Africa, Macao, and Timor as well. All these Portuguese territories and missions were affected by the ideas and ideals of the French Revolution, and these forces precipitated the vast changes of the nineteenth century.

II. THE CHURCH AND THE LIBERAL MONARCHY
(1820–1910)

While the invading French columns were hurrying toward Lisbon to prevent the royal family's escape to Brazil, the family left the Tagus estuary on November 29, 1807—the same day the French army, commanded by Junot, reached Sacavem, a few miles from Lisbon. While there, Junot received two delegations: the first represented the governors of the kingdom who, a few hours earlier, had received the charge to administer the country and, in that capacity, greeted the triumphant invaders; the second delegation, consisting of Freemasons, hailed the invaders as liberators. The invasion and the diverse personal reactions to it marked the emergence of the major contending parties in modern Portugal and initiated long years of warfare.

After the final defeat inflicted on the French at Waterloo in 1815, the royal family continued to linger in Brazil. The forces of Portugal's ally, Britain, remained on Portuguese soil and showed no signs of returning home. In such circumstances Portuguese patriots stirred with dissatisfaction.

On August 24, 1820, a popular revolution broke out in Porto, and another in Lisbon on September 15, 1820. The revolutionaries demanded the immediate preparation of a new constitution, which would end the absolute monarchy. Parliament began discussing it on January 26, 1821, and in Brazil King John VI bowed to the popular will and declared that he approved the constitution, even before he was aware of all its provisions. Hence, absolutism ceased to exist in Portugal. On July 4, King John returned to Lisbon and a country that was already a constitutional monarchy.

The years from John VI's death in 1826 to 1834 are times of internal dissension provoked by succession disputes between John's two brothers, Pedro and Miguel—the latter favored absolute monarchy, while the former backed the constitutional form. The resulting civil war ended on May 26, 1834, with the Liberals claiming a total victory.

The Portuguese, instead of uniting after so many trials and conflicts, remained divided. One party favored the 1822 Constitution; another supported the constitutional charter granted by Pedro in 1826. The 1822 Constitution, popular in origin, was considered more democratic and was favorable to local enterprises. On the other hand, the constitutional charter had issued from the king who had shaped it according to British fashion. It appeared to be more favorable to capitalistic forms and experiences. Only by the middle of the century (1851) did the country appear more or less settled.

From the beginning of the Liberal regime it was evident that, as far as religion was concerned, theory did not agree with practice. In theory, the Catholic religion continued to be the "official religion" of the State; in practice, the Church was expected to follow and obey the State almost blindly. Indeed there was a marked difference between the official Catholic religion and the Catholic Church, for it appeared that the State knew better than the Church how to deal with religious affairs.

After defeating the Absolutists, the Liberals on July 31, 1833, created a "Commission for General Ecclesiastical Reform." This reform, of course, was to the interest of the government as well as to its enrichment. The next year (August 23, 1834) the commission was replaced by another especially charged with disposing of all ecclesiastical benefices that had been declared vacant by the previous commission.

The government went further and broke off diplomatic relations with the Holy See. The main motive then adduced was that it could not recognize certain bishops who had been appointed during the civil war in response to the influence of the Absolutist government. The pope, of course, could do nothing regarding these governmental claims.

Popular opinion, however, forced the government to reconsider its attitude, and in 1835 Lisbon and Rome began negotiations to reestablish normal diplomatic relations. Pope Gregory XVI (1831–1846), seeing that Portugal was not fulfilling her obligations to maintain and foster the Eastern missions, published in 1838 the brief *Multa praeclare*, by which the royal patronage was simply abolished in all non-Portuguese territories. This brief aroused differing opinions both in Portugal and abroad, and forced the government to conclude that something urgent should be done to avoid further mishaps. The two courts came to agreement in 1842, and until the end of the monarchy, their relations remained quite normal and even friendly. On October 21, 1848, a Concordat dealing with the existing difficulties between Church and State was signed. Some historians consider the period, during which diplomatic relations were nonexistent, as one of schism. Such opinion, however, is not supported by the Holy See.

One of the measures taken by the 1834 government was the suppression (1836) of the canon law faculty at Coimbra University. Until 1911, there remained only one ecclesiastical faculty—theology.

The seminaries were also completely disorganized. From 1835 to 1837 the government did not allow any admission into Holy Orders. Subsequently permission was granted, but always on certain conditions. In 1845 the government decided that each diocese should run its own seminary; however, several years elapsed before this arrangement was implemented. Gradually conditions improved and at the end of the monarchical regime all seminaries were registering marked progress.

During the constitutional monarchy, the presentation of bishops belonged in fact, but not juridically, to the king; nomination remained with the Holy See. After 1862 canons and parish priests were also appointed by the State but had to undergo a previous examination conducted under a bishop's supervision. Admission to such exams, however, had to be requested at the Ministry of Ecclesiastical Affairs and Justice. Under such conditions parish priests were virtually civil servants.

During this period, kings, by using the royal *placet*, exercised control of all documents emanating from Rome. The appointment of bishops was generally a disputed question between Rome and Lisbon. Usually Rome agreed that Lisbon should *demand* a bishopric for a particular person in a Portuguese diocese. Where, however, royal patronage existed, the kings enjoyed the right of presentation.

Since monasteries and convents owned large tracts of land, the Church possessed great properties at the end of the absolutist monarchy. After the first liberal revolution (Porto, 1820), Parliament started the process of seizing such properties because 1) all religious orders had declined and, in fact, decayed and this was generally admitted by both ecclesiastics and laymen, and 2) there were very few inhabitants in the large religious houses. That convents which formerly housed fifty or more persons were now reduced to six or even fewer, that religious vocations dropped each year and that many who adopted a monastic life did so because of nonreligious motives—all influenced the recognition that reform of religious orders was essential. The government, however, took the opportunity not to "reform," but to "suppress." Thus, on May 30, 1834, a royal decree abolished all religious orders for men in Portugal and her overseas dominions. Their properties were incorporated in the Royal Treasury. Exception was made for sacred vessels and vestments that were to be distributed among needy parish churches. The government also promised to pay a fixed pension to all former friars who had been deprived of their residences. Later (April 15, 1835), a law authorized the government to sell such properties. These confiscations caused extensive national loss.

The campaign against the religious orders never completely abated. In 1901 it was so active that a mere spark caused a fiery outburst. For example, at Porto the Brazilian consul had a daughter who, so it seems, desired to enter a convent. Although she was of age, her father objected. On February 17, 1901, after attending Mass with her family, she tried to board a waiting carriage to begin her journey to the convent. This incident, as featured in the press, provoked spectacular outbreaks in a number of Portuguese cities. Succeeding days witnessed persecution of secular and regular priests and nuns and repressive action against religious houses, Catholic newspapers, and so on. The government finally intervened and on March 10 issued a decree ordering the closing of several convents and religious associations. One month later, another decree established the conditions under which such institutions were permitted to exist: 1) State approval of their rules and statutes was necessary; 2) their activities had to be restricted to charity, education, and the propagation of the faith overseas; and 3) novitiates and the professing of new religious should cease. The government was aware that several institutions could not comply with such injunctions. Thus these institutions led a precarious life and were always subject to legal prosecution.

Such uncertainty prevailed in the last years of the monarchical regime. In fact, the last government of the regime was particularly antireligious. It was particularly suspicious of priests who had studied in foreign seminaries or universities and on October 4, 1910, closed a Jesuit residence in Lisbon. The latter occurred only one day before the Republic was proclaimed.

In spite of these ordeals, religious orders exercised significant influence throughout the country. By the middle of the nineteenth century
most of the orders suppressed in 1834 had already succeeded in returning to Portugal. Jesuits, Franciscans, Holy Ghost Fathers, and
others maintained several houses and residences. Dominicans and
Augustinians, however, were absent: they had been unable to recover
from the suppression in 1834. For the Catholic press the days were
difficult; obloquy was directed at the Church, clergy, and religion itself.
Freemasons spread their propaganda not only against the Church but
also against religion. The clergy felt they could not complain because
the royal family and even the Crown were being attacked just as
violently. It was in these circumstances that King Carlos I was shot
when returning to Lisbon from the Alentejo (February, 1908).

But the missions prospered. Angola, Mozambique, and India were
again moving toward their missionary goals. Several religious orders,
well staffed by priests and lay brothers, were actively at work; not only
hospitals and schools, but also the missions were staffed by sisters
from various religious communities.

Two Concordats were signed with the Holy See, both relating to
the royal patronage in the Eastern Indies. The first one (1857) dealt
with the situation rising out of the brief *Multa praeclare*. The Holy See
was extremely generous in the negotiations: practically all Portuguese
demands were accepted. The Portuguese government thought that the
nation was ready to continue the old missionary traditions which, of
course, required not only great sums of money but also a considerable
number of priests. Actually both requirements were lacking, as was evident after only a few years. Negotiations for a new Concordat were
undertaken and in 1886 a settlement was effected that was more realistic and adapted to local needs.

III. THE CHURCH DURING THE REPUBLIC (1910–1968)

The Portuguese Republican Party was founded in 1873, during the
reign of Luis I (1861–1889). Deeply influenced by positivism and
laicism, the party from its first days systematically attacked monarchy
and religion, Church and the clergy. Enjoying full freedom of action
and expression, the Republicans soon became an active minority. Complaints of wrongs and injustices, whatever their origin, found a sympa-

thetic ear in the Republican Party while non-Republican qualities and virtues were made the subject for all sorts of jeers and mockeries. In the course of the African disputes, Britain imposed the 1890 Ultimatum upon Portugal. The Crown was held responsible for these humiliating developments. After the assassination of King Carlos I and the Crown Prince Luis Filipe (February, 1908), the monarchical politicians thought that participation in the challenge to Church and clergy would be a popular course. Mistakenly they believed that for the monarch to espouse a course hostile to the Church would deprive the Republicans of popular support. Instead, the Republicans increased in numbers and notably in Lisbon and Porto the monarchy lost influence.

A. THE REPUBLIC VERSUS THE CHURCH

1. 1910 *Proclamation of the Separation Law*

The proclamation of the Republic took place on October 5, 1910. Three days later there began a general offensive against the Church. On October 8, a decree ordered that all previous legal measures against both the Jesuits (from Pombal's days) and the religious orders be enforced immediately. The government took over all their properties and houses. Other anti-Catholic measures were prescribed: religious oaths were abolished; the University of Coimbra was deprived of its faculty of theology; catechism was no longer to be taught in primary schools; divorce was introduced; marriage became a purely civil contract; a number of seminaries were closed and only five of them were allowed to teach theology.

The new government again interrupted diplomatic relations with the Holy See, and the Portuguese chargé d'affaires left Rome in September, 1911. As early as the end of October, 1910, the apostolic nuncio had been invited to leave Lisbon. The climax of the attacks against Church and religion was reached with the "Separation Law," April 20, 1911. Its aims were so manifest that no doubts could be entertained about them: within two or three generations, many Republicans said, Catholicism would cease to exist in Portugal.

A Republican writer, Eurico de Seabra, published a book favoring the Separation Law. In its first edition (1913), he argued that in effecting separation the Portuguese government had three alternatives: 1) a free Church within a free State; 2) a free Church within a neutral State; and 3) a Church under suspicion within a State that is on its guard.[1]

Afonso Costa, the Minister of Justice, openly stated that the Separation Law was especially meant for the Portuguese, not for the French or Brazilians, and so emphasized its anti-Catholic purposes. It was a "hostile" law based on the belief that the Catholic Church was doomed to disappear within two or three generations and should only be considered as an anachronism, a useless tradition to be thrown overboard.

2. The Pastoral Letter

Catholics throughout the world were informed of the seriousness of the situation in Portugal by the encyclical *Jamdudum in Lusitania* (May 24, 1911) in which Pope Pius X protested against the unwarranted persecution. Portuguese Catholics, led by their bishops, followed the papal lead. As Portuguese, the bishops had to be discerning in their official statements. Indeed, a neat distinction had to be drawn between 1) the relations between Church and Republic and 2) relations between Church and persecuting Republic. The new Republican regime, as such, could be freely accepted by the Portuguese; continued persecution of the Church by the Republic, however, called for the protests of all Portuguese Catholics. The bishops accordingly prepared a pastoral letter which was finished on Christmas Eve, 1910. It avowed due respect and obedience to the newly constituted government and, at the same time, protested against all its exceptional measures affecting the Catholic Church. Catholics were told: 1) to obey the government in any lawful matter, 2) not to cooperate in any antireligious action, and 3) to foster, by all lawful means, the causes of religion and Church.

The Republican government responded by refusing to allow this pastoral letter to circulate. Incredibly enough, the government's recourse was to the old *placet*. Nevertheless, the pastoral letter was circulated throughout Portugal. Porto's bishop, D. Antonio Barroso, who had rendered distinguished service in the African missions, openly defied the government's orders and insisted that the pastoral letter be read aloud in all churches in his diocese. Afonso Costa, Minister of Justice and Cults, who had advocated many anti-Church measures and who had exercised unwarranted jurisdiction and power, deprived him of his bishopric and declared the see vacant.

[1] Eurico de Seabra, A Separaçao e as suas Causas: A Egreja, as Congregaçoes e a Republica. Estudio documental e critico (Lisbon, 1913), II, 527.

The pastoral letter stressed the need for an organization of Catholics to defend the rights of religion and the Church. Initially, very little could be accomplished since the letter was not unanimously accepted and since its spirit was not generally reciprocated. The bishops, having deliberately bypassed the question of the form of government, were prepared to demand a free Constitution for all and to accept the Republic: they further stated that the Church felt no objection to the Republic as such. They did, however, demand the freedom that the Republican constitution offered to all.

Although the Church as a single entity did not object, many individual Catholics did. Two divergent parties appeared: some Catholics were ready to accept the Republican regime and even to cooperate with it; other Catholics remained faithful to their monarchical convictions. The latter could not adapt themselves to the new form of government and, rightly or not, followed the then famous slogan" politique d'abord." The bishops encountered numerous difficulties in following their essential and indispensable "middle" course. Eventually recognition and acceptance of the division by Catholics was the only possible basis for common action, since the Church had deliberately ignored the political aspects of the question.

B. The Republic and the Church (1915–1926)

The year 1915 saw the establishment of the *Centro Católico Português* which, among other aims, proposed to defend Church rights in Parliament. The *Centro*, although run by lay Catholics, professed strict allegiance to the bishops' ordinances and concerned itself only with Church teachings and rights and not with the political preference of its members. Without discrimination Monarchists and Republicans were admitted to its ranks, although this "union" did not please those Monarchists who were expecting the imminent return of the fallen regime. The bishops did not waver from their position, which was theoretically sound as well as practical.

During Sidonio Pais' government (December, 1917–December, 1918), the religious-political situation appeared to settle. Diplomatic relations with the Vatican were resumed. After his violent death, however, division sprang up again. Gradually the Monarchists came to appreciate that for the general good it would be well to set their political opinions aside and to collaborate with the *Centro Católico Português*. Once this matter of principle was definitely settled, all Portuguese

Catholics regardless of political party could unite in order to defend Church rights.

On December 17, 1923, there appeared the daily *Novidades*, devoted entirely to the defense of these very principles. At first, its significance was variously interpreted. *Novidades* accepted the Republican regime, but it was not concerned with the form of government. Monarchist and Republican writers or collaborators were equally acceptable in its pages. This rather delicate situation persisted, although with decreasing acuteness, until the National Revolution of May 28, 1926.

This Revolution was prompted by a common desire to overcome not only the economic difficulties which had beset the Republican regime from its beginning, but also to reach a common platform of constructive action. Division after division had so fragmented the Portuguese that most of them longed for a union that might bring them all together, regardless of their political predilection, and thus prepare a brighter future for all. Because the Revolution sought to be "national," it was prepared by Republicans and Monarchists. The governments which came out of it accepted with equal warmth all Portuguese, irrespective of political opinion and so Monarchists and Republicans could meet again on a common ground for the common interest. The regime question was deliberately placed on a secondary level; what mattered most was the quality of men, not their monarchical or republican origin. This same principle is now fostered by the *União Nacional* (National Union) which, open to all Portuguese of good will, aims to provide effective government.

On various occasions Portuguese governments have shown their respect for the Portuguese royal family which has been allowed to return to Portugal, where it lives at present. Duarte Nuno, the Portuguese king, travels throughout Portugal and is received by all with dignity and simplicity. The princes behave with a similar dignity. The heir apparent now belongs to the Portuguese armed forces.

C. The Church and the Republic (1926–1968)

1. *Political Orientation*

The *Estado Novo* (New State) admits no parties, but only the *União Nacional*. The latter is open to almost all Portuguese and is therefore not a party.[2] Many differences exist in the ranks of the

[2] Only Communists are excluded from this party.

União Nacional. These differences are quite apparent even in newspapers, for the common good may be viewed from different angles. The
Parliament or National Assembly, thus, has to play a double role: the
deputies have to collaborate with the government in discussing the
principal national problems and in preparing laws; they also have to
play the role of opposition, as legitimate opponents to the government.
Students of political science appear to find this situation rather hard
to understand.

The absence of political parties does not mean that all Portuguese
agree with the National Union. There are many who, for different
reasons, aspire to the establishment of the same parties which, in the
past, have, on several occasions, led Portugal to the brink of disaster.

But private political opinions are no concern of the Church authorities, who try to follow the admirable but difficult "middle way." They,
like the members of Parliament, have a dual role. On one hand, they
desire to obey and collaborate with the legitimate authorities, that is,
the government authorities; on the other, they wish to remain free from
all political ties. Bishops and priests have to open their arms to all people, no matter what their opinions and desires. Theirs is a difficult
position, which few appreciated.

The "New State" has been identified by many with Salazar, the
Prime Minister until 1968. He has been called a dictator and even
worse. Those who do so have not properly studied the Portuguese constitution and have forgotten what they may have learned about other
European and American constitutions. A publicity-shy septuagenarian
as a dictator should appear quite extraordinary. Still there are many
who believe that he is one.

At Coimbra the Cardinal Patriarch of Lisbon, Cerejeira, was one of
Salazar's best friends. It was quite natural that being called to the
supreme direction of national affairs, material and spiritual, they
should continue their former friendship. Logic, however, gave place
to illogic when the conclusion was drawn that the "New State" had
the Church entirely at its disposal. And, although public statements
of the Cardinal's disprove this, the point is the theme of propaganda
conducted by those who wish to return to the "Old State."

On the eve of his thirty-eighth anniversary as Patriarch of Lisbon,
Cardinal Cerejeira, in addressing the clergy and faithful of his archdiocese, delivered one of his most impressive speeches. He was quite
outspoken on several matters including the subject of Church and

State. Cardinal Cerejeira insisted that the Church must be "depoliticized," that is, free from all political ties and attractions. Catholics, however, have their own duties toward motherland and country, and theirs is a different case. This "middle way" followed by the Church runs the risk of pleasing nobody. But that is a glorious risk, for it means obedience to true charity. All men belong to the Church and she is ready to embrace all of them. Pleasing nobody, the Church has also the opportunity of pleasing all men of good will. And this is what matters.

Two recent instances reveal some of the difficulties of the clergy's position: D. Sebastião Soares de Resende, the late Bishop of Beria (Mozambique), and the Bishop of Porto. Both men spoke out against the existing political stalemate. Both have been misunderstood and misinterpreted.

By continuing to remain silent, the Bishop of Porto perhaps has committed some error. Labelled anti-government, he has been hailed by opponents of the present government as "their bishop." To Church authorities, he appears a sincere patriot and an adherent to the Church's middle-way policy.

Bishop Resende, considered one of "the most influential of the dissidents, if not the most militant," has written numerous "pastoral letters on religious, social, and educational matters, and enjoys the reputation of having attempted—with little success and some risk— to liberalize the Portuguese administration in the territory [Mozambique]."[3] Nevertheless he sincerely regretted that his name had been classed with Holden Roberto, Ilídio Machado, António Neto, and Mario Pinto de Andrade, all confessed terrorists. From him the government received sincere collaboration, although he had disagreed with some of its measures. For its part the government printing press had printed several of his pastoral letters.

The opponents of the Salazar regime have done their best to entangle the Catholic hierarchy and the government in a fruitless and hostile dialogue. Cardinal Cerejeira has pointed out the route that had been followed and was to be followed by all. Right from the Apostles' times, the Catholic Church was to respect all legitimate powers and authorities. Why should the Catholic Church in Portugal adopt a different procedure?

The Monarchists, also, complained that the Church did not oppose

[3] Ronald Segal, *African Profiles* (London, 1962).

the Republican regime in 1911, when the Church was being openly persecuted. The bishops then had a clear view of their position as leaders of the Church. And, what is more, some of them were rather inclined toward the former regime. Still, as bishops, theirs was a unanimous voice. This position must be followed today particularly since the Church is not being persecuted.

2. Religious Orientation

When the National Revolution took place (May 28, 1926), preparations for a Plenary Council were already far advanced. With the participation of practically all bishops from home and overseas, its sessions lasted from November 24 to December 3, 1926, and it dealt with all problems affecting Catholic life in Portugal. Its decrees are still in force today.

Since 1926 all the governments have sought the complete restoration of old Portuguese traditions, including religious ones. The official steps toward this goal were taken in 1933, when a new Constitution was promulgated. Some of its principles are relevant to our subject:

1) Among the rights, liberties, and individual guarantees enjoyed by the Portuguese are a) liberty and inviolability of religious beliefs and practices, for which no one may be persecuted, deprived of a right, or exempted from any obligation or civic duty and about which no one shall be compelled to answer questions except in a legally conducted census; b) freedom of teaching (Art. 8).
2) The instruction provided by the State, in addition to aiming at physical fitness and the improvement of intellectual faculties, has as its object the formation of character and of professional ability as well as the development of all moral and civic qualities, the former along the traditional principles of the country and of Christian doctrine and morality (Art. 43 #3).
3) No permission shall be required for the teaching of religion in private schools (Art. 43 #4).
4) The Catholic religion may be freely practiced, in public or in private, as the religion of the Portuguese nation. The Catholic Church shall enjoy juridical personality and may organize itself in conformity with canon law and create thereunder associations or organizations whose juridical personality shall be recognized. The relationship between the State and the Catholic Church shall be one of separation, with diplomatic relations maintained between the Holy See and Portugal by means of reciprocal representation,

and Concordats or agreements entered into in the sphere of the *padroado* and where other matters of common interest are or need to be regulated (Art. 45). The Portuguese Catholic missions overseas and the establishments for training personnel for their services and for those of the *padroado* shall, in conformity with the Concordats and other agreements concluded with the Holy See, enjoy juridical personality and shall be protected and assisted by the State, as being institutions of education and assistance and instruments of civilization (Art. 140).

The Concordat and Missionary Convention—The Constitution gave ample satisfaction to Catholics. A few years later, when preparations began for the solemn celebrations of the Double Centenary of Portugal (the eighth centenary of her foundation in 1140 and the third centenary of her independence in 1640) the government decided to open negotiations with the Holy See for the signature of a Concordat and Missionary Convention. These diplomatic instruments were signed on May 7, 1940, three days before the German irruption throughout Europe. Both documents had the same object in view: the Concordat dealt with all religious situations then existing in metropolitan Portugal; the Missionary Convention covered all missionary matters. The principles previously laid down in the Constitution were also registered in both documents.

One of the main dispositions of the Concordat was the suppression of divorce for Catholic marriages celebrated after that date, although, under legally specified conditions, it was permitted in the case of civil marriages. The measure, however logical and legitimate, has been variously interpreted. Many Catholics illogically think that a Catholic marriage should enjoy the same rights attributed to a civil one. At present, among certain Catholics there is still talk of marriages "before" and marriages "after" the Concordat.

The appointment of bishops now belongs entirely to the Holy See. The government, however, is consulted about whether it has any objection to the nomination of a particular candidate. If no reply is forthcoming within thirty days, silence is considered as assent.[4]

The Missionary Convention, in turn, organized Portuguese missions in Portuguese territory. Angola was divided into three dioceses, one of them (Luanda) being raised to the rank of archdiocese, thus

[4] *Portugal e a Santa Se: Concordata e Acordo Missionario de 7 de Maio de 1940* (Lisbon, 1943).

forming an ecclesiastical province. Today there are seven dioceses in all. Portuguese East Africa constituted only a "nullius" prelacy. In 1940 it was subdivided into three dioceses, the main one (Lourenço-Marques) being made an archdiocese. Mozambique now has seven dioceses. Macao (China) continues to hold the same rank as before, but the Portuguese part of Timor Island was severed from the Macao diocese and became an independent bishopric.

The Portuguese government undertook to protect and aid all Portuguese missions. From 1940 to the present such aid has been given generously, and all missions seem to be flourishing. Various religious orders work in the area and many have seminaries either in metropolitan Portugal or in the Atlantic archipelagoes of Madeira and Azores. To the old religious orders other modern missionary associations have joined their initiative and enthusiasm.

There are no Apostolic vicariates in the Portuguese missionary organization. This is a policy long cherished by Portugal, that is, the existence of real dioceses. This has been in contrast with the policy followed by the Holy Congregation for the Propagation of the Faith, which originated the idea of Apostolic vicars. At the last Ecumenical Council, the decree Ad gentes omitted mention of such vicars so that it could speak exclusively of bishops, that is, true bishops. There is, however, an exception in Portuguese missionary organization: Guinea is not a diocese and it is not an Apostolic vicariate. Although it is still a mere Apostolic prefecture, it is hoped that very soon it will also receive the title of a real diocese.

Portuguese missions are not dependent on the Holy Congregation for the Propagation of the Faith. Like the other Portuguese dioceses, they correspond directly with the Holy Consistorial Congregation, for there is no difference whatsoever between metropolitan and overseas dioceses. In fact, some of the overseas dioceses are in a better position than some dioceses at home.

It must be remembered, however, that from 1910 to 1940 the development of Portuguese missions was stagnant. First of all, the Portuguese Republican government ceased to help them as it had done previously; thus most had to reduce their activities while others had to close down. Secondly, religious missionaries were expelled, and such colonies as Angola and Mozambique were left entirely in the care of the secular clergy. The Republican government went further and tried to replace Catholic missionaries with lay workers, soon called "lay missionaries." As the Portuguese politicians thought that they needed no religion to be good and faithful citizens, why should the same not apply to overseas Portuguese, the Africans? At first the same politicians preferred Protestant missionaries to the Catholic ones, but abandoned this preference. The "lay missionaries" did not meet government expectations and slowly such schemes were dropped. However, because of the government's disillusionment with the Protestant missionaries, it had to turn again to the Catholic missionaries, for only the latter consistently cooperated with the civil authorities. This did not mean that the government was disposed to alter the "separation" policy; consequently the Catholic missions were deemed "national institutions" or "civilizing missions," and as such were eligible for government subsidies. Although the word "religion" was carefully avoided in the first years, it eventually was openly acknowledged.

After 1917 the religious orders gradually began to work overseas again, and after 1940 they came in great numbers. Many of the missions continue to receive direct government subsidies. No government helps the missions as generously as the Portuguese government, but although this is to be praised, one should also be cognizant of the Portuguese people's deep awareness of their responsibility as a missionary nation. By and large they are convinced that it is the State's function to support overseas missionary work. In recent years, happily a healthy change in this outlook has begun.

According to the Missionary Convention (1940), all foreign missionaries are expected to help the government in fostering its national policy. They must know and teach Portuguese; they should obey Portuguese laws; they must accept the jurisdiction of Portuguese tribunals, and so on. Following several instructions from the Holy See, foreign missionaries must adopt the country where they work as their second "motherland" and obey the authorities there; moreover, they have the obligation to foster the education of good national citizens. This is done in every mission field throughout the world. The Portuguese authorities do not see why this same policy should not be pursued in Portuguese Africa, for it has been explained over and over again not only in official statements but also in books and in international meetings: Angola and Mozambique and Guinea are Portuguese provinces, not colonies. In spite of this, several foreign missionaries, mainly Protestants but including a few Catholics, have thought it their duty not to agree with Portuguese overseas policy, and consequently have not cooperated with the legitimate authorities, have not fostered the education of good national citizens and have favored Portugal's own enemies. The Portuguese authorities, therefore, have called them to account and in some cases have sent them away from their missionary posts.

Conscientious objections should always be highly respected. The Portuguese government desires that missionaries burdened by such objections should work elsewhere, and not on Portuguese soil. The expulsion of several of these missionaries has made a deep impression in many international centers and appears to provide one more reason to attack Portugal's policy in Africa. If some excuse may be offered for Protestant missionaries who do not have definite guidance in such delicate matters, Catholic missionaries are much less excusable, for they know or should know the teachings emanating from the Holy See, from the very foundation of the Holy Congregation for the Propagation of the Faith. Portugal occupies a unique position in Africa, and Catholic missionaries regardless of their objections, must accept this fact: Portugal is still in Africa, where she exercises a legitimate authority. Such authority must be obeyed. Because the Protestant missions did not collaborate with the State, they do not occupy a privileged position in Portuguese Africa, although their missions are superior to the Catholic ones. They do not feel as deeply as the Catholics the Lord's order ". . . go ye and teach. . . ." Rather they satisfy themselves with a few missions that are good. The Catholic missionaries, on the other hand, take, to a certain extent, a different attitude in fostering many, although inferior, missions. What matters to them is preaching the Gospel to as many people as possible.

3. The Ecclesiastical Structure

At present the ecclesiastical organization includes eighteen dioceses in Portugal divided into the three ecclesiastical provinces of Lisbon, Braga, and Evora. There is a diocese in each of the Portuguese Atlantic archipelagoes: Madeira, in Funchal; Azores, in Terceira Island; Cape Verde, at Santiago Island; the seven dioceses in Angola form an ecclesiastical province under the Archdiocese of Luanda; the seven dioceses in Mozambique constitute an ecclesiastical province, the Archbishopric of Lourenço-Marques. There is also the Archdiocese of Goa, in Portuguese India, the Diocese of Macao, and finally, the Diocese of Dili, in Portuguese Timor.

Under the terms of the 1940 Concordat all the bishops are Portuguese: two of them are Goans who govern the Dioceses of Sa da Bandeira (Angola) and Cape Verde. Portuguese Guinea is not yet a diocese, but merely a "nullius" prelacy.

Most of the dioceses own minor and major seminaries. Lisbon and Braga each have three seminaries. The religious orders also have their own seminaries. Many priests, both secular and regular, attend state universities and graduate in various branches of science in order to devote themselves to teaching either in seminaries or in colleges or even in state schools. Among the Portuguese clergy there is a long tradition of attending foreign universities, particularly the Gregorian University, Rome. The Portuguese bishops maintain a well-equipped college. The religious orders also follow the same policy, particularly for their theologians, most of whom are sent to their order's foreign colleges or universities. The religious orders have joined with the diocesan clergy in order to solve the problem of ecclesiastical education. The Jesuit faculty of philosophy of Braga was very recently established and is in fact the first faculty of the Catholic University of Portugal, a long desired goal now in process of achievement.

This does not mean that Portugal has enough priests. Far from it. In this respect, one may divide Portugal into two zones: the north is the more populous area and its dioceses provide the higher percentage of vocations. Here the religious orders have established their seminaries, and many of the priests working in other dioceses come from the north. In the north as well feminine vocations to the religious life are more numerous. In the rest of the country, where liberalism and positivism have made a greater impact, vocations are relatively few. Indeed, all central and southern dioceses are served by clergy coming from outside the area and so differ from most European dioceses, which are staffed by their own clergy. The exchange of priests, however, is likely to increase, as a result of the recommendations passed by the last Ecumenical Council. In some Portuguese dioceses a few foreign priests also serve.

The situation is even worse overseas. In Angola the Holy Ghost Fathers, many of them foreigners, man almost all the dioceses. In Mozambique the Portuguese Franciscans are the most numerous, followed by Portuguese Jesuits and Portuguese Fathers of the Society for Overseas Catholic Missions. For the next several years the dioceses of Angola and Mozambique will continue to need foreign help. Native clergy are being actively prepared in all missionary dioceses but vocations are not as numerous as they should be. Although the minor seminaries are practically full, the results are not proportionate. This, of course, is a universal trend and not simply African.

4. The Religious Revival

Catholic Action has played an important role in the religious revival of the nation not only in Europe but in the overseas territories. In April, 1932, the Episcopal Conference organized Catholic Action which by then had an enthusiastic following all over Europe. Young Portuguese priests, who had graduated mainly in Rome and Louvain, returned home convinced that Catholic Action was perhaps the most promising means of vitalizing popular religion left. Several months went into the preparation of statutes that were approved at the next meeting of the Episcopal Conference in November, 1933. Portuguese Catholic Action was entrusted to the able direction of the Archbishop of Mitylene, Ernest Sena de Oliveira, who had also supervised the drafting of the statutes. The Vatican had observed the preparations, for this official launching of Catholic Action in Portugal roused the deep interest of the Vatican. As a result, on November 10, 1933, Pope Pius XI addressed a letter to the Cardinal Patriarch of Lisbon, Manuel Gonçalves Cerejeira, in which were drawn the main lines to be followed in Portugal: spiritual care for the workers, religious instruction for all, the publication of good literature—books, magazines, and newspapers.

The whole nation was readily impressed by the zeal and fervor of the Catholic Action religious assistants, carefully chosen by the bishops, and responded to their leadership. They made use of all possible means of social communication, such as meetings, congresses, symposia, festivals, and retreats. Primary attention was paid to the proper preparation of lay leaders who were to work in their respective environments for Catholic Action, which without such leaders would be quite useless.

The organization followed more or less the same lines that had been previously adopted in Belgium for youths and adults. The JOC and JOCF (women's section), in particular, were vigorously active and made a forcible impact. The country's industrialization was then in full swing and this contributed in no small scale to the success then registered.

The Catholic revival was also aided by the monthly *Lumen*, a review of Catholic culture, which began publication in 1937. This as well as *Semanas Sociais Portuguesas* (Portuguese Social Weeks) were efforts to promote the study and knowledge of Church social doctrine.[5]

Still another influence in the revival was the appearance of the Virgin Mary to the three children of Fatima (May 13–October 13, 1917). The children declared that the Virgin Mary had appeared to them, that she had urged prayer and repentance and had foretold the coming of peace to the suffering world, that she wished a fervent recitation of the Rosary, and that she would like to be invoked on that same spot. The six apparitions marked an extraordinary change in Portuguese religious life. It may be a singular coincidence that in December of the same year Sidonio Pais led his winning revolution against the antireligious government.

At first the religious authorities kept aloof from the movement stirred up by the apparitions and were perplexed by the miracles, prayers, penance, and conversions. Vast crowds of both believers and unbelievers flocked to Fatima on the thirteenth of each month. The civil authorities, for their part, recognized what they believed their duty to be: to nip in the bud the fervent surge of devotion that was manifested every month. The children were threatened, jailed, and persecuted but to no avail. The "superstition," as it was called, triumphed. The Bishop of Leiria, who had jurisdiction over Fatima, decided in 1922 to pursue a thorough canonical investigation of the alleged facts and in a pastoral letter dated October 13, 1930, he authorized the cult of Our Lady of Fatima. The common people, however, had not waited for such permission: they had understood Fatima's message much earlier than the hierarchy. It was later said that Fatima gave the law to the Church rather than the reverse. The recent visit of Pope Paul VI to the sanctuary, following visits of several cardinals and many bishops from all parts of the Catholic world, provided a crowning touch to the devotion of Fatima.

Modern Portugal's spiritual revival practically began at Fatima. Today, however, Fatima is not an exclusive Portuguese affair—it is the world's meeting-place for all devoted to Our Lady.

IV. CONCLUSION

Relations between Church and State have consistently been a decisive matter in the history of the Catholic Church in Portugal. At

[5] Avelino Gonçalves, *Dez Anos de Acção Catolica* (Lisbon, 1945).

times, the State has quite dominated the Church and easily drew the Church into its own line of action. On other occasions, the Church authorities have reacted and protested. Such was the pattern in the beginning, in later centuries, and today, although on a minor scale, and the pattern will probably prevail in the future. It is expected, however, that the "depoliticization" of the Church, for which all men of good will are so concerned, will attain full realization.

The nineteenth century may be divided, according to historians, into two parts: the first part, extending to 1870, when France was easily overcome by Germany, was deeply influenced by liberalism; after the fall of the French Empire and the loss of the Papal States in the 1870's, the laicist period begins. Liberalism focuses on the general need for liberty. But in the name of this same liberty, all actions and reactions are allowed and freely explained. While in Protestant countries, liberty has meant that the Catholic Church is granted an opportunity for development, in Catholic nations, and in Portugal specifically, liberty has appeared as an aggressive weapon against the Church. Catholicism remains indeed the "official" religion of such countries and most Catholic politicians consider this fact as an all but inalienable privilege. Laicism then steps in and aims at the establishment of a lay state. In Portugal the liberal period continued until 1910 when the Republic straightaway attempted to establish a purely lay state removed from any religious influence.

Catholic visitors to Portugal have often remarked about a curious feature among Portuguese Catholics, and especially among those who live an indifferent Catholic life: they may be religious, some even very religious, but they are unable to conceal a certain anticlericalism. There is an outward distinction between religion and Church. Religion is rather impersonal, while the Church comes to them through the priests. Occasional scandals among the clergy are immediately enhanced and attributed not only to the offenders but to the whole class. This results from mutual unacquaintance and incomprehension, fostered by a tradition of propaganda against priests and monks. Often those who habitually criticize the clergy, upon becoming familiar with a priest, admit: "At least this one is different from the others! If the others were only like him!" And when questioned about the number of priests they know, they will confess quite candidly: "None save this one. But I know that the others are different."

This also explains the influence exercised by certain priests, whose apostolic lives have affected all public opinion. In recent years Portugal has venerated two such priests: Father Cruz and Father Americo. The first was known throughout Portugal for his charity and the second for his endeavors to care for abandoned boys. Throughout Portugal they were recognized and revered.

Thus one concludes that the clergy has remained too aloof from the common people. The gulf existing between them is being bridged, chiefly because Vatican II has stirred up in the clergy a deeper sense of responsibility.

The much disputed aftereffects of the Council, generally observed all over the Catholic world, have been less noticeable in Portugal. This can be partially explained by the Portuguese people's three principal devotions: the Blessed Sacrament, the Virgin Mary, and the Holy See. The opinions expressed by some theologians during the Council were regarded with some suspicion by the Portuguese people. Our Lady of Fatima has so deeply impressed the country that any slur on that devotion is at once rejected. There are, of course, some exceptions, and their exceptional character should be recognized.

Recently there has been some foreign propaganda against Fatima. Some Catholic newspapers and magazines criticized Pope Paul's visit to Fatima because it was thought that such a visit might strengthen the present political situation. If such reporters actually observed the way the government behaved during the pope's visit, they would have to agree that it could not have been more prudent and unobtrusive. This visit, on the other hand, produced a general effect on those who had hastily judged the visit Paul VI had paid to Bombay during the Eucharistic Congress, some years after the violent occupation of Goa by Indian armies. Portuguese crowds from all over the country flocked to Fatima in order to see and hail the Holy Father.

Today Portugal is generally criticized because of her overseas policy. This fact may have some influence on the severe judgment that anything Portuguese receives on the part of hurried readers. Portugal's case is unique. It deserves research and study.[6]

[6] The two standard works on Portuguese Church History are: Fortunato de Almeida, *Historia da Igreja em Portugal,* 4 vols. (Coimbra, 1910–1917), of which a second edition is in course of publication; and Miguel de Oliveira, *Historia Eclesiastica de Portugal* (3rd ed., Lisbon, 1958).

7 : SPAIN

Jean Becarud

INTRODUCTION

The Church in its history has been subjected to a twofold trial: persecution and, perhaps the more dangerous, triumph, that is, in the sense of temporal triumph. This observation made by Nikolai Berdyaev fits the situation of Spanish Catholicism today.

The vicissitudes that the Spanish Church has successively experienced during the last thirty-five years include: the anticlerical measures of the period of the Republic, proscription extending even to physical extermination during the Civil War, then, after 1939 and the victory of General Franco, the return to privileged status culminating in the Concordat of 1953. In recent decades the Church in Spain has been constantly placed in extreme positions. Only since the Second Vatican Council has it entered upon, and not without many difficulties, an apprenticeship to a new attitude, one both less extreme and less monolithic.

An analysis of the present state of a Catholicism now in full evolution requires as a preliminary a brief account of some historical antecedents which have helped to give the Spanish Church its special character. Such an account may serve to forestall misunderstanding of the particular forms that the conflict between the Church and civil society in Spain has assumed.

Essentially one must remember that only a very incomplete secularization of Spanish social life has taken place. Intimately involved in the existence of the nation from as far back as the Visigothic monarchy and during the period of the Reconquista, the Church remained present everywhere in the Peninsula under the Hapsburgs as well as under the Bourbons. The interpenetration of Catholicism and nationalism persisted practically without interruption until the end of the eighteenth century, despite the existence of a dissident intellectual current.

In a country where centrifugal forces and separatist tendencies have always been strong, the Church since the fifteenth century has proved to be the most effective element of cohesion and because of this was used extensively by the civil power. The official Catholicism of the Crown and the real and profound Catholicism of the nation coexisted until about 1820, after the clergy had played a decisive role in the War of Independence, that is, the struggle against the French invaders.

In spite of its ultimate failure, Napoleon's attempted conquest caused considerable turmoil in the spirits of men. "Traditionalists" and "Liberals" confronted each other. The opposition of the vast majority of the clergy to liberal ideas and their favor to the Carlists, defenders of tradition, helped to form, for the first time, a substantial barrier between the Church and a portion of the Spanish people. Violent anticlericalism soon appeared. Between 1830 and 1850 the burning of religious buildings, so characteristically Spanish, began to occur. During the same period, when avant-garde liberal governments were in power, they deliberately attacked the Church, seized the possessions of the clergy, and dissolved the religious orders.

This eclipse of the influence of the Church was short and superficial. After 1850, apart from the six years between the fall of Isabel II in 1868 and the restoration of the Bourbons in 1874, the Church recovered a position in national life different but no less eminent and privileged than that of the preceding centuries. This state of affairs endured with little change until the beginning of the Second Republic in 1931.

The liberal antireligious offensive, though superficial and limited in time, had important consequences. It did not achieve the laicization of society that had progressively occurred in France. By their confiscation of ecclesiastical property, in particular, Spanish anticlericals helped to throw the Church into the arms of the State which quickly decided to profit from a close alliance with the altar. After the clergy were deprived of the Church's lands which served to enrich the middle class and provided no assistance to less favored social groups, they turned to the civil power to assure their own material existence.

The Church as an institution, often the defender of the weak against the powerful and, because of the monks, in close contact with the masses, thus found itself, as early as the second half of the nineteenth century, on the side of the government and the rich. On the whole, the clergy, wishing to recover their former authority and a leading role for the Church in the life of the nation, sought to do so through a *rapprochement* with leading social groups. The shift of the Church as an institution to the side of the rulers instead of the ruled naturally increased the misunderstanding between the lower clergy and an important part of the lower classes, especially in the cities. Anticlericalism was thus sustained and expressed itself in sudden flare-ups well before the explosion of 1936—as in the riots of the "Tragic Week" in Barcelona in 1909. Gradually and until the fall of the monarchy in 1931, State Catholicism became more artificial and too often had the appearance of collusion between the civil power and the ecclesiastical hierarchy. It coincided less and less with the spontaneous movement of the people, except in regions of the Peninsula which were economically well-balanced or had remained separated from industrial life. State-dominated, bourgeois, and rural, the Spanish Church remained ignorant of an important social phenomenon—the migration of poor peasants toward the suburbs of the big cities where a largely dechristianized proletariat lived. After 1931 this proletariat, along with the landless agricultural workers, formed the backbone of the extreme leftist movements which were profoundly anticlerical. Even though we must not restrict ourselves solely to the political image of the Spanish Church, this summary sketch enables us to grasp a few of its principal characteristics:

1. The permanently acute problem of Church-State relations derives from Catholicism being the official religion of Spain. This is a factor of such scope and has played and still plays such an important role in the religious life of the country that it would be unjust to pretend that, all at once and without great suffering, the Church can free itself from such subjection.

2. A continuing and dominant idea is that peculiarly Spanish values are indissolubly linked to the Catholic religion. A whole school of thought persists in believing the Spanish people to be a chosen people with the mission of defending Catholicism lived in an integral manner. Persuaded that Spain has historically incarnated, and can continue to incarnate, a certain ideal relationship between the temporal and

spiritual powers, a rather large number of Catholics fight, no matter
what the odds, for the maintenance of a Catholic order of which, they
believe, the Spain of today, like that of the Counter-Reformation, must
remain the unshakeable bastion. It is clearly in these milieux, often described as "more Catholic than the pope," that the movement of renewal born of the Second Vatican Council meets the most resistance.

3. Powerful anticlericalism, although it has somewhat subsided at
the moment, remains latent. This anticlericalism by no means excludes
the maintenance of a more or less profound religious feeling. It often
represents the resentment of believers, or of the descendants of believers, who have been deceived by the conduct of the representatives of
the Church. We can even go further and say that in Spain atheists, for
there are some, and more than official statistics admit, have been much
more influenced, consciously or not, by centuries of authentic and
practically unanimous religious life than in most other Christian countries. This fusion of past and present makes the study of Spanish
Catholicism a study of complex distinction and delicate nuances so that
even a broad outline description of the evolution of the Spanish
Church since 1939 requires a historical background.

I. SPANISH CATHOLICISM SINCE 1939

A. From 1939 to the Concordat of 1953

In 1939 the Church in Spain, sorely tried by the Civil War, found itself
at the end of the conflict deeply committed to the side of the victors.
In its Collective Letter of 1937 the episcopate, with only two exceptions,
had in fact given its support without reservation to the "National Up-
rising." Only a substantial part of the Basque clergy and a few Catalan
priests espoused a position favorable to the Republicans.

Once peace was restored, the leaders of the Church exploited this
situation thoroughly in order to resume for Catholicism its centuries-
old role as moral guide of the nation. In this they were aided by both
the artificial and authentic religious renewal that became apparent in
the country after the terrible ordeal it had just undergone. On their
part, the civil authorities supported Catholicism with all their power,
since the cooperation of the Church was as valuable for supporting

the regime in the difficult political and diplomatic course it would have to follow as in establishing the regime. Several periods in this time span may be distinguished. Between 1939 and 1944, even though the Church recovered the position it had enjoyed before 1931—state aid for worship and freedom for Catholic schools and indeed other privileges affecting its civil status—the influence of the Falange, the only party and one jealous of its prerogatives in the State, predominated. Consequently there arose some friction between the religious and the civil authorities, especially regarding youth organizations and the nomination of bishops. On this latter point the Holy See, but not without difficulty, finally acceded to the demands of Serrano Suñer, Minister of Foreign Affairs. The agreement of June 7, 1941, stipulated that the pope would appoint bishops and archbishops. The appointment was to be made from a list of six, later of three, names submitted by the Spanish government. This is basically the system of the Concordat of 1953 still in force today.

After 1945 the Falangists, compromised by their sympathy for totalitarian countries, suffered an eclipse. They were, in part at least, replaced by militant Catholics; with the agreement of the Cardinal Primate, Martin Artajo, leader of Catholic Action, became Minister of Foreign Affairs. The "Fuero de los Españoles," dating from 1945 and a sort of fundamental Law of the Regime, expressly recognizes in Article 6 the Catholic character of the Spanish State. The years 1945–1950 are the high point of religious triumphalism. Ostracized by the United Nations, Spain wished to be the exception of the modern world. There was a veritable domination of certain sectors of national life by the Church, one inspired by a nostalgia to return to the paradise of the Catholic tradition. The Church was not only represented in numerous branches of the government such as the Council of the Realm, the National Council of the Falange; not only were official unions of Falangist youth groups assigned "religious advisors"; but even more the clergy exercised a vigilant control over the press, cinema, and radio. Public religious functions (processions and pilgrimages) in which a representative of the State participated, recovered their former splendor. In all the "pueblos" or villages of the Peninsula the curé was by far the most important person. Only a few with nostalgia for the monarchy, like Cardinal Segura, Archbishop of Seville, disturbed this euphoria by denouncing certain totalitarian aspects of the regime.

Today there are many Spanish Catholics, even those far from extreme positions, who judge this period harshly. One of them, Federico Revilla, has recently written:

> Distorted or not, the situation of the Church in Spain after 1939 provided it with a whole series of opportunities for action. It was protected, subsidized, defended, and supported. . . . Every initiative for religious propaganda was received favorably by the public authorities. Our generation has enjoyed the great opportunity of preaching the Christian message without interference, even to the most refractory of individuals, but it did not take advantage of it. We were lulled into complacency instead of profiting from these advantages in a missionary spirit, and nothing was done with them. We worked for years to maintain a pure and simple morality by the use of censure and prohibition. . . . Public religious functions were mass demonstrations, triumphalist spectacles whose only effect was to weaken even more the need for an in-depth apostolate.[1]

Nothing needs to be added to those harsh lines except to point out that after 1950, when Spain began to come out of its diplomatic isolation, a few farseeing minds like Bishop Herrera of Malaga understood that the superficial religious revival, born of certain favorable political circumstances, had run its course and that it was time to try to build more solid structures. Thus specialized movements of Catholic Action or other organisms like the "Cursillos of Christianity" were initiated.

B. From the Concordat to the Second Vatican Council (1953–1962)

The consolidation of the Franco regime in the 1950's and the spectacular *rapprochement* of Spain with the United States dispelled the doubts of the Holy See. In August, 1953, a Concordat provided a complete contractual basis for relations between the Catholic Church and the Spanish State. This Concordat is rather exceptional, at least in modern times, for it does not so much settle the rights of the Church with a State that could disrupt them, but rather harmonizes relations between two "perfect societies," each acting in its own sphere: the

---

[1] Federico Revilla, *Objectiones al Catolicismo español* (Barcelona, 1967), pp. 102–103.

Catholic Church and the officially Catholic Spanish State. The Church is recognized as a privileged body in the national community and this privileged body, by its very nature, is given supervisory right over the moral life of all Spaniards. Recognized as a legal and economic entity the Church administers its own property and has its own courts. The clergy is exempt from military service and episcopal directives escape civil censure. Furthermore, only religious marriage is recognized for baptized couples. The teaching of the Catholic religion is obligatory in state schools from the elementary grades through the university. On the one hand, the Spanish government retains the right to nominate the bishops[2], while prayers for the Caudillo, "Dux noster Franciscus," are to be said by priests during Mass. The State pays the salaries of the clergy. About 40 per cent of the budget of the Minister of Justice is devoted to ecclesiastical expenses. This along with the sums allotted to the Church by other departments of government, especially that of National Education, amounted in 1959, to 1.5 per cent of the whole budget.[3] In short, the Concordat established relations between the State and Church of such a nature as to justify more than ever the term "officialization" to describe the position of Catholicism in Spain.

After the signing of the Concordat, the Catholic hierarchy recognized that the clarification of the respective positions of the Church and the State enabled them to express reservations about the way in which civil power is used in certain areas. Since 1953, episcopal documents have more frequently criticized the regime's teaching on labor unions which was linked to monopoly in a way not in conformity with the social teachings of the Church. Some prelates also regretted the absence of a real law regarding the press which, while repudiating "license," would allow a relatively greater liberty. It was primarily in regard to social matters that the bishops adopted a firmer tone in order to criticize the unjust distribution of wealth, the low level of wages, and the selfishness of the rich.

Pastoral letters and episcopal directives, however, were not the most

[2] The complete procedure is as follows: the head of the State, in agreement with the nuncio, proposes six candidates to the pope who then chooses three of these. From these three names retained by the Sovereign Pontiff the head of the State chooses one on whom the pope confers the canonical office.

[3] W. Ebenstein, *Church and State in Franco's Spain* (Princeton, 1960), pp. 44–45.

significant of the changes in depth that Spanish Catholicism experienced after 1956. This date which marks the decline of militant Falangism is also the one marking the coming of age of a new generation less scarred than the preceding one by memories of the Civil War. In this new generation, especially in university circles, there is a much greater consciousness not only of the "abnormal" character of the Spanish regime, but also of the too evident collusion of the Church with the regime. Spain, it was said, was suffering from "religious inflation." Soon opposition groups appeared in which young Catholics played a preponderant role, as in the FLP (Popular Liberation Front) whose leader, Julio Cerón, a Catholic diplomat, was arrested and imprisoned in November, 1957. The next year there appeared in the ranks of the clergy a current of marked hostility to the spirit of the regime. In May, 1960, 339 Basque priests wrote a letter to their bishops in which they deplored the lack of liberty in the Spanish political community, the systematic distortion of truth in the press, and the use of torture by the police. These priests were, of course, disavowed by the hierarchy but it is no less remarkable that when, in December of the same year, a very heated polemic took place between the Cardinal Primate and the Secretary General of the Solís movement over the HOAC (Catholic Action Workers Brotherhood),[4] Cardinal Pla y Deniel energetically defended the HOAC who were accused by the head of the official unions. Soon, in Catalonia and in the Basque provinces, there tended to develop a permanent state of tension between the authorities and militant young Catholics. This was evidence of a real change of climate, a change which increases after 1962.

C. Since the Second Vatican Council (1962–1967)

The year of the first session of the Council, 1962, was for Spain one of intense social agitation. In the spring, there were big strikes especially in the Asturias. Thousands of Catholic workers took part and the HOAC played a leading role. In the areas affected by the movement, the parish clergy supported the strikers, but the bishops remained reticent and divided. One had to wait until 1963 to see an ecclesiastical dignitary, Dom Aureli Escarré, the Abbot of Montserrat, break with

---

[4] This is the principal worker movement in Catholic Action and later it will be considered at greater length.

the prudent line of conduct of the high clergy. Dom Escarré did not hesitate to condemn openly the attitude of the Franco government which, in his eyes, was guilty of refusing citizens the right to participate in public life. This nonconformism obliged the Abbot of Montserrat, after many incidents, to give up the headship of the famous monastery and to leave Spain early in 1967.

Meanwhile, the Council debates began in the autumn of 1962. The Council, according to the expectations of the Spanish bishops, would have a dogmatic character. The turn taken by these general sessions of Catholicity completely surprised the Spanish bishops while the whole Catholic world beyond the Pyrenees was shaken to its foundations as it had not been for centuries. As the sessions succeeded each other, the new ideas which the Council proposed were heatedly discussed by the various levels of the clergy as well as by militant Catholics: collegiality, the place of the laity in the Church, opening the Church to the world, ecumenism, and religious liberty. These were theses that put' to question many commonly accepted certitudes.

The very fact that a public discussion on problems of exceptional importance, a discussion which was respectful of the ideas of each discussant, could take place in Rome had immense repercussions in Spain. Numerous tensions, until then suppressed, came into the open. The confrontation which the Council permitted between the mentality of the Spanish hierarchy and that of other episcopates was in itself heavy with consequences. The Spanish bishops, at first uncertain and not very active, were themselves profoundly shaken by the contacts they made in Rome. If subsequently they intervened more, and sometimes quite to the point, especially on the question of the liturgy, they nonetheless joined as a whole the conservative minority at the Council. This was particularly evident during the final session.

Faced with episcopal reticence an important part of the young clergy became enthusiastic for the *aggiornamento*. The encyclicals of John XXIII, especially *Pacem in terris*, found an immediate response in Spain. A certain number of avant-garde Catholics, who had previously been suspect, could henceforth come into the open. One of the most representative of them, José Luis Aranguren, wrote:

This encyclical has just told us bluntly that in the political order at least—for the political order is more important than the personal order—we are far from what we think. The whole edifice of a retrograde Catholicism which turns its back on the modern world is henceforth considered uninhabitable. For the first time those Catholics among us who are not happy in this edifice can breathe freely without danger of condemnation.[5]

The real traumatic effect of the Council in the heart of Spanish Catholicism arises from a crystallization of contradictory tendencies. Partisans of "resistance" and followers of the movement are to confront each other more directly, as the application of some of the Council decisions touches certain crucial questions in Spain. One of the rare Spanish bishops who can be classified unequivocally as on the side of the Council's majority, Bishop Mauro Rubio of Salamanca, is perfectly clear on this matter. In 1966, after the Council was over, he wrote: "The present situation, subject to the Concordat of 1953, but even more to the Council which ended in 1965, is historically transitional. The Council necessitates a revision of the Concordat."[6]

Two series of particularly important clauses of the Concordat are in fact jeopardized directly by the Council: one concerns the manner of nominating bishops and the other the status of non-Catholics. Moreover, a certain number of prerogatives of a juridical or political character that the Concordat grants to the Church in Spain seem to be no longer compatible with the spirit of the Council. These various problems as well as those of the increasingly difficult relations between the hierarchy and Catholic Action movements have dominated the whole evolution of Spain during the last two years. As we shall see later, they are likewise at the heart of the differences between the hierarchy of the Church and a portion of the young clergy. A legislative measure on religious liberty was approved at the beginning of the summer of 1967, but the efforts of the Foreign Minister, Castiella, the tireless promoter of the law, encountered very strong opposition from the partisans of the "resistance." The final text of the law, though considerably toned down, does not seem to please the small Protestant minority and does not mention the rights of the non-Catholics who were more or less recognized as existing in Spain. Likewise, although the episcopate made a declaration of principle in which it renounced some of its privileges, this stand has had hardly any effect, and a number of ecclesiastical dignitaries still continue, for example, to sit in official bodies by right

[5] Quoted by Msgr. Jobit, L'Église d'Espagne à l'Heure du Concile (Paris, 1965), p. 205.

[6] Quoted in Informations Catholiques Internationales, November 15, 1966, 27.

of their office.[7] Finally and especially in regard to the nominations of bishops, the wishes of the Holy See, which ardently hopes to see the Spanish government freely renounce prerogatives now anachronistic, have not been fulfilled and the question at the moment seems to have reached a dead end. There are at present more than fifteen vacant episcopal sees.

As a result of all this, the Spanish Church is experiencing a real *malaise*. There is a growing cleavage between the clergy and those laymen who favor a rapid application of the decisions of the Council, an aggressive minority group, and an episcopate which is more prudent since it feels supported by a large conservative Catholic bourgeoisie. At the time of the workers' demonstrations during the "week of struggle" (October, 1967) which was supported by numerous priests and organizations of Catholic Action workers, the hesitant and, in fact, negative attitude of a person as important as the Archbishop of Madrid is in this connection particularly significant.

At the same time—as something entirely new in Spain—there is the birth of an anticlericalism of the right. The Church is accused of deserting its traditional social policy. It is reproached for resorting to demagogy. The growing political activity of the young clergy and of some bishops is denounced. The recent polemic between Bishop Añoveros of Cadiz and the writer Manuel Halcón, spokesman for the large landowners of Andalusia whom the prelate criticized for their lack of social consciousness, is one of a number of examples of this phenomenon. These few examples show that the Spanish Church in 1967 is no longer the almost solid bloc it used to be twenty or even fifteen years ago. Among the ranks of the clergy and of militant Catholics and even among the masses more or less faithful to the Church, there exists a variety of tendencies and currents.

II. THE CLERGY

In 1939 the Spanish Church was faced with the vital necessity of reconstituting its "sacerdotal ranks." The proportion of priests who were victims of the Civil War is painfully impressive: about one out of six

---

[7] In the new Cortès (Nov. 1967), four bishops, including Guerra Campos, Auxiliary Bishop of Madrid and Secretary General of Catholic Action, were named directly by General Franco.

in a country which, contrary to what is sometimes believed, lacked, in certain regions, at least, a sufficient number of diocesan clergy. Furthermore, fourteen out of some sixty bishops had been killed. These figures are for the Republican zone which at the beginning of the Civil War suffered from an anticlerical outburst of extraordinary violence. In Nationalist Spain some fifteen Basque priests, all autonomists, were executed, while 400 to 500 Basque curés or vicars were imprisoned, exiled, or relegated to distant parishes. Finally, two prelates had to give up their sees[8] because of their unfavorable attitude toward the new regime. Because of the religious renewal which followed the conflict and the support of the State which did not haggle over funds allotted for rebuilding seminaries and churches, the numerical reconstitution of the clergy was rapid. In 1964 Spain had 25,271 diocesan priests, 9,072 religious, and nearly 80,000 nuns.[9]

A. The Sociology of the Spanish Clergy

The remarkable studies of Father Rogelio Duocastella, the best Spanish authority on problems of religious sociology, describe with fair precision some of the sociological characteristics of the Spanish clergy.

First of all, there are important regional variations in the distribution of parish priests. In 1964 there was one priest for every 275 inhabitants in the diocese of Vitoria as against one for every 2,877 inhabitants in that of Malaga; the figures for Madrid and Barcelona are, respectively, one for 3,477 and one for 2,555.[10] There is a marked contrast between the North and the Center on the one hand and the South on the other —along a line extending from near Salamanca, Cáceres, Toledo, Albacete, and Valencia. Andalusia and the eastern provinces of the South are the most unfavored as well as the very large cities, Barcelona and especially Madrid.

The Spanish clergy come primarily from rural areas. Father Duocastella has shown that the mountainous areas and the predominantly rural provinces are the areas where vocations to the priesthood are most abundant. This phenomenon is not without importance, for a fair

[8] Bishop Mugica of Vitoria and Cardinal Vidal y Barraquer, Archbishop of Tarragon.

[9] *Anuario Estadístico de España* (edición abreviada, 1966), p. 385.

[10] R. Duocastella, J. Marcos, and others, *Analisis Sociologica del Catolicismo español* (Barcelona, 1967), p. 24.

number of Spanish priests, because of their background, find themselves rather ill-prepared to understand the problem of a predominantly urban modern world. Finally as a number of rural areas in Spain are at present losing their population to the big cities at an accelerating rate, there is a risk of an increasing disparity in the distribution of the clergy.

Perhaps this present decline of the countryside, the best area for recruiting vocations—45 per cent of seminarians come from farm families,[11]—is one of the reasons for the noticeable decline in the number of ordinations in recent years. The total of ordinations fell from 1,024 in 1960 to 801 in 1964. An increasing number of major seminarians drop out in the course of their studies—1,147 in 1965 as against 541 in 1962.[12] As in France, Spain is grouping together the major seminaries of several dioceses and transforming the vast number of minor seminaries into colleges for all. Yet the minor seminaries in Spain are still the essential sources for future priests. The elementary and secondary schools run by dioceses or religious orders furnish, on the contrary, only a very small number of priests. This is quite different from the pattern in other countries.

We have to make an essential distinction between the "young" and the "old" priests. Some will say that this is a trite distinction, but in Spain it has a very special importance. The "old" are those who lived through the Civil War. Obsessed by the trials of the past, they are above all sensitive to the positive aspects of the present situation. The "young," on the other hand, stress the compromises of the present and fear that the future may be dangerously mortgaged. This conflict between generations is more marked in Spain since the price in blood paid by those ordained between 1936 and 1939 often brings in contact the older priests with the recent graduates of the seminaries. The first, formed in the more traditional theology, have difficulty understanding the mentality of the younger clergy who, despite certain prohibitions, are very much influenced by men like Yves Congar and Karl Rahner. This is, of course, a rather simplified picture which does not allow for many individual exceptions. Since the Council, it is characteristic, nevertheless, that young priests look more and more not only to France and Germany, but also, and this is a novelty, to Rome, while the older generations prefer to emphasize the particularities of the Spanish "situation." This generation gap is increasing for seniority often plays a

[11] Duocastella, p. 24.
[12] *El Ciervo*, October 1967, p. 2.

predominant role in choices for ecclesiastical positions, sometimes at the expense of both specialization and personal competence.

Another contrast likewise merits notice. It is that which differentiates the regions where there is still a sentiment for autonomy from the rest of Spain. This phenomenon essentially concerns Catalonia and the Basque provinces. There the clergy evidence a solidarity and a remarkable *esprit de corps* which often reduces the conflict of generations to secondary importance. The solidarity of large portions of the Basque and Catalan clergy with "regional" and "separatist" opposition movements—according to the point of view one uses to characterize them— is an obvious fact. Numerous incidents have proved it in recent years, despite the satisfaction obtained in regard to the liturgy, because, since 1965, a part of the Mass can now be said in Catalan or in Basque. The appearance of several Basque curés in court and the events in Barcelona in May-June, 1966, when the police dispersed a street procession protesting against the naming of a non-Catalan as Coadjutor-Archbishop of Barcelona, were the subject of extensive comment in and outside of Spain.[13]

B. The Episcopate

Events like those of Barcelona in 1966 prove, like many others, that a lag in opinion and outlook has gradually developed between a portion of the clergy and its immediate superiors. This leads us to examine the composition and the behavior of the Spanish hierarchy. It is a delicate question but one impossible to avoid.

In *Spain, a Missionary Country?*, the Catholic writer Alfonso Carlos

[13] In a remarkable article published in *Études*, the French Jesuit review, A. Raymat wrote these penetrating lines on the demonstration in Barcelona: "To go into the streets, as the Catalan priests did, may or may not be an error. In any case it is evident that this step requires a remarkable courage: it presupposes an attitude of nonalignment when confronting the force of the State and what is no less difficult and dangerous, the affirmation of a certain liberty as regards the hierarchy. The risk is made even greater—which makes more dramatic the evolution of the Spanish clergy—by the fact that they risked, as events confirmed, incurring the antipathy of the majority: the Catholic right scandalized by the vigorous prophetism of these men of order which in their eyes the priests should be, and of the agnostic left, who were profoundly in agreement with the protest, but feared a new clericalism which would have the sympathy of the people." "Où va le laïcat espagnol?" in *Etudes*, September, 1966, p. 277, n.5.

Comin gives interesting details on the composition of the episcopate.[14] He emphasizes that the average age of the bishops is high: over 65 years. On the other hand, taking as his base 1956, which represents a turning point in the religious and political evolution of Spain, he notes that about 75 per cent of the bishops were named before that date. It is well known that the Holy See expressed the wish that bishops over 75 years old should resign their sees. Only four Spanish bishops of some twenty over that age have followed the recommendation of the Vatican. There is then an aged episcopate and one which, regardless of its good will, finds it difficult to keep up with the changing times.

But in evaluating the activity of the episcopate, it would be both unjust and too simple to limit oneself solely to the criterion of age. Another privileged observer of Spanish Catholic life, Lorenzo Gomis, director of the review *El Ciervo*, pertinently emphasizes the age of the Spanish bishops.[15] According to him, the old bishops who live on the margin of everyday life often join a narrow doctrinal traditionalism with a broad practical toleration regarding the conduct and ideas of their young priests. The younger bishops, some of whom, before their nomination, had a reputation for being open-minded, proved afterwards to be more jealous of their authority than the old prelates. Placed in an awkward position by the method used to nominate them, they wished at any price to avoid giving the impression that they are inclined to permit an evolution of their clergy and laity to the left. It seems to them that it would be both ungrateful and dangerous to let a part of the Catholics develop a political position somewhat hostile to the regime. Hence, they multiply rather tactful warnings and resort to more or less adroit acts of authority, as was evidenced in their handling of Catholic Action's crisis. When, in relations with the present government, they have the occasion to keep a distance both legitimate and in conformity with the decisions of the Council; for example, by declining to participate in this or that official arrangement, they hesitate and finally refuse to take the step.

In short, the "traditional spirit," to use a sufficiently vague formula, prevails among a majority of the Spanish bishops whether they be

[14] Alfonso Carlos Comin, *España, país de misión?* (Barcelona, 1966), pp. 270–271.

[15] In the course of an interview with F. Revilla, whose work was cited in the first footnote.

young or old. This was proved when the Episcopal Conference met in March, 1966. It is controlled by an almost constant majority of some forty votes and so the permanent commissions and positions of responsibility are in the hands of personalities who are "safe." Bishops considered too liberal have been kept out of certain positions, although their competence was often superior to that of those finally chosen. In the minds of the militant Catholics, most of the leaders chosen by the bishops are more disposed to hedge on the teaching of the Council than to hasten to apply it, except in certain limited areas like the liturgy. Herein lies the gap, already mentioned, between the hierarchy as a whole and a part of the Spanish Catholics. This gap is not without danger and tends, at least in certain sectors and in certain dioceses, to have the character of a real crisis in pastoral relations.

C. RELIGIOUS ORDERS AND MISSIONS

The religious orders seem, on the whole, to be less divided than the secular clergy. Viewed in only very broad outline some of them, preeminently the Jesuits and then the Capuchins, seem to be undergoing a complete renewal. The Society of Jesus which for a long time had, rightly or wrongly, a poor press in Spain is today viewed in a new light. Accused for centuries of being essentially interested only in the social elites, the Jesuits are now giving an eminent place to the apostolate among the masses. Alongside the admirable example given by Father Llanos in the most abandoned slums of Madrid, movements like *La Vanguardia Obrera* (The Workers' Vanguard) are making constant progress. On doctrinal matters the Jesuits are firmly and reasonably open-minded to all currents of Catholic thought in and outside of Europe. The Benedictine abbey of Montserrat in Catalonia, a traditional center of spirituality, liturgical renewal, and culture, is extending its preoccupations to all aspects of religious and cultural life through such publications as the review *Serra d'Or*.

The Spanish Dominicans appear to rely rather on tradition and, at present, their influence in the Peninsula seems to be relatively limited, but we should point out the development of their missionary activity which outside of Europe is a striking activity of the Church in Spain. More than 25,000 Spanish religious, men and women, are located in practically every part of the world. The secular clergy give important help to the Spanish-speaking countries of Latin America which are so short of religious. There are nearly 1,400 Spanish diocesan priests working in the New World.

Finally, in 1964 Spain had nearly 80,000 nuns in teaching, nursing, and convent life. Their social influence is enormous, although, especially among the teachers who come mostly from rural areas, contact with the rapidly changing urban mentality involves difficulties analogous to those encountered by the parish clergy, which also comes from relatively backward regions.

III. THE SOCIOLOGY OF RELIGIOUS PRACTICE

Spain as a completely Catholic country, according to one school of thought, is also ultimately the basis of the juridical construction which governs Church-State relations as drawn up in the Concordat of 1953. It is true that the Protestants are not very numerous, about 30,000, and that declared atheists are rare, but what does Spanish Catholic unanimity cover? Here sociological research concerning religious practice is relevant. Obviously these studies can only describe external expressions of religious feeling, not the feeling itself, but nonetheless they make it possible to avoid ready-made formulas and constitute an approach and method particularly useful in a country like Spain where people have a taste for cutting and contradictory assertions.

In Spain the unquestioned master of research in religious sociology is Father Duocastella. The following summary remarks are borrowed from his most recent work.[16] Anyone who wishes to have a detailed view of the sociological aspects of Spanish Catholicism should consult it. It is only recently, about 1955–1956, that systematic studies of religious practice were begun in Spain. This is quite understandable, for during the decade 1940–1950 the situation was distorted by the almost unanimous practice imposed, especially in small communities, by social pressure and by the need which many people felt to clear themselves of accusations involving their conduct during the Civil War. Later the letdown of constraints, if not their disappearance, awakened great interest in studies of religious sociology. Thus, interesting details have been obtained which can be grouped into two series: one concerns the geographical variations of religious practice, the other seeks to note the variations in practice according to social categories.

[16] See Duocastella, *op. cit.*

A. A REGIONAL STUDY OF RELIGIOUS PRACTICE

Among possible criteria the one used here is that of attendance at Sunday Mass. A number of studies have been made of it and Father Duocastella has synthesized the results. But, as he points out, the methods followed were not always the same for each diocese; hence the results obtained must be used with caution. In addition to those reservations, there must be initially a distinction between the predominantly rural areas and the big cities. In the rural areas of northern Spain, especially in Leon, Old Castile, and the Basque provinces, there is an intense practice of the faith; the percentage who attend Mass on Sunday varies from 60 to 80 per cent of the whole population. As one moves toward the East and South the figures decrease. Along the Mediterranean coast, in Catalonia and the Levant of Valencia, the percentage remains fairly uniform at about 35 per cent. In the center, in New Castile, La Mancha, and Northern Estramadura, the results are more variable and range from 20 to 40 per cent. In the South, from Badajoz to the Portuguese border and to Almeria on the Mediterranean, more fragmentary studies suggest an estimate of about 15 per cent. But in this last zone the percentage of Mass attendance goes up considerably at the time of big liturgical and local feasts. This is Andalusia, that is, the part of Spain where what might be called the "folklore stimulant" remains very characteristic and where the religiosity of the population is to be seen more in a series of traditional devotions than in respect for specific obligations.

The broad geographical contrasts just noted also apply to urban populations. In Vitoria, formerly the religious capital of the Basque provinces, 73.5 per cent of the people attend Mass. This is an impressive figure since the recent industrialization of the city has attracted migrants from the South who are very careless about the Sunday obligation. High also at Bilbao (over 50 per cent), the percentage goes down for a city like Valencia (27 per cent). This represents about 8 per cent less than for the rural part of the Diocese of Valencia. Seville and Malaga give figures analogous to those of Valencia, but it is worth nothing that, while everywhere else Sunday Mass attendance is less in cities than in the countryside, the contrary is true in Andalusia—perhaps as a result of the pastoral effort of the urban clergy. For Madrid and Barcelona we have unfortunately no figures—only fragmentary statistics for parishes belonging to different types of sections of the city.

Practice in the average residential section of each city ranges from about 30 to 40 per cent; however, there is a very sharp decline in the suburbs, especially where those from the South, moving from their villages with the rural exodus, tend to locate; here the figure drops below 10 per cent, and even below 5 per cent. These latter figures indicate the importance of a study of the distribution of practicing Catholics according to social categories.

B. A Social Study of Religious Practice

Father Duocastella tried to make a classification of religious practice according to professions. His analyses, though necessarily summary, led him to observe that the criterion of Sunday Mass attendance as a general rule produced very high figures (about 80 to 90 per cent) among industrialists, big landowners, high officials, and members of the liberal professions.

As one goes down the social scale, the percentages decline. This is true for employes, middle and lower echelon civil servants, and shop-keepers. Still, as regards these last three categories we should note that figures for Sunday Mass attendance are proportionally higher in the large rural villages of Andalusia and of Estramadura than in the rest of the country, for Mass attendance is a sign that one belongs to the social elite along with the big landowners and in opposition to the small land-owning peasants and agricultural workers. On the other hand, religious practice seems to be relatively homogeneous in the rural communities of the North where holders of small and medium-sized farms pre-dominate.

The tremendous effort which the Church in Spain is making in order to know better the religious life of certain social groups has re-sulted in relatively more detailed information on two segments of the population: the students and urban workers.

A recent issue of the review *Cuadernos para el diálogo* summarized a number of surveys of student groups.[17] Basically this reveals the growth of religious indifference in university circles. Avowed atheists are still rare—7 per cent according to a 1965 sample of the students of the University of Madrid—but the percentage tends to be higher in certain disciplines, for example 16 per cent of those in the faculty of economics. In interpreting these figures, we should keep in mind the natural in-

[17] *Cuadernos para el diálogo*, Numero Extraordinario, May, 1967.

transigence of youth. But the students who say they have broken completely with every religious idea seem, according to these same sources,
to be among the more dynamic elements. What would happen, then,
if the Church lost the opportunities for action which its privileged
status today makes possible? There is more reason to raise this question,
since the present organization of Church-State relations is criticized by
the vast majority of university people and indeed, only 11 per cent
among them look upon the present arrangement favorably.

Among the workers, a partial survey among different categories,
made by HOAC in 1958, featured two figures: a very high proportion
of anticlericals, almost 90 per cent and a great number of workers, more
than 86 per cent, who had recourse to the Church principally for baptism, marriage, and funerals. On the other hand, the average percentage of those who went to Mass on Sundays was very low—only 7.6
per cent.

The author of a more recent article on the religious outlook of the
Catalan workers quoted several characteristic phrases picked up here
and there: "I have the faith although I don't go to church"; "I believe
in God but not in the curés"; "I don't go to Mass but I am more Catholic than many of those who do"; "I don't go to Mass but my wife and
children go; it doesn't do them any harm."[18]

In short, along with a declared atheism no doubt important although
difficult to evaluate numerically because detailed studies have not been
made there are among the workers of the big cities both an old religious foundation and an open resentment regarding the visible structures of the Church. In general the Church is associated with a social-
political situation which is considered unjust. The Church, as a body, is
accused of profiting from this situation or at least of maintaining toward it the silence of an accomplice.

It is important, however, to emphasize that the accusation—the
clergy are indifferent to the social question—is not absolutely justified.
Alfonso Carlos Comin, a witness above suspicion, who is considered by
many as a dangerous extremist, has written: "If the Spanish hierarchy
has hardly spoken against the absence of political liberty, the same cannot be said of them with respect to the social question."[19] Either individually or in the form of collective letters, the Spanish bishops, espe-

[18] Pedro Negre Rigol, "Mentalidad religiosa del obrero en Cataluña," in *Annales
de Sociologia*, December, 1966, p. 46.
[19] A. C. Comin, p. 81.

cially in the last ten years or so, but for some as early as 1952, have denounced the egoism of the wealthy classes and have protested against the exploitation of the workers and demanded decent wages for them. This may be documented by many quotations from Bishop Olaechea of Valencia, from Bishop Morcillo when he was head of the difficult diocese of Bilbao, from Archbishop Bueno y Monreal of Seville, from Bishop Herrera of Malaga, not to mention the collective letter of the cardinals and archbishops of September 15, 1956, the positions taken at the Social Weeks, and the achievements of the Leo XIII Social Institute.[20]

But all these various texts scarcely reach the workers who can hardly read and have only a limited cultural level. Much greater influence on them is exercised by the attitude of an increasing number of parish priests now very close to their concerns. It is likely that for this reason certain prejudices are gradually disappearing and resulting in a decline of anticlericalism in comparison with 1958. Still, the religious situation in the workers' environment remains precarious. The hard core of militant Catholics is increasing and strengthening its influence, but the masses may even give up their religious conformism for the major events of life, once freedom of speech in political and religious issues again becomes a reality.

In conclusion, an overall view such as we have just sketched helps to put in just proportions the official conformism regarding Catholic Spain that prevailed until a few years ago. It should be said that the ecclesiastics in charge recognize the situation, although, for motives of self-interest, the civil authorities try to maintain certain fictions.

IV. CATHOLIC ACTION: ITS DIFFERENT FORMS AND ITS PROBLEMS

In Spain movements based on the notion of "Catholic Action," that is, various groups aiming to make the Catholic faith a living reality among laymen of every milieu, represent a particularly important element in the life of the Church as well as in national life.

Spain is a land of individualism and at present lives under a political

[20] In Spain there are more than 500 worker priests, commonly called "priests at work." They belong either to the secular clergy or to certain religious orders, but their status remains ill-defined.

regime that regulates freedom of assembly. Hence, Catholic Action has become in the nature of things one of the rare means of collective formation distinct from the State. By reason of its objective, which is to transform the milieu it works in, Catholic Action inevitably led to exercise an influence which if not political is at least civic. One should not be surprised then that Article 34 of the Concordat of 1953 is devoted to the conditions under which Catholic Action may function. There it is stipulated that it is free to carry on its apostolate under the direction of the hierarchy while remaining subject to the jurisdiction of the State in respect to its other activities. This ambiguous formula, of course, gave satisfaction to the Church, but by reason of the many conceptions of the apostolate that can be envisaged, it opened the way for numerous difficulties that did not fail to develop.

A. VARIOUS ASPECTS OF CATHOLIC ACTION

What are the present structures of Catholic Action? They have undergone profound changes since 1939. At the end of the Civil War, a period when Spain had at least the appearances of a traditional Christianity, Catholic Action represented the organized Christian masses, the disciplined soldiers of an army whose structures were assured by chaplains under the direction of the bishops. With the parish as its structure, Catholic Action combined the practice of traditional devotions with various social and charitable activities, while also being concerned with defending public morality. Little by little things changed: for effectiveness Catholic Action became oriented toward different conceptions. Alongside of general Catholic Action working within the parish structures there developed a specialized apostolate concerned with social groups: employees, students, and workers.

This evolution coincided with an awareness of the enormous task the Church had to undertake on behalf of the workers, especially those in industry. These movements solely concerned with the world of the workers soon became trailblazers and influenced the evolution of Catholic Action as a whole. The first groups of *Hermandad obrera de Acción Católica* (HOAC, Labor Brotherhood of Catholic Action), which today still forms the most important organization of Catholic Action operating among urban workers, were founded as early as 1946. Because of a few outstanding leaders who, according to the apt words of Raymat, had to sustain "a bitter and difficult struggle so that among their unbelieving and indifferent coworkers they could be witnesses to their faith and demonstrate that it had not removed them from their class,"[21] the HOAC made headway, but slowly. The militant workers not only had to work in an uncongenial milieu but they soon ran up against official labor unions which quickly saw in the HOAC the embryo of future Christian unions. For their part many bishops became reticent when faced with what they considered the too demanding spirit of the HOAC. Some of them even went so far as purely and simply to forbid the founding of the movement in their dioceses. On the other hand, the HOAC could always count on the determined and courageous support of Cardinal Pla y Deniel, Archbishop of Toledo and Primate of Spain. Without any doubt it was because of the Cardinal's intervention that the HOAC was able to surmount many difficult obstacles. The attitude of the Primate is even more remarkable, inasmuch as the militants of HOAC never hesitated to maintain contact with organizations of resisting workers, even the Marxists. They did this without renouncing any of their own religious convictions which were based on a highly developed doctrinal and spiritual formation.

The HOAC, moreover, merited respect because it evidenced a new type of completely trustful relationship between chaplains and militant members. As such it strongly influenced a part of the young clergy who, anxious to win over the masses, became deeply interested in the methods of the apostolate of the HOAC. The movement thus played a decisive role. In conjunction with the HOAC, which appealed to adult workers who had often been marked either by their experiences antedating 1936 or by the trying period following the Civil War, we must mention the rapid growth, after 1956, of groups for young workers, that is, basically Young Christian Workers (JOC). The progress of other specialized movements for students, employees, and others has been slower; however, it should be noted that they have been greatly influenced by the experiences of HOAC.

All the above-mentioned organizations depend on the secular clergy. In addition, there are movements initiated by religious congregations or orders. The aims of their movements, if not the methods, are analogous to the objectives of Catholic Action in the strict sense of the term. It is basically a question of the organs which the Jesuits created in this field a long time ago. These groups have their origin in the desire

[21] A. Raymat, p. 273.

of the Society of Jesus to extend its influence over the young men graduated from its schools. Thus *Congregaciones Marianas,* popularly called *"Los Luises,"* have been established. From the elite of the *Luises* has come a movement of limited membership but one that strongly marked Spanish political and civil life before and after 1936: the National Catholic Association of Propagandists. In recent years the *Congregaciones Marianas* have become modernized and have regrouped while at the same time a series of movements organized for different milieux, each with Jesuit chaplains, was created. One of them is *La Vanguardia Obrera* whose directors, instead of being appointed by the hierarchy as is still the case for "classical" Catholic Action, are democratically elected. There are other groups as well, including a dynamic one directed to employees.

There is also a series of groups, linked to Catholic Action, which are addressed to women's affairs. As a general rule the feminine organizations which bring together considerable numbers have remained more conservative than their masculine counterparts. The need for a regrouping of so many works and movements very soon made itself felt. To be sure, Catholic Action has its own periodical, *Ecclesia,* which for a long time was the only Spanish publication to escape the censorship. This gave special weight to its editorials. That, however, was not sufficient. A new organism was created to embrace the whole of Catholic Action, the National Union of the Secular Apostolate (UNAS). Two men play an essential role in it: Enrique Miret Magdalena, a layman, and Guerra Campos, the Auxiliary Bishop of Madrid and national chaplain of Catholic Action, but since the layman is in the spirit of the "movement" while the ecclesiastic leans rather to the side of the "resistance," the UNAS does not seem to have produced all the results expected of it.

Alongside of Catholic Action, but outside of it, there is an original and specifically Spanish movement called the "Cursillos of Christianity." These "Meetings on Christianity" combine the approach of study groups with days of recollection. Founded in 1949 by Msgr. Hervas, now Bishop of Ciudad-Real, the Cursillos have succeeded in shaking off the apathy of the middle class at a time when it felt self-righteous and lived in a quiet euphoria. Today the tendencies and methods of the Cursillos seem to be somewhat out of date.

Quite apart from Catholic Action and very jealous of its autonomy and its specific work is the *Opus Dei* which originated in Spain and then spread throughout the world. It is difficult to speak briefly of this famous Secular Institute. In Spain it is very often discussed and not always with competence. The conduct of *Opus Dei* in its original homeland has aroused much criticism. Suffice it to say that to an impartial observer it appears to be unquestionably involved in the political, social, and economic life of Spain. As such it is a "problem" in the Church and raises a series of complex problems which cannot be treated in a study of this kind.

B. The Difficulties of Catholic Action Today

In the case of Catholic Action one of the present paradoxes of the Spanish Church may be best perceived. While the word "Dialogue" is used and abused, dialogue is in fact becoming more and more difficult between the hierarchy, or at least the organs which speak in its name, and the most committed clergy and militant laity.

It was in 1966 that the relations between the hierarchy and Catholic Action began to deteriorate. At a plenary meeting in June, 1966, the leaders of Catholic Action formulated very specific criticisms of the way, despite the Council, Church-State relations were conceived. The Permanent Commission of the Episcopal Conference, dissatisfied with this stand, immediately replied by banning any meeting of the heads of Catholic Action. Then a few weeks later, a pastoral instruction from the Plenary Assembly of the Episcopate repudiated prudently but firmly all excessive "temporalism." During December, 1966, the two sides do not seem even to have tried to coordinate their points of view with the result that Catholic Action went through a real period of "hibernation." A certain number of periodicals published by various Catholic organizations were seized, often apparently at the request of ecclesiastical authorities. The weekly *Signo* and the review *Aun*, the latter inspired by the Jesuits, were even obliged to suspend publication completely. In March, 1967, the Episcopal Conference expressed a wish to undertake a real reform of the statutes and so moved further toward taking control of Catholic Action. Enrique Miret Magdalena's declaration on these statutes, published in the journal *Pueblo*,[22] expressed the wishes of the majority of those involved in Catholic Action: Election of the principal leaders instead of their appointment by the hierarchy; a sufficiently large initiative for the various movements

[22] *Pueblo*, October 14, 1967.

so that a real public opinion, not merely one that passively accepts the orders of the hierarchy, may be formed in the Church. In this way, according to Miret Magdalena, Catholic Action "could be an adequate vehicle for a free moral and religious expression of opinion on current questions" instead of being "simply an instrument of the hierarchy . . . a clerical apostolate."

A month after this declaration, following the "week of struggle" organized by various organizations of workers, the action of the Archbishop of Madrid seemed to prove that the hierarchy was little disposed to meet the aspirations of a large sector of Catholic Action. Bishop Morcillo, after hesitating a moment, replied in effect by refusing the request of worker movements of Catholic Action to authorize a prayer meeting for the freeing of imprisoned union workers. Was this not one proof among others that the distance between the conceptions of the two sides remained great and that the present crisis, which is perhaps after all only a crisis of growth, will not be easy to solve? At the same time, it is true, the general direction of the new statutes finally agreed upon by the Plenary Assembly of the Spanish Episcopate which met at the end of November, 1967, seems to take a step toward a real democratization in the designation of the leaders. If this tendency toward a reasonable increase in the role of the laity is maintained, one can hope it constitutes the beginning of a lasting solution of the still unresolved difficulties of Catholic Action. But the resignation of Enrique Miret Magdalena in January, 1968, does not make for optimism.

V. THE CHURCH AND TEACHING: THE INTELLECTUAL AND DOCTRINAL ACTIVITIES OF SPANISH CATHOLICISM

A. THE CHURCH AND TEACHING

Reacting against the prevalent policy of laicization of the Republican period, the Spanish Church tried to recover its place in the world of teaching as soon as the Civil War was over. To do this it agreed with the present regime, which was desirous of rebuilding the educational system so that traditional Catholic values would be given an eminent place. The first result of this identity of views was the introduction of compulsory religious teaching in all State schools up to and including the universities. Only recently have non-Catholic students been permitted to seek remission from classes of religious instruction and for this they must provide a justifying statement.

Even more significant is the place that schools and colleges, run by the secular or regular clergy, occupy in teaching elementary and secondary schools. At these two levels the Church has very largely made up for the absence of the State. We have to keep in mind that at present, despite notable efforts by public authorities in recent years, many children still cannot find schools to admit them. Since the State cannot do its job, Church schools and numerous private schools play an essential role. A few rough figures—statistics on this are not very reliable—permit us to see this. In the school year 1964-1965, Catholic elementary schools enrolled 18 per cent of all students and the secondary schools 40 per cent. Excluding private classes, one notes that although State grammar schools have four times as many students as the Church schools, the situation is reversed on the high school level, where religious colleges have twice as many students as the "institutos" dependent upon the State. There are indeed only 120 "institutos" or lycées, while there are more than 900 secondary Church schools which in general provide teaching of high quality. Their tuition charges, however, are high. In spite of the efforts of some congregations which specialize in teaching the lower classes, the Church seems to be oriented preferably toward secondary teaching which draws its students from the upper and middle classes, while elementary schools which recruit from the socially more modest classes, have been relatively neglected. The most advanced Catholic groups are beginning to consider this disproportion shocking. This critical reaction is repeated in the area of professional and technical teaching, where the Church plays only a rather modest role, although several religious orders have high-quality engineering schools that enjoy a well deserved reputation.

University teaching must be considered separately. In Spain there are several "Pontifical Universities" devoted exclusively to religious sciences, to the exclusion of secular disciplines. Their work is perfectly free and unrestricted by the State. But for universities covering all fields the State, until recently, enjoyed a monopoly which it surrendered only after long resistance by university circles. Since 1962, two Church-controlled universities called "Free Universities," one at Navarre founded by *Opus Dei* and the other at Duesto run by the Jesuits, have gained official State recognition for their diplomas. Thereafter, these universities, especially the former, which is conceived in a very modern way, developed rapidly. But in 1965 these two schools, along with the institutes attached to them, drew only 3 per cent of the whole student population.

B. CATHOLIC NEWSPAPERS AND PUBLICATIONS

After the Civil War, Spain had an extremely strict system of control over information. It involved prepublication censorship of papers, books, and journals. At first silent about this, the hierarchy after 1950 stressed that hindrances to freedom of expression were in no way in conformity with the traditional teaching of the Church and that the press needed a statute of its own. Cardinal Pla y Deniel and Bishop Herrera of Malaga (before 1936, and prior to his ordination, publisher of the very influential Catholic daily, *El Debate*) became very much interested in this question. Although inclined at first to be less demanding as regards Catholic publications, since the Council the spokesmen for the Church have insisted more and more clearly that all citizens have the "right of information" provided they avoid the excesses of "libertinage." Not until 1966 did they gain responsive attention. The Law of the Press presented by the Minister of Information, Fraga Iribarne, has given them partial satisfaction.

The best Catholic press organization is the *Editorial Católica* which published *El Debate* before the Civil War. Although this paper has not yet reappeared, the group publishes one of the most important dailies of Madrid, *Ya*, now a morning paper after having been the evening edition of *El Debate*. A chain of regional dailies affiliated with *Ya* have a large circulation. The *Biblioteca de Autores Cristianos*, directed until his death in 1965 by Luis Sala Batust, Rector of the Pontifical University of Salamanca, is also published by the *Editorial Católica*. This important collection which has several hundred titles gives a very large place to works in theology and patristics.

The Jesuits publish a doctrinal review, *Razón y Fe*, which is widely read, and a series of publications more or less linked to Catholic Action of which some, like *Mundo Social*, are clearly avant-garde. *Opus Dei* has a very active publishing house, *Rialp*, and a whole series of publications ranging from women's journals to a weekly of current events and a journal of opinion.

In the course of recent years the religious press has had a remarkable development drawing major impetus, it is true, from translations of foreign authors. For example, *Taurus* at Madrid publishes the Spanish translation of the works of Teilhard de Chardin, and is animated by Father Jesús Aquirre, one of those who introduced Rahner into Spain; *Fontanella, Nova Terra,* and *Estela* in Barcelona, and others. Reviews like *Proyeccion* and *Incunable* of priestly inspiration not only help to enliven the somewhat limited world of the Spanish clergy but also explore the present directions of theological, liturgical, and pastoral studies.

C. Movements of Thought and Intellectual Currents

The efforts of renewal in Spanish Catholicism have concentrated largely on the pastoral and liturgical. For work in the pastoral field mention may be made of Father Floristan, Director of the Pastoral Institute of Salamanca, who is now located in Madrid. The liturgy is one of the areas in which the Church in Spain immediately followed the directives of the Council. Prominent in this field is the influence of the monastery of Montserrat which is also a great center for biblical studies. Dom Gabriel Braso, Coadjutor, formerly Abbot of Montserrat, has published a very remarkable work entitled *Liturgy and the Spiritual Life.*

In theology properly so-called the situation is clearly less brilliant. This was noticeable at the Council where Spanish theologians played virtually no role. While seminarians and young priests study the works of German and French theologians, those who have official chairs often remain still respected but somewhat outdated representatives of an exaggeratedly scholastic Thomism. A few, however, are beginning to enjoy a following which extends beyond the borders of Spain, such as the Jesuit Diez Alegria and Canon Gonzalez Ruiz whose bold conception of the theology of work attracted attention at the time of the Council.

On the other hand the perspectives of the lay Spanish Catholic "intelligentsia" are quite different. The defenders of tradition in the strict sense of the word retain appreciable influence and continue to fight tenaciously for their ideal—but they are on the defensive. Opposing them are the partisans of all forms of Catholic openness and today they have clear sailing. Never in its history has Spain had such a constellation of philosophers and outstanding essayists who are laymen and profess the Christian faith. Thanks to them the narrow and limited notion of the Catholic intellectual that prevailed in Spain is disappearing.

Even before 1936, under the influence of Maritain and Mounier, a man like Professor Manuel Gimenez Fernandez had revealed social and communitarian preoccupations well in advance of the timid conceptions that still prevailed in the Catholic circles of the period. Since 1945, in men like Pedro Lain Entralgo, former Rector of the University of Madrid, and José Luis Aranguren, Spain's Catholic intellectuals have had leaders on a truly European scale. The influence of Aranguren on the evolution of Spanish Catholicism today is almost beyond measurement. As early as 1955 his book, *Day-To-Day Catholicism*, a reappraisal without hatred, but also without fear, of a certain number of false values to which Spanish Catholics have too long remained attached, won an exceptional following among university students. Aranguren's independence of mind cost him his chair at Madrid at the very time John XXIII and the encyclical *Pacem in terris* bore witness to the bold orthodoxy of conceptions that he had never ceased to defend.

Another of the outstanding personalities of the Catholic intelligentsia is Professor Joaquin Ruiz Gimenez. Minister of Education from 1951 to 1956, International President of *Pax Romana*, auditor at the Council and personal friend of Paul VI—Ruiz Gimenez is at the crossroads of many movements of ideas. He knew how to use his exceptional position in an effort to sustain the most continuous and remarkable openness that Spain today can exemplify. Since 1961 he has inspired the review *Cuadernos para el diálogo*, around which a group of intellectuals, mostly Catholic, pursue with tenacity and courage an inventory of the current problems of Spain in a spirit of broad understanding of the diverse points of view involved. It augurs very well for the future that the efforts of *Cuadernos para el diálogo*, which moreover had been preceded in this direction by a publication like *El Ciervo* of Barcelona, the remarkable review of the Gomis brothers, is inspired essentially by Catholics.

What will this future be? It is clear that the Church of Spain at this time, given the very particular political conditions under which the country lives, is in a period of truce. The Church should take advantage of this truce to accelerate its own apostolic transformation. As some of Spanish Catholicism's present leaders often prefer to take the easy way, the Church may face a difficult future there.

In conclusion, it appears that the present essay envisaged things perhaps too much from the political point of view and so fell victim to the usual trap that ensnares those who speak of Spanish Catholicism. Nevertheless, it should be noted that no matter how preoccupying may be the tensions between the hierarchy on the one hand and the progressive wing of the clergy and the laity on the other, these tensions in which politics have their role are not everything. The religious roots of a people profoundly tied to spiritual realities remain a positive factor provided they know how to present these realities without excessive temporal contaminations. After having described forthrightly the misunderstandings and friction which Spanish Catholicism is experiencing at present, it is good to conclude by quoting the witness of an unbeliever, which appeared in a recent issue of Cuadernos para el diálogo. The writer, Jorge Semprum, made the following observation: "The Church today is something very much alive in the Western World and in Spain it will succeed in becoming so despite inevitable delays. . . . It seems to me that the process has already started. This is a fact and certainly one of the greatest importance theoretically, politically, ideologically, and culturally."[23]

[23] J. Semprum, Cuadernos para el diálogo, Numero extraordinario, "Cultura hoy," July, 1967, p. 94.

8 : FRANCE

Robert Rouquette, S.J.

It is difficult to describe French Catholicism for an American public because the French and American historical backgrounds, social conditions, and major problems differ so greatly.

I. THE RUPTURE CAUSED BY THE FRENCH REVOLUTION

In order to grasp the complexity and the diversity in French Catholicism we must—perhaps more than for any other sociological phenomenon of the nation—see its evolution.[1]

To understand that evolution we have to go back to the French Revolution which produced a violent rupture in the whole life of the nation, particularly in its religious life. It was a rupture whose effects would be felt for a century and a half.

Prior to the Revolution, Catholicism had been an official institution for some fifteen hundred years; its clergy was the first privileged class

[1] There follows a listing of a few basic works: Adrien Dansette, *Destin du catholicisme français, 1926–1957* (Paris, 1957); A. Latreille, E. Delaruelle, J. R. Palanque, R. Rémond, *Histore du catholicisme en France*, t. III: *La periode contemporaine* (Paris, 1962), Book VII: *Les transformations sous les derniers pontificats* is by R. Rémond, professeur à la faculté des lettres de l'Université de Paris; *Forces religieuses et attitudes politiques dans la France contemporaine* (Cahier de la Fondation nationale des Sciences Politiques, 130, Paris, 1965); A. Coutrot and F. Dreyfus, *Les forces religieuses dans la France contemporaine* (Paris, 1965); F. Boulard, *Premiers itinéraires en sociologie religieuse* (2nd edition, Paris, 1967); J. Chélini, *La ville et l'Eglise. Premier bilan des enquêtes de sociologie religieuse urbaine* (Paris, 1958).

of the nation; and the Christian concept of life was, in theory at least, the official concept of the State. The Church had, in fact, monopolized education.

Almost from the beginning the Revolution, inspired by the philosophy of the Enlightenment, came into conflict with Catholicism; it provoked a schism, deprived the Church of its goods, and persecuted the clergy violently. Since the prevailing concept of the State was Jacobin, the law was made the final arbiter of right. Although the Church recovered a legal status under the Napoleonic empire and the restoration of the monarchy, it subsequently lost its influence on society. In the nineteenth century a part of the bourgeoisie recovered its faith; however, the intellectual elite was almost completely hostile to Catholicism which, for a century, was taken to stand for obscurantism.

For a long time France was divided by two ideologies. On the one hand, the ideology of the liberal bourgeoisie, the great beneficiary of the Revolution, was completely dominated by the mystique of "progress" according to which human reason was to bring into being a perfect humanity conceived in liberty, equality, and fraternity. In fact, it sought primarily political liberty as the panacea that would make possible an ideal political regime. The Church was considered an obstacle to this progress of reason and of humanity: its influence should be combatted.

In opposition, Catholic ideology was primarily negative and counter-revolutionary; it sought above all to overcome simultaneously the social, religious, and ideological consequences of the Revolution. Catholicism saw the necessary remedy first in the maintenance of the monarchy and, after its fall, in its restoration. Unfortunately, Catholic thought, preoccupied with the political struggle against the Revolution, did not confront a triumphant rationalism with a vigorous thought of its own; rather it took a completely negative attitude toward the rise of historical criticism. With the exception of a few farsighted minds, most Catholics could not see what was Christian in the revolutionary values of liberty, equality, and fraternity. An essentially conservative Catholicism prevailed in thought, politics, and conception of society.

Absorbed, however, by their political struggles, bourgeois liberals, aristocrats, bourgeois Catholics, and conservatives paid no attention to the great historical phenomenon of the nineteenth century, namely, the birth of an urban proletariat resulting from the emergence of big

industry: an uprooted people subjected to very hard working conditions, poorly paid, and completely separated from Catholicism. It was
not dechristianized, for it had never been Christianized. Rather the
Church had neglected it. It formed an enormous pagan people of a new
kind: behind it was no religious paganism as there was in the countries
of Africa and Asia which Europe was colonizing at the time. This proletariat was struggling violently for the improvement of its living conditions. While the Revolution of 1789 worked out to the advantage of
the bourgeoisie, the proletariat dreamed of another revolution, a social
one which would bring about equality between the classes. It turned to
a revolutionary socialism which, although at first romantic, was eventually seduced by a simplified Marxism. The overthrow of the social
foundations, which it aimed to bring about, frightened Catholic bourgeois who here again, with the exception of a few farsighted men, opposed it with a negative conservatism.

II. AN EVOLUTION: FROM NOSTALGIA FOR THE PAST
TO THE BUILDING OF THE FUTURE

Catholicism at the beginning of the Third Republic and in the later
decades of the nineteenth century was on the whole essentially conservative. It retained a nostalgia for the past which it had not yet forgotten, but saw in ideal colors. This idealized scheme presented a
picture of the Church with a privileged position among the institutions of the State and thereby able to exercise a direct influence over
the acts of the civil power in areas where the spiritual and temporal
domains encroached on each other. When the attempt to restore the
monarchy failed after the Franco-Prussian War of 1870–1871 and the
fall of the Second Empire, there ensued a tragic, vicious circle: the
republicans in power were anticlerical out of ideological conviction and
also because the hierarchy and Catholicism were antirepublican. The
Catholics were antirepublican because the republicans were anticlerical.
This vicious circle did not begin to break for more than half a century.
The habits and reactions it induced continue to be influential today.

Leo XIII tried to rally the French Catholics to the republican form
of government in 1888 in order to detach them from an irrevocable
past. This was, incidentally, an astonishingly direct intervention of a
spiritual power in the temporal order. It was astonishing and rare but

justified by its uniquely pastoral character. The pope counselled against a political option, legitimate in itself, which had paralyzed the evangelical mission of the Church. On this occasion the pope saw more justly and further into the future than the French episcopate and laity whose vision was limited by current events. Leo XIII likewise came closer to the aims of the new society born in 1789, while still retaining a paternalistic and, in fact, monarchical point of view. He thought of the State as under a prince. Nevertheless he established the principle which is at the foundation of modern democracy and which Pius XII would make one of the constants of his teaching, namely that the citizen should participate in public affairs. Although he did not recognize the civil liberty of religious option as a right of the human person, he accepted the ideological pluralism of modern societies as a fact. Finally, in *Rerum Novarum* he showed that the social problem was more urgent than the political one at a time when the leftist parties concealed a solid social conservatism behind their anticlericalism. He raised two fundamental principles: that action to suppress social inequalities was a duty in justice and not simply one of supererogatory charity, and that the law governing economic relations is not a matter determined by profit motives but by respect for the dignity and essential needs of the human person.

In fact, Leo XIII was not followed by the majority of French Catholics. The fruitful principles he laid down, however, ripened slowly in a germination that remains obscure; the growth took place because of a few pioneer spirits who were badly received by their fellow Catholics and who were suspect to anticlericals because of their Catholicism.

Apparently, historical contingencies also propelled most Catholics toward an unconstructive rightist opposition, for Catholicism was preoccupied more with defending rights than with building a new society —hence the disastrous Dreyfus case.

The radical parliamentary majority in power, inspired by a powerful antireligious Freemasonry, canonized a militant laicism that was basically dogmatic and considered the faith an alienation from which the national conscience should free itself. It withdrew the school from the influence of the Church: the laicized teaching given in the public elementary schools was an effective agent for the dechristianization of the masses through the activity of the teachers. It expelled the religious and confiscated their property. This real persecution culminated in the denunciation of the Napoleonic Concordat, the rupture of diplomatic relations with the Holy See, the separation of Church and State, and the confiscation of ecclesiastical property—seminaries, rectories, bishoprics, and churches, although the faithful were allowed to use the latter. This separation of Church and State, in fact, fostered the liberation of the Church: for it restored to the Church full liberty of action. Of course, the brutal and unjustifiable nationalization of her material goods reduced her to poverty, something glorious and pure to be sure, but having rather paralyzing effects.

However that may be, one can see how this violent crisis, although it quieted down quickly, drove Catholicism even further into a primarily defensive opposition as a political and social force.

World War I effected an initial change: the "Sacred Union," the human contact of the priest with the soldiers and the full participation of Catholics in the defense of the common good of the nation in danger, made it impossible to apply any measure of ostracism. Public opinion would not accept the anachronistic attempt of the Cartel of the Left which, for tactical rather than ideological reasons, tried in 1925 to revive a militant anticlericalism.

Diplomatic relations with the Holy See were resumed on the morrow of World War I: a *modus vivendi* signed with the Vatican gave the government a certain veto power over episcopal nominations, a sort of concordat without the name of one; dioceses were recognized as legal persons. With the establishment of a regime of "moderate separation," the State adopted a policy of benevolent neutrality. Henceforth, except for the school question, relations between Church and State were good.

Yet Catholics were systematically excluded from leadership in public affairs. Under the leadership of an old soldier, General de Castelnau, they formed the nationalistically inclined National Catholic Federation which was organized to defend Catholicism much more than to participate in civil life. Their activity, which, moreover, has been effective, continues to be defensive; in 1925 the assembly of cardinals and archbishops called upon Catholics especially to resist the laicism of the State.

A large segment of public opinion, particularly of the young, and a considerable part of the episcopate—out of repugnance for a regime whose faults were real and for the sterile interplay of parties—were strongly influenced between the two World Wars by the nationalistic *Action française* movement which expressed itself through the newspaper *Action française*, edited by Charles Maurras, an atheist. The latter saw in Catholicism a principle of order necessary to the life of the nation and favored an impossible monarchical restoration. The foundations of Maurrasism, which passed unnoticed by most of the supporters of the movement, rested on a positivist amoralism according to which the supreme norm is the interest of the nation. The youthful Charles de Gaulle, it might be noted in passing, did not escape the influence of Maurras. The movement was not constructive: its virtue lay in its ability to denounce mercilessly and violently and with unquestionable talent, the mistakes and the pettiness of the men in power.

The condemnation of the *Action française* by Pius XI in 1928 was a turning point, a clear breaking away from the primarily negative attitude of Catholicism. Although the condemnation was justifiable because of the ideological principles of Maurras and because of the violence the movement inculcated in youth, it was announced in awkward circumstances and was followed by severe, possibly excessive, measures against individuals—often those of good will. If it definitely turned away the most vigorous part of French Catholicism from a primarily negative and conservative activity, it also had an unfortunate consequence with effects that are still felt. It created division and real animosity among Catholics. It stiffened a number of the faithful in an attitude of anticlerical revolt, of political and social immobility which was often joined with a refusal to accept any pastoral change and any theological development. The integralists of today come from men who have been influenced directly or indirectly by the *Action française*; they are the heirs of those who could not accept or understand its condemnation.

III. THE RENAISSANCE BETWEEN THE TWO WORLD WARS

Yet during the period between the two World Wars, Catholicism underwent a profound transformation which gave it a new youth and dynamism whose effects are still evident today. We can speak of a true Renaissance—one with several aspects.

A. THE INTELLECTUAL AWAKENING

First of all, Catholic thought, which until now had been so lifeless and limited to an apologetics of defense, reasserted itself forcefully and commanded respect. Numerous conversions of intellectuals occurred in reaction to both the influence of an overabstract and desiccating Kantianism and an unrealistic ideology of progress. These converts, moreover, often burned what they had adored; they placed Catholicism in opposition to the errors of the "modern world" rather than attempting to grasp its positive values and to participate in it. Maritain's book *Antimoderne* was characteristic of this tendency. After the condemna-'ion of *Action française*, however, Maritain himself redressed the balance. In *Integral Humanism*, a book which was to have a profound influence, he presented ideas which have become today's commonplaces, for they are at the foundation of the Council's *Pastoral Constitution on the Church in the Modern World*, that is, the duty of the Christian to work for the progress of contemporary civilization.

However that may be, a substantial number of young students rediscover and practice the faith. It is something new to see thousands of students of the great scientific schools make their Easter duty publicly at St. Etienne-du-Mont in the heart of the Latin Quarter.

A great classical age of literature ensued in which Catholics have a considerable place. One has only to recall the names of François Mauriac, Paul Claudel, and Charles Péguy who obliged the public to pay attention to Catholic thought. Catholic journals of general culture increased in number and Catholic publications enjoyed a great development.

The Catholic Association of French Youth (ACJF) constituted a center of reflection for those top students who were preparing to participate in civic affairs, to act in society, not in order to clericalize it but to introduce into it the practical influence of the Christian conception of man. Most of these leaders would one day hold positions of great responsibility in post-World War II governments.

The same spirit inspired the *Semaines sociales* which each year have meetings in different places. These make known the social doctrine of Catholicism to a large public.

Under these influences a significant number of Catholics begin to accept fully not the antireligious dogmatic laicism but a lay state which, in effect, expresses the public power's respect for the ideological pluralism of the nation. Catholics taught in the secondary State schools. They were no longer excluded in practice from university chairs. They respected the neutral character of the State school and did not engage in proselytism, but by their presence gave witness to the Christian faith.

B. The Rise of an Apostolic Laity

The second great phenomenon is the rise of an apostolic laity. Gradually Catholicism began to become conscious of the problem of the proletariat, his conditions of life and his non-Christian character.

The incentive came from the Young Christian Workers (JOC), founded in Belgium in 1925 by Cardijn and introduced into France as early as 1926. The essential idea of Cardijn is that the profoundly dechristianized milieu made it impossible for a young Christian worker to keep his faith. This milieu, then, had to be transformed by the creation of living conditions that would not be dehumanizing but would permit effective teaching of the Christian message. This transformation could only be brought about by workers, not as individuals but as part of a movement which would group them into a dynamic community and, unlike earlier movements, would do this without cutting them off from their milieu in order to protect them from its influence. It was a simple idea-force, a naive one even, and it encountered difficulties which are still present. But in its first ten years its ideas attracted an admirable enthusiasm and generosity among a large number of young workers. In 1937 the Congress held at Paris to commemorate the tenth anniversary was a triumph: tens of thousands of young workers proclaimed their faith in Christ and their determination to give the workers their dignity. It was, as we shall see, an ephemeral triumph.

Still the Jocist fervor brought enduring values: a way of thinking that began with the concrete in order to know positively the reality of the milieu which was to be evangelized, and a fundamental awareness of the essential role of the laity for evangelization not only because of the shortage of priests, but because of the very vocation of the baptized. Finally, there was the recognition of the fact that the evangelization of a given milieu had to be undertaken primarily by men of the same milieu and not by an outside paternalistic elite.

These key ideas were the core of specialized Catholic Action which was peacefully supported at the time by Pius XI. Around the JOC there developed an analogous movement for each social milieu: a Christian Agricultural Youth (JAC), a Young Christian Students (JEC) which suffers from the inevitable weakness that the student world is not a stable one, and an Independent Christian Youth (JIC) for the bourgeois—also not a very homogeneous group. These were all necessarily movements of teenagers. Their transformation into adult movements would raise difficult problems.

However that may be, there gradually developed, to replace the earlier and primarily defensive movements, a new form of action based on clear observation of reality and on commitment to a specific service not only of the Church but of man. A new generation found in its faith the sense of duty to participate in the building of the city, not by a return to the past, but by creative research. Newspapers and journals were founded: *La vie intellectuelle, Sept,* then *Temps presents, Esprit, La vie catholique,* and *L'Aube.* No doubt they did not reach the mass of Catholics, but they did draw away from the conservative right a part of the youth and some of the intellectuals; in addition they tried to find out how Catholics could meet the healthy aspirations of the laity and collaborate with it in order to build a new society, more just and more human.

IV. THE RUPTURE CAUSED BY WORLD WAR II

World War II, defeat, German occupation, and Resistance produced a sudden rupture: freedom of the press was suppressed and movements forbidden. At the beginning most Catholics, like the rest of the nation, adhered to the regime of Marshal Pétain. The hierarchy long remained faithful to a, perhaps, too abstract and extrinsically juridical notion of legitimacy. It was too conscious of the material advantages granted the Church and the religious schools; soon Catholicism became as divided as the rest of the nation over the new regime. Catholics actively joined the Resistance and were among the first to organize a spiritual resistance with the underground paper *Témoignage chrétien* founded by the Jesuit, Father Chaillet. They, along with the non-Christians, anticlericals, and communists, paid dearly with their blood and their liberty. The bishops protested against the totalitarian organization of youth and against the persecution of the Jews. However, they recommended obedience to the established government, although from 1943 on they did so with a certain reserve. Some theologians—including the venerable Dean of the Faculty of Theology of Paris, Father J. Lebreton, a deeply spiritual man completely detached from every political passion —openly stated that the conscience of Christians is not bound to follow the political choice of the episcopate. This situation would later

accentuate the political disengagement of the bishops which had
clearly begun between the two World Wars.

A. The New Situation after the Liberation:
Participation in Politics

The great fact which characterized the postwar world was the participation of Catholics in political life. On the morrow of the Liberation
there was founded the Popular Republican Movement (MRP), which
was not a religious party like the Christian Democratic parties of Holland, Belgium, Germany, and Italy, but was inspired, nevertheless, by
Catholic principles. At first it attracted the votes of Catholics who, in
1945 and 1946, refused to vote for the old conservative parties compromised by Vichy. The success of the MRP was ephemeral. In the
following elections the Catholics reverted to the rightist parties, then
to Gaullism, while the leading young Catholics criticized the MRP for
not being sufficiently leftist. But in the traditional Christian areas the
rural population remained faithful to it. In 1967 it disappeared and
fused with a larger group the democratic Center which is trying to
prepare for the period after de Gaulle.

Henceforth, however, the profession of Catholicism no longer prevented accession to important positions in political life. Militant
Catholics can be ministers and heads of government. They no longer
hesitate to go into politics for they see it as a way of being effective.
They learned in the Resistance movement to collaborate with unbelievers:

> Less than thirty years after World War I which accelerated the
> integration of Catholics into political life, World War II led them
> to seek participation They were inspired less by the desire to defend
> confessional interests than to share the common ideal of all French-
> men. A new generation is assuming responsibility; it is to the left of
> its elders and contributes to the shift of the center of gravity of
> Catholic forces toward parties and programs which had long re-
> mained the exclusive property of anticlerical elements.[2]

In this new climate the hierarchy is accepting the lay character of
the State, according to the terms of the declaration of the cardinals
and archbishops on November 13, 1945, as "the sovereign autonomy

[2] Coutrot and Dreyfus, pp. 100–101.

of the State in the domain of the temporal order" as well as the duty of the State to leave each "citizen to practice his religion freely in a country of divided beliefs."

B. Awareness of Dechristianization

More important than this shift somewhat to the left is the reversal of perspectives which thereafter led a number of Catholics to look to the future and not to the past.

The first fact to note is no doubt contemporary Catholicism's awareness of dechristianization, thanks to the precise sociological studies of religious practice begun by Gabriel Le Bras, professor of Canon Law of the Faculty of Paris, and by Canon F. Boulard.

The Church in France can no longer live under its long-nurtured illusion that it represents the collective conscience of a Christian people. The nation remains theoretically Catholic in the sense that the population is almost totally Catholic in origin (94 per cent): Protestantism represents no more than 500,000 to 600,000. Most Frenchmen of Catholic origin are still baptized (97 per cent). But only 30 per cent of those over twenty-one make their Easter duty, 10 per cent to 25 per cent practice regularly, depending on the region, and a large proportion practice only occasionally in marking, more in response to social custom than out of a deep faith, the important events of life by religious ceremonies—birth, adolescence, marriage, death. Not only have whole regions abandoned Catholicism, but the working class has in large part been lost. Christianity is practiced and lived extensively only among the lower and middle bourgeoisie. Throughout Europe a practical and tacit atheism is developing. Men do not need God and even if they admit His existence in theory, they live as though He does not exist. Divorce is becoming general, although not on the scale it has reached in America. Ten per cent of the marriages end in divorce. French civilization is entirely areligious, although without any hostility to religion.

C. The Church Is Becoming Missionary

Because of these conditions, the Church in France recognizes that it must be a missionary one. This is what characterizes the Catholicism of the past twenty years. It has the duty to evangelize the dechristianized masses, especially the working class. The specialized Catholic Action movements are at the heart of this missionary activity. Before World War II they were primarily youth movements; today they are adult movements as well.

The enthusiasm which characterized their first years petered out and the transition to adulthood has not taken place without problems— which is a sign of life. Catholic Action has not failed, but we must recognize that it did not attain the goal it set itself before the war: the rechristianization of society. It has, however, and continues to have a real effectiveness. It forms militant Christians conscious of their responsibilities, ready to assume their role in the nation. It has deepened their faith which in the context of the dechristianized civilization in which it lives becomes more personal; a Catholicism of social habit is giving way to a religion of interior convictions and this deepening and personalizing partly compensate for material losses.

But this very fact raises a problem: the militant laity does not propose to remain passive. It has come of age, they constantly repeat, even if it is a slogan and even if the formula corresponds more to a need than to a reality. This situation raises the difficult question of the relationship of freedom of action and of obedience. This question is not tragic, but it has not yet been resolved.

It is primarily the missionary commitment of the laity that is strained by two demands, not opposed to each other but difficult to reconcile in practice: on the one hand, spiritual evangelization, and on the other, temporal action and humanization. It is clear that the Christian notion of the person requires a profound change in the social and economic temporal structures, a change which cannot take place without temporal, even political, if not revolutionary, action. Moreover sociological studies all reveal that the profession of Christianity is linked to a certain level of economic and spiritual liberty. There is then a social condition for evangelization properly so-called, which is inseparable from action on temporal structures. Contemporary Catholicism is thus caught in a dilemma: on the one hand, the Church as such does not wish to intervene in the temporal and especially in the political order except to judge it from the point of view of faith and morals. On the other hand, Christians, that is, the laity who are the Church, are discovering more and more their duty, in the name of their faith, to act in the temporal order. Shortly before World War II the French bishops clearly stated that the Catholic Action movements were movements of the Church, a participation in the apostolate of the hierarchy, a collaboration with that apostolate. The hierarchy intended to give an official "mandate" to Catholic Action, although the notion of mandate was hard to define exactly. It implied, however, that the positions taken by Catholic Action movements properly so-called commit the Church as such. The Council refused to generalize this notion of mandate and to make it the specific characteristic of Catholic Action as the French Bishops wished. Catholic Action movements, therefore, as official movements of the Church, are in the uncomfortable position of being prevented from committing themselves as movements to temporal action while their members have the duty to become involved in such action.

D. THE EXPERIENCE OF THE WORKER PRIESTS[3]

The worker movements in particular raised these problems—and recently, the student movements as well. The hesitation of the hierarchy when confronted with a movement's temporal commitment is explained by the experience of the years following Liberation and by the danger that then appeared either of abandoning all spiritual action in favor of the temporal or of political collaboration with communism.

The idea of the worker mission had two sources. First of all, during the occupation, the Germans forced young Frenchmen to work in the factories of Germany. Chaplains for this service were forbidden. Bishops therefore sent a few priests who worked as prisoners and assured a sort of secret chaplaincy; many paid for it with their lives. For those who survived, it was a veritable discovery of the worker's soul and of the world of the laborer: a closed world, a truly spiritual homeland to which a simplified Marxism gave the conviction that it was the bearer of the future of humanity. At the same time the chaplains discovered in this world the virtues of generosity, of brotherhood, of altruistic devotion too often alien to the bourgeois world. They had the very intense realization that the presence of the priest in the factory was the only way to understand the world of the worker.

On the other hand, in 1943, two young French priests, the Abbés Godin and Daniel, published a book called *France, pays de mission,* a report which overwhelmed Cardinal Suhard, the old Archbishop of Paris, a thoughtful man of rural origins. Nothing in his background apparently prepared him for the initiative he was about to take. The

[3] Cf. E. Poulat, *Naissance des prêtres ouvriers* (Paris, 1965).

two authors of *France, pays de mission*, relying on their experience, observed that the proletariat was absolutely impervious to evangelization because traditional Catholicism, linked to the bourgeoisie, was incapable of welcoming eventual converts: a worker convert breaks with his milieu, which is for him a true homeland, and cannot live his faith within the framework of bourgeois Catholicism; the parish milieu in particular is psychologically incompatible. The framework of religious life, the bond between bourgeoisie and Catholicism, must therefore be modified. But how? The authors were hardly able to offer any realistic solutions.

Cardinal Suhard, however, founded a group of priests, called the *Mission de Paris*, who were asked to study specifically and as a result of their own experience the means of making the Christian faith less inaccessible to the worker. It quickly appeared that the only solution was for priests to become members of the working class, that is, to become workers, first in order to know the milieu from within and not merely from a passing investigation, and secondly to devote their life to it. There was no question of direct proselytism but rather of making Christ present physically or almost sacramentally in the proletariat by living entirely the same life under the same working conditions as the working class. Only in this way could the Church understand that civilization so estranged from it and the values it possesses; only in this way could the world of the workers come to see concretely that Christianity is not the money power the workers think it is, an instrument of capitalistic interests. It is only in this way that this essentially concrete world, in constant contact with matter, could see how to live an authentic Christianity in its milieu. Although the *Mission de Paris* was not composed solely of worker priests—for Dominicans, Jesuits, and Franciscans have joined it—it was through it that the experience was gained which was followed in other great industrial cities. There were never more than a hundred worker priests out of the 50,000 priests of France, but the repercussions of their effort were enormous, too great in fact: for the press and novelists seized upon it and often distorted it in the eyes of public opinion. However that may be, the workers had the intense realization that the Church was no longer disinterested in their fate and that it was detaching itself from the bonds that tied it to the world of the owners.

Unfortunately, the experiment failed and it failed for two reasons. It had not been well enough prepared and thought out: those who

volunteered for it did not, if they were enthusiastic, have the necessary
balance. It developed without a unified leadership because the episcopate did not have effective means of unification. Frequently the
parochial clergy mistrusted the worker priests, and the latter, at least
the secular ones, were left too much to themselves. All these weaknesses
could have been gradually overcome.

But a second cause of failure was decisive. In fact, the Marxist mystique—I do not say the philosophy—formed an integral part of the
worker's world: it gave the workers their pride, their reason for being,
their hope. The communists defended the worker's world effectively.
It was impossible to become integrated with the working class without
participating in its struggle. This struggle was inspired by Marxism and
directed in fact by the union headquarters, General Confederation of
Labor (CGT), which is under the dominant influence of the Communist Party. It is likewise difficult, when becoming a part of the worker's
world, not to accept what has been called "workerism," that is to say, a
mystique which sees in the working class a chosen people all of whose
claims are just a priori and which has within it all the hope of a better
humanity. The worker priests did not succumb to the appeal of Marxist
theory which, for most of them, they knew badly, but they were led to
collaborate closely with a specifically political action which was com-
munist-inspired; they not only had to join the CGT—which was tolerated by the hierarchy—but because of their culture, their experience
in speaking, several were encouraged by their worker friends to become
union leaders in the CGT.

Part of the Catholic bourgeoisie were scandalized when they saw
priests engaged in manual labor—they forgot that St. Paul worked with
his hands. They readily admitted that a priest could spend his whole
life administering the finances of a bishopric or in teaching Latin grammar or mathematics—tasks just as profane. Right after the Liberation
people saw a Carmelite monk who had been an admiral and gov-
ernor-general of Indochina, and the fact did not arouse very much
indignation.

Reactionary circles multiplied their denunciations of the worker
priests to Rome. The Vatican authorities, one must admit, misunderstood the situation. They underestimated the enormous hope which
the experience had given rise to in the working class; they proposed
palliatives absolutely impossible for France, some even ridiculous. A
serious and well-informed historian of contemporary Catholicism,

Adrien Dansette, claims that Cardinal Pizzardo proposed encouraging boys to become altar boys and donating cribs for babies rather than advancing the worker priests! Yet the French episcopate decided that despite its weaknesses, its imperfections, and its dangers, the experiment should continue along with an effort to remedy gradually the deficiencies.

In September, 1953, however, the Vatican asked the bishops to withdraw the worker priests. After the intervention of the French cardinals a second measure limited their working time to a few hours per day. This made it impossible for them to go into the factories. Most of the religious submitted, about half of the seculars refused; several quit the Church. A few tried to work as artisans the half time permitted by Rome, particularly the priests of the Secular Institute of the Prado under their superior general Msgr. A. Ancel, Auxiliary Bishop of Lyon who had been a worker bishop for five years.[4] Rome finally forbade manual labor. This rigorous measure, as might be expected, caused great disillusionment among the working class. The Church seemed to be abandoning the proletariat. The breach between Christianity and the proletariat widened.

The French episcopate in its general assembly at Rome in October, 1965, during the fourth session of the Council won the right to undertake again the experiment of the worker priests on a new basis. At present some fifty priests, both seculars and regulars, are so working. They have been carefully chosen, they are in contact with parish communities where they exercise the pastoral ministry on Sundays. Their life of prayer is assured; they can join a union but they cannot assume positions of responsibility or participate in political demonstrations. Thus, in avoiding the errors of the first attempt, the experiment is being discreetly tried again on an improved and purified basis.

We have already seen how the first generation of the JOC ended in movements whose exclusive temporal commitments were judged by the hierarchy to be incompatible with the evangelical mission of Catholic Action.

Since then there has come into existence a Workers' Catholic Action (ACO), relatively few in numbers, but very dynamic according to an original formula which attempts to reconcile the exigencies of the spiritual and the temporal. The members must necessarily make a personal commitment to the worker movement—union, political, mu-

---

[4] A. Ancel, *Cinq ans avec les ouvriers. Témoignage et réflections* (Paris, 1963).

nicipal, civic action—but the movement itself does not become involved. Its aim is to nourish spiritually the individual commitment of its members. The formula is attractive but in fact is equivocal because in practice the groupings of the ACO are only workable if the members of a team have commitments of the same political and social inspiration.

The same tension does not exist in the rural Catholic Action movements, the Christian Agricultural Youth (JAC), and the Rural Family Movement (MFR), which have been extremely successful. "For the postwar world the success of the JAC is somewhat the equivalent of the Jocist miracle before 1939. It is probably the most successful experiment of a concept of Catholic Action which tries not to separate what is united in the existence of individuals as in that of societies."[5]

In fact, the JAC and the MFR give a spiritual and a human culture to young peasants by assuming responsibility for the human development of the agricultural class from the technical and civic points of view. The movement teaches the peasants to maintain their place in the nation at a time when mechanization, the disappearance of small property, and the competition of the European Common Market are provoking a veritable social revolution in the agricultural world. The JAC has given French villages a rather considerable number of young active leaders who are taking an important part in the conduct of the rural world.

E. A COMMUNITARIAN SPIRITUALITY

Two other movements, distinct from Catholic Action, have had a great development since the end of World War II. The Movement of Pastoral Liturgy has tried to make worship the center of the Christian community and the principal nourishment of interior life by making it accessible and intelligible, by giving it a theological basis again, and by making the faithful participate in it by virtue of their priesthood which comes from baptism. The Council's *Constitution on the Liturgy* consecrates all the inspiration of this liturgical movement.

Moreover, groups of families have the aim of making the permanent, sacramental value of marriage effective in daily life and of making conjugal life a source of total Christian life as well as a witness to it.

All of these movements, Catholic Action, the Liturgical Movement,

[5] Rémond, p. 656.

and family groups have introduced a communitarian spirituality, the characteristic of the Catholicism of the young. They have passed from an individual religion preoccupied first of all with personal perfection and salvation to a living communitarian religion in a shared spiritual communion concerned with the salvation of all men as well as with personal salvation, with the promotion of humanity, and not with individual perfection alone. They give a collective witness to others. This spirituality is based on a rediscovery of the mystery of the Mystical Body between the two World Wars and, since the Council, of the reality of the People of God. There is here unquestionably a real force and great hope.

F. THEOLOGICAL RENEWAL[6]

During the past twenty years there developed a powerful movement of theological reflection which was at first more or less suspect at Rome but which the Council confirmed. One has only to recall the names of Fathers Congar and de Lubac, both unjustly banned, silenced, and forbidden to teach, who were rehabilitated by John XXIII and Paul VI and were among the good workers of the Council. This theological movement led to a return to biblical and patristic sources by substituting for a notional and scholastic theology a theology of the history of salvation which analyzes the privileged and religious experience of the people of Israel, its termination and perfection in Christ, and then its development in the life of the Church. It is this theology of the history of salvation which Paul VI in his famous reply to Professor Skisgard, speaker for the non-Catholic observers at the Council, settled as the essential end of research in the age which is beginning (October 17, 1963).

V. AFTER THE COUNCIL

The Council was well received in general by Catholic opinion in France. In fact its principal results corresponded to the latent aspirations of the Church of France. Thus French Catholicism is presently calm. It is not experiencing the crisis of adolescence which the churches

[6] Cf. A. Aubert, *La théologie au milieu du XXe siecle* (Paris, 1954).

of Holland and England, for example, are undergoing. In particular, there is none of the latent misunderstanding between the hierarchy and the laity that may be observed elsewhere.

A. INTEGRALISM

The small group of integralists, more noisy than numerous, who have lost the excessively large influence they once had at Rome, protested vehemently against liturgical reform. These extremists are recruited primarily from the former adherents of *Action française* and from the partisans of the extreme political right: North African colonials expelled from their own country and angered by the anticolonialism of the government; soldiers exasperated by the useless sacrifices which the Indochinese and Algerian wars imposed on the army; anticommunists of the McCarthyite type who see in all social reform a concession to Marxism with which they are obsessed. They pretend to defend the prerogatives of the pope which are endangered, they say, by the Council, the doctrine of collegiality, and the episcopal synod. One must not exaggerate the importance of this opposition.

B. THE EPISCOPAL CONFERENCE

One of the principal immediate benefits of the Council has been the creation of a coherent episcopate. Hitherto, one might say, we had bishops but not an episcopate. Most of the crises of the last twenty years were due to the fact that problems of national importance could not be considered by a body large enough to handle them.

Out of fear of Gallicanism, which completely disappeared long ago in France, Rome feared a centralized organization of the episcopate. Since the Revolution of 1789 there has been no general assembly of bishops except once under the First Empire and twice at the time of the separation of Church and State in 1905–1906, and then only to face particular questions which the new situation of the Church in France presented.

Between the two World Wars, however, under the pressure of necessity organs of coordination between dioceses appeared and have multiplied: the assembly of cardinals and archbishops, the secretariat of the episcopate, the national chaplaincy of the Catholic Action movements. But these new organisms, unforeseen by law, had no canonical authority and could only give directives which bishops were not obliged to follow.

Beginning in 1951 Rome authorized a general reunion of the episcopate which in fact met every three years and had fifteen permanent commissions. The Council made this assembly an episcopal conference, an annual institution, and gave it canonical authority for decisions taken by a two-thirds majority. It is very well structured with a permanent committee of specialized commissions and it permits directed and coordinated action of the hierarchy. Collaboration with religious orders is made possible by a mixed commission of bishops and of major superiors.

On archaic ecclesiastical provinces, ill-adapted to pastoral needs, has been superimposed a new structure of dioceses; apostolic regions have been established that group neighboring dioceses having common problems.

The Church of France thus structured faces numerous urgent problems. There is, first of all, the reapportionment of the clergy. Despite a noticeable decrease of priestly vocations, the number of priests in France remains relatively high—higher than in Italy or in Spain—50,000 for a population of about 49,000,000. But this clergy is very badly allocated. In particular, rapid urbanization, the rapid migration from the countryside to the cities, especially to the urban region around Paris—8,000,000 inhabitants, one sixth of France—has meant that the pastoral service of the big cities, the vital centers of the country, is ill-provided for. There are parishes of 60,000 people in Paris with one priest for each 12,000 inhabitants, while in Brittany there are still parishes with one priest for only 500 parishioners. The same disproportion exists between the number of priests assigned to teaching secular subjects in Catholic schools and the number of chaplains in the state *lycées* which have a uniquely spiritual ministry calling for special effort. The official policy of the Church of France is to seek out people where they are, not to wait for them in the halls of the churches. A more equal distribution of the clergy, regrouping parishes which are too small, is necessary and is currently under study.

At the end of the German occupation Cardinal Suhard had already created an original institution, the *Mission de France* whose purpose was to form a team of priests in a special seminary for the dechristianized regions. This seminary raised many problems. It inaugurated new ways of living and of teaching candidates for the priesthood. At the beginning its tendencies were the same as those of the *Mission de Paris* and of the worker priests, although, contrary to what is often believed, it was not destined exclusively to train worker priests. It aroused suspicions in Rome which, after several crises, endowed the *Mission de France* with a special stature. It is a *prelatura nullius* symbolically attached to one place, the ancient abbey of Pontigny, where the seminary was located until October, 1967. The mission had a French bishop especially assigned to look after it, at first Cardinal Liénart, Bishop of Lille and the present Archbishop of Reims. The priests of the mission are incardinated in this diocese and form an interdiocesan clergy at the disposition of bishops short of priests.

During the course of the Council the episcopate studied a profound reform of the seminaries. Seminaries with few students have already been reorganized into a few interdiocesan houses. The life of the seminarians is henceforth open to the world and to its problems so that the education of the clergy does not take place in a closed and isolated world. Regulations have in large part been made flexible; the course of studies has been changed so as to initiate clerics from the beginning in the history of salvation and biblical theology and not just in profane philosophy or a notional theology.

Along with episcopal collegiality, priests' councils for the bishops are being set up everywhere; most of the members are elected by their fellow priests. Councils of the laity are under study in order to establish a participation of the laity in the direction of diocesan and parochial life; the modalities which would permit this participation and yet leave intact the final authority of the bishops have not yet been worked out —to no one's surprise.

Another study is being made of the necessity of transforming parochial structures.[7] In big cities the parish is an artificial milieu distinct from the working environment; the territorial parish is a dormitory where during the day one finds only the aged, women, and children. In Paris especially, the assembly of the clergy is considering projects for the rearrangement of parish boundaries. The parish clergy would be replaced by rather large communities of priests, including not only priests charged directly with the parish ministry, but also chaplains of

[7] F. Connan and J. C. Barreau, *Demain la Paroisse* (Paris, 1966).

different movements. At their head would be a coordinator to unify pastoral work within the boundaries of the former parishes which would maintain their places of worship.

C. CATHOLICISM AND MEANS OF ACTION IN THE CITY

Labor unionism, inspired by Christians, has taken on great importance, at least in that part of the salaried world near the level of the lower bourgeoisie. In his speech of May 22, 1966, in connection with the seventy-fifth anniversary of *Rerum Novarum*, Paul VI recalled that the Church recognizes the legitimacy and necessity of workers' associations and has overcome its earlier historical preference for corporatism and mixed organizations (salaried workers and owners). Unions are not movements of the Church and hence are freer in their temporal options. Thus it is even more striking, as a sign of the transformation of mind and of the desire of collaboration with all, that recently Christian unionism felt impelled to give up its confessional character while continuing to be inspired primarily by Christians. Moreover it should be noted that the hierarchy recognizes or at least tolerates a freedom of choice of unions and that Christians often adhere to neutral ones.

The Catholic press with its magazines, newspapers, and journals is extensive. It is read largely by Catholics, although a study of it revealed that 56 per cent of French adults read a religious publication at least from time to time.

On the other hand, the larger secular press and even certain provincial journals which had hitherto been anticlerical give extensive coverage of religious information, more no doubt than before the last war. But usually this information is largely superficial and factual, although done with good will. There are two exceptions: a bourgeois paper like *Le Figaro* which, for some years at least, has published substantial chronicles written by outstanding men like Abbé Laurentin and Father Maurice Villain, an able specialist in ecumenical questions. Another exception is the high level intellectual daily *Le Monde* which has an excellent religious chronicler in Henri Fesquet who is both a deeply religious man and a liberal Christian.

But a decisive weakness of French Catholicism is that it has no access to those powerful agents of influence on public opinion: radio and television. The state monopoly of the Office of French Radio-Television (ORTF), which assures a certain standard for broadcasting and saves it from excessive vulgarity, grants only a very limited time to religious programs, and these only during hours with few listeners. Protestantism, Orthodoxy, and Judaism are allowed a half-hour; Catholicism, one hour and a half on Sunday mornings. Most of the Catholic program is taken up with the Mass. On the radio there are the Lenten sermons at Notre Dame and one weekly Mass at a time when there are few listeners. It would be very unwise to ask for more. Thus in Germany and England the religious programs are more important. In the United States the audiovisual mass media are not monopolies, and the Church can use them more easily, either by establishing its own stations or by buying time on existing stations. In France that is not possible, even in the case of the accessible peripheral stations, because of the limited financial resources of the Church.

Does Catholicism exercise an influence on French culture? That is a difficult question to answer. Unquestionably Catholics participate freely and to a great extent in the intellectual life of the country. It is also true that the problem of the opposition of faith and culture, and especially of faith and science, no longer comes up. But there are no more great Catholic novelists. There is no Catholic philosopher who is an idol of the young generation. Those who had great influence —Maritain, Gilson, Gabriel Marcel—are now old. Alone, the posthumous work of Teilhard de Chardin exercises a vast influence outside of Catholicism.

D. The Political Impact of Catholicism

Can one measure or see any influence of Catholicism on French political life? We have already seen that there is no specifically Catholic party in France which has the support of the mass of Catholics as in other countries of Europe.

The hierarchy refrains from intervening in the elections and the life of the parties. It recognizes the right of Catholics to free political choice to the extent that the ideological doctrine of a party, such as the Communist Party, does not imply any fundamental opposition to the faith. Doubtless, it has an influence in reminding people of their duty to vote. One notes in fact a much greater proportion of participants in regions where traditional religious practice prevails.

We have pointed out that Catholics voted for the right for a long time. But for a long time too "the opposition between the right and left has had a tendency to reduce itself to an opposition between partisans and adversaries of the Catholic Church," to such an extent that a conservative social and bourgeois party like the Radical Party is considered leftist—"leftist in principles but as much as possible not left in its achievements."[8] Today we can say that this classification is in large part outdated except for the Socialist Party (SFIO). Moreover, it is difficult to determine just how the right and the left differ. On the whole, however, we can say the right tends to an economic liberalism which limits state intervention and defends the capitalistic system, while the left tends toward a state-controlled levelling to a more or less socialistic economy, it being understood that it often happens that parties or men who wish to be leftist have characteristics of the right and vice versa.

How do the majority of Catholics vote? There have not been enough sound polls of opinion to permit answering this question with certainty. Yet a comparison of maps showing religious practice and electoral results permits certain conjectures.

Until 1936 there was no electoral district located in an area of religious practice which did not give at least 40 per cent of the votes to the right. The three strong zones of the right coincided with zones of religious practice: West, East, and South of the Massif Central.

In 1945 and 1946 the MRP which in its leadership could be classified as left of center, because of its policy of levelling and of nationalization, and was inspired by Catholics, picked up its followers from the traditional right except in the non-Catholic areas. It took root also, incidentally, in regions which were not very Catholic and which in 1936 did not vote for the right. It has been assumed that this success was due to the women's vote in areas where men always refused to vote for a candidate accused of being sympathetic to the Church.

The appearance of a Gaullist party in 1951, which had certain characteristics of the Bonapartist right and which cannot be considered a Catholic party, caused the MRP to lose half of its supporters; it went from 5,600,000 to 2,400,000 votes. Thereafter, Catholic voters were divided among the center and rightist parties. A poll taken in 1952 shows that for every 100 interviewed, 54 voted MRP, 20 independent, 18 Gaullist; some voted more to the left: 5 Socialist and 1 Communist.

Gaullism was not a political party, although a large number of Catholics voted for de Gaulle. If the General did not deny he was a

[8] F. Goguel cited by Coutrot and Dreyfus, p. 190.

practicing Catholic, it seems clear that his religious preoccupations did not play any role in his decisions and choices. The episcopate, wiser after the experience of Vichy, avoided giving hostages to Gaullism.

Thus, the Catholic electorate was divided between the center, Gaullism and the moderate right. Certain sociologists, however, think that the Catholic press seems to show a certain sympathy for the left, in the sense that it became open to theses which before 1940 were not characteristic of the right: anticolonialism, collaboration with unbelievers, social equality, sense of community. "After considering for several decades order and authority as definite values destined to govern the conduct of societies, and moral reform as the most effective means of overcoming political errors, other theses appeared and supplanted the first. Today we invoke rather the requirements of justice than those of order; we seek more often the conditions for a democratic participation than the means for making authority triumph."[9]

But this Catholic press and its theses have obviously only a feeble impact on elections. The Catholic press reaches only the intellectuals and the militants. Thus, there appeared a break between an active and reflective minority and the mass of Catholics oriented as always toward conservatism.

A large part of these militants tended to the formation of a labor party in which one might find democrats of Christian leanings, a part of the radicals and the socialists, whose economic, social, and political doctrines are not irreconcilable.

E. THE SCHOOL PROBLEM

This evolution which completely changed French political life runs head on into the problem of laicity, or, more exactly, into the problem of the school which remains a cause of division between the right and the left. This is the only point where religious considerations weigh strongly on political life. It is this problem which prevented France from signing the European Convention of the Rights of Man of UNESCO, which included freedom of teaching among the Rights of Man. Two theses confront each other: one, which in virtue of the principle of the laicity of the State, refuses to admit that public funds be given to confessional schools, although the question causes no trouble when hospitals are involved. The other considers confessional teach-

[9] Coutrot and Dreyfus, pp. 167–168.

ing a semipublic service and freedom of teaching illusory without State aid. It points out that private school teaching, in practice almost exclusively Catholic, relieves the burden on the public school—15.4 per cent of primary school education and 40 per cent of secondary school education in 1958. In 1961–1962 the maintenance of Catholic education would have cost more than a billion francs. In the last few years the teachers in the Catholic schools, who have the degrees required of teachers in public schools, are paid by the State on the condition that they follow official programs and are subject to the control of the public school. This measure provoked an increase of anticlericalism in traditionally leftist circles.

But the school question is evolving. First of all, Catholics accept State control of the subsidized schools and no longer demand that a proportional share of the public funds be allocated to State and confessional schools. The school problem, although important both in theory and in practice, is not the most urgent; since 1945 the hierarchy has, on the whole, taken moderate and prudent positions. It is more and more conscious of the duty of evangelizing children where they actually are. It proclaims its respect for the public school and its teachers. In 1928, on the contrary, the Assembly of Cardinals and Archbishops saw the public school as "a school of impiety of which crime is the natural result."

Another section of Catholic opinion thinks that in the present concrete situation it should be wise pastorally to give up subsidies on the condition that public schools not be under the exclusive control of the State and that they offer children a proper religious instruction by means of a system of chaplaincies. The supporters of this course include *Esprit*, the University Parish, and the General Union of National Education affiliated with the French Democratic Confederation of Labor (CFDT). There are powerful groups of lay Catholics who work to defend the confessional school: the Parents Association for Private Schools (APEL) and the Secretariat of Study for Freedom of Teaching exercise an effective pressure on the legislator.

Vulgar anticlericalism, however, has almost completely disappeared as a result of the mixing of peoples brought about by the war and the Resistance, of the withdrawal of the Church from politics, and perhaps especially of widespread religious indifference.

Militant anticlericalism is rather artificial, especially among the teachers, including Catholics, who dispose of powerful means of action, particularly the state-subsidized League for Teaching which, along with the Federation of National Education and the National Union of Teachers, has now constituted one of the most powerful pressure groups—the Committee of Lay Action.

It is primarily this pressure which prevents the Socialist Party from allying with Christian Democrats, a number of whom feel closer to the Socialists than to the independents or Gaullists of the right. Indeed, the Socialist Party (SFIO) has to take teachers into account, for it is estimated that two-thirds of the teachers vote Socialist and that they form one-fifth of the militants of the party. On the other hand the Socialist Party is up against the higher bid of the Communist Party, which accuses it of not being "laic" enough. In the heart of the Socialist Party, however, there are those who are tempted to go beyond this outlook: parliamentary commissions set up to study the question were presided over by Socialists. Guy Mollet himself, General Secretary of the Socialist Party when he was President of the Council, negotiated with the Holy See an agreement for aid to the confessional school. In 1963 Gaston Deferre, Socialist candidate for the Presidency of the Republic, refrained from reviving "a passionate quarrel" on this subject. The failure of the Federation of the Left in 1965 certainly reveals that the SFIO is still bound by its anticlerical militants and that the religious issue, in the form of the school question, continues to be a source of endless division between Catholic Democrats and Socialists. It has been asked "whether laicism was not rather a pretext than a real obstacle to the coming together of the MRP and the Socialist Left." According to Deferre "if the problem of the laity is raised it is to prevent a majority in favor of progress" from coming into existence. The young find this quarrel anachronistic and do not see any urgent political problem in it.

Outside of the school problem the direct influence of Catholics on political and parliamentary life is weak.

G. CATHOLICS AND INTERNATIONAL POLITICS

On problems of international policy the Holy See from Benedict XV to *Pacem in terris* has clearly encouraged the creation of an international organization and, in the last decades, autonomy for colonial peoples.

Until World War II French Catholicism was nationalistic. Since then an evolution has taken place: "When toward 1930 the Church (in France) or the majority of Catholic organizations speak, it was to recall the rights of the country and of the West; in 1965 it is to call the faithful or the adherents to the Defense of the Rights of Man or of human dignity." But the episcopate remains prudent regarding the means to use and leaves the faithful complete freedom of choice—a choice they use extensively.

Thus, if on the problem of atomic armament the French bishops took a position courageously at the Council, the assembly of the episcopate has said nothing so far on the position taken by the French government which seems difficult to reconcile with the Constitution *Gaudium et Spes.* The episcopate has not spoken out on the war in Indochina. As regards the Algerian war, the Assembly of Cardinals and Archbishops in 1955 and in 1957 specifically condemned the use of torture although it refused to take a political position. However, dropping their habitual reserve, the bishops discreetly recommended—in veiled terms—that Catholics vote "yes" in the referendum on the Evian agreements which granted autonomy to Algeria

In regard to European problems we must recognize the widespread myth of a Vatican Europe: there is no liaison between the Christian Democratic parties of Europe. Still, the Holy See has not ceased to recommend supranationality and a small Europe. The French hierarchy did not intervene to support this prospect because it involved choosing a concrete solution and because French Catholics are divided on this issue. The action of the youth movements, however, is clearly in the direction of a united Europe.

Thus, no doubt the most active part of French Catholicism is receptive today to the future rather than to the past; it tries to welcome with understanding the search for a new civilization. Militant Catholics wish to collaborate in the building of this civilization. Although it is not possible to measure the extent to which they are influencing it, they do constitute a social and civilizing force which is not negligible.

9 : BELGIUM

Jean Delfosse

"A FREE CHURCH IN A FREE STATE"[1]

The Belgian State was the issue, in 1830, of a coalition between the Catholic Church and the liberal bourgeoisie. Neither had been able to get along with the Dutch regime: the Church because King William intended to rule its internal life and to limit its rights to open and direct schools; the liberals because public opinion was not free. Thus, the Belgian Constitution of 1831 set up a regime of liberties which at the time seemed to be of unprecedented boldness from the viewpoint of the states of the Holy Alliance as well as from the viewpoint of Rome. The fundamental law recognized the liberties demanded by the Church: freedom of teaching and of association, and the freedoms dear to liberals: freedom of opinion,[2] of the press, and of assembly. It set up freedom of worship and its corollary, separation of Church and State.

Cardinal de Méan, Archbishop of Malines, had told the people that the Church "asked for no privilege: a complete freedom with all its consequences, such is the sole object of the wishes of the faithful, such is the advantage they wish to share with all their fellow citizens." The position of the Belgian bishops was inspired more by practical motives than by truly theological reflection. They were less concerned with

---

[1] For the history of the Church in Belgium today see the very complete bibliography in A. Simon, *Le parti catholique belge* (1830–1945) (Brussels, 1958).

[2] Cardinal Lambruschino, who was to become the Vatican Secretary of State shortly afterwards, wrote in 1831 on the freedom of conscience recognized by the Belgian Constitution: "This freedom at bottom is nothing else than the proclamation of religious indifference and the expression of incredulity."

revealing the principles of the freedom of the act of faith than with obtaining the most favorable conditions for maintaining the influence of the clergy. Since, at the time, the country was on the whole "Catholic," the hierarchy considered that they had everything to gain from a regime of freedom which would permit them to organize, as they pleased, Catholic seminaries and schools, charitable and other institutions, and which, on the other hand, limited the power of the State.

The separation of Church and State incorporated in the Constitution does not, however, deprive the Church of State aid. Rather the ministers of worship (Catholic, Protestant, and Jewish) are paid by the State which also participates in meeting the costs of construction and maintenance of places of worship. Moreover, certain institutions dependent upon the Church, like schools and hospitals, receive subsidies. In view of the very low proportion of the population which adhere to Protestant and Jewish faiths (barely 5 per cent), the Catholic Church seems to be a Church privileged beyond what the mutual independence of Church and State requires. It has, in short, kept all the advantages of the Concordat of 1801, signed by Napoleon and Pius VII, but none of its inconveniences.

These privileges which the Church enjoys in fact and in law have been gradually contested first by the liberal bourgeoisie and then by the socialist movement. Until recently, the whole political life of the country was dominated by the regrouping of forces for the defense of the rights of the Church on the one hand and of anticlericalism on the other.

The Belgian Government will find no more loyal supporter than the clergy. Since 1830 the bishops have played the role of defenders of legality and national institutions, beginning with the monarchy. They did not limit themselves to defending the interests of the Church. Instead they have intervened, in the name of the requirements of Christian morality, in great national questions each time that the stability and unity of the country were at stake. Thus Cardinal van Roey,[3] Primate of Belgium, intervened between the two World Wars against the Flemish extremists and against the Fascist Rexists, in 1940 at the time of the Belgian Army's capitulation, during the Occupation against Nazi demands (1942) and against the deportation of workers

[3] Cf. R. Aubert, "Le Cardinal van Roey" in *La Revue Nouvelle*, XXXIV (nos. 8–9, August, September, 1961).

(1943), after 1945 in defense of the royal right and legitimacy of King Leopold III, and again in January, 1961, at his death, in order to condemn the general strike unleashed by Socialist unions against the government of Eyskens.

It is not surprising, therefore, that certain national crises like the royal question between 1945 and 1951 have inevitably taken on the air of religious conflicts to the great detriment of priests and militant laymen who in the industrial regions of the Sambre-et-Meuse valley were facing the problems of the dechristianization of the masses of workers. All Christians concerned with a "missionary" Church have constantly demanded dissociating the taking of political positions from the witness of the faith.

ILL-ADAPTED PASTORAL STRUCTURES

That the law assures a minimum of the resources necessary for worship poses at least one inconvenience: a lack of flexibility in adapting bishoprics and parishes to population changes. Nothing, of course, prevents the Church from increasing the number of bishoprics and parishes, but if it wants the new ecclesiastical territories to benefit from the advantages provided by the State, it cannot simply increase parishes but must establish them legally—and this involves political negotiations.

In the nineteenth century it was easier to reestablish those parishes that had been suppressed at the time of the annexation of Belgium to France—the Concordat between Napoleon and Pius VII foresaw their reestablishment—than it was to create new ones. This is one reason why the distribution of the clergy was not adapted to changes in population. Thus, in Brussels the average number of inhabitants per parish which was 6,000 in 1800 increased to 15,000 in 1880. It was to Cardinal van Roey's credit that he tried to arrange a better distribution of the parishes of the capital. In 1961 the average number of inhabitants per parish had been reduced to 11,000.[4]

It was especially the working-class population that was the victim of the maldistribution of the clergy in the nineteenth century. The industrial centers were simply not given enough priests to reach the immigrant populations. Thus, at Charleroi they had to wait until 1930 before additional parishes were created. Is it surprising then that the

[4] F. Houtart, Les Paroisses de Bruxelles 1803–1951 (Louvain, 1955).

most dechristianized populations reside in the big cities and especially in the old industrialized areas?[5]

It is not impossible to overcome the difficulties involved in establishing a new parish for they are purely administrative, but the creation of a new diocese necessarily raises political questions. First of all the parties in power must be in agreement; but, except for the years 1951–1954, the governments since 1919 have had to be coalition governments and, therefore, include a certain number of ministers more or less influenced by nineteenth-century anticlerical ideology and little inclined to increase the financial burdens of the State in favor of a Church toward which they are prejudiced. Moreover, considering the centrifugal tendencies which in the last few years have expressed themselves with a new vigor on the political front, political authorities are suspicious of any change of diocesan boundaries that would upset the national equilibrium or that would even seem to give encouragement to the partisans of a Federalist regime.

However that may be, it is clear that the present distribution of dioceses does not correspond to pastoral needs. At the death of Cardinal van Roey in 1961, *La Revue Nouvelle*,[6] making use of the religious sociological studies of Canon Houtart and P. Kerkhofs, S.J., proposed making eleven dioceses out of the existing six dioceses. Until now these suggestions have been only partially realized. In 1961 the Archdiocese of Malines was divided into two parts by creating the Diocese of Antwerp and the Archdiocese of Malines-Brussels. Malines had been one of the most important dioceses in the world because of the number of baptized (3,338,500), its 3,221 priests, 4,371 religious and 15,339 nuns, and its numerous institutions. It included more than one-third of the population of Belgium. The new Diocese of Malines-Brussels is still very large: it includes, besides the area of Malines, the Province of Brabant, the most populous of Belgium, and the most diverse as well, since it is the meeting place of the French and Flemish languages. Brussels has an important international population that includes civil servants of European communities and members of private international organizations which have established more and more centers in the vicinity of the European communities, members of SHAPE, and the Spanish and North African workers.

[5] L. Dingemans and F. Houtart, *Pastorale d'une region industrielle* (Brussels-Paris, 1964), deals with the agglomeration of Charleroi.

[6] Cf. "L'adaptation des dioceses en Belgique" in *La Revue Nouvelle*, XXXIV (nos. 8–9, August, September, 1961).

Despite the assignment of a vicar-general by the Archbishopric to each of the four regions of the Diocese (Malines, Flemish Brabant, Walloon Brabant, and Brussels) dialogue—the watchword when Cardinal Suenens inaugurated his episcopacy—is just as difficult as in the time of his predecessor. It is too soon to say whether the new structure of dialogue, the priests' council, established in 1967 and based on direct election by the clergy, and the parish council,[7] which is to be created in 1968, will be able to remedy the inconveniences arising from the size of the archdiocese.

In 1967 the Diocese of Liège was divided in order to make possible the new Diocese of Hasselt which covers the whole Province of Limburg. The creation of this diocese was delayed for quite a while: its creation was believed to involve support for divisions along linguistic lines. The decision to divide the diocese was seen as a movement in a direction that worried the defenders of the unitary regime established in 1830.

Today, Belgium has eight dioceses. This means that each diocese has on the average more than 1,000,000 Catholics (95 per cent of the inhabitants are baptized),[8] that is each diocese has more than four times the average number of baptized per diocese, if Europe is taken as a whole.

Dioceses	Deaneries	Parishes	Priests	Area (Sq. Km.)	Inhabitants
Malines-Brussels	66	645	2,035	3,603	2,273,644
Antwerp	21	287	1,234	2,552	1,298,423
Bruges	24	383	1,514	3,235	1,101,435
Ghent	33	410	1,347	2,935	1,310,650
Liège	49	825	1,870	6,354	1,656,364
Namur	38	738	1,172	8,078	597,556
Tournai	36	561	1,078	3,756	1,261,162
Total	267	3,849	10,250	30,513	9,499,234

[7] At Pentecost in 1967, Cardinal Suenens inaugurated a vast consultation in the dioceses soliciting their opinion on the Pastoral Council to be created. The answers were returnable until December 31, 1967.

[8] But has not baptism been a rite without importance for very many? According to the investigation of C. d'Hoogh and J. Meyer, *Jeunesse Belge: Opinions et Aspirations* (Brussels, 1964), 84 per cent of Belgians between 16 and 24 declare themselves baptized Catholics; 14 per cent have no religion; 69 per cent practice regularly—among the 69 per cent there are three girls for every two boys.

ORDERS AND CONGREGATIONS, CONVENTS

| | MEN | | WOMEN | |
Dioceses	Congregations	Convents	Congregations	Convents
Malines-Brussels	42	160	180	663
Antwerp	29	67	92	405
Bruges	26	64	91	589
Ghent	22	68	77	525
Liège	39	104	128	469
Namur	28	67	72	295
Tournai	32	66	95	346
Total	218	596	396	3,292

Figures are cited from the *Annuaire Catholique de Belgique*, 1966–1967, and before the subdivision of the diocese of Liège.[9]

The Belgian bishops to some extent are the prisoners of their administrative responsibilities. Contacts between pastors and laity, and even between priests and their bishop, are not easy, even if the bishop is warm-hearted, open, and immediately hospitable. A vicar-general once told me: "If you wish to submit a problem to my bishop do it in two pages, for he won't read more than that."

The Belgian bishoprics give an impression of being solidly structured administrations, but they are not free of the defects of bureaucracy. It is not surprising to hear laymen and clergy sometimes complaining that their bishops, who at the Council sought to disengage the Church from the Vatican Curia, have until now barely remedied the "curialism" of their own diocesan administration.[10] Will the priests' councils and the pastoral councils remedy this situation? It is too soon to say, since these councils are only beginning to be set up.

Each diocese has organized its councils in its own way which is quite in accord with our tradition that each bishop sees to it that there is only "one crozier in his own diocese." Under the circumstances the

[9] According to *Het Belang van Limburg* (July 21 and 23, 1966), there were in the diocese of Liège about 900 priests who came originally from Limburg, 70 women's congregations and 30 congregations of priests and brothers devoted to teaching and caring for the sick. 99 per cent of the population of Limburg is baptized.

[10] Cf. Jan Grootaers, "Concilie en Paus, te Rome en Thuis" in *De Maand* (no. 1, January, 1965).

variety of methods is fortunate so far as diocesan councils are concerned, but when problems go beyond the limits of a diocese, a more structured interdiocesan institution is desirable. There is to be sure a national conference of the bishops of Belgium, but the rule of unanimity which was adopted for each decision does not permit the president of the conference, the Cardinal Archbishop of Malines-Brussels, to commit himself very seriously when his views are sought.

The rule of unanimity lacks flexibility. On the other hand, it is difficult to rescind it in the present situation, when there is such an awareness of the very diversity of the country with all the consequent questioning of the political and ecclesiastical structures.

CENTRIFUGAL TENSIONS

A few months ago I asked a Flemish Jesuit to join a working party which *La Revue Nouvelle* had organized for consideration of "The Post-Conciliar Belgian Church." He refused and said: "There is no Belgian Church." The incident may very well suggest the movement of ideas in Flanders today.[11]

Since the settlement of great problems like that of the monarchy, the school question and the decolonization of the Congo, all of which made it necessary for a party to avoid raising divisive issues, that is, since 1961, the worsening of the linguistic conflict has heavily burdened the life of the Church at least regarding institutions and places where French-speaking and Flemish people meet, as at Louvain, Brussels, or along the seacoast. In Flanders the use of French in the liturgy has been denounced by the *Vlaamse Volksbeweging*—the Flemish popular movement which brings together the most varied cultural associations and which is organized as a pressure group to promote the Flemish language and the Flemish people—as an attack on the "linguistic homogeneity of the region." The extremists have not hesitated systematically to disturb Masses celebrated in French in the churches of Antwerp, along the seacoast, or on the outskirts of Brussels. So much was this the case that Bishop Desmedt of Bruges had to decree that Masses should be said in Flemish, even during the summer vacation

---

[11] On the Church in Flanders, cf. the important collaborative work under the direction of P. Kerkhofs, S.J., and J. Van Houtte, *De Kerk in vlanderen* (Tielt-Lattage, 1962).

season, when more than half of the vacationers are Walloon. Similarly, Bishop Daem of Antwerp had to suppress the few religious services said in French in certain parishes.

On the whole, the Walloons have taken badly the rigor of these episcopal decisions. They point out that in the tourist areas of Walloon provinces Masses in Flemish are said during the vacations and occasion not the slightest trouble. In so arguing they fail to appreciate that the Flemish have social and cultural motivations which do not arise for the Walloons. The Flemish movement is so aggressive toward the use of French because French has been used by the traditional bourgeoisie of Flanders and, therefore, is considered an instrument of social discrimination.

Many Flemish Catholics blame the bishops for not committing themselves sufficiently to the complete Flemishization of life in Flanders. The least one can say is that there is some tension between diocesan authorities and certain groups of intellectuals and religious. The latter, especially the Jesuits who exercise a notable influence through their colleges and their review, *Streven*, and the Dominicans with their review, *Kulturleven*, charge that the bishops are too closely linked to what they call the Establishment, that is, the leading older classes, especially the industrial and financial circles which are mostly French-speaking, to be able completely to understand specific Flemish needs.[12] These tensions have always existed, but the Council, by the free discussion it favored, permitted underground currents to surface. It favored in particular an intense reflection on the pastoral consequences of the political evolution which in recent years has increased and culminated in the legislative recognition of Flemish and French-speaking "cultural communities."

In 1962 and 1963 a series of laws were voted to establish in a radical way a single language for the regions. Henceforth provincial and communal administrations are no longer authorized, without penalty, to use a language other than the official language of the region. Likewise the language of the schools must be that of the region. This legislation restricting linguistic freedom on the level of administration, teaching, and business was in response to Flemish demands.

In reaction there developed the idea of a Walloon community in Walloon territory. But this idea did not have the strong supporting

12 Cf. Jean Kerkhofs, "Naar nieuwe kerkstructuren in Belgie" in *Streven* (January, 1967).

bond provided by the defense of a language threatened by the competition of a culturally and socially more prestigious tongue. The idea did not have the same cohesive force and remained ambiguous: sometimes it was aimed at the French-speaking people of the capital and the inhabitants of the Walloon provinces, and sometimes only at those who found in the economic decline of their region a justification for creating a Walloon community. Contrary to what is taking place in Flanders, where the movement to promote Flemish is directed by Catholics and sometimes presents very confessional aspects, in Walloon provinces the Walloon movement is led principally by leftists; and Catholics show themselves rather reserved.[13]

Until now Catholic Walloons have been more inclined to defend the traditional unitary Belgium because unitarism seems to work in favor of the maintenance of their position of strength related to the whole Christian institutional system in the country. Certainly, for example, the settlement of the war over the schools in 1958 involved a law relatively favorable to the Catholic school which was obtained at the end of the "school year"; the result would not have been secured without the collaboration of the Flemish Catholics who provided balance for the political and social minority position of the Catholics in both the Walloon area and Brussels.

Such a course of action as the representation of Christian organizations on a national scale also depends in large part on the contribution in men and money of the Flemish regions. There are, however, Walloon Catholics who think that from a pastoral point of view, the abandonment of the unitary system, which until now has prevailed for Christian institutions, would be preferable. This would free the Church in Walloon areas from a whole institutional, school, and social system considerably overdeveloped in proportion to the real number of Walloon Catholics.

The necessity of maintaining a whole institutional network which the majority of the people reject calls for energies that would be more effectively used if the Church adopted a frankly missionary stance. Rather than rendering "services" in competition with the "services"

---

[13] There are, however, Catholics involved in the Walloon activity. Cf. for example, Robert Royer, *Vivre sa foi aujourdhui en Walloonie* (Brussels, 1967), and Msgr. Jacques Leclercq, *Les Catholiques et la question flamande* (Liège, 1963). See also *Notes Pastorales* (no. 2, March-April, 1967) on the topic "Le rôle des chrétiens dans l'avenir économique de la Walloonie" (Brussels).

offered by society, should not the Walloon Church try to be productive of "testimony"? This is the question which the Walloon Christians more and more ask themselves. In general they tend to agree with P. Kerkhofs, S.J., who suggests that every attempt to think out pastoral problems is paralyzed, for both the Flemish and the Walloons, when it is insisted that the problems be considered from a unitary point of view. Father Kerkhofs further suggests that two episcopal conferences be set up in Belgium, one Flemish and the other Walloon. The link between them would be assured by the Archbishop of Malines-Brussels who as titular head of the only bilingual diocese and Primate of Belgium would have the right to participate in both conferences. There would also be coordinating organs between the two conferences.

Are there any opportunities to apply solutions of this kind? It is hard to answer this question because the situation is so complex. One obstacle to such an organization is that it inevitably has political implications which are feared by some and welcomed by others: can the Church, which has been one of the unifying factors of Belgium, accelerate a process of federalization of the country? That is one of the questions that inevitably comes up in the present political context. However that may be, one cannot deny that for the moment people are thinking in terms of a greater autonomy for the two regions and a greater awareness of what differentiates them. The difference is not simply one of language; people think differently because their situations are different. Christianity is seemingly coherent and predominant in Flanders;[14] in the Walloon areas it is socially divided and in the minority. Besides, the Walloon clergy and Catholic militants are influenced by French theology while the Flemish are more interested in German and Anglo-Saxon theologians whose works are immediately translated into Dutch. Thus, works like *The Secular City* of Harvey Cox or *Honest to God* by John A. T. Robinson were published in Dutch well before they were published in French. *Honest to God* had a much greater success in Dutch than the French translation had in France and in the Walloon provinces. Finally, the movement of ideas which is stirring Dutch Catholicism in such a spectacular manner has direct repercussions in Flanders where Catholicism had until only recently rather similar characteristics: a strong clerical atmosphere and social control organized by the Church.

[14] Hence the more violent reaction of numerous circles of Flemish intellectuals against "triumphalism" and "clericalism."

According to research on Sunday Mass attendance,[15] it is estimated that about 60 per cent of the inhabitants in Flemish regions attend Sunday Mass; in Walloon areas the figure is 40 per cent and in Brussels 35 per cent. According to a map of Sunday Mass attendance made from an October, 1962, census of the country, a certain number of factors are common to both Flemish and Walloon areas: the proportion of those who practice is greater in rural areas than in industrialized concentrations. A comparison of the number of ordinations in proportion to the population likewise shows that the differences between Flemish and Walloon areas are relatively unimportant: a rural Walloon diocese like Namur has no reason to envy the most Catholic diocese of Flanders.

The figures for ordinations are given in terms of 10,000 young men old enough to be ordained (24 to 26 years of age) for the years 1951 to 1960: Malines, which had not been divided at the time, 9.66; Bruges, 13.94; Ghent, 10.43; Liège, which had not yet been divided, 11.12; Namur, 18.93; Tournai, 7.55. For the country as a whole, towns of average size (those with more than 20,000 inhabitants) have the highest rate of ordinations and big cities the lowest.

Today the visible differences between Flemish Catholicism and Walloon Catholicism are perhaps more superficial than would appear at first sight. In the long run the problems which each faces are basically the same as those facing all countries of Western Europe, that is, to make the transition from a Church which up to now has sought to preserve as much as possible of Constantinian Christianity to one which, according to Karl Rahner, sees itself in the situation of a *diaspora* in a desacralized and laicized world.

THE CATHOLIC WORLD

Belgian Catholicism has not structured itself with the view of conducting a dialogue between the Church and the world, a view which largely came out of Vatican II with the collaboration of Belgian theologians. The Council produced a lively sense of disquiet, but the

[15] Works of the Center of Socioreligious Research of Louvain cited in "Structures et évolution du 'Monde catholique' en Belgique" in *Courrier hebdomadaire* of the Center for Research and Sociopolitical Information (CRISP) (nos. 352, 353, 354, February 10, 1967).

structure is too solid and the importance of the whole Catholic institutional apparatus in Belgian society too considerable to expect any spectacular changes.

Belgian society is a strongly segmented society.[16] As Catholicism has occupied a relatively strong position in it from time immemorial, the divisions came into being in terms of the Church or as a reaction to it.

Seen from the outside, the Church appears to be a strongly structured political-religious society in which Christians find an answer to all their needs, not only the spiritual ones but also those on the level of education, health, and the preservation of their social and economic interests. This society is apparently organized in competition with other societies structured around non-Christian political parties. These, doubtless, do not present themselves as counter-churches; yet they organize themselves parallel to the churches and try to meet all the needs of man.

It is primarily the Socialist Party, the party of the workers which is organized in the same way as the Catholics.[17] The only service non-Catholics have not created is teaching; they have preferred to develop the official schools of the State, the provinces, or the communes. The only important exception in this area is the Free University of Brussels founded in 1834 as a reaction to the reestablishment by the Belgian bishops of the Catholic University of Louvain which the French republic had suppressed in 1797. The University of Brussels is, therefore, officially freethinking and requires its professors to sign a declaration explicitly affirming their rejection of all dogmatic authority.

From the ideological point of view, the Free University of Brussels appears to be less free from the past than the Catholic University of Louvain which has abolished the antimodernist oath required of professors since Pius X. It has even named some notoriously non-Catholic professors. So far as students are concerned, it has since the 1950's dropped the ancient requirement that a student present a baptismal certificate of the Catholic Church in order to register at the university.

[16] A good analysis of the system of compartmentalization of society has been made by Professor Val R. Lorwin, in "Conflits et compromis dans la politique belge," CRISP, (no. 324, June 10, 1966), a translation of a communication made to the 1965 annual meeting of the American Political Science Assn., Washington, D.C. The same author has written, "Belgium: Class and Language in National Politics" in *Political Oppositions in Western Democracies* (New Haven, 1966).

[17] Cf. Jean Delfosse, "Der Belgische Sozialismus" in *Katholizismus und freiheitliches Sozialismus in Europa* (Cologne, 1965).

The University of Louvain, complemented by other institutions of higher Catholic learning, is the focus of a whole network of schools of all sorts, scattered throughout the country, although the density in Flanders is greater than in the Walloon provinces.

In 1964–1965 the distribution of school population between the official system of the communes, provinces, and the State, and the almost completely Catholic system of religious schools was: 768,483 students (43 per cent of the total) in the former, and 1,018,861 (57 per cent) in the latter.

These totals do not include those in technical or professional schools on the secondary level; in 1963–1964 the official technical schools were attended by 102,959 students or 37 per cent of the total as against 175,518 students, or 63 per cent in the religious schools.[18]

Finally, almost half of the country's university students were registered in Catholic universities which in 1966 enrolled 23,634 students, of whom 19,222 were at Louvain.

These figures help us to understand why the Belgian bishops at the Council were so keenly interested in the Declaration on Christian Education. In particular, Bishop Daem of Antwerp, former Director-General of the National Secretariat of Catholic Education, played a decisive role in writing it.

In 1957 the bishops created the National Secretariat of Catholic Education in order to assure coordination and unity in Catholic teaching. The increase in the school population required rationalizing the development of schools, for some depended on the bishops, others on various religious congregations.

The need to defend the very conditions of existence of the free schools, which had been made rather precarious by legislation voted by a Socialist-Liberal majority, worked in favor of the coordinating effort for which the bishops had asked: generally religious congregations are wary of yielding on the independence of their schools. The Secretariat established at Brussels became a powerful administration, well equipped and organized, and in overall control of the Catholic school system.

The school pact, signed by the three big national parties in 1958,

[18] Most of the statistics quoted here are taken from the issue of CRISP referred to in note 15 or are based on information supplied by the organizations concerned. For the bishops' views on the schools see Cardinal Suenens, *La question scolaire* (Paris-Bruges, 1956).

after elections which constituted an outright disavowal of the war on the schools waged by the leftists, gave the arrangement of two school systems, one the official and the other the Catholic, a rigidity which is not ideal from either the democratic or the religious point of view. On the one hand, it may be asked whether the Catholic schools, in surrendering their liberty to a centralizing organ which tends to impose a single model, can still claim to represent the value of liberty by which they justified their existence with respect to the State; on the other hand, there is the fear that the existence of a well-subsidized school system[19] at the disposition of Catholics, will gradually lead those responsible for the official schools to consider them as schools for unbelievers and, therefore, to interpret the principle of the ideological neutrality of the official school in such a way as to exclude Catholicism and even Christian values.

Finally, now that the school accord has lessened tension, it becomes more evident that the bishops' concern for Catholic schools contrasts more with their indifference to those attending the State schools. In them the baptized are numerous. Between 60 to 70 per cent of the students in the public schools enroll in the course of religion in preference to the course in ethics: students are obliged to select one of them.

It is not easy to raise questions on the Christian school. Before the school pact of 1958, all energy was devoted to the defense of the religious school; in the emotionally charged climate of the period and faced with the aggressiveness of the anticlericals, how could one doubt the accepted ideas about the Catholic school? The school accord was made for twelve years. The forthcoming occasion for its renewal invites Catholics to reconsider their positions in the light of the whole body of Conciliar texts, especially *Lumen gentium* and *Gaudium et spes* and not simply the decree on Christian education. In November, 1967, *La Revue Nouvelle* undertook a study on the future of the religious schools.[20] The violence of the very diverse reactions shows that it is a very delicate question to raise. In my opinion the question will become more relevant and urgent: there are the practical grounds, notably the decline of religious vocations; and there are intellectual and psychologi-

---

[19] The only costs not paid by the State are the costs of construction. All other costs—professors' salaries and administrative costs—are paid by the State.

[20] Cf. Cincinnatus, "L'enseignement libre en Belgique aujourdhui et demain" in *La Revue Nouvelle*, XLVI (no. 11, November, 1967), and "Le Dossier Cincinnatus" in *La Revue Nouvelle*, XLVI (no. 1, January, 1968).

cal grounds, for example, the idea of pluralism appeals to younger people. However that may be, a serious scientific study of the effectiveness of the religious formation given by the Catholic school would be desirable, for it would suggest which directions should be taken. Of what use is it to mobilize so much effort for teaching, if it turned out, as certain comparisons of religious practice between students of the two systems suggest, that the Catholic school does not have the influence claimed for it and that in fact it is the example of the parents that is decisive?[21]

There is no human need, as we have said, which does not find its answer in a Catholic institution or organization.[22] It is not possible to list them all: from checkups for babies to homes for the aged, not to mention cooperatives, mutuals, and recreation services. Here only the most important will be named along with the figures or their membership or their beneficiaries. The distribution according to linguistic regions will be indicated. The elements for comparison with similar non-Catholic institutions will be provided.

All the organizations and services which reach salaried workers are federated in the Christian Worker Movement (MOC) which assures unity in program and collaboration in action. The Young Christian Worker (JOC and JOCF), a Catholic Action movement which likewise assumes responsibility for the interests of young workers belongs to MOC. The Young Christian Worker movement has from 8,000 to 10,000 young men and women in the Walloon provinces and 61,000 in Flanders. The apostolate and education of adult women is carried on by the Women's Christian Workers League (LOCF) which has

[21] Cf. P. Delooz, S.J., "La mesure de l'efficacité de l'enseignement catholique" in Du cri à la parole, "Cahier Lumen Vitae de psychologie religieuse," IV (Brussels, 1967); and Abbé Van Ruyskenvelde, "Enquête sur la Foi de 83 collégiens," Pro manuscripto (1967). The investigation "confirms the fundamental importance of the religious practice of parents; it is possible that the level of certitude of the faith of children is linked to parental religious practice, which in turn is a probable sign of the level of certitude of the faith of the parents; and that the incidence of the other variables, notably attendance at a confessional school, has only a secondary effect, the milieu being what it is. Here, however, it is a matter of possibility, not a certainty."

[22] The apostolate is understood by most movements and good works not in the sense of witness among unbelievers, but in the sense of the maintenance of the baptized in a Christian milieu. "We use," writes the Abbé Comblain, "the word apostolate to designate activities which in fact constitute the care of the Christian people."

125,000 members in the Walloon provinces and 260,000 in Flanders. The counterparts for men are the Catholic Worker Association (*Katholieke Werkliedenbonden*, KWB) in Flanders and the Popular Teams (*Equipes Populaires*, EP) in Walloon areas. The former has some 132,000 members and the latter 2,200. The interests of the workers are protected by the Confederation of Christian Unions (CSC) which in 1965 counted 884,410 associates—compared to the General Belgian Federation of Labor (FGT), socialist in tendency, which has 734,805 members. The total number of salaried workers is 2,850,886. Flemish federations of the CSC account for 74.5 per cent of the members, that of Brussels 7.7 per cent, and those of the Walloon provinces 17.8 per cent.

When the French Christian unions decided to give up their confessional character by transforming themselves into the French Democratic Confederation of Workers (CFDT), the question arose as to whether the Belgian CSC would not follow their example. But August Cool, President of the CSC, made it very clear that "the question had not come up in Belgium."

Since passage of legislation obliging practically every Belgian to be insured against sickness, mutual insurance companies have increased considerably in recent years. In 1966 the National Alliance of Christian Mutuals had 1,467,874 participants or 44.3 per cent of the total number of participants, while Socialist mutuals had only 900,873 subscribers or 27.2 per cent of the total. If one takes into consideration the beneficiaries (the spouse and children of participants) of the system, the difference between Christian mutuals and Socialist mutuals is even more evident: 4,098,090 or 46.2 per cent versus 2,275,478 or 25.6 per cent. Finally, the MOC includes powerful consumer cooperatives, insurance companies, and savings banks. The resources obtained by membership fees, premiums, and the profits from the economic organizations, permit the MOC to support study groups, education, and recreation. The MOC publishes two daily newspapers: one Flemish, *Het Volk*, which with a circulation of 220,000 ranks second among Flemish papers; and the Walloon *La Cité* which has a circulation of about 30,000.

There is no national coordinating federation for the peasants equivalent to that existing for the workers. In Flanders, the *Boerenbond*, the Peasant Alliance, unites into a federation all movements dealing with the apostolate among farmers and with their professional, economic, and educational interests. In 1964 their agricultural guilds had 90,233 men; circles for peasant women 136,067 members; their youth sections accounted for 23,901 boys and 19,971 girls. The *Boerenbond* is an economic power because of its various consumer and producer cooperatives, its credit unions, and insurance companies: in 1964 loans outstanding amounted to more than 8 billion Belgian francs ($160,000,-000). It is also an important pressure group. In Flanders it has a virtual monopoly in the protection of farmer interests. It reaches into a few Walloon regions where, although it has only few members, it plays a certain economic role. In the Walloon region the Catholic Action movements for the young and for adults are organized independently of the professional organizations: the Agricultural Union with an obvious confessional tendency has 25,000 members and the Professional Agricultural Unions (23,000 members). The religious authorities have long regarded the outlook of the latter with suspicion.

The middle classes likewise are more institutionally organized in Flanders than in Walloon areas. The National Christian Middleclass Association (*Nationaal christelijk Middenstandverbond*) with 40,000 members is devoted to the defense of middle-class interests and seeks to permeate the life of its members with Christian principles. Its Walloon counterpart, the Movement of Independents and of Cadres, is not at all comparable in importance.

All these social organizations of workers, peasants, and middle class consider themselves officially independent of every political party, but they do have links with the Christian Social Party (PSC). Each has a political committee with PSC parliamentarians who belong to the organization. The authors of *La Décision politique en Belgique* (Political Decision in Belgium) quite rightly say: "From the sociological point of view the PSC seems to be the political guarantee of the whole institutional edifice in which 'the Catholic world' is incorporated."[23]

When in 1945 the PSC was established upon the remnants of the old Catholic Party, it wished to give up its confessional character. Nonetheless, it has remained the Catholic party. In 1945 some leftist Catholics tried to form the Belgian Democratic Union, a sort of Labor

[23] *La Décision politique en Belgique* under the direction of Jean Meynaud, Jean Ladrière, and François Périn (Paris, 1965).

party in which Catholics and non-Catholics would unite on the basis of a progressive program. The venture was a complete failure. It was sabotaged by the Socialist Party whose leader of that period, Max Buset, said in 1945: "Two ideologies confront each other in Belgium, the socialist and the Christian; in ten years the second must be eliminated in favor of the first." The Union was condemned by Cardinal van Roey who thought that Catholics must support only the Christian Social Party. The conclusion of the school pact of 1958 ended the ideological blocs. The elections of 1961 were the first since 1884 in which the bishops abstained from giving the slightest directions to Catholics. The first party to draw the lesson of this development was the old liberal party which dropped its nineteenth-century anticlerical positions and opened up its ranks to Catholics. Under the name Liberty and Progress Party (PLP), it seeks to attract the middle classes and conservative circles.

The parties, apart from the PLP, that have benefitted most from the breakup of the ideological blocs have been the small parties with nationalist or linguistic leanings, like the *Volksunie* in Flanders, the French-speaking Front in Brussels, and the Walloon parties in the south of the country. The PSC and the Socialist Party, the two most important parties, find it harder to free themselves from the past and from the bonds which tie them to either or all the Christian or all the Socialist groupings of social, economic, and educational institutions. These parties are no less torn by internal nationalistic and regional tensions: the PSC, in particular, no longer can claim the role of defender of the Catholic school and so has lost a major cohesive force.

In the PSC as in the Socialist Party, however, there are very strong currents working to preserve the unity of the party and of the social organizations. Flemish Socialists do not wish to face without allies those they call the proponents of clericalism, the majority group in Flanders: similarly the Christians, a minority in the Walloon areas, fear the excessive power of a left that is still impregnated with anticlerical traditions.

Since the war the PSC has received the following percentages of votes:[24]

---

[24] In 1950 the monarchy was at stake; in 1958 school legislation. In 1961 the bishops gave no directives. In 1965 the big issue was mostly the linguistic conflict which favored the small parties at the expense of the PSC.

Elections	Flanders	Wallonia	Brussels	Kingdom
1946	57.3	29.9	32.9	42.5
1949	54.6	31.2	31.0	43.6
1950	60.4	32.9	34.7	47.7
1954	52.2	29.9	30.3	41.1
1958	56.6	34.2	33.5	46.5
1961	51.3*	30.5*	31.8*	41.5
1965	43.8	23.3	19.6	34.5

* Indicates that a dissident party is included.

THE CRISIS AT THE UNIVERSITY OF LOUVAIN[25]

The intermingling of strictly political conflicts with the questioning or the defense of confessional institutions may obscure the real forces at work. The intermingling makes it difficult to distinguish the real motivations of the attitudes taken by Flemish and Walloon Catholics in the post-Council debates concerning certain Christian institutions. The most crucial issue centers around the Catholic University of Louvain.

The old university, founded in 1425 by the Duke of Brabant, suppressed in 1797, and reestablished in 1832, is the most important university of Belgium. It has almost as many students as the three other universities together. It is also the Belgian university with the greatest international reputation.[26] Louvain, a Catholic university, has always sought to work for two objectives: to be the crown of the whole Catholic school system and to be a center of thought and research in the service of the universal Church. The fact that the faculty of theology is incorporated in an institution where all the profane sciences are the subject of research and teaching has given it a tradition of rigorous

[25] The most objective documentation on the crisis is published by CRISP in its *Courrier Hebdomadaire*, "L'Université de Louvain et la question linguistique" (no. 173, November 9, 1962, and no. 178, December 7, 1962); see also "L'Affaire de Louvain" (nos. 333–334, September 16, 1966) and "Évolution et implications de l'affaire de Louvain" (no. 358, March 17, 1967, and nos. 364–365, April 28, 1967).

[26] As of January 15, 1968, the university had 25,000 students divided about equally between the two language sections. The French section had a little more than 2,500 foreigners (685 North Americans); the Flemish section had 250 foreigners.

scholarship which constitutes one of the reasons for its authority in the Church, especially as regards the Congregation of Seminaries and of Universities at Rome.[27]

At the very moment when a whole team of Louvain professors played a role which was often decisive at the Council and which earned for the university unquestioned glory on the international scene, at home the very structure of the university was more and more violently questioned in Flemish circles.

Since 1911 the university has progressively introduced more courses in Flemish: twenty-five years later practically all the courses were taught in both Flemish and French but the structure of the university remained unitary. Since 1961 this unitary structure and the maintenance of French-speaking faculties in the area of Louvain, a Flemish section, have been challenged.

When the government's proposed legislation on languages was made known in 1961, French-speaking professors were disturbed by the legislation's possible consequences for the French-speaking section. For the area of Louvain the legislation proposed to make Flemish the sole language to be used in the administration, including its dealings with the inhabitants, and in the schools whatever the origin or the wishes of the parents. The French-speaking professors started a campaign to demand at least a special arrangement for the members of the university who had to reside in Louvain.

The Flemish saw in this demand a maneuver to prevent the "homogenization" of Flemish Brabant that the new legislation was meant to assure. They expressed the fear that given the projected expansion of the university—several studies showed that by 1980 the student population would total between 38,000 to 43,000, of whom 16,000 to 17,000 students would be in the French part, the numbers of professors, assistants, researchers, and French-speaking employees coming to settle at

[27] At Louvain there are numerous contacts between the secular disciplines and theology, but interdisciplinary research is only beginning to be organized somewhat systematically. Its first achievement to attract attention was the "Colloquium on interdisciplinary reflection and research as a method of the Church-World dialogue," held November 10–12, 1967, on the initiative of FERES (International Federation of the Social and Socioreligious Institutes) with the collaboration of the International Center of Research, Studies and Cultural Exchanges of Paris, of the Protestant Center of Studies at Geneva, the Department "Church and Society" of the Ecumenical Council of Churches, of the International Federation of Catholic Universities, and of the Kerk Weredienstituut of the Netherlands.

Louvain would be large enough one day to require a bilingual status for the city.

As the French-speaking side stiffened, the Flemish side became more radical. It not only opposed any provision for exception, but even demanded the immediate separation of the administrative organs of the university so as to assure the autonomy of the Flemish section. The purely linguistic demands were accompanied by a demand for a more democratic system of powers in the administration of the university.[28]

In April, 1962, the bishops appealed for understanding on the part of the legislators in order to preserve for the two linguistic sections conditions that were viable and would allow each to grow. This amounted to favoring the wishes of the French-speaking professors, the only ones whose section would have suffered from the effects of the proposed law.

In August, 1962, the bishops announced a plan of university reorganization. The plan was intended to assure its unity while providing a basis of relative autonomy for each linguistic section.

The declarations of the bishops, the measures taken in 1963 which organized double faculties, except for theology and canon law, the nomination of a pro-rector for each linguistic regime, and the establishment of separate French and Flemish university parishes, did not bring about the desired pacification.

Meanwhile, the idea of transferring the French-speaking section to a Walloon area and of the total autonomy of the Flemish section had become the dominant idea of the Flemish movements.

In January, 1966, the bishops created a commission headed by Professors Leemans and Aubert to study the different aspects of the future of the University of Louvain. The members of the commission reached unanimous agreement on the distribution of the power of decision within the university. On the other hand, the French-speaking members could not accept the Flemish proposal to transfer a part of the French section—the candidacies. They refused for pedagogical reasons to separate the candidates for the licentiate and the doctorate. Moreover, they feared that this sacrifice, which was asked of them as proof of

[28] The idea of democratizing the university regime expressed the wish of a majority of the professors and students in the two linguistic sections; but the idea was sustained by the Flemish with all the fighting ardor of a younger group conscious of winning a place for itself.

good will toward Flemish claims, would be considered by the extremists as a step toward a complete transfer.

On May 13, 1966, the bishops finally made their long awaited solemn declaration. It caused an astonishing explosion of rage among Flemish Catholic youth, which their clergy generally looked at benevolently, while French-speaking circles believed they had finally received the guarantees they sought.[29]

Among the reasons for this outburst of rage was primarily, according to all observers, the authoritarian tone of the declaration; the appeal to the argument of authority came too late to be effective. To say too late is to suppose that authority would have been effective even in a matter in which the competence of the bishops was strongly contested by the whole current of thought on the subject of secularization.

In their declaration the bishops reaffirmed "their unshakable will to maintain the unity of alma mater and to assure the maximum expansion of the two linguistic communities in perfect equality of rights and of duties." "There is no question," they said, "of founding, right away or by stages, a new French or Dutch university, or of dividing the patrimony, or of dismantling the University of Louvain in any way. We refuse to envisage two Catholic universities in our country, even if their realization was financially or politically possible." They announced, however, that unity caused no obstacle to a greater autonomy of the two sections and to the scattering of candidates across the country to meet the rapid increase of students.

On July 15, 1966, the bishops made a declaration intended to appease Flemish opinion. Flemish circles interpreted this rather ambiguous declaration as a surrender by the bishops of the positions taken in May, while the French-speaking people stuck by the declaration of May 13, 1966. Thus, the relative calm that reigned in 1967 does not justify thinking that the tensions have been definitively overcome.[30]

The future of the University of Louvain awakens so many passions throughout the country, because it is considered by public opinion as

[29] On the significance of an objective Flemish point of view of these events, cf. "Louvain dépasse Louvain" in *Les Dossiers* (Brussels, no. 7, September, 1966), a translation of the article "Leuven Buiten Leuven" which appeared in *De Maand*.

[30] At the time of this writing (February, 1968) Flemish demonstrations have begun again in favor of ridding Louvain of its French-speaking section as a result of the declaration (January 25, 1968) of the Academic Council of the French-speaking section in favor of maintaining a complete French-speaking section at Louvain.

foreshadowing that of the State. One of the conclusions of a poll taken in 1967 was this: "The most fundamental point to become clear is that the battle over Louvain is, for public opinion, a stage in a struggle involving all the institutions of the country."[31]

But the political problem is not the only one to be raised at Louvain. Such problems as the declericalization,[32] and the deconfessionalization of the university, problems ultimately of greater import to the Church, have been taken up. In the atmosphere of linguistic conflict which has prevailed there for nearly ten years, it is difficult to distinguish to what extent the reform proposals are purely tactical or inspired by a new vision of the Church. Thus, the hope of seeing the bishops cede a part of their powers to the laity is not always free of ambiguity on the part of those who hope to see the University of Louvain become the great Flemish university.

On the other hand, some on occasion regard a certain insistence of the French-speaking group on the international role of the Catholic university and an appeal to the authority of bishops as convenient means of defending existing positions.

It is possible that the political aspect of the Louvain problem has somewhat worked against a frank revision of the definitely clerical character of the university which looks more and more anachronistic in terms of the great perspective of the Council, notably the idea of the responsibility of the laity in the Church and in the world.[33]

The bishops of Belgium affirmed on May 13, 1966, that the future of Louvain should be seen "in a perspective not only regional or national, but European and worldwide." The whole question is to see whether there is a way of following regional, national, and worldwide objectives at the same time.

Some wished Louvain to assert, first of all, its universal vocation and to subordinate its national or regional vocation.[34] The policy set by the bishops in 1966 remains in conformity with tradition: it tends to offer

[31] *L'opinion publique belge et l'Université de Louvain* (Louvain, 1967), p. 79.

[32] Msgr. Dondeyne wrote: "A modern Catholic university cannot have a clerical character. That is why laymen must have a share of the responsibility at the highest administrative level."

[33] Cf. Jean de Bay, "L'Expansion Universitaire" in *La Revue Nouvelle*, XL (no. 12, December 15, 1964); Georges Van Riet, "Décléricaliser l'Université catholique" in *La Revue Nouvelle*, XLIII (no. 3, March 15, 1966).

[34] Jacques Drèze, "L'Université dans la société contemporaine et le devenir de Louvain" in *La Revue Nouvelle*, XLI (no. 6, June 15, 1965).

in Catholic institutions preparations for the most varied careers to as many students as possible. Is this preoccupation compatible with the maintenance of the unity of the French-speaking and Flemish sections which have already become quite autonomous? Does it not involve from the more or less long-term point of view the transfer of the French section away from Louvain? The majority of the French-speaking section oppose any idea of transfer; they fear the rupture of a tradition, the difficulties of moving since, for lack of sufficient resources, this could not be done quickly enough. They see in it the negation of the catholicity of the university since the harmonious meeting of the two close linguistic groups could not be assured. How, they say, can one assure a common thought and will, when each one is primarily preoccupied with saving its autonomy?

To this objection the partisans of transfer answer that collaboration would be much more fruitful when the causes of tension will have disappeared, and each section will have found the basis for its own flowering. The fact that this theme is developed every day by the professors of the university shows at least that the solemn declaration of the bishops has not succeeded in closing the debate definitively. There is nothing surprising in this since essentially the debate is linked to the ensemble of Belgian problems and these are not close to being settled.

RESEARCH AND CONFLICTS

Belgian Catholicism, as we have seen, presents the image of a strongly organized institutional system made somewhat political by the fact the Christian Social Party, although in principle free from all allegiance to the hierarchy, was the only party open to Catholics until the end of the School War (1958) and moreover the only one which still has direct and systematic, although informal, relations with Christian institutions.

The first to criticize this situation of the Church in Belgium—in the years around 1945—were small groups of priests and militant laymen of the industrial Walloon regions. They had become aware of the dechristianization of the working classes and wanted to undertake missionary action.

This questioning took on much greater scope at the time of the important National Congress for the Lay Apostolate organized in 1956 at Louvain. Its theme, "The Laymen in the Crisis of the Modern World," was a preparation for the Second World Congress that was to be held the following year at Rome.

One of the fundamental reports, that of André Molitor, made the notable point concerning institutions with confessional tendencies: "We should know that they have rendered and still render great service but they are imperfect, and their existence risks arousing in us a sense of power and of domination far from the message of the Beatitudes as they sometimes risk, by their appearance, separating men of good will from the Kingdom."[35] The Flemish section of the Congress came to similiar conclusions. This constituted a veritable revelation for the great movements of the apostolate in Flanders.

This Congress was the origin of a regrouping of Flemish intellectuals and militant laymen around a new monthly, De Maand (1958), whose general policy was similar to that which La Revue Nouvelle, also run by laymen, has tried to follow since its foundation in 1945: to deconfessionalize political life and to renew religious life by a return to biblical sources, by liturgical reform and opening up theology to present world problems, and by effective recognition of the place of the laity in the Church.

The Louvain Congress, although it had great repercussions and had notable effects in certain areas—better coordination between the various movements of the apostolate, enlarging the scope of the idea of the apostolate, liturgy, and catechetics—did not have all the fruits expected of it because it lacked an organ which could assure continuity.

The Council, however, reawakened interest in questions that had been raised at the Congress of 1956 and had not yet received an answer. Since 1965 discussions on "Christian Institutions"[36] have been part of the program but they remain theoretical. In practice, the desire to open and broaden these institutions conflicts, even apart from the instincts of those responsible for them, with the very extent of Christian temporal institutions: their importance in Belgian society means

---

[35] Les laics dans la crise du monde moderne (Brussels, 1957).

[36] The General Council of the Lay Apostolate thus created a commission to study Christian institutions. The report said in part: "One criterion that should permit Christian institutions to justify themselves is the effectiveness of their action in rebuilding the world either by the original contribution they make directly as institutions or by the spiritual and doctrinal help they bring to the Christians who collaborate in the work of all."

that their disappearance would seriously endanger the whole social order itself.

There are then hardly any very characteristic changes; at most a few nuances in the expression of principles which are at the basis of a given social or cultural institution. The argument most often used to defend Christian institutions is that the blocs on both sides should break up in a parallel progress: that Christians cannot open up their institutions unless the opposing institutions likewise evolve. One point at least has been won: the demand for the monopoly of Christian institutions for Catholics is made with less assurance. It is no longer a rigid obligation that Catholics join Christian institutions.[37] Another point which is settled is the need for dialogue: the word is very often used to hide the absence of it in practice, but it is impossible to turn back. The idea is making headway, especially among the younger generations who have grown increasingly allergic to any system of exclusionism and segregation.

It is symptomatic, to take an example, that Youth Homes which have been set up in different parts of the country, most often on the initiative of Catholics, have been established on the principle of internal pluralism. This is a change from the duplication of youth hostels which prevailed before the war: the neutral network and the Catholic network. Catholics used to maintain pluralism in the form of institutions with an ideological basis: today they rather visualize institutions which are themselves pluralist.

On the other hand, certain movements of the apostolate, especially in the Walloon areas, seek more openly to signalize their independence with respect to political and even social organizations. This is notably the case of the Popular Teams which, although linked to the Christian Worker Movement, did not hesitate in 1965 to protest against the fact that the presidents of Christian social organizations for workers, farmers, and business men, had on the eve of the elections published a manifesto in favor of the Christian Social Party. The intention of the Popular Teams was not to oppose the Christian Social Party in which incidentally some of its members were active, but rather to emphasize the freedom of Christians in their temporal commitments.

In short, the aspiration to real personal responsibility is making itself felt more and more strongly, even within big organizations. The aspira-

[37] Cf., for example, the report of the 1966 Congress of the National Alliance of Christian Mutuals, *Pour ou contre une mutalité chrétienne*; L. Lindemans, "Les organisations chrétiennes profanes" in *Les Dossiers* (no. 5, June-July, 1967).

tion was forcibly expressed in a report on pluralism recently issued by the committee on "Research and Common Objectives" which includes leaders of all French-speaking apostolic movements: "Christians must be permitted to discover more clearly what is essential to the faith: in this way they will be helped in distinguishing the essentials of faith from sociological structures established by the Christian community of a given period to serve its specific needs; and in this way they will be helped to act on the moral level as adults who dare assume their responsibilities according to their conscience and not according to sociological conformism and conditioning."

CONCLUSIONS

During the nineteenth century and until the Council, Belgian Catholicism played the role of avant-garde in the universal Church. It was preeminent in missionary ideas with men like Father Charles, the Jesuit founder of *Semaines de Missiologie*, and notably, Father Lebbe. In proportion to its population Belgium remains the first missionary country in the world and second in absolute figures: in 1960 it had 4,317 priests, 926 brothers, 4,611 sisters, and 216 laymen working in Asia, Africa and Latin America.[38] Under the leadership of men like Cardinal Mercier it gave the example in philosophical and theological studies of a "dynamic devotion to objective research," an ideal pursued by the University of Louvain of which a particularly enlightened Roman cardinal said: "It was one of the great avenues of Catholic science."[39]

After World War I, Cardinal Mercier also undertook an ecumenical action which was daring for its time; the Malines Conversations with Lord Halifax were discreetly interrupted by Rome after the death of the great Cardinal. His friend and counsellor, Dom Lambert Beauduin, founded at the same time the Benedictine monastery devoted to the union of Churches: the monastery of Amay, now at Chèvetogne. At the Council some of its monks, especially Dom Olivier Rousseau, played a role that gained considerable attention.

In the area of Catholic Action and the lay apostolate, Belgium also did pioneer work. Cardinal Cardijn played a dominant role in this sphere by founding the JOC. The latter, as Abbé Dhanis has stressed,

[38] *Bilan du monde: Encyclopédie du Monde Chrétien* (Tournai-Paris, 1964), II, 134.

[39] Msgr. Edouard Beauduin, *Le Cardinal Mercier* (Paris-Tournai, 1966).

had a decisive influence on the very vision of the Church. "Upon its breakthrough into history, the JOC set into question the separation of faith and secular life and so compelled the undertaking of a long study, still continuing, on the relations between the Church and the world, of which *Gaudium et Spes* is an essential step."[40]

In the area of the liturgy, too, Belgium has been at the head of the movement thanks to the influence of a man like Dom Lambert Beauduin,[41] and the monasteries of Mt. César at Louvain and of St. André at Bruges. The school of Msgr. Cerfaux has won for Louvain an important place in exegesis, while in the renewal of the Christian vision of the world, personalities like Msgr. Leclercq,[42] Msgr. Dondeyne, Msgr. Moeller and, more recently, Jean Ladrière, have been outstanding by reason of the boldness and the solidity of their works.

Belgian Catholicism lives on its thrust. There is not the effervescence which agitates Holland. By comparison it gives the impression of having some difficulty in making the transition, of having lost the creative *élan* that characterized it in the nineteenth century and during the period between the two World Wars. It seems to be somewhat the prisoner of the structures which until now have been its strength and which, in certain respects, no longer fully correspond to the ideal, outlined by the Council, of a Church at once a sign and instrument "of the unity" of all men in Christ.

The future depends on two things. The first—which goes beyond Catholic circles although they can play a decisive role because of their importance in the country—is the overcoming of the linguistic and regional conflicts which disturb social life. The second is the success or failure of the priests' councils and pastoral councils which are beginning to take shape and should in principle assure a dynamic integration of priests and laity in the Church. If these councils manage to awaken a large participation of all the People of God in the problems of the Church in Belgium, they will give impetus to the changes which are sensed to be necessary—although no one, even today, realizes their exact nature.

[40] T. Dahnis, "Cardijn, prophète" in *Les Dossiers* (no. 6, August-September, 1967).

[41] Louis Bouyer, *Dom Lambert Beauduin, un homme d'Église* (Paris-Tournai, 1964).

[42] Cf. the collaborative work, *Jacques Leclercq, l'homme, son oeuvre, ses amis* (Paris-Tournai, 1961).

10 : IRELAND

Desmond Fennell

In the Catholic regions of Continental Western Europe the modern history of the Church has been so characterized by common features as to be a common history, largely shared by all the peoples concerned. The general pattern of this history is widely familiar. What is more, the history of the Church from the French Revolution to the early twentieth century in Italy, France, Germany, Austria, and to some extent in Belgium and Spain, has been widely accepted not only as the history of the Church in Western Europe, but as the essential *history of the Church* during this period. Church historians writing in English have done little to revise this classic, monolithic story or to make the adjustments necessary in the overall account if the history of Catholicism in the British Isles and in the other English-speaking countries is to be seen not as notes in the margin, so to speak, but as a component, as an integrated part of the whole story.

Consequently, while an account of the contemporary Church in the Catholic regions of the Continent can assume a broad familiarity with the historical background on the part of the interested reader, this is not the case with an account of the Church in contemporary Ireland. Though it is fairly well known that the modern history of the Irish Church has differed substantially from that of the Church in other Catholic regions of Europe, the nature and the degree of this difference are not generally known.

An account of the Church in modern Ireland must describe a Church and a people whose modern history, present circumstances, and present consciousness differ in decisive ways from those of Catholics on the Continent. It seems advisable, therefore, to recapitulate those features

271

of the Irish Catholic past which made this history decisively different from the well-known Continental pattern. This will also indicate the extent to which certain features of American and Australian Catholic history, often held to be specific to the Church in those countries, originated or were paralleled in Europe.

Furthermore, since the sociological and other experience of the Church on the Continent continues to a large degree to be regarded as normative for the Church in Europe and even, in a thoughtless manner, for the Church as a whole, it will be useful to lay some stress on those sociological and other circumstances of the Church in Ireland today which contrast with Continental experience.

The Irish divergence from the West European norm had nothing to do with essential doctrine. Throughout its long history the Church in Ireland has been singularly free from doctrinal heresy; the documentary evidence bears witness to a continuously maintained orthodoxy. Only insofar as Roman teaching in the past century and a half has included evaluations of particular political forms or activities has the Church in Ireland deviated occasionally in conviction and practice. Likewise, in the spheres of devotional practice and of ecclesiastical administration and discipline, the Irish Church, at least since the nineteenth century, has been at one with Rome on the one hand, and with the Church in the larger urban centers of Western Europe on the other. The divergent development of the Church in Ireland arose out of the special political, social, and cultural history of the Irish people. In its decisive features this history had no counterpart in Western Europe.[1]

A truth which has often been ignored in the Church's view of itself in history is exemplified with unusual clarity in the history of the Catholic Church in Ireland: that the Church is by and large what its people are and what its people make it—through their clergy, together with them and in opposition to them—and that its people, in what they are and what they do, are conditioned by the general course of history as it affects them. Nowhere more clearly than in the case of Irish Catholic history is the equation of church history with the doings of clerics and with works of ecclesiastical piety seen to be a false equation, as historically unsound as it is theologically erroneous.

To a large extent, the history of the Irish people from the Reforma-

[1] The nearest comparison is afforded by the history of the Dutch Catholics, but even here the important differences are of an overriding nature.

tion to the nineteenth century was not chosen or willed by themselves. The scope of their self-determination was incomparably narrower than in the case of any other Catholic people in Europe during the same period. In many instances the divergence of their history from the European Catholic norm resulted from conditions and pressures that were imposed on them by a foreign people who had subjected them. Moreover, in the nineteenth century, when modern Irish Catholicism took shape, the Irish were culturally and politically integrated—albeit as a provincial, Catholic variant—into a British civilization which differed in many important respects from that of Continental Western Europe. But the fact that there is an Irish Catholic history to tell, and that it is the history not of a relic but of an entire, self-conscious people, points to the fact that their free determination of their history, while extremely narrow in scope, was intense and enduring in one vital respect—religion.

By the normal standards of post-Reformation European history, the Irish Catholic people should have ceased to exist, should have been absorbed, as citizens of Protestant religion, into the British realm. No people in modern times except the Jews have been so deeply penetrated by alien ways and language and yet maintained a sense of their separate identity and, even more, of their right to express that identity politically. But the will to political self-determination recurred and in the end became paramount because loyalty to the Catholic Church endured. This loyalty insured the continuance and development in extremely exceptional circumstances of a Catholic people and of a Church and retained within that Church conflicting political viewpoints and social forces which elsewhere, especially during the nineteenth century, resulted in large defections from Catholicism. The containment of these conflicts within the Irish Church contributed to its special development, while enriching its experience and keeping it in extremely close touch—often despite itself and unknown to itself —with contemporary history.

Alone among the old Catholic nations of Europe, the Irish, in modern times, suffered a radical break in cultural continuity. They changed their language, thereby losing the medium which embodied their historical memories, their indigenous view of life, their traditional prayers and devotions, their characteristic theology, and the lives of their saints. In the seventeenth century Irish was still the Church's chief vernacular; by the first half of the nineteenth century English was the language normally used by the clergy and most of the people. Irish Catholicism also lost its medieval church buildings and schools, its monasteries and abbeys, its hospitals and almshouses, its statues, paintings, and other sacred artifacts. The cathedrals and parish churches were taken over by the Reformers, the monastic buildings suppressed and, in many cases, destroyed. Until the last decades of the eighteenth century Catholics were prevented from constructing any substantial buildings for religious purposes and widespread building activity did not get under way until the 1830's. Cathilicism in Ireland (there were many Irish exiles on the Continent) did not participate in the Renaissance or Baroque periods of European culture. Neither did it join actively in the European Enlightenment, although many of the values of this movement were later to be accepted by Irish Catholics as their own.

Repeated military defeats in wars with the English had resulted, by the end of the seventeenth century, in the destruction of the native aristocracy and social system and in the suppression of Irish law. Catholics were outlawed; a century later only about 8 per cent of land remained in Catholic hands. As material and cultural proletarianization proceeded, Irish society fell into *anomie*, a state of radical social disintegration and cultural disruption. This development was dramatically quickened by the Great Famine of 1846-47. When Catholics regained their full civil rights in 1829, and the rebuilding of their Church —the building of *modern* Irish Catholicism—got under way, the Irish were the only Catholic nation in Europe without an inherited culture of aristocracy and burghers, of town and castle, farms and schools. This lack of a palpably surviving past, intensified by the loss of the Irish language-culture and the neglect of Irish history, made them about as rootless as a people can be in its ancestral land. Their urban middle class, relatively small in numbers, lived as second-class citizens in towns and cities whose traditions were hostile to their own.

By and large, then, modern Irish Catholicism, developed in conditions which were culturally and socially "American" or "Australian," all the more so in view of the fact that it was in the nineteenth century that Catholic Ireland became predominantly English-speaking and was culturally assimilated into the Anglo-Saxon sphere. Psychological and material conditions very similar to those which immigrant Catholics experienced in the American cities existed throughout Ireland, either earlier or simultaneously. Even language change, with all that it entails, was part of the experience common to the majority of Irish Catholics and to American immigrant Catholics—insofar as the latter were not themselves English-speaking Irish.

The new Irish Catholicism which developed in the nineteenth century was trained in liberal democratic politics by Daniel O'Connell and the parish clergy. The Irish Catholic members in the British House of Commons were frequently allied with the British Liberals and before its demise in 1918 their Home Rule party evolved into a liberal party pursuing Irish interests within the framework of the United Kingdom. The clergy were not paid by the State and the Church had no corporate existence at law.[2]

The ecclesiastical and cultural leaders of the resurgent Irish Church turned their backs on the Gaelic Catholic tradition as it had endured into the seventeenth century and, in a broken manner in rural areas, even into the nineteenth, and built instead on the new English-speaking Catholicism which had developed during the eighteenth century in Dublin and in other cities and towns. Due to the abandonment and decay of the old religious and rural cultures, there was little in Catholic Ireland to compete with or to modify the ultramontane, romanizing religion of Pius IX and the utilitarian, Nonconformist-style culture of Victorian Britain. Both were embraced eagerly by the leaders of the people and gradually penetrated the remotest countrysides.

There was little attempt to rebuild even those ruined abbeys and churches to which the established Church of Ireland did not lay claim. The traditional peasant Catholicism, with its native piety and devotions, its old customs and saints' festivals, wilted or else succumbed to active discouragement. The new forms of religion, including a new spirituality, spread out from the cities and towns and from newly-founded seminaries and convents. Urban and contemporary in origin and outlook, these new ways of being Catholic and viewing life were derived from the writings of the English Douai school and from the religious temperament of the Italian and French bourgeoisie. The saints whose imported statues filled the new churches, and to whom

---

[2] No change has been made in these arrangements since the establishment of an independent Irish State, so that the formal and financial relationships between Church and State such as exist in most European countries, including several East European Communist states, have no counterpart in Ireland.

the Irish learned to pray, were those of the contemporary Church in the Latin countries. Devotion to the native saints decayed. Similarly, in the sphere of general values and attitudes: because of the lack of a coherent or satisfying rural culture, the moral and other valuations of the urban middle class were accepted by the countryside to a degree unparalleled in any other Catholic region of Europe. These are among the chief reasons why rural immigrants from Ireland, in contrast to those from Continental Europe, adapted readily to the conditions of urban Catholicism in the United States: their Catholicism was not a traditional "peasant religion" and their aspirations were urban and lower middle class.

Many historical factors which loom large in the consciousness and writings of Continental European Catholics are absent from the historical consciousness of Irish Catholics, insofar as this relates to their own local Church. The Irish Church, looking back into its history, does not find that it was ever a persecuting Church. Even during those short periods in the sixteenth and seventeenth centuries when, due to the vicissitudes of English politics, the Catholics in Ireland found themselves substantially in control of the country, the imprisonment or execution of heretics was not part of their program or practice. The Irish Catholic past throws up no "union of throne and altar" or *ancien regime* to hark back to or to deplore, no execrable "bourgeois morality" juxtaposed to a "working-class" or *Jugendbewegung* morality, no socially entrenched, politically conservative "Catholicism of the Right," no "dechristianization" (in the accepted sense) or "lost working class."

Except for specialists, "modernism" and "integralism" are merely strange words found in books. Talk of the "Constantinian era" as a phase of Church history which must now at last be finally overcome sounds very much like twaddle in Ireland. No event or period in Irish Church history bears the tag "secularization." Secularization did occur, especially of work and recreation and of the countryside (the "Protestant" cities always seemed "secular"), and the dichotomy of the sacred and the secular was obtruded into Catholic consciousness. But the Irish Church itself led the way in these developments—it did not yield to something forced upon it and it did not call its desacralizing process "secularization." As for political parties or trade unions calling themselves "Catholic" or "Christian," or priests sitting as members of Parliament or personally leading political parties, these are not things which Irish Catholics think about or recall for the good reason that they have not occurred in their history.[3]

"Revolution" is a special case. This has a place in the consciousness of Irish Catholics, but their relation to it is different from that of Continental Catholics. For the Irish, "revolution" is first and foremost the Irish revolution, something which Catholics, their own kith and kin, carried out half a century ago for a purpose they approve—an event and a legacy whose willing heirs they are.

Again, the Church in Ireland has not been involved on its home ground in those epic struggles against liberalism, syndicalism, socialism, and anticlericalism which played such large roles in the modern history of the Church on the Continent. The degree to which Irish Catholics in the nineteenth century made the methods of political liberalism their own caused recurrent disquiet in Rome. Anticlericalism has never assumed a systematic political form; it has occurred either as resentment over clerical opposition to specific political policies or as a literary mode. Socialism, under that name at least, has never presented itself as an important ideological force. What was considered socialism elsewhere was often absorbed into the nationalist cause (specifically, into land-reform and republican nationalism) or else, after 1922, selectively implemented, without the name, by successive governments. Besides, such socialism as has been propounded in Ireland has hardly ever borne antireligious overtones. James Connolly, the most famous Irish socialist, and one of the few in Ireland who ever really deserved the name, is a national hero. Executed as leader of the Easter Rising of 1916, he professed himself a Catholic all his life and had come to share the view of Pearse and several others of the 1916 leaders that the rising they were planning should be a blood sacrifice, in the image of Calvary, for the redemption of the Irish people.

As with historical consciousness, so too with sociological circumstances. The most remarkable sociological feature of the Church in Ireland today is that it is virtually coextensive with a historic people and its contemporary society. The term "ghetto," indicating a situation which the Church must break out of, does not occur in public discussions of Church affairs in Ireland. The Irish Church comprises all the

[3] In the century previous to World War I, priests often played a very active part in politics, but, in contrast to practice on the Continent, in neither of the capacities mentioned.

typical social groups of a modern Western-style democracy. Urbanization and industrialization have not been accompanied by any substantial falling away and are not obviously related to such loss of faith as does occur. Low-brow egalitarianism, along with the almost complete disintegration of the old rural culture and the relatively open and classless nature of Catholic society, has produced a Church whose social composition is remarkably homogeneous, its religious forms and pastoral methods excessively so. The strength of this homogeneity on the ideological plane was evident during and after the Second Vatican Council: the Church in Ireland, though it engaged in vigorous public debate, did not throw up opposing camps of die-hard conservatives and runaway progressives. One of the causes of this homogeneity—the cultural and, to a large extent, institutional break with the past which occurred in the eighteenth century—has given a uniformly "modern," unhistorical tone to the contemporary Irish Church: Irish Catholics do not worship in medieval or baroque churches or pray before old statues or carved altarpieces; none of their cathedral chapters has existed continuously since medieval times.

The supply of clergy in the middle decades of the present century far exceeded home requirements; more than 50 per cent of the priests ordained each year left for service in Britain or overseas. In a word, the sociological circumstances of the Church in Ireland do not present many of the standard "problems" of the Church in Continental Western Europe.

Catholic Ireland has 26 dioceses grouped into four ecclesiastical provinces: Armagh, Dublin, Cashel, and Tuam. Each province is headed by an archbishop. The title of Primate of All Ireland is borne by the Archbishop of Armagh, that of Primate of Ireland by the Archbishop of Dublin. Both titles date from the Middle Ages and are purely honorary. In the present century the Archbishop of Armagh has always been a cardinal, the present incumbent being Cardinal William Conway.

Armagh, traditionally the see of St. Patrick, is in Northern Ireland. Since 1920 a state boundary has divided Northern Ireland (a part of the United Kingdom) from the rest of the country. Of the estimated 3,240,000 Catholics in Ireland in 1965, 2,730,000 live in the Irish Republic, 510,000 in Northern Ireland. With nearly 4,000 diocesan priests, Ireland has one priest for about 820 faithful. If the 2,000 regular clergy are included, the ratio is 1:540. The number of priests working abroad is the same as the number at home, nearly 6,000. There are about 3,600 religious brothers and about 18,000 sisters, of whom several thousand are serving abroad.

The Church has no corporate status in civil law, but it is publicly recognized in the Republic of Ireland by the Constitution of 1937. In the matters of religious freedom and relations between Church and State in a predominantly Catholic state, this Constitution anticipated the Second Vatican Council by a quarter of a century.

The preamble begins: "In the name of the Most Holy Trinity, from Whom is all authority and to Whom, as our final end, all actions both of men and States must be referred, we, the people of Eire, humbly acknowledging all our obligations to our Divine Lord, Jesus Christ, Who sustained our fathers through centuries of trial. . . ." In Article 44 the State "acknowledges that the homage of public worship is due to Almighty God" and undertakes to "respect and honour religion." It goes on to declare:

> The State recognizes the special position of the Holy Catholic and Apostolic and Roman Church as the guardian of the faith professed by the great majority of the citizens.
> The State also recognizes the Church of Ireland, the Presbyterian Church in Ireland, the Methodist Church in Ireland, the Religious Society of Friends in Ireland, as well as the Jewish Congregations and the other denominations existing in Ireland at the date of the coming into operation of this Constitution.

Freedom of conscience and the right to practice religion are guaranteed, subject to public order and morality, to every citizen. No religion is to be endowed, no disabilities imposed, and no discrimination made on the grounds of religion. Every religious denomination shall have the right to manage its own affairs, acquire, and administer property.

Catholics constitute 95 per cent of the population of the Republic. The "special position" of the Catholic Church, which the State recognizes on the purely pragmatic grounds of its being the majority religion, has never been defined in law. Essentially this recognition expresses the state of affairs which in fact results when the majority of the people and almost all members of parliament and of the government are practicing Catholics.

Divorce is prohibited by the Constitution. The sale of contraceptives, as well as writings advocating artificial contraception or abortion, is forbidden by law.

The provisions of the Constitution relating to religious liberty and to discrimination on religious grounds have been scrupulously adhered to in practice. Protestant and Jewish spokesmen have frequently borne witness to this fact in public statements. Practice has in fact been more generous than the constitutional obligation would require. The first President of the Republic, Douglas Hyde, was a Protestant. The Protestant share of the time allotted to religious programs on the national television network is much greater than 5 per cent.

In December, 1967, an informal inter-party committee on constitutional reform presented an interim report. It recommended, among other things, that the clauses recognizing the "special position" of the Catholic Church and giving express recognition to other religious bodies be removed from the Constitution; further, that the clause prohibiting legislation for divorce be removed and another clause substituted allowing for divorce legislation to cover cases where divorce was not contrary to the religious tenets of the persons concerned. A referendum would, of course, be needed to give these recommendations effect and it seemed unlikely that this would take place in the near future. Cardinal Conway and both archbishops of the Church of Ireland made statements rejecting divorce on behalf of their churches. Leaders of other Protestant denominations seemed to welcome the committee's recommendation on the subject.

In Northern Ireland, in contrast to England and Scotland, there is no State church. However, the fact that the subordinate government in Belfast has always been in the hands of the Unionist Party has resulted in a generally disadvantageous situation for Catholics. The Unionist Party, an exclusively Protestant body, is controlled by the militantly Protestant Orange Order. All leading Unionists belong to the Order, which is in fact the decisive ideological and political power. On the other hand, the spokesmen of the Catholic minority have always denied the legitimacy of the Belfast regime and advocated a united Ireland, an idea which is abhorrent to the Orange establishment. Systematic discrimination against Catholics in local government bodies, in the higher public appointments, in housing and employment, has occasionally been justified by Protestant spokesmen on the grounds of the political disaffection of the Catholics.

In recent years a more conciliatory policy toward Catholics has been attempted by the more liberal wing of the Unionist Party under the Premier, Captain Terence O'Neill, and Catholics have shown a greater degree of political cooperativeness. But these efforts are being thwarted by the extremist Protestant element, whose principal spokesman is the Reverend Ian Paisley. Through their influences within the Orange Order and the electorate these diehards hold the Unionist government in check.

A conjunction of historical and cultural factors has made Catholicism in Northern Ireland a sort of "depressed area" within the Irish Church as a whole. In this respect there is a certain parallel with the condition of Catholicism in Scotland in the context of British Catholicism. In both Scotland and Northern Ireland, Catholics are a minority in an area where Presbyterianism has been the dominant cultural and religious force for centuries. Northern Ireland has no diocesan major seminary, the intellectually eminent religious orders have no establishments there, and not a single Catholic journal of note is published. (Northern intellectual life is barren anyhow; there are *no* periodicals of any importance.) Although the missionary movement has played a predominant role in Irish Catholic activity in recent decades, there is only one major missionary center in Northern Ireland. Only in the field of catechetics, in recent years, have valuable impulses came from the North to the Irish Church as a whole. The literary renaissance and the revolutionary movement, which stimulated creativity in most parts of the country in the first decades of this century, left the Catholics in Northern Ireland relatively unaffected. Their political dilemma since Partition, and their ineffectual obsession with it, have blocked important development in any direction, leaving lowbrow parochialism virtually unchallenged.

For several decades after Partition the Catholics of Northern Ireland allowed this issue to dominate their politics and thus to a great extent their lives outside the private sphere. An end to Partition was seen vaguely as an escape from discrimination. In fact, however, as the course of events has shown, the Northern Catholics never regarded union with the Republic as vitally important. Their calls for an ending of Partition and their complaints about discrimination were not accompanied by any imaginative policy or any decisive action. Even in the areas contiguous to the Republic, where Catholics are in the majority, there has never been any attempt at secession or civil disobedience. Meanwhile, local "Ulster" patriotism was allowed to become a Protestant monopoly. In effect, the Northern Catholics were unconsciously using the political situation to justify feelings of frustration and resentment which went deeper than politics. By admitting to themselves, as they are now beginning to do, that they accept Partition for the present and wish to improve their status within Northern Ireland, they are dispelling an illusion which has prevented them from facing up to their cultural negativism and to the challenges and possibilities of their actual situation.

In *The Church in Contemporary Ireland* (Dublin, 1963), the French jurist Jean Blanchard, after remarking that there are "no official legal relations between Church and State" in the Republic of Ireland, goes on to say: "An examination of the general *practice* will reveal that, although the two powers are separated, there is in fact interpenetration of the two systems, civil and religious; and the two powers enjoy a fruitful cooperation." Separation but cooperation of the powers with *formal* interpenetration of the two systems is a fair description of the practical relationship of Church and State in the Republic. It is the kind of relationship which might be expected in a state where almost all the citizens are practicing Catholics whose political ideology is *étatiste* liberalism, in a republican context, with strong secularist undertones.

The Church cannot possess property directly or take legal proceedings; it must use the trustee system. The civil and religious calendars do not coincide, so that certain major Church feasts which are public holidays in some Continental countries, even in Western Germany, are not observed as such in Irish cities and towns. The State has no legal rights in the appointment of bishops. On the other hand, solemn religious services on St. Patrick's Day, at Christmas and Easter, are attended by the high civil dignitaries in their public capacity. Important public events, such as the installation of a new government or the opening of a new Parliament, are marked by religious ceremonies of all the leading denominations. There is no Concordat with the Vatican, but the papal nuncio is *ex officio* dean of the diplomatic corps. Civil and religious marriages are both recognized at law; a double ceremony is not required. (As a matter of fact, Catholics hardly ever have recourse to civil marriage.)

The clergy take a less active part in politics than they did before independence. It was not unusual then for a parish priest to preside at a political meeting; this does not occur today, and the clergy remain

aloof from party politics. There are no permanent areas of direct conflict between Church and State; relations are normally harmonious.
Occasionally, however, individual bishops and priests make public
criticisms of government policy, and direct clashes between government ministers and clerics occur from time to time. Since independence, the bishops as a body have intervened very rarely in political
affairs. In 1951, when a measure providing for a limited degree of state
medicine was due to be implemented, the bishops privately conveyed
to the government their disapproval on moral grounds of certain provisions of the measure. In face of this, and of strong opposition from
the medical profession, the measure was withdrawn. But the next
government introduced a modified version of the measure, and subsequent social welfare measures have met with no opposition from the
bishops. In 1956, following a militant campaign by the illegal Irish Republican Army across the border into Northern Ireland, the bishops
supported government policy by publicly condemning the use of violence as a means of national policy and reiterating their interdict on
membership of secret societies acting in defiance of the lawful civil
authority.

The Church in Ireland possesses no official or semiofficial organ issuing moral evaluations of books, films, or theatre, and the bishops do
not normally make pronouncements on these subjects except in general
terms. But a state censorship of books, which was established in 1929,
made itself notorious for its frenzied bannings of contemporary fiction,
Irish and foreign, during the 1930's and 1940's. These bannings were
undone by a law of July, 1967, which freed all books, except those advocating artificial contraception, banned before July, 1955, and set a
twelve-year limit, with the possibility of renewal on all future bans.

Contrary to what has often been assumed abroad, there has been
nothing specifically Catholic or even religious about this book censorship, except insofar as its ban on writings advocating artificial contraception might be regarded as reflecting Catholic teaching rather than
state policy. Neither was it ever as comprehensive as has often been
suggested. Works included on the Roman Index continued to be freely
available in bookshops and libraries. In contrast to the Australian book
censorship and the British theatre censorship—to take two other examples of state literary censorship from English-speaking countries—
blasphemy is not included in the terms of reference of the Irish censorship. Apart from writings advocating the "unnatural prevention of

conception" or abortion, its scope extended only to obscenity and indecency and, in the case of magazines, to an excessive emphasis on crime. Unlike most twentieth-century censorships, especially in revolutionary regimes, it has not affected philosophical, historical, or political writings. When priests and Catholic lay people agreed with its heavy bannings of literary works—and some priests came to be among its critics—they were subscribing to a view of life and literature which was as much at home in the North of England, New South Wales, or New England as it was in Irish Catholicism or Irish Protestantism.[4]

The rigors of the book censorship relented in the 1950's and its function today is largely the exclusion of pornography or near pornography. Its bannings are few and they are poorly enforced. The censorship board can act only when books are submitted to it. There are no common-law prosecutions of booksellers, as in Britain or America.

There is also a state film censorship of similarly restricted scope, which likewise went through a period of extreme severity. In recent years it has established a grading system and bans outright only extremely indecent or pornographic films. There is no censorship of the press or of the theatre.

Primary education is officially nondenominational. Religious instruction is permitted in schools outside the state-regulated hours, but no pupil is obliged by law to attend. In practice, however, primary education is *denominationally organized*. Under an arrangement which dates from the British regime, the primary schools (called National Schools) are managed by Catholic parish priests, Protestant ministers, or in one case, a Jewish rabbi, while the State assists financially. The parish priest appoints the teachers in his school and is responsible for maintenance. He manages the school according to the State's regulations and the national teaching program. Most primary schools are staffed by lay people, but some are conducted by sisters or by male religious.

Tuition in National Schools was always free. Since 1967, postprimary schooling is also provided at public expense; for Catholics this is given mostly in state-assisted secondary schools run by religious or by diocesan priests. Some Catholic secondary schools are run by lay people. There are also state-run vocational schools, with shorter courses, which spe-

---

[4] It was simply the "normal" view in English-speaking countries until James Joyce and the new literary establishments of New York and London from the 1920's onward challenged it.

cialize in technical and commercial subjects. In recent years the State has also opened a few "comprehensive" schools in districts where post-primary educational facilities were inadequate. This new kind of school combines features of the traditional secondary school with features of the vocational school.

In Northern Ireland the arrangements for primary education are the same as in the Republic. Catholics have their own state-assisted post-primary schools called grammar schools.

Ireland has no Catholic university and no State university. The structure of university education in the Republic is at present being re-organized. Hitherto the National University of Ireland, established in 1908, had constituent colleges in Dublin, Cork, and Galway. Its charter, granted by the British government, made it undenominational and forbade the establishment of a theological faculty. The great majority of staff and students were, of course, Catholic, and Catholic chaplains were attached to each of the colleges. There was also Trinity College, Dublin, the oldest university institution in the country. Founded in the sixteenth century by Queen Elizabeth I, its history was closely con-nected with that of the Protestant Ascendancy; it has a Protestant chapel and a faculty of Anglican theology. Even after the establish-ment of the new State, its links with Britain continued to be very close. Less than 30 per cent of the academic staff were Catholics in 1967. Catholics were forbidden by their bishops to attend Trinity College, but permission was in fact granted quite frequently if sufficient grounds were given. Both National University and Trinity College receive sub-stantial financial assistance from the State. Queen's University in Bel-fast, a secular foundation, is attended by students of all denominations.

In April, 1967, the Minister of Education of the Republic, Donogh O'Malley, announced that the government intended to establish a "multidenominational" University of Dublin with University College, Dublin, and Trinity College as constituent colleges. The National Uni-versity of Ireland would be dissolved, with the colleges in Cork and Galway becoming autonomous. Two months later, the Catholic bishops, in a public statement, wished the new venture well. Negoti-ations are proceeding with a view to finding a formula of unification for the two Dublin colleges which will be acceptable both to the gov-ernment and to the colleges concerned.

All the larger religious orders and congregations have their own semi-naries or houses of study. St. Patrick's College, Maynooth, is both the national seminary and a recognized, degree-conferring college of the National University. With few exceptions diocesan priests intended for work in Ireland study either at Maynooth or at Clonliffe College, Dublin, the seminary of the Dublin Archdiocese. Maynooth has recently embarked on a policy of admitting students from religious orders and congregations and even lay students. Previously there had been no opportunity for lay Catholics to take a full university-level course in theology. However, it is not yet clear how this development at Maynooth will be related to, or affected by, the reorganization of university education in Dublin, which is only a few miles away. Besides Maynooth and Clonliffe, six other seminaries for diocesan priests are engaged almost exclusively in supplying the needs of the other English-speaking countries.

The formal interpenetration of the Church and State systems in Ireland is not accompanied by an integrated unitary view of all spheres of public and social life. An outsider can easily fail to notice this if he goes by the formal evidence alone. The dichotomy of the religious and the secular has long been sensed as a reality, and acted out in practice, in Ireland as elsewhere. There have been several notable instances during the last century or so of churchgoing Catholics, and even numbers of priests, rejecting the validity, or at least the literal force, of episcopal pronouncements when these were held to have gone beyond the bounds of ecclesiastical competence. The tangible influence of Catholic principles on the policies of Catholic politicians and on government has by and large been negative only; in the sense that the principles in question were at most allowed to designate things, such as divorce and contraception, which were not permissible. References to religion are rare in the national parliament and are regarded by the deputies as "bad form." Irish premiers and cabinet ministers, unlike Nikita Khrushchev, are slow to mention God or Jesus Christ in their speeches and ill at ease when they do so. Nowhere is this secular-religious dichotomy so obvious, despite the formal interpenetration of the two spheres, as in the field of social policy and doctrine.

Even before Pope John brought papal social teaching up to date, the earlier papal social encyclicals had been held in high regard. Since *Mater et Magistra*, government ministers and trade union leaders have frequently called Pope John to witness in support of a policy or a claim. Nevertheless, it cannot be said that "Catholic social teaching" has been consciously or consistently applied to the shaping of social and economic life in the Republic. It is not that the principles of social and economic relations set out in the papal teachings have not been operative in Irish life: there has been a great deal of effective concern for the common socioeconomic good, a widespread willingness to ensure a just distribution of wealth and a decent standard of living for all. But the motivation of social reform and shared economic betterment has seldom been consciously related to religious principles.

The reason for this is the deep underlying conviction that the world of work, business, and state action is "secular" and subject therefore to "secular" norms. For Catholic social principles to become directly applicable to this sphere, theology and the day-to-day teaching of the Church would need to have related it effectively, and as a whole, to "religion"; this was not done. In effect, then, there has been next to no radical examination in the light of Catholic social doctrine of the *de facto* socioeconomic order. This basically capitalist, market-economy *status quo*, along with the social relations and norms of action arising out of it, has been taken as the given framework within which socioeconomic reform and amelioration shall take place. To the extent that reforming and ameliorative measures seem to coincide with Catholic principles, this is regarded as a good thing. But where Catholic social teaching seems to run counter to the divine right of established system and practice, it is dismissed as unrealistic and Utopian.

Although socialism has never been an issue in Irish politics, the economy is in fact more socialized than that of Sweden or of several other countries where there are so-called "socialist" regimes. One result of the piecemeal, pragmatic implementation of quasi-socialist policies in the Republic was that when Pope John in *Mater et Magistra* approved and advocated "socialization," he caused no flurry in Ireland. The social-economic structure of the Irish Republic is the product of state action of several different kinds applied to an economically underdeveloped society in which capitalist enterprise and the market economy were regarded as given factors. Numerous publicly owned commercial enterprises and agencies—semistate bodies, as they are called—have been established in fields where private capital was inadequate or centralized action in the national interest seemed desirable. Equalization of opportunity and diminishment of hardship through redistribution of wealth are accepted public policies. In recent years the State has encouraged the establishment of industry by foreigners through tax concessions and grants-in-aid.

The secular-religious dichotomy is again reflected in intellectual life. The exclusion of theology and religious studies generally from the colleges of the National University is a palpable example. But the schizophrenic effects of the secular-religious dichotomy are reinforced by the unchallenged dominance in intellectual life of the positivistic breed of academic specialization. Church history and secular history—the latter is usually called "history" *tout court*—go their separate ways, as if it were not the same people who were involved in both cases. As a result, although there is a flourishing school of university historians, the history of the Church in Ireland is extremely neglected and there is hardly a book available on the overall history of the Irish Catholic people. Neither on the philosophical-theological nor on the literary-poetic level has Ireland produced any original Christian analysis, vision, or interpretation either of contemporary Irish life or of the contemporary European experience as a whole.

Not surprisingly, then, "the press" is regarded as synonymous with the "secular press," the "religious press" being a special, marginal category that includes a wide spectrum of weekly, monthly, and quarterly journals ranging from the century-old *Irish Ecclesiastical Record* and *The Irish Theological Quarterly* (founded in 1906) through dozens of missionary journals and special cult magazines to the weekly newspapers, *The Irish Catholic* and *The Catholic Standard*. Some of these magazines, such as *The Word*, a well-made pictorial monthly published by the Society of the Divine Word, and *Reality*, a popular monthly review of Christian life and comment, have large international circulations, something which cannot be said of any Irish "secular" journal. Besides *The Irish Ecclesiastical Record* and *The Irish Theological Quarterly*, several other quality journals emanate from Maynooth: *Philosophical Studies*, an annual publication; *The Furrow*, a pastoral monthly for priests; *Christus Rex*, a journal of sociology; *An Sagart* (The Priest); and *Irisleabhar Mhá Nuat* (Maynooth Annual).

In general, the appellation "religious" tends to be given to journals which deal mainly with religious or theological topics or to journals which give prominence to an expressly Christian view of life. Most of the periodical press, apart from specialist and trade journals, belong to one or other of these categories. There are very few diocesan newspapers. The two weekly newspapers already mentioned are owned and edited by laymen and cater to a mass readership. The scope for

"Catholic newspapers" is very limited because the ordinary daily press, which is almost entirely in Catholic hands, gives good coverage to news which would rank as specifically "Catholic" in Britain or America. Since the Second Vatican Council this coverage has been expanded to include, for example summaries of new documents on the liturgy or lectures by prominent theologians.

"Lay Catholic comment" is not institutionalized in certain journals, but is integrated into both the "secular" and "religious" press—and is frequently heard on television. Literary journals are a *genre* of their own, none of them falling into the "religious" category. The Jesuit quarterly *Studies* ranges over the entire cultural and intellectual field, including theology.

Since the 1920's, when the majority of Irish Catholics achieved political independence, their collective energies have been expanded principally in two directions, one internal, the other external: they have been engaged in state building at home and in the Christian apostolate overseas. Their most creative single achievement in the internal sphere was the Constitution of 1937; in the external sphere the Legion of Mary. The Legion, which a small group of lay people founded in Dublin in 1921, was not intended expressly as a missionary venture overseas. It simply grew—and became the largest organization of the lay apostolate in the world and an auxiliary to missionary endeavor in all the principal mission territories. It provided the backbone of Catholic resistance in China after the Communist take-over. In 1966 the Legion was active in 1,500 dioceses. Its *Handbook*, a manual of the Legion apostolate written by Frank Duff, the Dublin civil servant who founded the Legion, has been translated into 31 languages. *Maria Legionis*, the Legion journal, is edited from Dublin and has a North American edition and a Spanish-language edition, printed in Quito. The Dublin edition runs to 100,000 copies. More than 70 Legion envoys have spent periods overseas organizing the Legion. One of them, the heroic Edel Quinn, who died in Africa, is a candidate for beatification.

Though the declared aim of the Legion is to penetrate all sectors of society, its failure to make much headway in Irish universities has restricted its apostolate in the home country. Apart from some progress made in recent years by *Opus Dei*, the organized lay apostolate in Ireland is practically identical with the Legion and the Society of St. Vincent de Paul.

The modern missionary movement proper got under way in 1916 with the foundation of the Maynooth Mission to China, later called the Society of St. Columban. In 1922 Father John Blowick, co-founder of these "Columban Fathers," founded the Missionary Sisters of St. Columban. Between that year and 1952 there were four more Irish missionary foundations: The Holy Rosary Sisters of Killeshandra, founded in 1924 by Bishop Joseph Shanahan, a Holy Ghost Father and the great missionary pioneer of Nigeria; St. Patrick's Foreign Mission Society (1932), better known as the Kiltegan Fathers, which was a response to Bishop Shanahan's appeals to the Irish bishops for priests; the Medical Missionaries of Mary, founded by Marie Martin in 1937; the Franciscan Missionary Sisters for Africa, founded by Mother Kevin of the Franciscan Sisters of the Five Wounds, the beloved "Mama Kevina" of Uganda (she was born Teresa Kearney).

During the same decades the Holy Ghost Fathers and the Society of African Missions, which had established themselves in Ireland in the nineteenth century, increased their membership dramatically, sending hundreds of priests to Africa. Some Irish teaching congregations had old-established foundations in Africa and Asia: the Loreto and Presentation Sisters, the Irish Christian Brothers, and De La Salle Brothers. These too were able to extend their activities, and many other religious congregations of men and women, infected by the general missionary enthusiasm, established missions abroad. Finally, lay people joined the movement in substantial numbers, both as auxiliaries to already existing missionary societies or in societies of their own, such as the *Viatores Christi*, a Legion of Mary offshoot. In May, 1965, the Missionary Service Center in Dublin published the first full statistical report on the modern Irish missionary movement. These statistics, based on figures supplied by 92 mission-sending bodies in Ireland, gave the following overall picture:

I. Continent	Priests	Brothers	Sisters	Laity	Totals
Africa	1,443	230	2,004	445	4,122
Asia and Oceania	651	257	1,047	7	1,962
Latin America	210	54	139	30	433
Totals	2,304	541	3,190	482	6,517

Priests Ordained for Service in English-Speaking Lands

II. College	Great Britain	Australia and New Zealand	North America	South Africa
All Hallows, Dublin	380	360	436	45
Irish College, Rome	17	24	21	5
St. Kieran's, Kilkenny	314	107	189	4
St. Patrick's, Thurles	· 142	100	246	33
St. Patrick's, Carlow	269	131	533	10
St. Peter's, Wexford	139	42	112	
Totals[5]	1,261	764	1,537	97

Taken together, these two sets of figures amount to more than 10,000 and represent the largest missionary effort abroad of any Catholic people at the present time. Insofar as they concern Africa, Asia, and Latin America, they also represent one of the largest contributions now being made to the development of underdeveloped countries.

The impact of this missionary movement on Irish life has been much less than might reasonably have been expected. The missionaries have produced no literature worth mentioning. There is no chair of comparative religion; no school of ethnology in any Irish university; no institute of African or Asian studies has been established.

The second half of the nineteenth century in Ireland had been marked by a decline in the crude rate of natural increase and by a very low marriage rate. Between the decade 1910–1920 and the 1950's the rate of natural increase rose from its nadir of 4.0 (per 1,000 of population annually) to 9.0. In the late 1940's this rising curve of vitality began to affect marriage habits. In 1945–1946 the marriage rate per 1,000 single or widowed males aged 20 to 24 was 18.2; by 1964 it had risen to 48.5. At the same period the corresponding rates for women were 45.1 and 96.8 respectively.

[5] Sum total 3,659, but the real total is larger since figures from St. John's College, Waterford, are not included.

The latter part of the 1950's witnessed a surge of economic, largely industrial, growth within the framework of the First Economic Program: annual growth rates of 3 to 4 per cent were recorded. This economic development has continued into the 1960's and has transformed material living standards and the horizons of businessmen. The annual rate of emigration, very high in the early 1950's, had been more than halved as the sixties began. Since the late forties a groping movement of creative initiatives and new expectations had become perceptible in the Irish Church at home. Television was introduced in 1961. Pope John was issuing his great encyclicals. For the first time an Irish-American Catholic, John F. Kennedy, became President of the United States and visited Ireland, where he addressed the assembled houses of the Oireachtas (Dáil and Senate) and drank tea in the cottage of his ancestors.

It was against the background of these events and developments that the Irish bishops attended the Second Vatican Council. Like the vast majority of Irish Catholics, they were not aware of any urgent need for an *aggiornamento* of such scope and magnitude as was envisaged by the driving forces behind the Council, mostly theologians and bishops from France, Belgium, and Central Europe. But certain stirrings in the Irish Church in the fifteen years before the Council now assumed, retrospectively, the role of an anticipatory movement.

During those years two journals had been founded which gradually served as focal points for the new currents: *The Furrow*, edited from Maynooth by Dr. J. G. McGarry, and *Doctrine and Life*, edited by Austin Flannery, O.P., in Dublin. New institutes and congresses were founded: an annual Irish Liturgical Congress in the Benedictine Abbey of Glenstal; the Dublin Institute of Catholic Sociology (now the Institute of Adult Education), sponsored by the Archbishop of Dublin, Dr. John Charles McQuaid; the *Christus Rex* movement of priest-sociologists (with its journal of the same name edited by Dr. Jeremiah Newman of Maynooth); the Social Study Congress in Dublin. The Jesuits opened a college for trade unionists which has since become the College of Industrial Relations. Publishers, with the Mercier Press of Cork in the lead, translated many German and French theological works. Old-established Catholic journals passed into the hands of new editors and showed marked improvement. Biblical studies made some progress. Premarital courses for engaged couples were established at several centers. *Doctrine and Life* began the publication of a special journal for religious sisters. Summer courses and study meetings of all kinds multiplied. An excellent vernacular ritual in Irish and English was adopted. Some architects, priests, sculptors, and painters began to collaborate fruitfully for the renewal of church architecture and sacred art. In short, when the Conciliar movement affected Ireland, it encountered some receptive groups who were not entirely unprepared.

Since the ending of the Council, the excited public debate which it occasioned has gradually died down. The liturgical reforms, introduced in varying degrees from diocese to diocese, have occasioned neither fuss nor yet a truly transformed liturgy. The bishops have maintained their long-accustomed collegiality and reticence. Although none of them stepped forward as an inspired spokesman of the Council program, none of them showed reluctance to implement it at least formally. By character and by their studies—mainly in old-style theology and canon law—they are circumspect men and no heaven-stormers. Their predominant view is the long-term one that reform of religious instruction in the schools and of priestly studies in the seminaries will best serve the purposes of the Council, and in both spheres important work is being done. There has been a considerable spontaneous growth of locally organized, church-sponsored social services of all kinds. The rapport between the clergy and architects, painters, and sculptors has been deepened, but no equivalent rapport has yet been established with writers, musicians, or composers—a serious lack, since language, music, and song are the typical media of cultural expression in modern Ireland. By and large, active involvement in religion and in things religious has declined: pious associations and sodalities have been losing membership, attendance has fallen at various kinds of devotions. There has been a sharp rise in dropouts among students for the priesthood. But there has been no movement among priests to abandon the clerical calling. Various new associations have been formed in the wake of the Council: an Irish Theological Association, a Catholic Biblical Association, an Association of the Religious Press, and a Catechetical Association.

Essentially, of course, what the Council has to offer is a renewed Christian view of God and man, out of which, through liturgy and sacraments, a new life can grow. The Council can take effect in Ireland only in the degree that its theology and anthropology are rendered indigenous and concretely applicable by Irish Christians, but first and foremost by their theologians.

There are several reasons for the stagnation of Catholic thought in Ireland in the period preceding the Second Vatican Council, the most important being the low valuation of reflection and theory in modern English-language culture, the provincial mentality permeating Irish intellectual life, and the exaggerated status of canon law and moral casuistry in the seminaries. Another contributing factor was doubtless the absence from the past and present of the Irish Church of the standard great problems of the Church on the Continent at that time. Direct confrontation with great problems is a major incentive to creative thought, theological or otherwise.

It was not merely that the standard problems of Continental Catholicism did not impinge directly on the Church in Ireland and that there could not therefore be any direct confrontation with them. Great issues, some of them common to the Church as a whole, some of them shared with modern European culture generally, and others arising precisely out of the differences between Irish Catholic experience and that of the Church on the Continent, were latent in the Irish Church. If these had been perceived, and perceived as the great theological issues they were, theology in Ireland would have had plenty to grapple with to the benefit of the Church in general. But for the great issues latent in the Irish experience to be perceived at all, Irish theologians would have had, in the first place, to regard Irish experience as thoroughly valid experience of the Roman Catholic Church in modern times and thus deserving of intense, theologically-informed scrutiny. They were prevented from doing this by the provincial-mindedness already referred to and by the belief—a gratuitous act of faith—that the condition of the Church in the world was essentially monolithic, the same everywhere, regardless of the actual variations of human culture and historical experience.

Thus, for Irish theologians the Church "over there" was the essential Church, the issues which it noticed and called great the only ones which merited profound theological concern. Not finding themselves directly confronted with *these* issues on their home ground, they had a choice of two courses, each of which they followed. Either they could try bravely to believe that these issues, as discussed and as understood on the Continent, were in fact present in the Irish Church, or they could regard their particular part of the universal Church as, by a special grace of God, unproblematic—at least in respect to such problems as merited their concern *qua* Catholic theologians. Since neither course resulted in thoughtful grappling with the Christian experience as actually presented in Ireland, theology had a barren time.

For awareness of great theological issues latent in the Church in Ireland, Irish theology had to wait until certain German, French, and Belgian theologians, after intense scrutiny of the Church in their respective countries, restated the problems of the contemporary Church as they saw them there. To the extent that this restatement had obvious relevance to Irish conditions, it has resulted in a certain quickening of theological thought in Ireland. But even in this restatement, many of the issues are not real issues in Ireland *or would require reformulation* to be made relevant to Irish experience. For the most part, the theologians have hitherto lacked either the courage or the inner freedom to do this.

For as long as Irish Catholics, in the belief that valid Catholic experience is essentially monolithic and "over there," continue to await delivery of their theological themes from the Continent and in Continental packaging, they will fail to emulate the best Continental theologians by theologizing out of their own historical and contemporary Christian experience. As a result, theology in Ireland will be thin, derivative, and only superficially relevant to life, quite inappropriate to a part of the Church whose role in modern Church history has been so epoch-making and seminal, quite inadequate to the program of new Christian life offered by the Second Vatican Council.

Nevertheless, inasmuch as the history of the Church on the Continent and its present circumstances there have, since the Council, burdened Catholic consciousness with a great weight of guilt and induced a great deal of breast-beating, the "escape" of the Church in Ireland from much of that history and from many of the present consequences thereof gives it a comparative advantage. Too much consciousness of guilt, as has so frequently been said these last years, can have a laming effect on life and induce a morbid sort of thinking. The comparative "innocence" of the Irish Church—however much or little by its own merits is of no consequence—gives its arduous past a sunny aspect and its present an untrammelled freedom which is at the same time a

challenge and a responsibility. How and to what extent this circum-
stantial freedom will be used is a momentous question now facing Irish
Catholic Christians.[6]

[6] A bibliography of Irish Church history should include: Jean Blanchard, *The Church in Contemporary Ireland* (Dublin, 1963); Seán de Fréine, *The Great Silence* (Dublin, 1965); relevant articles in *The Irish Ecclesiastical Record, The Furrow,* and *Christus Rex,* all edited from Maynooth; Desmond Fennell, ed., *The Changing Face of Catholic Ireland* (London, 1968); Patrick J. Corish, ed., *A History of Irish Catholicism* (in fascicules). Four fascicules have been published so far by Gill and Son (Dublin and Melbourne, 1967).

11 : SCOTLAND

Thomas Hanlon

Under the blanket of "British," Scotland tends to lose her identity abroad to England. Yet historically, nationally, culturally, and religiously Scotland has been and remains different from her neighbors in the United Kingdom. It would be false to assume that Scottish Catholicism has no distinctive features of its own; its origin and history, particularly in the post-Reformation period, have ensured its peculiar character and at the same time have defined its problems. Although extremely proud of their heritage, Scottish Catholics have been chiefly to blame for the confusion of their identity.

Christianity in Scotland owes its origin to Ireland and it is especially to the lifelines from Ireland since the Reformation that the Church in Scotland today owes its vigor. Because of the zeal of the early Presbyterian reformers who capitalized on the sorry plight of the pre-Reformation Church in Scotland, the Reformation in Scotland met with tremendous success. Since there was little organized resistance such as there was in England, Catholicism was almost wiped out. It survived mostly in remote pockets in the Highlands to the north and in the Hebridean group of islands lying off the west coast. Without doubt the faith would have perished in these areas too through neglect, except for the advent of Franciscan and Vincentian missionaries from Ireland, who interested themselves in these Gaelic-speaking communities. Little detail is known of this missionary activity which began early in the seventeenth century, but the areas in which these missionaries worked never succumbed despite later bitter persecution; in addition, they have retained their own strong brand of devotion. The Church in many other parts of the English-speaking world owes much to these communities. After the ill-fated rebellion of 1745, romanticized by the tragic figure of "Bonnie Prince Charlie," the less-publicized "Highland Clearances" took place, when in order to create large estates for the landlords (many of whom were English), whole communities in the north and in the islands were driven from their homes, herded onto ships whose destinations were frequently not revealed, and deported mainly to Canada, Australia, and New Zealand accompanied generally by their priests.

Since it was believed that the pope was behind the rebellions of 1715 and 1745, Catholicism in Scotland was associated with Jacobitism, the cause of the exiled Stuart kings. Unlike the Episcopalians, however, who were committed to the Jacobite cause by the expectation of privileged status under a restored Stuart dynasty, Catholics were guided in their allegiance by politics rather than by religion; the Stuart dynasty had done little for the advancement of the Church either by policy or by personal example. The unfortunate association, implying disloyalty to the established government in London, did the Catholic cause no good but was used as an excuse for the continued repression and blocked Catholic emancipation.

Between the death of Prince Charles (the last pretender to the Scottish throne) in 1788 and Catholic Emancipation in 1829, the face of Catholicism in Scotland changed immensely. In 1800, when the population of the country was around 1.5 million, there were only 3 bishops, some 40 priests, and 30,000 Catholics with 12 churches. By 1827 there were some 50 priests, over 70,000 Catholics with 31 churches. This rise resulted from the immigration of the Irish who were driven out of Ireland by famine, rack rents, and the hope of a livelihood elsewhere. The industrially expanding west of Scotland was a haven. By 1835 in the southwest alone there were over 70,000 Irish immigrants, and in Glasgow the Catholic population had jumped from 50 in 1795 to 24,000, and in Edinburgh from 700 to 8,000. By 1841 there were over 120,000 Irish-born Catholics in Scotland and although they had settled mostly in the southwest many had spread to other areas and led an almost nomadic existence in search of employment. Unfortunately no Irish priests accompanied this wave and many of them lapsed when they finally settled in areas where there were no Catholics and no priests. Elsewhere they settled down, built churches, increased, and multiplied. Most Scottish Catholics today are descended from these and subsequent immigrants from Ireland.

The Irish were not the only immigrants in the industrial west. Native Catholics from the Highlands and Isles, driven by the same causes, were also arriving, and unfortunately there was strife between the two parties, with the Irish complaining of discrimination. The hierarchy was restored in 1878 and today in Scotland there are eight dioceses, over 1,000 secular priests, 275 regular clergy, for a Catholic population of over 800,000. These are unevenly distributed over the country; more than one-third of the Catholics are concentrated in Glasgow and almost two-thirds in the dioceses of Glasgow, Motherwell, and Paisley, the main industrial centers of the country. The Catholics constitute a little less than 20 per cent of the total population.

Before the convening of Vatican II, one could detect a certain complacency in the Church in Scotland. The difficult period was over and the problems which were acknowledged were slight in comparison to those which had been faced and successfully overcome during the previous century: the supply and training of priests to meet the demands of the surge in population; the establishment of schools and colleges for the education and training of the laity; hostility, bigotry, and discrimination on the part of established Presbyterianism. Fortunately during that period Church affairs had been entrusted to a succession of zealous pastorally-minded practical bishops and priests. The future was bright and the only problems were the building of churches for the ever-increasing Catholic population and the stopping of the "leakage," the term used to designate the defection of Catholics.

The once steady flow of priests from Ireland, without whom the Church in Scotland would never have prospered, became a trickle. The generations succeeding the immigrants, however, provided a fertile seedbed for vocations. The two major seminaries at home and the two national colleges abroad (Rome and Spain) were providing sufficient priests to meet the demand and were likely to continue to do so. New churches were being built where and when required, for incurring debt in this field was not feared. The education problem no longer existed and had been solved in such a way that the system and facilities provided for Catholics were the envy of Catholics elsewhere. A new professional class of Catholic laity, who had availed themselves of the educational system and had entered the various professions and positions in civic life, had come into existence. While other churches were declining in membership, closing establishments, and generally losing influence, the Catholic Church was expanding rapidly, despite the leakage, and not merely as a result of the attitude to birth control. Moreover no one could doubt the caliber of the Scottish Catholics: by and large they were voluntarily practicing, devout, and loyal with a faith that had been buttressed over the years by the persecution and discrimination of a non-Catholic, even anti-Catholic majority.

The ecclesiastical vital statistics compared favorably with those of any other country. Complacency in such circumstances was almost natural and to some extent understandable. Pope John's calling of the Council with its program of *aggiornamento* came as a surprise: there was no obvious need of reform and no patent errors requiring correction. Yet it highlighted the deficiencies in the ecclesiastical set-up in Scotland. Concern with domestic problems over the years had obscured other issues, movements, and currents in the universal Church. The agitation for liturgical reform, the ecumenical movement, the trends in biblical and other branches of theology had been either unnoticed or shrugged off as the trivia of Continental clerics unwilling to perform even the basic pastoral duties of the apostolate in their own countries.

Over the years members of the hierarchy, with few exceptions, had been drawn from the ranks of the secular clergy and were not academically inclined men or visionaries with their fingers on the pulse of the intellectual life of the Church. They were practical men who met urgent practical problems successfully, but they remained apparently unaware of, or at least uninterested in, the new movements, new outlook, new horizons, new problems, and new thinking of the Church in the mid-twentieth century; and consequently they were not likely to lead or to encourage growth in these fields. Opportunity for priests to become involved in the new life of the Church was almost nonexistent because of the policy of keeping them actively engaged climbing stairs and knocking on doors. A priest engaged in any field other than parochial was almost considered a waste of priestly potential.

Nor did the clergy, by and large, seek guidance in these new fields that were opening up. They had been trained for one thing, the active pastoral mission, in institutes which were bastions of conservatism in post-Tridentine theology and kindred disciplines; in the Gregorian University, in the seminary at Valladolid (Spain), in the West of Scotland seminary, in the seminaries of Ireland and England, and (a few) in the seminaries of France. Theology, the whole of it, or at least what was relevant in it, was considered to have been imparted during the semi-

nary course and little taste was left for more. What was imparted then
—and worse still, what was retained—was considered sufficient to meet
all needs.

In such conditions it was not likely that Scotland would possess a
laity enlightened in the new thinking or even prepared to assimilate it.
In school the laity were given a good grounding in the faith of their
fathers through a catechism which was an excellent summary of post-
Tridentine theology, but of dubious value in the instruction of children. Little opportunity existed for further instruction after schooling,
apart from the Sunday sermon. On the whole the Church failed to
convince the laity of their part in the apostolate; the lay apostolate itself, "male sonans" in many clerical circles, failed to attract members
of the educated professional classes.

No doubt pastoral solicitude for the needs of a rapidly expanding
Church dictated this outlook. Nevertheless, even before Vatican II
that era was ending in Scotland. The home seminaries were opening
their doors and were already beginning to reformulate theology and
present the new emphases. The second of these major seminaries was
opened in Edinburgh in 1953 and since then only a few priests have
been trained abroad. Two Catholic training colleges for female
teachers, in Glasgow and in Edinburgh, were imparting new catechetical methods and the catechism itself was undergoing drastic revision.
The recently emerged professional class of laity were beginning to think
for themselves and to criticize. The new atmosphere was not welcomed
everywhere and required Pope John's call and the Council to convince
many that innovation was called for: "Roma locuta est" traditionally
settled matters for Catholicism in Scotland.

Scotland possesses an educational system which has attracted attention from abroad, not least from Catholics. The system combines principles for a high standard of secular education with education in the
various beliefs of her people. Things were not always thus. It was only
after Catholic Emancipation in 1829 that Catholics were allowed to
establish and maintain their own schools. This added to the already
existing heavy financial burden. Even when in 1872 the government
established a program for state-aided schools, which were to be managed by locally elected school boards, Catholics only qualified for half
the grants, since they decided to retain the management of their own
schools, the appointment of teachers, and the freedom to have religion
taught according to their own beliefs and practices. This withdrawal of

control from the local school boards disqualified them from benefitting from the levy raised by these boards, even though Catholics like others had to contribute to the local levy.

The result was that Catholic school buildings were generally inferior and Catholic teachers were paid less and were fewer in number, so that classes were proportionately larger and accommodation accordingly more crowded. There were naturally comparatively few Catholic secondary schools, and these only in the more populous districts. Opportunities for Catholic children to earn scholarships which would assist them in higher education were consequently few and thus few Catholics attained professional status. By 1918 Catholics comprised one-tenth of the whole population and one-seventh of the children attending state-aided schools. They had kept up an unceasing campaign against the injustice of the situation until finally the government recognized the injustice and desired the Catholic schools to benefit to the same extent as others in a new reorganization of the system which it was then contemplating. The desire was to bring them under the control of new local county authorities, which would also be responsible for the appointment and payment of teachers.

After much deliberation and opposition, agreement was reached under which Catholics transferred their schools to the county authorities (either by sale or by lease). These were henceforward responsible for the management, appointment, and payment of teachers, but were bound by law to manage and make appointments exactly as Catholic managers themselves would have done and to make no appointment which was not first approved by representatives of the Church. A religious supervisor, likewise approved by the Church, was to be appointed to each school by the county authority (in practice almost invariably the parish priest), and time was to be set aside for religious instruction and examination. Moreover Catholics were to be represented on the administrative bodies. Like any other citizens they may be elected to the county council and so find their way onto the education committee, but over and above that a Catholic representation or representative must by law be co-opted ex officio to the education committee of the county; such representatives are nominated by the local ordinary. Besides, each county is divided into school management areas, with committees charged with the day-to-day running of the schools; wherever there is a Catholic school in any such area, the law provides that there shall be a Catholic representative on the committee. The local priests may enter the school at the time set aside for religious instruction, which forms part of the school curriculum and which must be given daily under the supervision of the ecclesiastical authorities.

That such an agreement is advantageous to Catholics is obvious: Catholic schools were improved in every way, teachers were given salaries equal to others, Catholic children were granted equal opportunities for scholarships, maintenance grants, travelling expenses, and hostel allowances, if required. Primary and secondary schools are erected at no expense to the Church and in areas where, if left to her own resources, they would never have been erected. Equal opportunities exist for Catholics in the sphere of higher education in training colleges and universities; such education is absolutely free. Seminarians qualify for the same aids as university students, the grants amounting to £480 per year; when tuition fees, books, and board have been deducted, the major seminarians are left with around £100 for personal expenses, the grants covering the operating cost of the seminaries.

Those Catholics who offered most opposition to the settlement in 1918 were subsequently satisfied and could testify that the education act was administered not only impartially but generously and that their fears had been groundless. In the early years after the act, there was naturally an insufficiency of qualified Catholic teachers, especially for the secondary schools. However with the present advantages, the shortage of Catholic teachers is no greater than the general shortage and is determined by well-known social and economic factors. The average shortage, apart from Glasgow where it is higher, is just over 10 per cent. The odium of making appointments to school staffs and the danger of being accused of favoritism is removed from the priests; likewise there is no criticism involving accommodation, upkeep, equipment, and payment of teachers, such as the priests received when they controlled school management.

No provision was made for religious as such. To have asked a Protestant legislature to give Catholic religious privileged status would probably have wrecked the settlement with all the attendant benefits; it was essential to consider what was best for the children and for the Church in general, not what was best for religious. However religious in no way suffered under the act, for although transferred like other teachers so as to hold their appointments from the county authorities, they were given equal pay for equal qualifications, promotion, increased emoluments in due course, and pension on retirement; moreover, although not provided by law, a religious was appointed to succeed a religious when the religious applicant had the necessary academic qualifications.

Such a system has been frequently alleged by educationists to be the finest in the world. If there is any flaw in Catholic education in Scotland it is on the Catholic side in not making full use of the advantages. One anomaly that puzzles educationists, both at home and abroad, is why the Church considers it imperative for women teachers to be trained in a Catholic training college before being considered fit to teach Catholic children (nongraduate teachers undergo a three-year course, graduates one year), while mere attendance at twelve lectures (generally in the university chaplaincies) is considered sufficient Catholic training for the male teachers. Until now there have been no nongraduate male teachers, although at this moment some nongraduates are training in a Catholic training college. This question of the graduate male teachers has been raised frequently over the years but so far nothing has been done to remedy the situation, which is no doubt at least partially responsible for the fact that instruction in the faith in secondary schools is not always adequate.

With the government's projected scheme for comprehensive schools, other questions are being raised. In an age of increasing specialization in education, some educationists, including Catholics, foresee the necessity of integrated secondary schools. A prima facie case for these can be made on the basis of the shortage of qualified specialists coupled with an emotive ecumenism. One can only foresee stubborn resistance to such a project, although ultimately some compromise may be necessary.

Ecumenical dialogue was unknown and unthinkable a decade ago. The climate was very unfavorable: Presbyterianism in Scotland ever since the Reformation has been fanatical in its denunciation of papistry and has continually fanned hostility. The official confession of faith of the Church of Scotland still refers to the "Pope of Rome . . . that antichrist, that man of sin and son of perdition." Bigotry, discrimination, and distrust of Catholics have always permeated almost every sphere of life, and still do to a large extent, despite the softening of the climate. In such conditions it is remarkable that any progress should have been made in this field. A general assessment is difficult to make: even though the community is small, there are great differences in attitude, for example, in the isolated pockets of Catholics in the north and north-west, in the densely populated industrial west, and among the scattered and heavily outnumbered Catholics elsewhere. It is even more remarkable that the initiative and lead among Catholics should have come from a man in a contemplative order, Dom Columba Mulcahy, Abbot of the Cistercian Abbey at Nunraw. Today ecumenical gatherings are frequent, and in them sincere, frank discussion and criticism are possible without fear of offense.

Before this the Protestant churches in Scotland had been attempting, with a fair measure of success, to put their own house in order. The various moves to heal the divisions which had arisen over the centuries were motivated by a variety of considerations: the divisions were a source of scandal and were responsible for large drops in the numbers of practicing Protestants, especially among the younger generations which were no longer interested in theological controversy or tradition. The consequent fall in revenue and in vocations to the ministry made it more and more difficult to support separate establishments. In addition, many ministers had become skeptical of doctrine, which at best appeared uncertain and not worth permanent divisions, and for some their religion had deteriorated into mere humanism.

Dialogue involving Catholics is principally with the Presbyterian Church of Scotland, which claims some 35 per cent of the adult population as communicant members. To a lesser degree there is dialogue with the Scottish Episcopal Church, claiming some 1.5 per cent of the population. Both Catholics and Protestants prefer dialogue with each other to that with Episcopalians, who betray no clear-cut beliefs and who are suspected by the Church of Scotland at large of using the dialogue as a cover for a take-over.

The change in the atmosphere has not been welcomed everywhere. Only a small minority on both sides is actively engaged, but it is a vocal, articulate minority, sincerely convinced that the Spirit is at work in the movement and that concerted action in the promotion of spiritual, religious, and moral values is a desirable thing in a country where Christian values are no longer the norm. For the vast majority the change has been too sudden, and the difficulty is to know where, and above all, how, to begin. The barriers are high; respective positions have been well clarified and instilled over the years; no one has any illusions about the gulf which separates Catholic and Protestant. Thus while theoretically admitting the principles which underlie and inspire ecumenism, many cannot see beyond or behind the dividing doctrines and so view the movement with anxiety and fear. They feel that a movement which, however well-meaning and charitable, limits itself to discussing and clarifying what is held in common, cannot last forever and that cooperation on the social plane will give the wrong impression; differences must finally be discussed and an inevitable impasse reached, which will define the respective positions more clearly. For non-Catholics, a general union with papism would be an unthinkable betrayal of the Reform; for Catholics anything less would be equally unthinkable.

Catholics actively engaged in dialogue experience other types of difficulties. The Reformed Churches in Scotland appear in practice to recognize no rule of faith or authority, so that it is difficult to find a group or spokesman for a group, who will claim to be, or be recognized as, representative of a church, even on fundamental issues. Rejection of fundamental Christian doctrines is not so very rare among ministers of all these sects and it is a source of embarrassment to the orthodox, who appear powerless or unwilling to intervene and remedy the situation. Nor do the aims of non-Catholic ecumenists always coincide. Hardly anyone among them contemplates a form of reunion that would mean one visible church, one teaching and legislative body, one ministry and one liturgy. Something in the nature of a federation of independent churches, with freedom of worship, freedom of the sacraments, and interchange of pulpits would be more acceptable.

Catholics engaged in dialogue feel tolerated by the hierarchy and by the majority of their brethren; they sense little encouragement, little lead or policy, have embarrassing restrictions imposed on them and are at a disadvantage when it comes to taking any initiative even along lines indicated by the Council and Rome. Despite everything there is general agreement in the churches that the new sympathetic atmosphere is already indicative of progress, which it is hoped will continue and is likely to do so.

The lay apostolate has never been an effective organ of Catholic public opinion on any major social issue. Although over fifty societies are listed in the directory, the laity as a whole have remained unconvinced of their share in the apostolate. In this field, however, things are moving with a view to implementing the recommendations of recent popes and the Council. In 1966 there was formed a National Council for the Lay Apostolate composed of representatives from diocesan committees (where these exist) and from national societies. Perhaps it is still too early to expect anything valuable from this body, but nothing of value is likely to emerge without cooperation at diocesan and parochial levels. Here there is much to be done: instruction of the laity in their role as apostles and in the renewal of the Church and the reorganization of the existing societies. The National Council has undertaken this task and one training center for the laity has been established in Edinburgh to which selected parishes are required to send groups.

It is in the liturgical field that the effect of renewal has been felt most. Prior to the Council little interest was shown in things liturgical and it was considered an achievement to have a dialogue Mass in Latin or a whole congregation joining in the Gregorian chant. The introduction of the vernacular aroused little reaction and in all the dioceses was prepared by conferences for both clergy and laity and by a course of sermons explaining the changes and the necessity for them. Now of course there is uniformity throughout the English-speaking world.

The implementation of the Council's program will depend almost entirely on the lead given by the hierarchy; in many quarters it is believed that the hierarchy itself is not always convinced of the necessity for renewal. Perhaps this is understandable in a country devoted to its traditions and noted for its conservatism. Little remote preparation existed and there is much leeway to make up. At the moment interest among the clergy and laity is very much alive and it would be a great pity if this is not sustained. Refresher courses for the clergy, conferences for summer schools for the laity, and the establishment of truly consultative bodies at diocesan and parochial levels, are indicated. In some dioceses these have already been instituted, in others it is doubtful that they are envisaged.

One feature of Catholicism in Scotland which is disturbing and which amazes outsiders is intellectual apathy. This is reflected in the fact that Scotland has no periodical or review of its own for the clergy nor have any of the clergy contributed anything of theological significance to any of the theological periodicals. It is reflected too in the nature of the Catholic press (two papers) which are little more than glorified parish magazines, notoriously untrustworthy in their factual presentations and generally uninformative in the new thinking within the Church. In fairness, one is bound to say that there has been improvement here too within the last few years and with only lightweight theologians on hand and a comparatively limited circulation, responsibility must be shared.

12 : ENGLAND

M. A. Fitzsimons

I. HISTORICAL CHARACTER OF ENGLISH CATHOLICISM

In recent centuries the English Catholics have successively been a defeated remnant, a tolerated religious group whose numbers multiplied, and, in the twentieth century, members of a Church that enjoyed a measure of national recognition and encouragement.

In the latter half of the sixteenth century, after the Elizabethan church settlement, the numbers of English Catholics began to dwindle. The decline lasted, with few interruptions, for more than two centuries. In 1780 Catholic numbers were estimated to be 56,500, that is, less than 0.7 per cent of the population. In the nineteenth century numbers and percentage increased. Calculations based upon the census of 1851 led Msgr. Philip Hughes to put the number of Catholics in England and Wales at 679,067 out of a population of 18,000,000.[1] Today, they total perhaps 8 per cent of a population numbering more than 50,000,000.

These figures reveal a history of growth in sharp contrast with the decline that many Continental countries experienced. A large part of

[1] "The English Catholics in 1850" in *The English Catholics, 1850–1950* (London, 1950), pp. 45–46. The Newman Demographic Survey which considered statistics of Catholic marriages and Catholic baptisms has generally presented much higher figures: more than 4.5 per cent in 1851, 10.7 per cent in 1951, and 12.2 per cent in 1961. See A. E. C. W. Spencer, "The Demography and Sociography of the Roman Catholic Community of England and Wales" in Lawrence Bright and Simon Clements, eds., *The Committed Church* (London, 1966), pp. 61–63. *The Catholic Directory's* figures are much less scientific in claim and considerably lower in numbers. The English Census has not dealt with Church membership and attendance since 1851.

the increase, however, consisted of Irish immigrants and their descendants. It was the boast of some of the English bishops at Vatican Council II that the Church in England had not lost the working class. But English Catholicism consists of groups in addition to the Irish. Each constituent group has good reason to recognize its separateness from aspects of English life.

The defeated remnants consisted of old Catholic survivors of the Penal Laws. Their numbers are suggested by the estimate of Catholics in 1780. Even at that time the Catholics had largely become an urban people. The leaders of the old Catholics, however, were the survivors of a now vanished rural world of hierarchy in which their estates had been centers of Catholic worship. Even after the toleration achieved in the eighteenth century and political emancipation (1829), these old Catholics bore in their consciousness the marks of defeat: for them the English world was not to be provocatively disturbed— not to mention talk about the conversion of England. Their religion was individualist and their piety sober and unostentatious.

To this group were added the converts from Protestant English society who for more than a century after the Oxford Movement provided a substantial number of the leaders and apologists of English Catholicism.

The numbers of the converts rose from about 1,500 annually in 1850 to about 7,700 annually in 1911 and to 12,304 in 1961. Since then the figure has somewhat declined. This influx of converts from Anglicanism and agnosticism provided English Catholicism with a mythic hope of converting England. Curiously enough little systematic study has been made of the converts as a group—or of the losses of Catholics, the "leakage" problem. Presumably, in recent decades, many converts were marriage partners of Catholics. At any rate, the converts increased the small middle class and professional element in the Catholic population. Many of the converts from the Oxford Movement were mainstream English in formation, well-educated, independent minded, and endowed with the habit of authority. Conversion set them apart from their Anglican and Protestant countrymen, for they believed the Roman Church to possess divinely established authority in doctrinal matters. They had the self-confidence to bear active witness and their piety was not retiring. Their relations with the old Catholics were often troubled. In his tireless witness the convert Archbishop Henry Edward Manning, who rejoiced in exercising the ecclesiastical authority that he magnified, encountered the passivity and hostility of the old Catholics. Their Catholicism, in his eyes, was a low form, anti-Roman and lazy. Almost a half century later the tension was still observable: the old Catholics "rather awkwardly, but very wrongly,—think that every convert is a wolf, or rather an ass in sheep's clothing. . . ."[2]

In 1852 the convert John Henry Newman in a sermon "The Second Spring" recalled the low estate of Catholics in the century past to dramatize the development that he celebrated: the forming anew of an English people unto God, a new Catholic community provided in 1850 with a hierarchy.

But tragic events in Ireland were already flooding the new people unto God in England with unexpected recruits. "The Second Spring" brought not the conversion of England but the addition of an impoverished and non-English people to English Catholicism. The Irish of the Famine (1846) and later decades usually passed from a subpeasant level to the lowest paid of the English proletariat. This Irish immigration may have slackened from the 1880's to the 1920's. Since the 1930's the movement greatly increased so that today in England alone there are almost one million Irish-born who provide not only unskilled labor but a considerable number of doctors and nurses. The number and distribution of the Catholic clergy and churches were entirely inadequate to serve this human movement. Indeed, Irish migration strained the pastoral resources of the Catholic Church in Britain for almost a century. Cardinal Manning once described his work as an apostolate to the Irish and for this work he required all his belief in the ordering of the world by providence, which he saw as a "progressive" dispensation of "imperfect outline and discordant preludes." For the clergy this service meant a constant preoccupation with raising voluntary contributions for building churches.

Until recently the Irish did little in the way of creating institutions in Ireland, England, and the United States to equip the migrant for his ordeal and to assist him in settling down. The beginning of an explanation of this may be found in the social disintegration that the Irish had experienced. They were, as Engels wrote, "almost without civilization," that is, a culture of range and depth. The great silence of a distinctive Gaelic culture had begun. Many of the Irish of Famine Years had not

[2] Edmund Sheridan Purcell, *Life of Cardinal Manning* (London, 1896), pp. 88–89; C. C. Martindale, *The Life of Monsignor Robert Hugh Benson* (London, 1916), I, 317.

the range of cultural inheritance that German, Polish, and Sicilian villagers possessed. Loss of leaders, oppression, and rack-renting potato agriculture diminished Irish culture: many Irishmen were left with little more than a sense of identity that was mainly religious in form.

Their ill-instructed piety was largely confined to simple and individualist devotions. In their new surroundings many of them either were far from a Catholic Church or found the Church overcrowded. Assimilation, generally slow at first, was often accompanied by adopting English Evangelical morality. Tens of thousands of Irish drifted away from Catholic practice. This loss of Irish and other Catholics to the Church rendered all talk of the prospective Catholic conversion of England romantic chatter.

Few Catholic bishops were selected from the numerous Irish clergy in England. In matters of public concern the Irish supported Irish Home Rule and Catholic educational interests. Some were active in the organizational endeavors of unskilled labor in the 1880's; some were supporters of the infant Labor Party. Apart from the play of religious and racial prejudice, however, two circumstances limited Irish participation in English public life: the conflict of English and Irish nationalisms and the nearness of Ireland. The latter meant that many Irish could readily return to Ireland or, at any rate, believed that they soon would.

These diverse groups of the Catholics in England were united in a common faith and professed it with varying degrees of assertiveness. As the Irish became settled in England, they began to share the memories of English Catholics and to venerate the martyrs of English Catholicism. Each constituent group, however, apart from many of the clergy, had little knowledge of the others and neither theology nor their devotions promoted a lively corporate sense.

The Catholic minority professed its English loyalty and patriotism. After 1921 the Irish question lost its bitterness. As a group Catholics had few quarrels with the government of the United Kingdom; they and their leaders supported it in two World Wars; they received public assistance for many of their schools. When World War II began, Archbishop Hinsley of Westminster was a solid patriot whose Englishness and leadership made him a genuinely national figure. The reassurance provided by the converts continued. Until the thirties, at the very least, the roll of converts included some very distinguished names: Ronald Knox, Christopher Dawson, Eric Gill, G. K. Chesterton,

Graham Greene, and Evelyn Waugh, who became the prose laureate of the old Catholic view. Some of the converts expressed a troubled awareness of the decline of religion among their fellow countrymen.

The English Catholics viewed their country with loyalty and their society generally with a sense of apartness. The end of apartness would come presumably with the conversion of England and its return to medieval Christian unity. The Catholic Truth Society and the Catholic Evidence Guild were founded to foster conversions. A Converts Aid Society helped to ease the difficulties converted and married Anglican clergy might encounter. Where the Catholic Truth Society was intended to remove misapprehensions by providing correct information about Catholicism and Catholic views, the Evidence Guild bore witness in the free public forums of England.

Conversion and preaching meant the spreading of the Gospel's good news. At the time, however, the Church generally took a formal and institutional view of its work. In England Catholics spoke of submission to Rome. The historical memories of English Catholics as well as their own interpretation of the Church and the world generally made for a defensive and aloof attitude that ran counter to the hopes that inspired the Catholic Evidence Guild. Church policies and Catholic institutions were intended to reach out into English life in order to extend Catholic influence and to provide assurance of Catholic loyalty and conformity to aspects of national life. But they were also meant to protect Catholic interests and believers. There were Catholic associations for the protection of animals, the care of sailors, and, in order to promote marriages among Catholics, the holding of dances. The necessity of financing church buildings and schools inspired other forms of associations. There were as well guilds of Catholic journalists, actors, lawyers, teachers, doctors, nurses, and university students. Where some have seen in this construction of a Catholic world an imitation of the Establishment, other Catholic critics have called it an artificial world, the refuge of a "devout sectarianism" lacking in apostolic zeal.

The social views of a religious minority are likely to be a complex matter: on the one hand, their sense of apartness implies a judgment on their society and an aspiration to change it; on the other hand, the minority's very apartness may deprive it of effective means to influence the society and may foster views of little relevance to the society or views that remain at best intellectual or even verbal formulations.

Apartness and defensiveness had special English sources among the old Catholics, the converts, and the Irish. They were, however, rooted in the general defensiveness and minority attitude of the Catholic Church and its papal leadership. Nineteenth-century and early twentieth-century Catholicism encouraged a hostile passivity to the moving forces of the contemporary world.

Rome's guidance reenforced the antimodernism of some Catholics and converts. For them the modern world was ugly, sin-breeding, based on error, and doomed to destruction, and the Church was an ark of escape and salvation. For some Rome's pervasive guidance was the order of infallible authority and the exaggeration of its authority was at most an emergency dictatorship over the Church conceived as a mighty fortress. From obedience and the subjection of conscience the Catholic appeared to derive peace and certainty in a troubled world. Implicit in this attitude was the view that the Church and Catholics had all the answers, at any rate, all the answers to questions worth raising.

Here the Church was the beneficiary of those critical of the freedom of the Anglican Church which they saw as doctrinal chaos, and of some antiliberal movements. From outside the Church, George Wyndham wrote to Wilfrid Ward: "You are an army with generals who may be dilatory, or retrograde. We are a mob, with individuals who may be brilliant and impulsive." For his part, Ward believed that the Church was passing through a necessary but transient, autocratic stage in which martial law was necessary. Lord Hugh Cecil replied: "The vigour and severity of martial law are only to be justified by success, and the notable thing about ultramontanism is that it is a failure."[3]

At the same time Catholicism meant for many Catholics a wider world than the English-speaking one. It frequently entailed sympathy and even partisanship for Austrian and Latin people and their governments, particularly the governments of Dollfuss, Salazar, Franco, and Mussolini.

Catholic writing reflected this English situation. The English Catholic world, a world of unbourgeois extremes, of an upper class and an abundant mass, attracted men of literary talent. Additionally, English Catholics as writers, publishers, and lecturers enjoyed the advantage of a market and audience in the United States and other parts of the English-speaking world. On occasion English Catholics acted as middlemen of ideas in adapting Continental Catholic writing (notably

[3] Maisie Ward, *Insurrection versus Resurrection* (London, 1937), pp. 546, 566.

French and Belgian). There was some flourishing Catholic medieval scholarship. As contrasted with publicist work and creative literature, however, scholarship was not notable in range, for English Catholic intellectual life did not have institutional bases such as Catholic universities sometimes afford. This situation was to change: the transition time is the interwar period, when there was a marked growth of Catholic middle and professional classes.

II. THE ENGLISH CATHOLICS SINCE 1945

During World War II, Catholics were conspicuous in the general support that the government received. The war also increased the Catholic population of Britain which became the center of governments-in-exile. The course of the war and its aftermath meant that more than 150,000 Poles settled in Britain.

In the war years Catholic leaders sponsored welfare and relief services and took three noteworthy initiatives. In 1942 appeared the Joint Pastoral on the Social Question of the Bishops of England and Wales. Their recommendations included a family wage, family allowances, and adequate housing. The second initiative was a response to government plans to reorganize the national system of education. As the proposals appeared to deny the possibility of growth to Catholic schools, the hierarchy initiated a campaign to assert Catholic educational interests. Thirdly, the Sword of the Spirit movement, inaugurated in 1940, was an attempt on the part of such Catholic spokesmen as Cardinal Hinsley, Christopher Dawson, and Barbara Ward, to articulate the spiritual values in the United Nations' wartime cause and to emphasize the necessity of spiritual revival for the prosecution of the war and the making of peace. Apart from Hinsley's leadership, Catholic participation was primarily lay. In a limited way the movement was ecumenical. After losing its momentum in the postwar period, the movement took on new vigor when Cardinal Griffin asked it to educate Catholics in international relations. In 1965 it became the Catholic Institute for International Relations which has also sponsored aid to underdeveloped countries. Its special concern with Africa finally led to the separate establishment of Africa House.

The period since 1945 in English Catholicism may be divided into two phases: the years until 1959 may be seen as largely characterized by the Catholic schools campaign and by the reassuring stocktaking that went with the centennial celebration of the restoration of the hierarchy; since 1959 there is the slow, cumulative impact of Vatican Council II.

The Westminster careers of Bernard Griffin (1944–1956) and William Godfrey (1956–1963) are conservative stories. Griffin's archiepiscopal career was initially characterized by a vigorous pursuit of familiar policies. In his first four years at Westminster, Griffin energetically sponsored the case for Catholic schools for which he subsequently organized the Westminster Diocesan School Fund. The Archbishop believed that the English Catholics had come of age or, at any rate, out of the catacombs. He and his successors at Westminster took pains to indicate that they opposed the formation of Catholic blocs for political and social purposes. They did so to urge upon Catholics the duty of active participation in public life. For activity with Englishmen of other faiths and churches, Archbishop Griffin laid down the ground rules: "We have already agreed between us that on religious matters we work on parallel lines, but with regard to social matters or the welfare of the community we work in harmony and full cooperation. . . ." He stressed the necessity of "Catholic people penetrating and finding their place in the different spheres, civic and professional, of the nation's life" so as "to bring the benefits of our religion to a country which we hold most dear. . . ."[4]

The Archbishop drew perhaps very limited implications from his recognition that the mission of the Church was not at an end and that the future would not necessarily repeat past patterns. The penetration of lay society, for example, required an apostolate of the laity but this apostolate had to be trained by the clergy and directed by the hierarchy.

The Cardinal, as he became, had genuine gifts of command: he could choose able subordinates, which was fortunate, for he suffered a physical collapse in 1949 and a coronary thrombosis in 1951. Although the Cardinal would have rebuked any overt profession of complacency, nevertheless, he believed that "the Church in this country now approaches a degree of glory."[5]

His successor, William Godfrey, was sixty-three years old in 1956 when he was appointed to the Westminster Archdiocese. Behind him were careers as a seminary professor at Ushaw, Rector of the English College in Rome, Apostolic Delegate to the United Kingdom, and

[4] *The Tablet,* June 15, 1946, pp. 303–304; Sept. 22, 1956, p. 221.
[5] *The Tablet,* Sept. 22, 1956, p. 222.

Archbishop of Liverpool. In Rome he had gained a doctorate and at Ushaw served as Classics Master and as teacher of theology and philosophy. Such seminary teaching was, of course, not scholarship, which, indeed, was not his preference.

Labels annoyed him but his views were conservative, which he took to mean "regard for tradition and for the long history and experience of the Church . . . I can see no necessity for making changes for change's sake. But that is not to say that we have no regard for real progress, for the proper application of the Church to the needs of the time."[6] During his six Westminster years, the Catholic population of his diocese increased by 50,000; thirty-seven new churches were opened, and 11,000 additional school places were provided in Westminster schools.

At the first session of Vatican Council II, Godfrey was ranked with the conservatives. His eyes, of course, were not on the problems and urgencies that preoccupied the reformers. He knew that Continental Catholics had their great anxieties, but on the whole he did not think that these were of primary concern to the Church in England. For Godfrey Vatican Council II, as it developed, might be described as the unnecessary Council. A similar position is implicit in the views of a number of his episcopal colleagues.

Indeed, a reading of the bishops' pastoral letters (pre-1963) and the Catholic weekly newspapers seems, at first, to suggest that the Council's work of reform had no English prehistory. Nevertheless, the Council sweepingly fulfilled the idea of the Lay Apostolate which the English hierarchy had endorsed, and in many other respects the Council's reforms and the response to them had long been prepared. Renewed scriptural studies had promoted new efforts in theology. Behind a surface of noncontentious uniformity was a widespread, though rarely expressed, sense that existing policies had reached an impasse. This questioning ranged from Catholic teaching on birth control to apologetics, philosophy, and theology and was the starting point for a new generation in English Catholicism: the growing Catholic middle class and particularly university students and intellectuals. Some of them profess to find many of the views of English Catholicism irrelevant to the world they faced. To this generation, that articulated the unspoken doubts of their predecessors and sometimes exaggerated them, faith and authority had new meanings.

The course of this transformation, still in process, is difficult to de-

[6] Derek Worlock, "Cardinal William Godfrey," *The Wiseman Review*, No. 495 (Spring, 1963).

scribe. I propose here to deal with manifestations of the change in a number of areas: the hierarchy and clergy, the schools issue, higher education and theology, Catholic social views, the impact of the Council, liturgical reform, ecumenism, and the crisis of authority.

A. THE HIERARCHY AND CLERGY

The hierarchy consists of about twenty bishops and three metropolitans. With the Archbishop of Cardiff and the Bishops of Wales the number is small enough for semiannual meetings of two to three days under the presidency of the Archbishop of Westminster. Although each bishop is master of his own diocese, there is little evidence of episcopal pluralism, for the bishops avoid public disagreement and controversy. Generally they have been educated in seminaries and in Rome. Few of them have had systematic study of sociology, economics, politics, or critical history. As a rule only the converts and those with late vocations have had intimate association with lively modern universities.

In their writings the bishops emphasize the pastoral aspect of their office, although they are frequently preoccupied with administrative work. Indeed the largest number of them have emerged from careers as episcopal assistants, administrators, papal diplomats, or rectors of colleges. Generally they see themselves as practical men, burdened by responsibilities and thoughts of consequences, rather than as prophetic teachers. Their lives have been passed under a system of authority which it is now their duty to wield. Questioning is not welcome and they have been averse to English Catholics engaging in the controversy that the implementation of Vatican II's reforms is likely to provoke.

Finally, these wielders of ecclesiastical authority have been somewhat inaccessible to their subordinates, at any rate in matters that involved authority. The word has been given but only too often without preliminary discussion and persuasive work. The sources of episcopal information are often conservative. Instead of widening these sources the Catholic press sometimes has acted as an episcopal claque suggesting that the solid Catholic laity simply await episcopal word before moving.

Apart from the priests from Ireland, the clergy are trained in five interdiocesan seminaries or in Roman and Continental training centers. It is almost a convention to contrast the zeal and enthusiasm of seminarians with the intellectual drabness of the training they receive. The core of the curriculum has been a nonproblematic philosophy and theology. Until recently the relevance of theology to the problems of English life was rarely established or even considered.

The seminaries have sought to train pastoral priests. The priest has been expected to visit his parishioners and to be on terms of acquaintance with them. Sheltered tutelage, however, provided little preparation for such pastoral work. Recently seminarians have been encouraged to broaden their social experience, especially in vacation periods.

Only some of the regular clergy, Dominicans, Jesuits, Benedictines, and Franciscans, have had university training and the freedom from pastoral duties that a scholarly and intellectual life requires. For the future, it is recognized, those engaged in pastoral work will have to be able to speak to congregations of an advancing level of education and to convey to them a livelier sense of the relevance of religion to their living and its demands.

B. THE SCHOOLS

The kinds of Catholic schools reflect the social condition of English Catholics and the needs of religious orders of women. Several Catholic secondary schools, catering to the upper classes and people of means, may claim to rank with the leading "public schools." Secondary schooling for girls is more abundantly provided by convent schools, voluntary schools maintained by fees. Secondary schooling for boys has been more limited, because until well after 1945 the major Catholic effort was directed toward building primary schools.

Separate Catholic schools were originally a defensive necessity, when schools, orphanages, and institutions for the destitute and delinquent were maintained by voluntary effort and generally were Anglican controlled. A world of Catholic institutions had to be created.

The schools were required because the vast majority of Catholic parents were ill-instructed in their religion. Successive generations of Catholic educated parents should have substantially changed this situation. Many Catholic parents, however, did not assume direct responsibility for the religious education of their children: in some cases they themselves were ill-educated religiously; in other cases the prevailing attitudes in the Church induced parents to regard religious education as the task of Church authorities and schools. The case for Catholic schools and for government financial support of them welled out of a view in which the parental role was seen in a limited way. The Catholic case, nevertheless, was broader than defensiveness and parents' rights: it insisted that education should include knowledge, methods, character formation, and example; in short, it should have wholeness and harmony. But this admirable conception was often vitiated by inadequate means and the spirit of implementation. The defensive spirit sometimes had a dualist effect: there was the sheltered Catholic world and then there was the world into which the student finally emerged. Surveys of religious practice among the young attest to the shock that this abrupt transition caused.

The major Catholic educational effort has extended over 120 years. As universal education became an accepted goal and voluntary efforts were recognized to be insufficient, a national system of English primary education was proposed. Cardinal Manning vainly argued for the support of denominational schools as part of the national system. Instead, the Forster Education Act (1870) provided that schools established at public expense, that is, local schools maintained by rate-payers and controlled by locally elected education boards, were to offer strictly nondenominational religious teaching. Voluntary schools, however, might continue to receive support from the Privy Council.

The Balfour Education Act (1902) brought Catholic and other voluntary primary schools into the national system by providing rate support for the operation, but not the construction, of voluntary schools.

The Education Act of 1944 proposed to complete the national system of education by extending the years of schooling and by reorganizing secondary education. Nondenominational religious instruction was to be provided in all publicly maintained elementary and secondary schools. The denominational schools, it was assumed, had reached their full development; they were not to be replaced but no allowance was made for their growth. If Catholic primary schools and the smaller number of secondary schools met the standards established by public authority, they would be "aided" to the full extent of their operating costs, apart from those imposed by the exterior of the buildings and the sites. In turn, building costs to replace existing schools might be provided up to 50 per cent. An "aided" school would provide denominational instruction and would be governed by managers, two-thirds of whom were to be named by the school's denomination. The managers appointed teachers who met publicly set standards. The alternative was "controlled" status, that is, the public authority's government and maintenance of the school with provision of two hours of denominational instruction per week. Consequently, Catholic authorities everywhere sought to qualify for "aided" status.

The Catholic financial burden for this terminal development was estimated by the Board of Education to be about £ 10,000,000, a gross underestimate. Not even the most alarmed Catholic critics in 1943 foresaw the magnitude of the school crisis. By 1949 the sum needed for Catholic schools was £ 60,000,000.

The hierarchy saw the financial crisis as a crisis of survival. First of all, the material standards of aging Catholic school buildings had declined. Secondly, the growth and mobility of the Catholic population necessitated the construction of schools in numbers that no one had anticipated and that the Education Act was not designed to meet. Thirdly, many secondary schools had to be constructed to achieve the goal once formulated as "Every Catholic child in a Catholic school."

To press the Catholic case the Catholic Parents and Electors Association was formed in 1943. The campaign of the hierarchy and the Association had several achievements registered in new enactments and the amendment of administrative policies. For example, the Education Act of 1959 permitted the contribution of 75 per cent of the building costs of new schools from public funds; in 1966 the figure was raised in a blanket way to 80 per cent. The hierarchy and Catholic representatives displayed considerable ingenuity as well as persistence in arguing their case.

The Catholic effort was accompanied by some unexpected developments. Its demands touched almost all Catholics. The public argument required figures and forecasts. This prerequisite for planning was provided by the Newman Demographic Survey. In addition, a few dioceses placed school financing on a more centralized basis: for example, the Westminster Diocesan School Fund, established in 1952, proposed to raise £ 150,000 a year for the ensuing thirty years.

The limits on even a diocesan approach were emphasized in comments on the Government's White Paper on Southeast England in 1981. A writer for the *Catholic Herald* (March 26, 1964) noted that Catholics would probably comprise 500,000 to 750,000 of the area's expected increase. Such numbers would require schools, new churches, and priests on a scale far beyond the resources of, say, the Diocese of Brentwood.

The struggle for the schools evoked some far-ranging criticism. Major targets have been the policy of maintaining Catholic teachers' colleges, the teaching of religion, clerical control of schools, and the objectives of Catholic schools.

The existence of Catholic schools was the primary occasion for establishing Catholic teachers' colleges. With the growth of Catholic schools, the colleges have increased in number and have been supported by public money. There is little serious criticism made of their professional competence. What is sometimes questioned is the desirability of separate education for Catholic teachers. The main line of defense has been that Catholic teachers must be educated in the religion they will teach.

This has been the very subject for severe attack. Religion, it has been argued, has not been taught at a college or university level. Even more critical inquiry has been made into teaching religion to children. The inspiration of the *Lumen Vitae* group on the Continent prepared the way for changes affecting the very young for whom the memorized question and answer catechism is no longer used as a principal means of instruction. The greatest deficiency, critics alleged, was in the secondary school, especially for students in the fifth and sixth forms. Effective teaching there required that the teacher have some measure of serious theological training. In turn, the training colleges required theology professors of a competence equal to the teachers of other subjects. Until they are provided, went one criticism, "we are in fact treating the supernatural needs of Christian minds as the *Cinderella of the syllabus*."[7]

The necessity of theological studies was also stressed by Dr. Monica Lawlor, a psychologist. In speaking of the immaturity and lack of commitment of Catholic university students, she looked back to their earlier schooling: Catholics, she contended, had paid attention to the problem of securing Catholic education at the cost of not evaluating its achievements. Some subjects had been inadequately taught and more serious were the defects of an authoritarian education, which she listed

---

[7] David Collieer and Margaret Bendelow, "Training the Crew," *The Tablet*, April 11, 1964, pp. 400–402; April 18, 1964, pp. 429–430. The authors quoted from a "Report of an Enquiry into Divinity Courses and Religious Life in Catholic Training Colleges, November, 1963." They argue that some 19,000 Catholic teachers are in longer formative contact with children than the clergy. To prepare these teachers, higher religious studies are necessary. Without such provision "we are not manned to stop the leakage, let alone dress the ship and fly the flag."

as the lack of self-discipline and self-reliance. In her eyes the student's vocation required an openness of mind. Without a serious study of theology the Catholic student was condemned to live in separate worlds of faith and of science. For him the consequence would be spiritual and intellectual mediocrity.[8]

Cardinal Heenan responded to criticism of Catholic religious instruction in two moves. In appealing to Catholic secondary school teachers to help "a generation facing a crisis of faith," he promised the intensive training of priests as school chaplains (*Catholic Herald*, April 17, 1964). His second move was to establish in London a residential Catechetical Center for laity, religious, and clergy.

Other criticisms have been directed to the clerical control of education. Noel Hughes, addressing a Catholic Education Council Conference, insisted that Catholic schools should be controlled by the laity. Twenty years earlier, he admitted, the social condition of Catholics necessitated clerical leadership and control. He recognized the difficulty of getting lay acceptance of responsibility but argued that, if Catholic schools were demanded on the grounds of parental rights, then the schools should not be run by the clergy (*Catholic Herald*, May 7, 1965).

Finally there are those who want to know more about the results of Catholic schools: what do they achieve and what kind of Catholic emerges from them? Some misgivings are equally fundamental: if the massive Catholic effort cannot assure that all Catholic children will be taken care of, what must be done for those who cannot be served (better than one in three in Westminster Diocese)?

C. Universities: Higher Studies: Theology

In recent Catholic controversies in England the increasing number of Catholic university graduates have played a major role. In 1914 there were about 150 Catholics in Oxford; today the number has more than quadrupled. A similar account could be given for Cambridge and London. At Liverpool the Catholic percentage is higher and Catholic students form an appreciable part of the new universities. The number and activity of Catholic university teachers grow in importance and include impressively zealous Catholics. But it is unlikely that the present un-

[8] This matter is discussed in John Coulson, ed., *Theology and the University* (London, 1964).

dergraduate generation will be passive or voiceless. One university chaplain has called contemporary undergraduates the "autonomous generation," because they feel that nothing, especially in religion, is acceptable simply because it is traditional.

The prominence of university Catholics is a consequence of Catholic educational effort, the growth of English society, and government policies that extended educational opportunities. In the first half of the nineteenth century the requirements of Oxford and Cambridge debarred Catholics. Later, Catholics were inhibited by the Congregation of Propaganda in Rome and by their own hierarchy. A virtual prohibition was in force from 1867 until 1895. When in the 1870's Manning talked of establishing a Catholic university at Kensington, Newman's severe judgment was that the Kensington project would not provide a university education and was primarily a gesture to allay criticism. Newman, also, voiced a fear that still sways some critics: "I am inclined to think that the Archbishop finds only an ignorant laity manageable."[9]

The failure of the Kensington project supported the judgment that English Catholics did not have the resources to sustain a university. When Catholics were permitted to attend Oxford and Cambridge, Catholic chaplaincies were established there. This arrangement has been extended to the new universities. Their number is now so large that a case has been made for establishing the chaplaincies with general instead of diocesan support. In 1964 the lay businessman's organization, the Catenians, offered to raise £ 1,000,000 for the support of the chaplaincies. The offer, which had the approval of several bishops, was turned down by the hierarchy.

Catholics have two major university associations: the Newman Association for graduates and the Union of Catholic Students for undergraduates. These organizations emerged from the University Catholic Federation (1920), which was to provide, among other functions, an opportunity for the inevitably few members of some university Catholic clubs to associate with a more numerous body of Catholics. By the early 1940's increasing Catholic numbers at the universities made desirable separate organizations for graduates and undergraduates.

The newly-organized Newman Association declared its objectives to be: to support the Catholic student movement and to assist in found-

[9] Quotation in J. Derek Holmes, "Newman and the Kensington Scheme," *The Month*, Vol. 33 (1965), 12–23.

ing university chaplaincies; to promote cooperation among Catholic
graduates, particularly in spreading knowledge of Catholic principles
and their application; "to encourage Catholic graduates to assume
positions of responsibility in public life"; "to represent the Catholic
graduate body of Great Britain so as to enable it to take part in the
intellectual and cultural life at home and abroad . . ."; "to provide facilities for the higher education of the Catholic laity."[10]

The Association offered university extension lecture courses in theology, history, philosophy, psychology, and sociology. Its most significant work was the Newman Demographic Survey and the fostering of
discussion groups devoted to a special subject, such as the Philosophy of
Science Group initiated in 1953.[11]

The Survey, founded in 1953 and sponsored by the Newman Association, pioneered for Catholics the serious and empirical study of contemporary religious sociology. It brought together social scientists and
professional people to collect statistical information on the Catholic
population of England and Wales. Initially it was sustained by voluntary labor. Its statistics and projections aided the presentation of the
case for Catholic schools and teacher training colleges.

Within a decade the Survey had incurred debts beyond the Association's capacity, and Archbishop Heenan in 1964 requested that all data
concerning education be placed in the official and efficient hands of the
Catholic Education Council. The head of the late Survey, Anthony
Spencer, became Senior Resident Lecturer in Cavendish Square College. Spencer retained stores of statistical material but has lacked the
resources to make extensive use of them.

The division of the Survey's functions occasioned by financial crisis
has a propriety that may obscure a serious consequence of the division.
Understandably the hierarchy does not wish to appear as direct sponsor
of sociological works, and Spencer has used some of his work to criticize the authoritarian structure of the Church for inhibiting communications and reducing available means of problem-solving. But this

[10] P. H. Harris, "The Newman Association: The First Twenty-One Years," *The
Wiseman Review*, No. 497 (Autumn, 1963), 200.

[11] Within three years the Group had a membership of more than 500. Its
purpose has been summarized: to complete the education of the scientists by philosophy and theology and "to assist and guide Catholic scientists to achieve their own
personal integration, and then to encourage and stimulate them to play their full
part in the life of the Church." P. E. Hodgson, "Catholic Scientists in Britain:
Increasing Responsibilities," *The Tablet*, December 15, 1956, Vol. 208, 528–529.

termination of the Survey and some subsequent statements reveal an underprizing of the study of sociology and of the part it may play in a minority's understanding of itself and in the renewal of Church life with an emphasis on community.

On the university level, then, there has been no separate Catholic world. From the work of the Newman Association and from a group of priests and laymen who have met regularly at Downside Abbey since 1952 and from other Catholics have come pointed reminders of the limitations of this arrangement in that educated Catholics need the study of theology. The Downside discussions, involving the laity and members of religious orders, highlight the prominent role played by a few religious orders in the intellectual life of English Catholicism. These religious orders, it should be noted, have houses of study at Oxford or Cambridge Universities.

Since the end of World War I Catholic theologians have paid serious attention to areas that also preoccupied Protestant theologians: the liturgy, biblical and patristic theology, ecclesiology, and Christian sociology. These studies prepared the way for many of the liturgical reforms and doctrinal statements of Vatican II. The study and explication of the liturgy encouraged and drew upon biblical and patristic studies. Interest in biblical studies was reflected in translations such as that of Msgr. Knox and in the *Catholic Commentary on Holy Scripture*, edited by Dom Bernard Orchard and others (1953).

Liturgical, biblical, and patristic studies served to undermine the generally held simplistic view of Church worship as unchanging and of Church teaching as rigorously formulated for all time. Such researches inevitably challenged the view which saw Thomism as an inexhaustible computer. The study of the liturgy involved raising questions about the nature of the Church, the Christian community, and society. The direction of theological studies within the Church was toward the theological study of the problems of modern society that has become the formulated objective of the Dominicans of Blackfriars, Cambridge, and of their journal, *New Blackfriars*.

A major problem in this movement was how to relate the Catholic study of theology to the university world. In 1952 Msgr. H. F. Davis paid tribute to his own university, Birmingham, which had invited Catholics to serve as teachers of theology. Elsewhere, however, Catholics faced unsatisfactory conditions. The universities, he insisted, recognized that theology was concerned with Divine Revelation and the order of grace. As theology's sphere was more than that of the order of nature, he concluded that separate Catholic and Protestant theological faculties, as at Tübingen, should be established in the English universities. Five years later Father Adrian Hastings stated: "We do not want our own university, but we do need a theological faculty."[12]

Later, as ecumenism required dialogue, more attention was paid to Catholic participation in university departments than to insistence upon separate Catholic theological faculties. The theologians wanted a university setting and university graduates insisted that the availability of theological studies of university level was essential to the fruition of their inquiries. To that end a broader project, an Institute of Advanced Studies, was proposed.

The English hierarchy responded favorably and with deliberate speed. In 1965 they announced plans for the Heythrop Athenaeum to be established at Heythrop College, a Jesuit institution. The Chancellor of the Athenaeum is the Archbishop of Westminster; the Vice-Chancellor is the Jesuit Provincial, and the teaching staff is primarily Jesuit. The Athenaeum offers studies in philosophy and theology leading to the baccalaureate, licentiate, and doctorate for priests and laymen. In the early planning it was announced that several religious congregations would be in residence at Heythrop and that the Athenaeum would be "something like a national seminary." The Athenaeum was also to be the temporary seat of the Institute of Advanced Studies. It was emphasized that the national seminary was close to Oxford and that the prospective association with Oxford would encourage the university's recognition of Catholic theology which might then advance to "playing an integral part in the higher academic life of the country as a whole."[13]

The Athenaeum is a noteworthy response: the response also seems curiously reserved and incomplete. This appears in the seminary aspect and in siting the Athenaeum more than a small distance (16 miles) from the milieu of the University of Oxford.

D. Social Teaching and Social Issues

Cardinal Griffin expressed the hierarchy's views on Catholic social action when he endorsed parallel action in religious matters and cooper-

---

[12] *The Tablet*, May 10, 1952, Vol. 199, 386; January 26, 1957, Vol. 209, 82. The charter of the University of Liverpool specifically excluded theology.

[13] Statement from Archbishop's House quoted in *Herder Correspondence*, May, 1965, p. 148.

ation in social and political affairs. These views, also, expressed a measure of contentment with the English political system. Indeed, a Catholic political party in England would have been insignificant and was in fact never a serious possibility. There have, however, been public issues that challenged Catholic positions and ran counter to the Catholic view of what was morally acceptable. In these matters, and generally on an *ad hoc* basis, Catholics have mobilized across party and social lines and have sought to persuade as much of the nation as possible.

Catholics have generally opposed legislation to make divorce more easily obtainable, to make knowledge of contraception readily accessible, and to permit abortion. Here the argument is that these matters contravene a moral and natural law binding on all men. Often it was assumed, today with dwindling warranty, that many English Christians would support this position. For the future Catholics and their bishops are unlikely to rally a body of English opinion to gain the sanction of public law for their moral positions.

The Abortion Bill of 1967 was not a government or party measure. The unsuccessful parliamentary resistance to the measure was led by Norman St. John Stevas, a Catholic, Conservative MP. Cardinal Heenan's position on the bill was alarmist, as he told the World Congress of Catholic Nurses at Brighton (*The Times*, June 11, 1966). The role of Catholic nurses, the Cardinal said, will become more important as the decline in recognition of the moral law accelerated. He opposed abortion because he believed in the sanctity of life, even in the womb: "For, make no mistake, once the Abortion Bill has gone through, the next move will be euthanasia, the destruction of the old." In that eventuality the Cardinal expressed confidence that the Catholic nurse would stand up and say no.

On birth control the hierarchy is publicly committed to the earlier teaching of Church authorities but the laity is divided. For many of the clergy, however, the old position has been weakened in several respects: the acceptance of the rhythm method for controlling conception and the limited credibility of the argument that the overriding primary end of marriage is procreation. This position has, in effect, been rejected by many married people who ignored the ecclesiastical prohibition of contraception. The rejection of the Church's position of the recent past is usually defended on the grounds that the welfare of the family requires control of births, that there is a world population problem for which a necessary measure is contraception, and that the

Church teaching of recent centuries underrates the significance of human sexuality and so deals with marriage inadequately.

No other issue poses more difficult questions for the teaching authority of the Church and the hierarchy. Historical and moral justification of change does not affect the practical dilemmas for teachers and confessors who rigorously insisted that artificial birth control was forbidden by unchanging natural and moral law. On the English bishops these considerations have weighed heavily and, indeed, contributed to Archbishop Heenan's attack on the Council draft dealing with the Church in the modern world.

Pope Paul reserved this matter for his future pronouncement. For the intervening period the earlier teaching of the Church was to prevail, and the hierarchy of England and Wales issued a firm and much criticized statement to the effect that contraception "is not an open question, for it is against the law of God" (*Catholic Herald*, May 8, 1964). The dilemma persisted: some Catholics are in doubt and some, supported by their confessors and the acquiescence of the bishops, insist that for the time being the matter may be decided by the individual conscience. The debate continues on a public and private level in spite of Cardinal Heenan's request for an end to public controversy until the pope speaks (*Catholic Herald*, March 5, 1965).

The birth control controversy cuts across all social lines, even though the lineup of public proponents of birth control largely consists of educated and professional people.

Concerning international affairs the English bishops have urged Catholics to support the United Nations and efforts to promote the reign of law in international affairs. In recent years the hierarchy have been at pains to stress the duty of aid to underdeveloped nations. The bishops have adumbrated the horror and unacceptability of nuclear weapons: they have refrained from extensive criticism of the deterrent policy. The Catholic laity with varying nuances and growing criticism of nuclear weapons have similar views.

In domestic social questions Catholics have agreed that there is a common good as well as norms of justice that regulates the responsibilities of individuals of each class and provides the context for their rights. This agreement in principles embraces left and right but the extremes may be in sharp conflict over the course of action the principles may require.

The historical memory of a Christian society and the belief that re-

ligion should be the guide of life have directed attempts to elaborate a
Catholic social philosophy. The theorists largely have been idealists or
historical romanticists, lacking in social catholicity or in realism. The
concern with social philosophy received inconspicuous episcopal support and encountered general popular indifference. To explain this
popular indifference, it should be noted that the persisting antimodern
views of the Church made Catholic social philosophy largely a conservative exercise that would have drawn Catholics far from the major
stream of English public life and into ineffectiveness concerning immediate interests. Additionally, Catholic social theory did not close the
social divisions that characterize English and English Catholic society.

The career of the Catholic Social Guild (founded in 1909) may
serve as a paradigm of English Catholic social thought. It passed
through a phase favorable to social welfare legislation, but after World
War II its leadership, influenced by Paul Crane, S.J., and Colin Clark,
expressed reservations about the servile potentialities of the welfare
state. In 1958 the hierarchy placed the Guild under a priest director,
Henry Waterhouse, S.J., who was also made Principal of the Catholic
Workers' College at Oxford. The hierarchy expressed the wish that the
Guild be a center of serious study for supplying the Church in England
with expert advice and up-to-date information. Seven years later (*The
Month*, December, 1965), Father Waterhouse explained in reply to
criticism of the Guild's popular journal, *The Christian Democrat*, that
the Guild had been unable to raise funds for a serious journal. In
August, 1967, the Guild voted to dissolve its activities on the national
level. The Guild could not gather support even from the religious reformers whose aim was to adapt Catholicism to English culture. As its
Director said, using the standard word for an ill-supported cause, the
Guild was a "brotherhood" (*The Tablet*, September 9, 1967).

The Workers' College and the Guild limited themselves to educational work. In the late thirties and after the War, however, the Young
Christian Workers provided a vigorous example of the Lay Apostolate.

During the interwar years Social Catholicism was distracted by the
idealism of romantic medievalists and distributists, among them Eric
Gill, Father Vincent McNabb, and G. K. Chesterton. In spite of their
ingenious advocacy, it was always questionable as to how a distributist
England could support the population of England as well as the immigrants from near-distributist Ireland. Distributism was an antimodern
phenomenon that steadfastly rejected industrial society. For the class

division of society it proposed a solution that won few adherents.

Social division is a challenge that stirs a number of theological reformers as well as the Catholics of the New Left associated with *Slant,* a journal founded at Cambridge in 1964. One of the most frequently used words of the reformers and the New Left is "community." Their starting point is the absence of community: some, then, hope to build community on a local level through discussion and common action and through the newly emphasized corporate conception of the liturgy; for *Slant* and the Catholic New Left this is not enough. Like the American New Left they are prophetic and melodramatic protesters impatient with the limitations of existing political and social structures. For them the possession of nuclear weapons as well as modern war itself is wrong and the logic of deterrence only testifies to the corruption of society which cannot be reformed but must be transformed in revolutionary fashion. For that future the necessary roles are those of the revolutionary and martyr whom they are inclined to equate. Understanding and dialogue are important but their wish for dialogue appears reserved for forces of the future—the socialist parts of the world which, though in their eyes suffering from perverted developments, nevertheless hold within themselves the approaches to the future kingdom of man, a union of Catholicism and socialism.

A critical assessment of the Catholic New Left in its present stage is difficult. It is an affair of intellectuals who in the manner of Raymond Williams come to the criticism of society through literature. So far, they are very young intellectuals talking to one another and about one another's works. Apart from Rosemary Haughton and a few others, they feature some very bad writers, unusual naiveté, and the intolerance characteristic of the New Left.[14]

They talk of community and devote themselves to attacks on the cohesive forces that society may have. The New Left may welcome the crumbling of minority positions, but they dismiss these changes as inadequate reformism.

E. Vatican Council II: Ecumenism: the Liturgy

Bishop Derek Worlock, describing the astonishment that in 1959 greeted the summoning of the Council, recalled a seminary professor

---

[14] See the editorial on the police handling of the demonstration and riots at the American Embassy, *Slant,* April-May, 1968.

who had said that the Vatican Council of 1870 and the Declaration of Papal Infallibility had rendered councils unlikely, and added: "I did not realize that the *aggiornamento* had begun."[15]

Initially, reform and *aggiornamento* through a council of bishops and abbots might have appeared unlikely *in excelsis*. On the diocesan level, the bishops were major beneficiaries of the centralized, authoritarian regime that would have to be reformed; and few of the bishops had prepared the laity and priests, not to mention themselves, for the criticism and exploration of new courses that reform entailed. The early period of the Council was educational and broadening: it was then that the bishops discovered themselves as Council Fathers, as teachers and reformers of the Church. After the first session, Bishop Worlock wrote, many bishops returned to their dioceses appreciating, if not holding, views which earlier they might have thought had been condemned. Open deliberations on Church matters and the currency given to radical, and sometimes new, formulations of theological ideas advanced by theologians and by the *periti* soon began to affect a portion of the laity. The *periti*, expert theological advisors to the Fathers of the Council, readily took advantage of communications media to reach a world audience for ideas that previously had but a limited circulation. To authority-conscious pastors the *periti* appeared to be forcing the pace for the Council Fathers.

Against this background Archbishop Heenan made a memorable intervention in the Council on October 22, 1964. The occasion was a discussion of the draft for *The Church in the Modern World*. His address was at once recognized as unusual for the severity of its criticism and the anxieties it expressed. The Fathers, he argued, had painstakingly elaborated theological definitions but Schema 13, dealing with questions of immediate concern to people, was unworthy of the Council, for it had been prepared without the benefit of expert opinion. As examples of inadequate statements the Archbishop later cited those on family life, nuclear warfare, and world hunger. He therefore urged the rejection of the text of a pastoral document that was inadequate on pastoral grounds. He went on to propose that a new commission including married couples, doctors, economists, and scientists as well as priests with long pastoral experience, should be charged to submit a

[15] "Aggiornamento in Embryo," *The Wiseman Review*, No. 498 (Winter, 1963–1964), 316–334.

new text in three or four years to what would then be the last session of the Council. The effect of this proposal would have been to head off for some years a direct statement on birth control.

The Archbishop's insistence that a Pastoral Council needed the expertise of many fields in addition to theology was very much in order. His defense of authority and attacks on the *periti*, however, have an anti-intellectual character. Some of the latter he attacked for inflicting suffering on the Church and caring not at all for the teaching authority of bishops and the pope. The Archbishop later passed more reflections on the *periti* and other experts "who, since their youth, have spent their lives in monasteries, seminaries, or universities." "These eminent men hardly know the world as it really is." "We must protect the authority of the teaching Church."[16]

Reform and updating required an abandonment of past defensiveness, exclusiveness, and polemical severity. As the future Bishop Butler put it later: the primary mission of the Church was not to preserve the faith of Catholics but to preach the Gospel to all men. With this universalist concern ecumenism gathered life. The ecumenical spirit was no matter of tactics, for it as well as liturgical reform grew out of new developments in biblical theology, historical studies, and the theology of the laity and the Church. The Church was now described as a pilgrim Church, always in need of reformation, and not as a mighty citadel of unchange, as though it were a Platonic idea.

These new developments confronted the English bishops with special problems. Ecumenism proceeding by dialogue and exploration of what was held in common meant an end to Catholic exclusivism and a decided change in the hope of conversions. The hierarchy, themselves, however, shared the pre-Conciliar attitudes and temper that created special English problems. This pre-Council temper is expressed in the statement (1956) of the present Archbishop of Birmingham, George Patrick Dwyer, that the ecumenical movement would interfere with conversions. This position was sometimes supported by the further argument that Catholics, possessing truth in fullness, could best show their love for non-Catholics by refraining from any action that would encourage them to be content with their errors. There was, however, a

---

[16] The speeches and press conference remarks are in *Council Daybook: Vatican II*, Session 3, September 14 to November 21, 1964 (Washington, 1965), pp. 171, 173, 175–176.

positive approach that saw in conversion the deepening and fulfillment of what the convert had previously held.

The English bishops found ecumenism worrisome for its likely effect on conversions, for its foreseeable effects on some converts, and for the psychological difficulties in undoing the habits of a large part of the Catholic population. Another practical concern disturbed some of the bishops: ecumenical discussions with Anglicans might be conducted by Continental bishops and theologians and take place outside of England. Here, the English bishops insisted, their authority should be respected. After all, they knew the Anglicans better and would have to live with the daily consequences of such discussions.

This reserved attitude strengthened the suspicion that the English bishops were minimalist in ecumenical matters. Archbishop Heenan's anxieties led him to insist that the decree on ecumenism, which he then accepted, was incomplete. Additionally, he cautioned against anyone seeking advantage in ecumenical activity and, yet, said that its final aim "is, of course, the visible union of all Christians in the one Church of Christ." The decree, he argued, should affirm the obligation imposed by Christ to teach the whole truth. Archbishop Dwyer (November 27, 1963) reminded the Council Fathers that some of them had had no experience with the problem, for they lived in countries almost wholly Catholic. The English Catholics, on the other hand, lived as minority in what was decidedly not a closed community and they knew that words and kindness are not enough.

Upon his enthronement at Westminster, the Archbishop had spoken with warmth of his good friend, the Archbishop of Canterbury. Under his jurisdiction English theologians, priests, and laity had a number of meetings to prepare the way for ecumenical activity. But the Cardinal was aware of public feeling which, while generally favorable, has manifested some bitter complaints from converts about the abrogation of authority and the defeatism of the ecumenists. The Cardinal insisted that ecumenism is no bar to conversions, for the converts are mainly drawn from unbelievers and those without formal religion, who are so numerous in England as to offer the proper field for convert work. He has said that no one has any right to be scandalized by Christians praying together (*Catholic Herald*, September 18, 1964). He has also observed that until recently ecumenism had primarily attracted people living in the academic world. These, he thought, were the least likely ones to present matters to the faithful who in their jealousy for the faith recoiled from any attempt "to soften the lines of defense." The ecumenical task must be taken up by priests with pastoral experience who would lead the people gently (*Catholic Herald*, February 27, 1964).[17]

In the ecumenical field, then, the Catholic bishops proclaimed their intent to proceed. Criticism of their slow and gentle pace continued. The Directive of the Bishops (December, 1967) on ecumenism was thought to be quite liberal. But ecumenical work still suffers from lack of mature preparation. There has, for example, been little enough ecumenically inspired work on the English Reformation.

Pastoral interest motivated the Council Fathers in choosing liturgical reform as their first order of substantive business. Significantly the Council's decision to amend the liturgy itself involved a commitment to further reforms, for the liturgical changes could best be explained in terms of the theology of the Council reformers. If the desire was for services more meaningful and engaging for the people, greater popular participation was dictated. This change was justified theologically by the concept of the Church as the People of God. In one form the Church is the worshipping community of the parish joined in the Eucharist. From this it followed that at least parts of the Mass should be in the vernacular and that the Eucharistic worship of the Church was primarily communitarian.

The English bishops moved with deliberation in implementing the decree on the liturgy and made no major effort to explain the full theological grounds of the changes. They were, after all, only too aware that for English Catholics the use of the vernacular was identified with Protestantism and sometimes was regarded as the mark of heresy. If use of the vernacular was presented as a tactic, so that the Mass would be understood, it was argued that the Anglican Church used a vernacular text of incomparable beauty and had only a limited appeal to the English people. Late in 1964 at Advent, the vernacular liturgy was introduced. Opinion polls testified to the acceptability of the liturgical

---

[17] Michael Ramsey, Archbishop of Canterbury, in discussing the possibility of the removal of obstacles to the reunion of Rome and Canterbury, was asked about the position of the English Roman Catholic bishops, if the obstacles were removed. He replied: "They might find themselves unnecessary. I won't say more than that. They might find themselves unnecessary." (*The Economist*, June 13, 1964).

changes to a large percentage of Catholics. The bishops also encountered firm, though minority, opposition from the Latin Mass
Society, whose views reveal something of the quality of English Catholicism of the past. Bishop Dwyer, speaking to a Council Press Conference (October 22, 1964), indicated the core of the difficulty: "The
Liturgy Schema, for example, is not just about dressing and acting in
Church. It has launched a movement which will uproot all kinds of
age-old habits, cut psychological and emotional ties, shake to the
foundations the ways of thought of three to four million Catholics—
all this so that the emphasis on the individual's personal concern will
give place to an emphasis on communal responsibility."[18]

The Latin Mass Society, organized in 1965 and soon claiming 1,000
members, was a conservative response that rejected compromise. It
wanted an all-Latin Mass and regarded use of the vernacular as a concession to human frailty. The vernacular, associated "with the triviali-
ties and worldliness of everyday life, is sadly inadequate for the expression of the sublime mysteries. . . ." Latin, the Society's members
argued, was the language of the English martyrs and had the hieratic
quality proper to mysteries. Further, and this is reminiscent of the Old
Believers, the timelessness and universality of Latin made the Latin
Mass a source of spiritual strength and refreshment. The Society, then,
was for those who "wish to *hear* [my italics] the Mass entirely in Latin."
Some of the Society's conservative speakers saw Church reform
as internal subversion, inspired mainly by seminary and university
professors.

English Catholics are generally inclined to say that the needs of the
Society's members should be met. The significance of the Society's
protest is its revelation of the individualist piety of recent decades. For
their part the Society's members never refer to the theological conceptions that animate the liturgical changes.[19]

Later the liturgical reforms were extended. On liturgical reform *The
Tablet* (February 1, 1964) editorialized under the heading *Festina
Lente*. The editorial noted that there was no widespread desire for
liturgical change: "Our history has made us as Catholics afraid of losing

[18] Printed in Msgr. Derek Worlock, ed., *English Bishops at the Council: Third
Session* (London, 1965), p. 160.

[19] Detailed accounts of the Latin Mass Society and its meetings appear in the
Catholic Herald, April 30, May 28, July 16, and December 3, 1965.

one jot or tittle of a heritage for which great sacrifices have been made."[20]

Bishop King of Portsmouth believed that after a while English liturgy could make its impact. After people hear parts of Scripture they have not heard before, he was sure "that the people would appreciate, be it little by little, the motives which have caused the Church to make this big change" (*Catholic Herald*, November 27, 1964).

Some English Catholics are doubtful of their preparation for the ecumenical work of renewal. The Dominican Provincial, Father Henry St. John (*The Tablet*, March 9, 1963), contended that the English were hardly prepared for the encounter and recommended do-it-yourself programs of preparation. The implementation of renewal will indeed tax the resources and efforts of Catholic churches everywhere. English Catholicism faces a particular difficulty in that its educational resources in theology, even for the clergy, are not abundant.

F. The Transformation of Authority

Aggiornamento became a program of many changes at once and of change leading to further change. Its impact may be seen in the reorganization of the Catholic Evidence Guild, which has shifted from an apologetics-centered witness to a program of training its members in biblical and theological studies as well as in the training of seminarians and the joint prayer meetings of Anglicans, Free Churchmen, and Catholics.

The changes have begun the transformation of a Church that in recent centuries has been characterized by defensiveness and exaggerated emphasis on papal authority. The papacy, involving headship of the Church as well as a temporal monarchy, early developed a court and bureaucracy. The popes, however, could not continuously and effectively control the Congregations, that is, the bureaucracy.

Criticisms of the Congregations were frequently resisted as attacks on authority. At the Council the cry that authority was under attack

[20] *The Tablet's* spread-eagle rhetoric is rather more surprising than that used in 1923 to increase school facilities in Liverpool so that "not one child of the Church of the martyrs should stand for an hour in danger of apostasy." Quoted in John Barron Mays, *Growing Up in the City*, Social Research Series (Liverpool, 1964), p. 56.

was not unfounded. There was and is a crisis of authority in the Church. The crisis is in part psychological, for the transformation of the anti-modern Church inevitably unsettled believers and habits of obedience. Reform was usually justified by arguments that in emphasizing the limits of time, condition, and culture upon the Church, concentrated not on the inerrancy of the Church but upon the inevitable incompleteness of past formulations of religious teachings. With this development there was advanced a conception of authority that stressed participation and consent instead of the duty of instant obedience.

This new formulation challenges one dominated by a conception of order. Peace is seen as the tranquility of order which involves hierarchy which in turn demands obedience. The conception has its truth and grandeur but its recent historical form was incomplete in failing to allow for the individual, his conscience, and moral development. Another formulation of this position is that the crisis of authority arises from the way in which authority has been exercised: there has been a confusion of teaching authority with administrative policies and exigencies.

The broad conception of authority is presented in Archbishop Heenan's admirably straightforward address to the British Council of Christians and Jews (March 5, 1964), explaining his reappearance at the Council from which he had resigned in 1954. The withdrawal of Catholic members was in response to an order from the Holy Office. Rome, as the Archbishop explained, had been alarmed by reports that the International Council of Christians and Jews was about to favor policies indifferent to religion and hostile to state support for schools offering denominational instruction and that the British Council would approve such a course. These reports were not accurate but "had sufficient basis to make them hard to refute." Concerning the British Council it "is possible and even probable that the Vatican was misinformed. . . . In the event, the Holy See took immediate and vigorous action." Despite Cardinal Griffin's plea for further investigation the Catholics were ordered to resign. The English bishops submitted because those who expect obedience must also give obedience.[21] Here appears a concept of authority as a system with obedience as an imperative justified by the necessity of maintaining the habit of obedience.

Nevertheless, Cardinal Heenan does not profess to be a speculative thinker and systematizer and his responses to problems may belie all

[21] Address printed in *The Wiseman Review*, No. 499 (Spring, 1964), pp. 3–7.

prophecies. In 1966 he and the bishops of England proceeded to the establishment of diocesan senates of priests to provide means of consultation with the clergy. Later would follow the establishment of councils of the laity. The sequel of this participation—association with the order of authority—will very likely involve a reorganization of many Catholic organizations.

In the structural changes in the Church two approaches are visible. On the one hand, the Bishop of Plymouth, Derek Worlock, has sketched out areas of episcopal activity but insisted on seeking information, consultation, and participation from his clergy and people. In setting the tone for his episcopate he described himself as a coordinator and not a dictator. Cardinal Heenan representing the older view emphasizes authority and its necessary role. When he mentions the developing theology of the laity, his formulation is restrained. The priesthood of the laity, he says, has been recognized and it is now time for the laity to take responsibility on a scale comparable to what priests have done in the past. It should be recognized, however, that the Bishop and the Cardinal are moving in the same direction.

The emerging conception of authority involved both a critique of the institutional order of the Church and a theory of authority. In the past authority has involved an authoritarian structure and failed to develop a sense of responsibility and commitment. Charles Davis made the same point: Catholic education had failed to foster personal judgment in moral matters. The necessity for personal judgment, however, did not derogate from authority. "But the authoritative guidance must be personally appropriated if it is to count for a truly personal decision."[22]

Individual participation and responsibility may prove unsettling in many matters that were once handled with greater formalism and little probing. The Catholic psychiatrist, J. Dominian, who has worked with the Catholic Marriage Advisory Council, has advocated a study of the causes of marital breakdowns and a reexamination of the criteria of a valid marriage. If the validity of a Catholic marriage depends upon the sincerity of the vows exchanged, then it must be established that the couple involved are "physically and psychologically capable of effecting a minimum expression of what these vows signify."[23]

Theology, too, must be freed of the heavy-handed authoritarian

[22] "Theological Asides," *Catholic Herald*, August 12, 1966.
[23] "Vatican II and Marriage," *The Clergy Review*, LIII (January, 1967), 26.

structure. If it is to be a culturally influential study, theologians have
to be concerned with questions raised at the creative center of an age.
Theology's special preoccupation, therefore, is with hard issues, and
theologians have a particular duty to avoid the temptation of an easy
life. They required an atmosphere that encouraged far-ranging speculation and this meant relaxing the exercise of authority in the field of
doctrine, where authority had been conceived as issuing the "commands of a sovereign power." Theologians could warily avoid the disturbing only at the cost of keeping their subject at the level of a past
culture. "Much of the policy of protecting the faith of the people by
the exclusion of disturbing ideas is in fact a policy of jettisoning the faith
of the next generation in an ill-directed attempt to salvage the faith
of this."[24]

The new concept of authority has been strikingly formulated by
Professor J. M. Cameron. His argument is that the individual ruler,
pope or king, does not possess authority but is possessed by it. The
feudal and early modern age, however, confusing the concept of authority, saw it as vested in persons. This has proved to be unjustifiably
favorable to habits of obedience. The Church, Cameron argues, is the
people of God; and authority, which should always be under judgment, is the servant of the people. Obedience, in turn, is linked with
understanding the point of a command and the purpose it serves.[25]

The publisher, John M. Todd, contends that renewal in the Church
and the changes necessary in English Catholicism cannot be made by
the old methods and under Canon Law. He has called for a change in
methods of selecting bishops that will allow local knowledge and wishes
to play a major role. On the diocesan level his demand for consultation
of priests and laity is in the course of being met. He has, also, complained that, though the hierarchy have, on occasion, consulted the
laity, they were not consulted before the hierarchy issued what he

[24] The phrase, "commands of a sovereign power," is from J. M. Cameron,
"Problems of Religious Editors," The Times, February 25, 1967. The paragraph
is based on Charles Davis, "Theology and Its Present Task," in John Coulson, ed.,
Theology and the University (London, 1964), pp. 107–132; the final quotation
is from p. 12.

[25] Cameron's ideas are developed in an essay in John M. Todd, ed., Problems
of Authority: An Anglo-French Symposium (London, 1962) and in Images of
Authority (New Haven, 1966).

called the "jejune" statement on birth control (1964). He argued further that when professionally prominent men speak out, they are undercut by the hierarchy.[26]

In 1965 an editorial in *The Month*, a Jesuit magazine, agreed that there was a crisis of authority among English Catholics, although it was not of long standing and was not radical. The crisis persists and where in 1965 a few priests abandoned their priesthood, the number has increased. For some of the grounds of this statement as well as an explanation of the absence of a specific figure, see *The National Catholic Reporter*, June 12, 1968. One result of the hierarchy's gentle leadership in gradual reformism is that many priests and laymen encounter the disturbances with incomprehension. At any rate the crisis is clearest among intellectuals and university people and theological reformers.

The crisis, mainly on familiar lines, appeared with some sharpness when late in 1966 Father Charles Davis announced that he was going to marry and leave the Catholic priesthood because the existing structure of the Church in fostering dishonesty made the task of reform impossible. In itself the decision might have caused disarray among Catholic reformers, for to critics of the reformers Davis' action pointed to the direction in which they believed the reformers to be moving. Charles Davis had been something of a chaplain-theologian for some of the reformers. One of them, Rosemary Haughton, wrote that Davis' departure was a "shattering blow."[27]

Charles Davis' decision may have been long in maturing and during that time of internal debate he wrote much and lectured. His decision meant that he repudiated some of the things he had been expressing. From his writing it appears that the hierarchy's position on birth control played a large role in his decision. Thus, in the *Clergy Review* (November, 1966), he described the prevailing position as "passive suspense" which he believed to be "actually corrosive." "What is corrosive

[26] Summary of John Todd's chapter on the Church in England in *Die Kirche nach dem Konzil* (Mainz-Grunewald, 1966) in *Herder Correspondence*, III (November, 1966).

[27] In a characteristic action Cardinal Heenan invited Rosemary Haughton to discuss her anxieties and the Cardinal then proposed and she agreed that they write a book on some issues confronting Catholicism. The book, *Dialogue: The State of the Church Today* (London, 1967) is well worth reading, although dialogue is not its most striking feature.

is the pervading sense of dishonesty and frustration in the present uncomfortable position of postponing any frank confrontation of the
issues involved."[28]

Davis' statements were careful and dignified and there was remarkably little heat in the public comments of his critics. Some of his priest
friends even attended his wedding.

The case acquired explosiveness when another reformer, Herbert
McCabe, O.P., published an editorial in New Blackfriars. Father Mc-
Cabe wrote sympathetically of the work of Charles Davis. His own
position, he affirmed, was that membership in the institutional Church
put him in communion with transcendent spiritual realities. Here,
then, was a line drawn to mark what he believed to be Davis' mistaken
course. At the same time he elaborated on the personal dissatisfaction
of many English Catholics with the institutional Church in England
and endorsed Davis' judgment that the Church was corrupt.

Father McCabe was removed from his editorship and suspended
from his priestly faculties. Catholic academics and some members of
the Slant group wrote critical articles. Dr. John Bryden of the Newman
Association presented to the Dominican Master-General in Rome a
petition asking for Father McCabe's reinstatement as editor. A Pray-In
at Westminster Cathedral was scheduled for March 11, 1967. Then,
on February 28, it was announced that on the same day as the Pray-In
Cardinal Heenan would be joined in prayer with Archbishops Dwyer
and Beck and Bishops Butler and Worlock at Westminster Cathedral.
The Cardinal would say Mass and prayers would be offered for the
Church, clergy, laity, and all those who had lost the faith. In a brief
address at the Mass Cardinal Heenan insisted that the prayers were
directed against no one.

Two days later as something of an anticlimax a Teach-In on liberty
of expression in the Church took place in the Central Hall of Westminster.

In New Blackfriars, April, 1967, Father Ian Hislop, Dominican
Provincial in England, affirmed the devotion of the Dominican Order
in England to the Church and insisted that Father McCabe had written the editorial directly to affirm that one could work in the Church
for the cause of reform on lines that Charles Davis had declared to be
impossible. The Provincial further said that the Dominicans would

[28] Charles Davis' restrained and well-written account is in his book, A Question
of Conscience (London, 1967).

inevitably shock people, would be misunderstood by some of the laity, and would make mistakes in discharging their task of viewing society and its problems theologically. Father McCabe's successor as Editor explained to critical contributors that he had accepted the post as a matter of religious obedience.

Father McCabe was soon restored to his priestly functions. Cardinal Heenan, it was revealed, had written in favor of McCabe's reinstatement as Editor, if he apologized for having attended Davis' wedding and for his charge that the Church was corrupt. The strains inevitable in the interplay of changing views of authority appear in the Davis-McCabe affair. Perhaps, in the long run, the example of Davis may be more serious than the consequences of the McCabe controversy. Members of the *Slant* group have described the action of Davis as one of witness, a kind of martyrdom.

The Catholic Church in England is in the course of renewal on lines agreed upon for the whole Church. The bishops, with such exceptions as Worlock and Butler, preside over the work of renewal with assurances that improvements and changes are being made and that no revolutionary turmoil is called for. The abandonment of defensiveness comes at a time when the cause of Catholic schools has achieved the remarkable victory registered in the government policy of 1966. The facile criticism of Catholic schools as socially divisive is in many ways belied by the lively examination that Catholics now direct at their own schools.

The work of renewal has also involved the working out of new conceptions of authority. On the one hand, the hierarchy have initiated changes that may begin to meet the new conceptions. On the other hand, university Catholics are critical of the surviving power of past structures and outlook. The criticism and frustration of these reformers is too often met by tactical concessions or by the statement that the Church is for all conditions of men and not for an intellectual elite alone. The latter point is fair enough but is used in irrelevant ways, for renewal means a development of studies and ideas that has not yet made much advance. The vehemence and uncharitableness of some reformist critics and the esoteric quality of some of the *Slant* group reduce their effectiveness as critics and serve to appear to justify opposition to them. These deficiencies are particularly regrettable because the English Catholic Church and its leaders have accepted the reforms of the Council without apparently catching its spirit of renewal and concern with the world. So it has enacted the specific reforms but has not moved, as the Dutch have tried to do for their nation, to work out a characteristically English Catholicism and not an adaptation of Rome.

The English Catholic Church is too much the Church of the past and in prospective view is not reassuring. So it is well that many English Catholics are critical of their Church. It is well that there is concern about change and renewal. The zeal that the cries for change call for may, however, inspire misgivings. Perhaps the past order was too willing to settle for passive and even marginal Christians—and even helped to make some people so. But can one hope to find all England ablaze with zeal as some speakers have hoped? Can one even hope to foster a pervasive sense of community in the urban parish?

For the Christian the tension between experience and aspiration must always exist. This is an ecumenical possession and renewal is not just a Catholic concern.[29]

[29] The most useful general books on English Catholicism are: David Mathew, *Catholicism in England* (London, 1936); E. I. Watkin, *Roman Catholicism in England from the Reformation to 1950* (London, 1957); G. A. Beck, ed., *The English Catholics, 1850–1950* (London, 1950); David Mathew and others, *Le Catholicisme Anglais* (Paris, 1957); George Scott, *The RCs* (London, 1967). For a *Slant* view, see Terence Eagleton, *The New Left Church*; or Brian Wicker, *First the Political Kingdom* (Notre Dame, 1968). Cardinal Heenan's thought and accents are conveyed in *Council and Clergy* (London, 1966); meditations in the new religious style are in Dom Sebastian Moore, *God Is a New Language* (London, 1967); for theology consult Bishop Christopher Butler, *The Theology of Vatican II* (London, 1967).

INDEX

Action française, 219, 220, 221, 233
Adam, Karl, 52
Adenauer, Konrad, 49
Agagianian, Cardinal Gregoire, 100
aggiornamento, see modernization
Alfonso I (Portugal), 158
Alfrink, Cardinal Bernard, 10, 17, 26, 27, 28
Amery, Carl, 51
Amon, Karl, 66
Ancel, Msgr. A., 230
Annuario Pontificio, 122
anticlericalism, 164–166, 167, 181, 184, 186, 193, 216, 217, 219, 240–241, 246
antimodernism, xi, 314
Aranguren, José Luis, 191, 212
Arbeitsgemeinschaft für Entwicklung-shilfe, 38
art, 85–86
Artajo, Martin, 187
Assumption, 52
atheism, 149, 150, 151, 186, 201, 202, 205
Augsburg, Peace of, 29, 30
authority, xiv, xvii, 5, 16, 19–20, 27, 223, 337–340

Baldelli, Msgr. Ferdinando, 135
Balfour Education Act (1902), 320
Balthasar, Hans Urs von, 89, 103, 108
Barth, Karl, 103
Basques, 190, 196
Bea, Cardinal Augustin, 90, 105
Beauduin, Dom Lambert, 269
Bekkers, Msgr. W., 6
Benedictines, 66, 70–72, 198
Berdyaev, Nicholai, 183
Bible Oecumenique, 92
biblical theology, 64, 317
birth control, *see* contraception
bishops, 5, 32, 33–35, 40, 56–57, 58,

71–74, 89, 123–124, 168–169, 174, 186–187, 189, 191, 192–193, 194, 196–198, 230, 246–249, 263–266, 283, 285, 300, 316–319, 327, 328, 329, 332–337, 338–339, 343
bishops' conference, 52–53, 71, 76, 99, 123, 207–208, 233–234
Blanchard, Jean, 282
Böll Heinrich, 51
Boy Scouts, 95, 131
Breslau, diocese of, 41–42
Brussels, University of, 254
Burgalassi, Father Silvano, 147

Calvinism, 2
Cameron, J. M., 340
canon law, 293
Cardijn, Cardinal Joseph, 222, 269
Catalans, 196
catechetics, 13–14, 154, 281, 301
Catholic Action, 80, 128–133, 179, 187, 193, 203-208, 222–223, 226, 231, 257–258, 259, 269–270
Catholic Emancipation, 2, 274, 301
Catholic Evidence Guild, 313, 337
Catholic Herald, 321
Catholic People's Party, 4
Catholic Social Guild, 330
Catholic State Party, 3
Catholic Truth Society, 313
Catholic Workers' College, 330
Cecil, Lord Hugh, 314
celibacy, 7, 14–15
censorship, 283–284
Center Party, 32–33
Central Committee of German Catholics, 42
Centro Católico Português, 169
Cerejeira, Cardinal Manuel Goncalves, 171–172
Christian Agricultural Youth (JAC), 231

Christian Democratic Party, 76
Christian Democratic Union, 37, 49–50
Christian Democrats, 144–146, 241
Christian Education, Declaration on, 255
Christian Social Party, 259–260, 266, 268
Christian Worker Movement, 257, 268
Church and State, 49–50, 58, 76–81, 139–142, 158–159, 160–162, 163–166, 167–169, 172, 173–178, 180, 184–186, 216–220, 224–225, 239–241, 243–245, 279–280, 281–285, 302–303, 309–310, 313, 316, 320–321
The Church in Contemporary Ireland, 282
Church of England, 314
Civiltà Cattolica, 138
clergy, 3, 59, 152–153, 192–196, 247, 275, 278–279, 300
Coimbra, University of, 164, 167
collegiality, 7, 40, 73, 96, 235, 293
Collegium Germanicum, 32
Comin, Alfonso Carlos, 196–197, 202
Communist Party, 144, 145–146, 149–151
concordats, 34, 77–79, 123, 140–142, 164, 166, 174, 178, 183, 186, 188–189, 204, 218–219, 244
confession, 9
Congar, Yves, 232
Connolly, James, 277
conservatives, x–xi, xiii, 6, 13, 31–32, 70, 109, 112, 184, 191–193, 216, 217, 218–219, 300
constitutions, 106, 141, 142, 173–174, 243, 279–280
contraception, xvii, 93, 279–280, 283–284, 328–329, 341–342
converts, 44, 68, 310–311, 312–313
corporative state, xi–xii
Costa, Afonso, 168
Counter-Reformation, 32, 55, 67
Cuadernos para el diálogo, 212
Cullmann, Oscar, 90, 103
culture, xiv, xv, 274–276, 293–295, 306
Cursillos, 188, 191, 206

Daniel, Abbé, 227–228
Dansette, Adrien, 230

Davis, Charles, 339, 341–343
Deferre, Gaston, 241
Delp, S. J., Rev. Alfred, 35
Denis, King of Portugal, 159
Deutsche Caritas-Verband, 38–39
dialogue, 29, 30, 46, 83, 207, 268, 305–306
dioceses, 41–42, 61, 96–97, 122–123, 159, 178, 233, 245–249, 278, 299
Dirks, Walter, 51
distributism, 330
divorce, 142, 151, 174, 279
Doderer, Heimito von, 85
Dominian, J., 339
Dominicans, 198
Downside Abbey, 326
Duff, Frank, 289
Duocastella, Father Rogelio, 194, 199–201
Dutch Catechism, 12–14
Dwyer, Bishop George Patrick, 333–334

Ecclesia, 206
Ecumenical Institute (Fribourg), 92
ecumenism, 6, 10–12, 23, 36, 52, 55, 74, 75, 89, 102–104, 105, 106, 118, 269, 300, 304–305, 306, 315, 333–335, 336–337
Education Act (1944, Butler), 320–321
Education Act (1959), amended (1966), 321
Engels, Friedrich, 311
Escarré, Dom Aureli, 190–191
Estado Novo, 170–171
Eucharist, 9, 11
Eucharistic World Congress, 52, 182

Falange, 187, 190
farmers' organization, 258
Fascism, 128, 144
Fasquet, Henri, 236
Fatima, 180–182
Feiner, Johannes, 89, 90
Le Figaro, 236
Flemish nationalism, 249–253
Forster Education Act (1870), 320
Fraga Iribarne, Manuel, 210
France, pays de mission, 228
Franco, Francisco, 189
Freemasons, 166, 219

French Revolution, 2, 162, 215–216
Fribourg University, 100
"Fuero de los Españoles," 187
Die Furche, 83

Galli, S.J., Mario von, 118, 119
Gasperi, Alcide de, 144, 145
Gaullism, 238–239
General Confederation of Labor (CGT),
    229
German Democratic Republic, 41, 42
German Peoples' Republic, 58
Girl Guides, Italy, 131
Gleason, Philip, ix, x
Goa, 161–162, 182
Godfrey, Archbishop William, 316–317
Godin, Abbé, 227–228
Gomis, Lorenzo, 197
Gregorian University, 127, 128, 178
Gregory XVI, Pope, 163
Greinacher, N., 41 (n. 1)
Griffin, Cardinal Bernard, 315, 316,
    327–328
Grosche, Msgr. Robert, 36
Guardini, Romano, 36
Günther, Anton, 65, 66

Heenan, Cardinal John Carmel, 323,
    328, 332–334, 338–339, 342
Henry the Navigator, Prince, 160
Herr, Friedrich, 83
Herrera, Bishop Angel, y Oria, 188, 210
Herwegen, Abbot, 36
Heythrop Athenaeum, 327
Hinsley, Archbishop, 312, 315
Hislop, O.P., Rev. Ian, 342–343
Hitler, Adolf, 33–34, 35
HOAC, 190, 202, 205
Home Rule Party (Irish), 275
Houtart, Canon, 246
Hughes, Msgr. Philip, 309
Humanae Vitae, xvii

Index Librorum Prohibitorum, 283
Innitzer, Cardinal, 76
integralism, 233
Inquisition, 160
intercommunion, 10–11

Jachým, Archbishop Franz, 62, 70, 77
Jaeger, Cardinal Lorenz, 52–53
Jesuits, 32, 67, 106, 139, 161, 198, 206,
    210, 250
Jews, 23
John VI (Portugal), 162
John XXIII, passim
Jong, Cardinal de, 4, 5
Joseph II, Emperor, 61, 70
Journet, Charles, 93, 94
Jungmann, S.J., Josef, 67, 72

Karrer, Otto, 89
Katholikentag, 42, 52, 77
Kathpress (Austria), 83
Kennedy, John F., 292
Ketteler, Bishop von, 31
Kerkhofs, S.J., P., 246, 252
Klostermann, Ferdinand, 65–66
KNA (Catholic News Agency), 43
König, Archbishop Franz, 61, 72, 79
KRO, 25, 26–27
Kulturkampf, 109
Küng, Hans, 88, 89

laity, 54, 59, 108, 117–118
Lange, Dr. D. de, 7–8
language and nationalism, 249–253,
    273–274
Lateran Pacts (1929), 140
Latin America, 38, 136, 198, 199
Latin Mass Society, 336
Lawor, Dr. Monica, 322–323
lay apostolate, 266, 267, 301, 306
leakage, 68, 299, 312
Le Bras, Gabriel, xiii, 225
Lebreton, Father J., 223
Legion of Mary, 134, 289
Leo XIII, 217–218
Liberal Party (British), 275
liberalism, xv, 162–165, 181, 184, 216,
    243, 277
Liénart, Cardinal Achilles, 88, 235
liturgy, 8, 9, 57, 70–72, 211, 231, 270,
    293, 300, 307, 326, 335–337
Lortz, Josef, 36
Louvain, University of, 254–255, 261–
    266
Lubac, Henri de, 232
Lumen Vitae, 322

De Maand, 267
McCabe, O.P., Herbert, 342–343
Manning, Cardinal Henry, xii, 310–311, 324
Marian Congregations, 133, 206
Maritain, Jacques, 22
marriage, 6–7, 12, 48, 55, 77, 79, 104–106, 142, 151, 174, 282, 291
Marxism, 7–8, 205, 229
Mater et Magistra, 286, 287
Maurras, Charles, 219, 220
Maynooth, 285–286
Méan, Cardinal de, 243
Mercier, Cardinal Désiré J., 269
Messner, Johannes, 66
Miret Magdalena, Enrique, 206, 207–208
Misereor, 37
Mission de France, 234–235
Mission de Paris, 228
Missionary Convention, 174–177
missions, 3, 38–40, 136–137, 160–161, 162, 174–179, 198–199, 269, 281, 290–291
Modernism, 254
modernization, ix, xi, xii–xiii, xiv, xv, xvii, 8, 20, 154–155, 191–192, 267–268, 293–295, 300, 332, 337
Mollet, Guy, 241
Le Monde, 236
Movimento dei Focolari, 134
Mozambique, 172, 177
MRP, see Popular Republican Movement
Mulcahy, Dom Columba, 305
Müller, Alois, 112, 113 (n. 14), 119–120
Mun, Albert de, xi
Mussolini, Benito, 144

National Civic Committee, 132
National Socialism, 32–35, 68, 76
nationalism, xv, 183–184, 185–186, 241–242, 246, 260–266, 270, 273–274
Nenni, Pietro, 145, 146
Neue Zürcher Zeitung, 110
New Left, xvi, 331
Newman Association, 325–326
Newman Demographic Survey, 321, 325–326

Newman, John Henry, 311, 324
Nierman, Bishop of Groningen, 15
Non Expedit (1874), 143–144
Nova et Vetera, 93

O'Connell, Daniel, 275
Old-Catholic Church, 10
O'Malley, Donogh, 285
O'Neill, Captain Terence, 280–281
Opus Dei, 107, 138, 206, 207, 209, 210, 289–290
Order of Christ, 159, 160
orders (religious), 3, 16–17, 64, 125–126, 159, 164–166, 198–199, 248, 290–291
Orientierung, 118 (n. 16), 119
Ottaviani, Cardinal Alfredo, 93
Oxford Movement, 310–311

Pacelli, Cardinal Eugenio, 34
Padroado, 160–163
Paris Match, 11
parish councils, 10
parishes, 98, 124, 153, 234, 235, 245, 248–249
Parsch, Pius, 71, 72
Partito Popolare Italiano, 144
Pastoral Council (Holland) 12, 21–28
Pastoral Institute, 9, 14
Paul VI, 14, 90, 123, 180, 182, 232, 236
Pétain, Marshal, 223
pilgrim church, xvi
Pius IX, xi, 7, 139–140
Pius X, 144, 168
Pius XI, 128
Pius XII, 128
Pizzardo, Cardinal Giuseppe, 230
Pla y Deniel, Cardinal Enrique, 190, 205, 210
Placet, 158–159, 161, 164, 168
pluralism, 109
Poland, 41–42
Pombal, Marquis of, 161
Pontifical Assistance Work, 135–136
Popular Republican Movement (MRP), 238, 241
population, 1, 298–299, 309
practice (religious), 3, 44–45, 68–70, 146–149, 200–203, 225, 253
Presbyterianism, 281, 297, 304

press, 4, 42–43, 50, 83–84, 137–139, 170, 207, 210-211, 223, 236, 288–289
priests, 15, 18, 45–46, 62–65, 97, 234, 299
priests councils, 55, 235, 247, 270
Protestants, 47–48, 67, 103–104, 114, 176–177, 192, 199, 225, 244, 280–281, 297, 304

Quinn, Edel, 289

radio and television, 4, 75, 82–83, 236–237
Rahner, S.J., Hugo, 67
Rahner, S.J., Karl, 67, 72, 75
Reformation, 2, 30, 55, 272–273, 297
reformism (Catholic), xvi
Rerum Novarum, 218
Resende, Sabastião Soares de, 172
Resistance, 36, 223
Revilla, Federico, 188
revolution, 277
La Revue Nouvelle, 246, 249, 256, 267
Riedmatten, Henri de, 92
Rinkel, Msgr. A., 10
Risse, H. T., 41 (n. 1)
Roey, Cardinal von, 244–245, 260
Roman Curia, xvi, 20, 27, 32, 48
Rossum, Bishop von, 3
Rouquette, S.J., Robert, xii
Rubio, Bishop Mauro, 192
Ruiz Gimenez, Joaquin, 212

St. John, Henry, 337
St. Vincent de Paul Society, 134
St. Willibrord Association, 10
Salazar, Antonio de Oliveira, 171
Santvoort, Harry van, xiv
Sartory, Thomas, 54
Scharf, Adolph, 78
Schillebeeckx, Rev. E., 17–21
schools, 6, 57, 79, 81–82, 109, 126–127, 138–139, 143, 173, 189, 208–210, 218, 239–241, 244, 250, 255–257, 266, 284–285, 302–304, 315–316, 319–323
Schoonenberg, Piet, 11
Schott, Father Anselm, 70

Scripture (Holland), 20
Seabra, Enrico de, 167
secularization, xv, 183, 276
Segura, Cardinal Pedro, y Saenz, 187
seminaries, 15, 46, 63–65, 66, 125, 153, 164, 167, 178, 179, 195, 235, 286, 301, 318–319
Semprum, Jorge, 213
Separation Law (Portugal), 167
sisters, 125–126
Sjaloomgroep, 11
Slant, 331, 343
social action, 16, 113–114, 132–133
social teaching, 189–190, 202–203, 218, 236, 283, 286–287, 315, 327–331
Social Weeks, 132, 179–180, 203, 221
socialism, 5, 49, 50, 54, 77, 78, 80–81, 113–114, 145, 146, 277, 286–287
Socialist Party, 238, 241, 254, 255, 258, 260
Society for the Propagation of the Faith, 39–40
sociology, 4, 43–45, 64–65, 68–70, 97–99, 116–118, 146–149, 185–186, 194–196, 200–203, 225–227, 239, 246, 253–254, 273–276, 277, 278, 292–293, 298, 299–300, 313–314, 325–326
Sonderbund, 106, 113
Spain, a Missionary Country?, 196–197
Spencer, Anthony, 309 (n. 1), 325
State and Church, see Church and State
statistics, 41, 61–63, 64–65, 225, 246, 278–279, 309–310
Stevas, Norman St. John, 328
students, 201–202, 223
Sturzo, Don Luigi, 144
Stuttgarter Schuldbekenntnis, 47
Suhard, Cardinal Emmanuel, 228, 234
Sword of Spirit Movement, 315
"Syllabus of Errors," xi
Synod of Bishops, 12

Taize, 102–103
teachers, 303–304, 322
teachers' colleges, 81–83, 303, 322
Teilhard de Chardin, 211, 237
theology, xvii, 15–16, 65–67, 87, 107, 127–128, 211–212, 232, 288, 293, 294–295, 307–308, 323–327
Todd, John M., 340

Togliatti, Palmiro, 145
toleration, 243, 279
Tour du Pin, Marquis de la, xi
trade unions, 5, 49, 257–258
Trinity College (Dublin), 285
triumphalism, 47–48, 187

Una Sancta, 36
Una Voce, 59, 60, 72
União Nacional, 170–171
universities, 44, 285, 327
University Catholic Federation, 324
University of the Sacred Heart (Milan),
    127
urbanization, 151, 152, 153, 195, 234–
    235, 275–276

Vatican II, 331–337, and passim
Vet, Msgr. G. de, 21–22
Villain, Father Maurice, 236
Vlaamse Volksbeweging, 249
vocations, 15, 65, 136, 178–179

Vonderach, Bishop Johannes, 105

Walloons, 250, 251–253
war, 242, 329
Waterhouse, S.J., Henry, 330
Waugh, Evelyn, xi, 313
Weber, Leonhard, 89
worker priests, 227–231
workers, 69, 131–132, 136, 185, 202–
    203, 204–205, 208, 216–217, 222–
    223, 227–231, 236, 245–246
Worlock, Bishop Denis, 331–332, 339
Wort und Wahrheit, 67, 83–84
Wyndham, George, 314

Young Christian Workers (JOC), 205,
    222, 231, 257, 269–270
youth movements, 75, 129–139

Zauner, Bishop, 72, 73